HAMMERSHØI
AND EUROPE

STATENS MUSEUM FOR KUNST

KUNSTHALLE DER HYPO-KULTURSTIFTUNG

PRESTEL PUBLISHING

HAMMERSHØI
AND EUROPE

KASPER MONRAD

With contributions by:

MARYANNE STEVENS

ANNE HEMKENDREIS

PETER NØRGAARD LARSEN

ANNETTE ROSENVOLD HVIDT

TONE BONNÉN

HAMMERSHØI AND EUROPE IS SUPPORTED BY

BIKUBENFONDEN

C.L. DAVIDS FOND OG SAMLING

THE GEORGE JORCK & EMMA JORCK FOUNDATION

CONTENTS

PREFACE

Vilhelm Hammershøi is among the pre-eminent Danish artists from the late 19th and early 20th century, and his reputation has reached further beyond the shores of Denmark than that of any other Danish painter. Over the course of the last 30 years a range of retrospectives of his works in Europe, Northern America, and Japan have served to consolidate his position as the equal of all the other great artists of the era. The predominant themes in his art – loneliness, isolation, and alienation, yet also an intense sensuality and a sense of contemplation and quiet serenity – continue to appeal to a very large contemporary audience that reaches far beyond the ranks of art specialists. He is undoubtedly the one Danish artist who has been most frequently "discovered" by new generations of art lovers!

Hammershøi has always been regarded as a true individualist within Danish art – a monumental figure that towered among his contemporaries and vas virtually without equal, both within Danish and international contexts. This view has been a staple of Danish art history for many years and has undoubtedly contributed to our understanding of Hammerhøi's art. Yet such a perception has also had a restricting impact on the angles of approach used for his art. Hammershøi himself was very sparing with statements about his art and his sources of inspiration, a fact which has prompted several art historians to assume that he was neither interested in the art of his own day nor inspired by it – which in turn prompted them to largely refrain from including works by his contemporaries when discussing his paintings. The only exception has been the US painter Whistler – with good reason, for Hammershøi himself actively sought to get in touch with Whistler. Yet even in this case there has been a certain resistance to seeing a direct connection or impact.

In Hammershøi's own time, however, several observers noticed obvious parallels between his art and that of certain artists from abroad. In addition to Whistler, such observers make specific mention of Puvis de Chavannes and Carrière. However, this has only recently had an impact on art history, and hitherto the subject has not been treated in depth.

The objective behind this exhibition and this book is, then, to place Hammershøi's art within the international context in which it was created. Yet our primary goal is not simply to identify Hammershøi's role models and shed light upon direct influences that may have transpired between the artists. Rather, we will showcase artistic endeavours that share a certain kinship, thereby accentuating how there are obvious parallels to be found between Hammershøi and several of his contemporaries, particularly within the non-literary side of the international Symbolism movement. He was not alone in the world, and several other artists also focused on phenomena such as atmosphere and existence rather than narrative.

In view of Hammershøi's own silence about the art he saw while travelling in Europe we fully realise that we are moving into a field where very few tangible points of reference exist and where the claims made can only be supported by qualified assumptions. We can point to likely connections, not prove them conclusively. Yet we view this approach as necessary if we are to set Hammershøi free from his isolated position within art history and shed new light upon his art. The exhibition arises out of many years of research into Hammerhøi's universe. Over the course of the last decades, senior research curator Kasper Monrad has addressed significant aspects of Hammershøi's art, not least within the context of the international painting scene of Hammershøi's time, and the results of this research is summarised in the exhibition and in the book. The exhibition itself has been created in close co-operation with art educator Annette Rosenvold Hvidt, who has also conducted research on Hammershøi's art on previous occasions. The opportunity for collaborating with Kunsthalle der Hypo-Kulturstiftung arose when where the planning had already reached an advanced stage; after this point curator Roger Diederen was actively involved in planning the exhibition.

The exhibition catalogue is intended as a companion to the exhibition itself, but also as an academic publication in its own right. Kasper Monrad addresses the exhibition's overall theme in the book's main article, and two other members of staff at Statens Museum for Kunst contribute essays on significant aspects of Hammershøi's art. Head of Collections and Research Peter Nørgaard Larsen discusses homelessness as a theme in his paintings, and Annette Rosenvold Hvidt writes about how Hammershøi works with intimacy and a sensuously recording gaze in his works, thereby working within a vein of Intimism. What is more, two scholars from abroad turn their attention to issues that have engaged art historians in the past, but not yielded any satisfactory answers before. Director of Academic Affairs MaryAnne Stevens elucidates why Hammershøi travelled to London on so many occasions, and Anne Hemkendreis discusses why the German poet Rainer Maria Rilke never wrote the article he was planning to do about Hammershøi's art. The graphic design of the book has been beautifully executed by Mette Secher.

In Copenhagen the final selection of works and the exhibition structure was determined in a process of fruitful interplay with exhibition architect Mads Kjædegaard. During a crucial stage of the planning the rhetorician Signe Hegelund contributed ideas on how best to structure the display.

In Munich the works for the exhibition were selected by Roger Diederen, while Matthias Kammermeier designed the exhibition rooms.

The exhibition could not have been realised were it not for the kind and open responsiveness of private collectors and of our colleagues at all the museums and collections who have helped stage this exhibition by loaning us their precious paintings. We wish to extend warm thanks to all who have loaned works for this event.

An exhibition on this scale cannot be staged without substantial donations towards the costs. In Copenhagen the exhibition has received crucial support from the Bikuben Foundation, from the C.L. David Foundation and Collection, and the George Jorck & Emma Jorck Foundation. Support has also been provided by Bruce Lauritzen and John L. Loeb via The American Friends of Statens Museum for Kunst. While preparing the exhibition Kasper Monrad also received support from the Dutch Embassy in Denmark in the form of a study trip to The Netherlands. In Munich the exhibition was funded thanks to a donation from the HypoVereinsbank/UniCredit.

A project of such ambition could not possibly have been realised without these donations, and we wish to offer our warmest thanks for the generous support received.

Karsten Ohrt	Christiane Lange
Director	Director
Statens Museum for Kunst	Kunsthalle der Hypo-Kulturstiftung

PARIS 1891

INTRODUCTION BY KASPER MONRAD

The year is 1891, the place is Paris. Vilhelm Hammershøi has sat down in front of the mirror in his hotel room and is painting his own portrait. As he paints, in the nature of things he has his gaze fixed on his own face, and he paints what he sees. But in the finished painting his gaze is neither fixed nor firm [1]. It appears to be directed at the viewers of the picture. Still, when standing before the painting, one does not really have eye contact with the man in the picture, and one begins to doubt whether he is focusing on anything in particular. Is he looking at anything at all, or is his gaze turned inward?

The painting was done at one of the most epochal and dramatic points in the history of Danish art. A group of young artists had just taken steps to break the almost 150-year-old stranglehold of the Royal Academy of Fine Arts in Copenhagen on the Danish art world. The reactionary artists on the Academy Jury had abused the adjudication rules for the annual exhibitions at Charlottenborg to repeatedly reject works by several young innovative artists. Worst affected was Hammershøi himself: the rejection of his works in 1890 by the Jury was the direct reason for the establishment of Den Frie Udstilling (The Independent Exhibition) the following year. The first exhibition had been held shortly before Hammershøi's departure for Paris and had been a grand *succès de scandale* in Copenhagen. It would not be too much to say that all artistic renewal in Danish art in the 1890s was associated with Den Frie Udstilling.

Hammershøi went on his honeymoon to Paris in September 1891 and spent a long period in the city, two years after his first journey there in connection with his participation in the Universal Exposition in 1889. That he chose Paris rather than Rome, the traditional destination of the Danish artists, is highly symptomatic of the artistic orientation of the young Danish artists at the time. They had their sights on the Parisian art scene, and for the first time in several decades many of the Danes were aware of the absolutely contemporary currents in French art. In comparison, it took 15-20 years beforse French Impressionism evoked a response in Danish art; that is, until after the French artists' struggle for recognition was in reality over. On the other hand the new Symbolist and Synthetist art won a hearing with several young Danish artists while the new modes of expression were still fresh, and a few of the Danes forged personal contacts with the French painters.

When it came to the shift from Naturalism's and Impressionism's focus on external, visible reality to dwelling on an internal, psychological world, Hammershøi was in fact one of the first to signal the new artistic orientation – in the international context as well as at home. His breakthrough work, *Portrait of a Young Woman* from 1885 [32, p. 55], already marked a striking break with the prevailing norms of portraiture in Denmark. With her inward-looking, faraway gaze and her almost ethereal appearance, the woman in the portrait is entirely removed from the specific momentary situation in which portrait subjects were otherwise depicted.

Hammershøi used his stay in Paris to find his bearings in current French art. Specifically, in January 1892, at a gallery in Paris, he had the opportunity to see an exhibition on

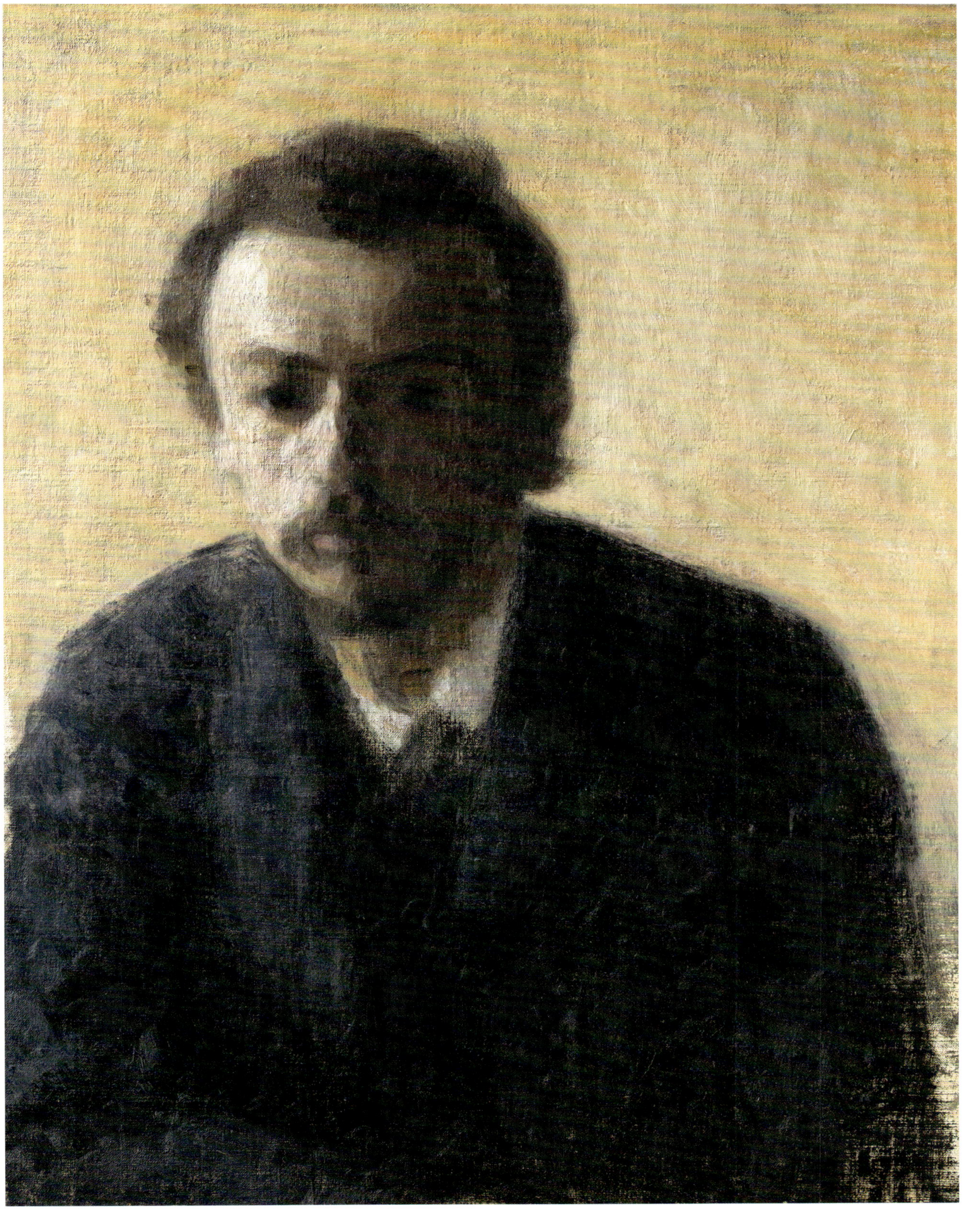

[1]
Vilhelm Hammershøi 1864-1916 Danish
Self-portrait 1891
Oil on canvas 54 x 42 cm
Private collection

which he commented very ironically in a letter to his close acquaintance Johan Rohde (p. 41). What he saw at the exhibition was clearly not to his taste!

This comment is one of the very few cases where he had anything to say about the art of his time. So if we are to take Hammershøi at his word, we can note that he did not care much for Symbolist art. But should we take him at his word?

Just a few months later, shortly after his arrival in Paris in the autumn of 1891, Hammershøi had sent his mother an often-quoted report: "I shall learn more from the old art than from the new." This suggests a one-sided interest in older art. But viewed in its context the statement is not quite so simple: "After all, I have travelled here to Paris to see a great deal and also preferably to learn something, but I believe I shall learn more from the old art than from the new. The many ideas that are around I have not seen so much of, but only [heard that] there were many ideas around."[1] In reality he was not denying that he could also learn something from contemporary art. But as yet he had not seen enough to take a stand.

In the letters preserved, primarily addressed to his mother, Hammershøi only exceptionally wrote about the art he may have seen on his travels. If we chose to conclude on the basis of this taciturnity that he only saw the art he explicitly mentioned, we would for example have to infer that during his seven-month stay in Rome in 1902-03 he saw not a single work of art! However, this is quite unthinkable. We know with certainty that on his way home from Italy in 1903, during a brief stay in Berlin, Hammershøi spent every day from morning to evening in the city's art museums.[2]

It is equally unthinkable that Hammershøi would in general have remained ignorant of what was happening in the international art world – not least considering that he was a frequent traveller. In 1885, six years before Hammershøi would be sitting in front of the mirror in the hotel room in Paris and paint his self-portrait, he made his first journey abroad, to Berlin and Dresden, and two years after that his next trip went to Holland and Belgium. In 1889, as mentioned, he went for the first time to Paris in connection with his participation in the Universal Exposition. Over the next 25 years he went on many journeys abroad. However, in Denmark too he had good opportunities to see the foreign art of his time. In 1888 both a large pan-Nordic art exhibition and a comprehensive exhibition of French art were held in Copenhagen. Five years later, in 1893, an epoch-making exhibition of works by Vincent van Gogh and Paul Gauguin was held at Den Frie Udstilling. A further four years later, in 1897, a large international exhibition of contemporary art was shown at the Ny Carlsberg Glyptotek. In addition, Hammershøi must inevitably have listened to – and perhaps also participated in – the discussions that were taking place among his colleagues. Several of the artists in his circle of acquaintances – especially Johan Rohde and Jens Ferdinand Willumsen – were actively keeping abreast of what was happening on the international art scene.

As early as 1886 the painter and critic Karl Madsen was mentioning his later friend Hammershøi in the same breath as the two prominent foreign painters Pierre Puvis de Chavannes and James McNeill Whistler, in his review of his paintings in the exhibition at Charlottenborg.[3] The critic Emil Hannover expanded on this six years later: "He belongs to a circle of artist-phenomena who have their most notable representatives abroad in Puvis de Chavannes, Eugène Carrière and Whistler, but who in this country found no pioneer until Hammershøi appeared. These are painters who differ in many ways from one another, and among other things apply their art to different ends, but [...] they use more or less the same kind of artistic expression."[4]

The only case where we have certain knowledge that Hammershøi decidedly sought contact with a contemporary foreign artist was during his first stay in London in 1897-98, when he tried to visit the American painter James McNeill Whistler, who was living in England. The Dane was unsuccessful in his venture, since Whistler was away. The idea for the visit was of course not a sudden whim; it must have grown out of several years' interest in Whistler's art. It therefore seems reasonable to assume that Hammershøi similarly kept a watchful eye on other European artists of the time, although he was apparently relatively introverted, and perhaps even quite shy. From statements in his letters we know, however, that he spoke both German and French to some degree and later learned English. Although he is unlikely to have created a wide network of contacts on his travels, we *cannot* therefore conclude that he did *not* share Johan Rohde's great interest in current international art.[5]

In the autumn of 2008, when the present exhibition and book were being prepared, a large retrospective exhibition of Hammershøi's art was mounted at the Royal Academy of Fine Arts in London, and in her review in the prestigious art periodical *Burlington Magazine* Rachel Sloan wrote, summing up on Hammershøi: "[...] there is much to suggest that he was keenly alive to the artistic currents of his time, and we can only hope that this avenue will be investigated more thoroughly in the future."[6] The aim of this exhibition is precisely an attempt to fulfil this hope.

NOTES

1 Letter to Frederikke Hammershøi, October-November 1891, quoted in Vad, 1988 (1992), p. 100.
2 Cf. Vad, 1988 (1992), pp. 125, 130.
3 *Politiken*, 4 June 1886; cf. Scavenius, 1883, p. 46.
4 Emil Hannover in *Politiken*, 8 May 1892.
5 See for example H.P. Rohde, *Journal fra en rejse i 1892*, introduction by N.G. Sandblad, Copenhagen 1955.
6 Rachel Sloan, "Vilhelm Hammershøi", *Burlington Magazine*, vol. CL, 2008, p. 625.

INTENSE ABSENCE

KASPER MONRAD

STORIES THAT ARE NOT TOLD[1]

At the Charlottenborg exhibition in 1886 Vilhelm Hammershøi showed a painting of an old woman sitting alone in an absolutely empty room [2]. The picture is all in grey, brown and black shades, and only a red hanging or curtain in the right of the picture breaks up the highly limited colour spectrum. Like so many of Hammershøi's other paintings from this time, it aroused considerable surprise among the exhibition visitors. Even a reviewer who later became one of the artist's most faithful supporters, the painter and critic Karl Madsen, seems to have been confused about his intentions and about the content of the picture; he couldn't resist the temptation to quote a remark he had heard at the exhibition: "A lady remarked that it looked as if the poor souls had been thrown out of their apartment and all their furnishings had been taken from them except for an old chair or chest [...]. Now they were sitting out in the lobby meditating over the vagaries of fortune."[2]

Today this anecdote may seem quite irrelevant to Hammershøi's picture, for if there is anything the picture is *not* about, it is people being evicted. But it does turn the focus on the widespread expectation of the period that a picture should tell a story. And indirectly it touches on something quite central to Hammershøi: his art grew out of a tradition where the anecdotal played a very important role. Simply put, he painted the same types of subjects as the contemporary genre painters; but he removed all the layers of meaning that referred directly to external reality and contemporary life, and consistently omitted all elements of narrative. In other words he painted genre pictures without any real genre content. The picture in question is presumably about loneliness and isolation.

Formally speaking, Hammershøi's painting of a *Young Girl Sewing* [3] is a genre painting. But no story is told, and we learn nothing about her. She is frozen in a movement, but the needlework as such is of minor importance. Although we can identify the model (the painter's sister, Anna), this is a person with no individual identity. Instead of focusing on narrative details, Hammershøi has aimed at tight, compact form and condensed expression. In the depiction of the woman he has taken a huge leap away from the standard pictures of women in a working situation that could be seen in the preceding years at the Charlottenborg exhibitions in Copenhagen.

In other words there is a duality in Hammershøi's art, and in this very respect he stands out from his Danish contemporaries, practically all of whom insisted on giving the picture a content. This was of course the case with all the artists who, like his teacher, Peder Severin Krøyer, continued in the Naturalist tradition, but also with the artists who either devoted themselves wholeheartedly to Symbolist art or moved on the borderline between Symbolism and Realism. No matter how much his colleagues of the same age, Laurits Andersen Ring and Ejnar Nielsen, infused their pictures with Symbolism, the subjects kept their specific meaning, and the narrative that was associated with them as such retained its validity.

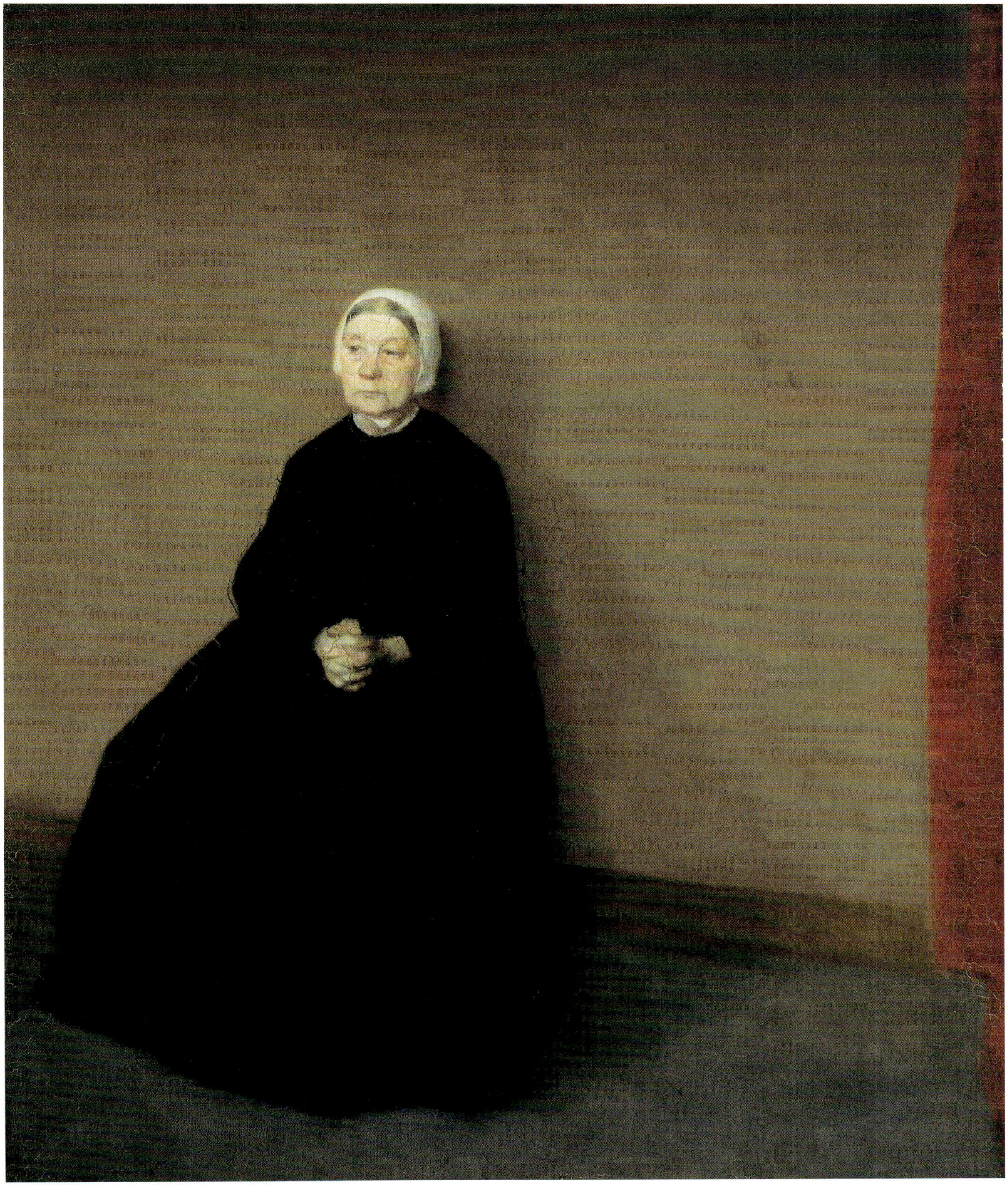

[2]
Vilhelm Hammershøi 1864-1916 Danish
An Old Woman 1886
Oil on canvas 69.7 x 56.7 cm
The Hirschsprung Collection, Copenhagen

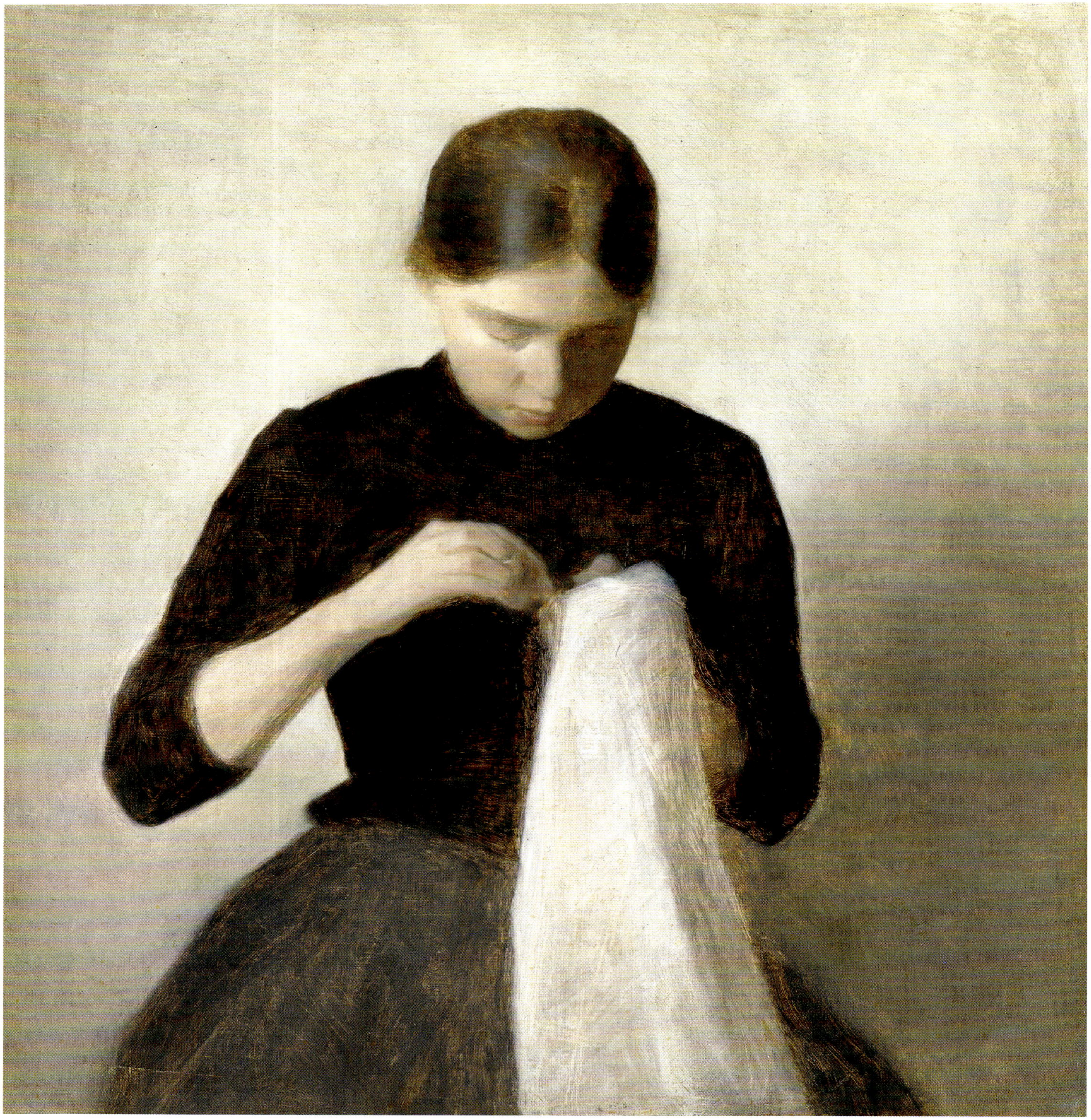

[3]
Vilhelm Hammershøi 1864-1916 Danish
Young Girl Sewing. Anna Hammershøi, the Artist's Sister 1887
Oil on canvas 37 x 35 cm
Ordrupgaard, Copenhagen

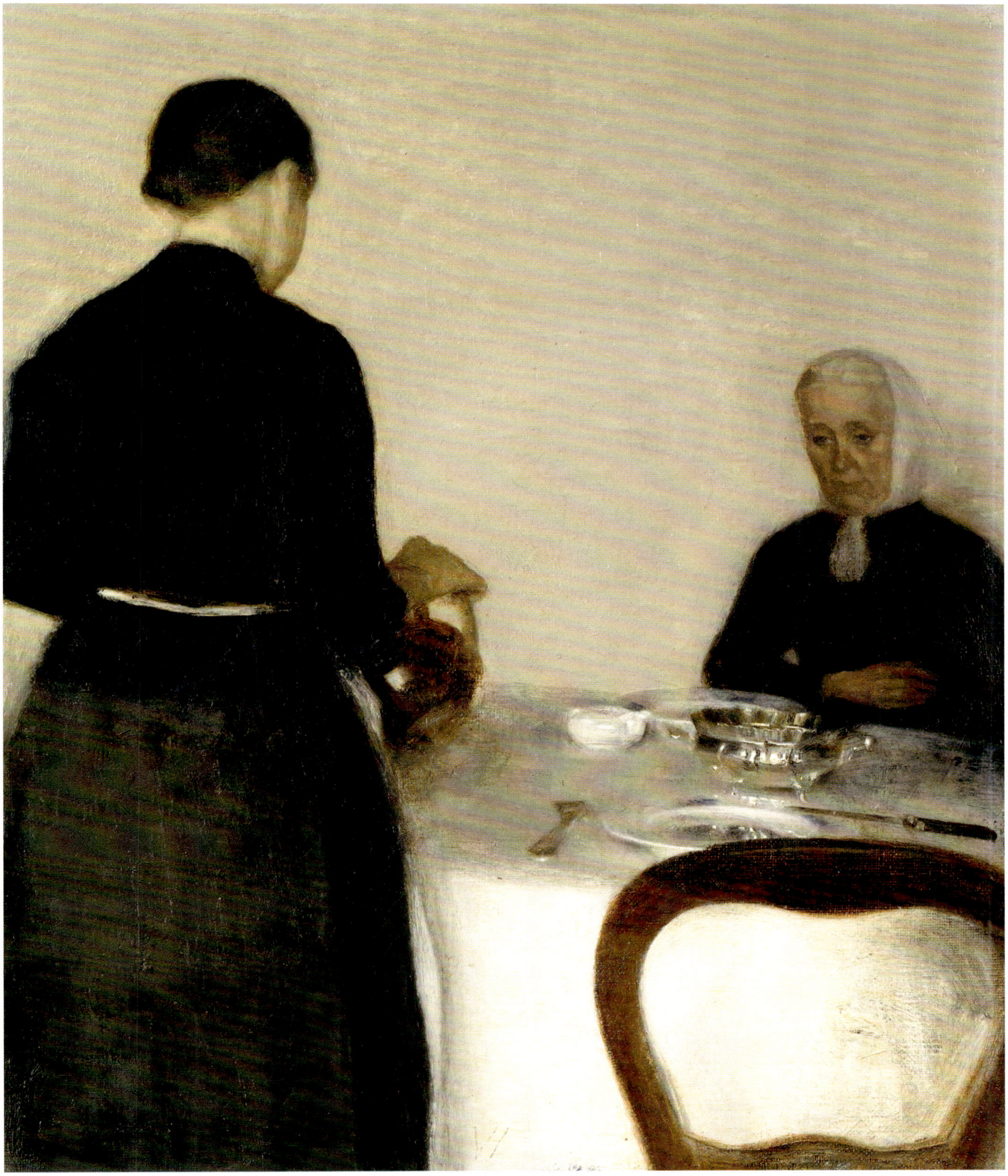

[4]
Vilhelm Hammershøi 1864-1916 Danish
Interior with the Artist's Mother and Sister 1884
Oil on canvas 40 x 34 cm
Private collection (Dep. Ordrupgaard, Copenhagen)

Solitary figures in empty rooms

Hammershøi's duality is expressed not least in the group of subjects that were to be central to his art: the interiors.[3] There can be little doubt that he was familiar with the tradition for this picture type, in both European and Danish painting; which means first and foremost the Dutch painting of the 17th century and that of the socalled Danish Golden Age of the early 19th century.[4] But he took his primary point of departure in the many Danish interiors of his own time. In the 1880s there seems to have been a whole wave of pictures of bourgeois homes – paintings that often focused on the sequestered, limited universe where the women of the time lived their sheltered lives, protected but also isolated from the surrounding world. Although the painter Carl Holsøe was later to become greatly indebted to Hammershøi, there are indications that at first it was Holsøe who was the debtor. In April 1888 a reviewer wrote that Holsøe had "a good grasp of the Copenhagen parlour atmosphere in the peculiarly closed 'home' where wives and daughters could live a whole life without the least sense of the world outside."[5]

By and large Hammershøi took over this theme, but purged the pictures of the anecdotal. In the drawing-rooms we often see a single woman, perhaps formally engaged in some chore. But in reality she is doing nothing, she is frozen in her movements, and time stands still. Nor did Hammershøi make any attempt to give a more detailed characterization of the solitary – and presumably also isolated – women we see in his interiors. Their life-situation is only hinted at, and the impression is reinforced by the often oppressive, sometimes claustrophobic atmosphere that typifies the paintings. Strictly speaking, he delivers the same message as the period's more anecdotal pictures, which straightforwardly tell the stories of the women of the day. He simply peeled the narrative away and left the core. Already in the early painting of the artist's mother and sister from 1884 [4] he has settled into his narrative form. The two women appear to be in the middle of a meal. But the viewers inevitably begin to doubt whether the young woman will ever get the tea poured, or whether the older woman will get started on her meal. Nor are we told what relationship exists between the two women in the picture – or indeed in real life! (The picture was not conceived as a portrait, and the artist's mother and sister are only to be considered as models.) Even when the figures are carrying out specific actions that constitute a single moment in a time sequence, time and all motion have stopped. A woman who is sweeping a floor [5] will never complete her task.

In a few pictures we see a woman absorbed in reading a letter. This subject has several classic antecedents, especially in the 17th-century Dutch paintings of Johannes Vermeer and Pieter de Hooch, who in several pictures depicted a woman reading a letter. This action – the reading of a letter – had a special meaning in the Dutch paintings, since the reading women must be assumed to have been married to merchants who were travelling abroad, running their businesses. The letters thus testify indirectly to a societal type and a family pattern. But there is none of this in Hammershøi. Nor did he take the line of his older and contemporary colleagues, who frequently signalled that the letters being read were of an amorous character. We are given no hint of who has sent the letter, or of the situation of the recipient, and the letter as such has no symbolic meaning. This is underscored in several paintings where the letter has been replaced by a book [6]. Only the absorption remains. Similarly, the action has been removed from the subject in the paintings of women who sit at a piano or are busy doing needlework. In most cases the woman, with her back to us, conceals what she is occupied with, and the figure seems completely self-enclosed [64, p. 87].

Hammershøi's *The Coin Collector* from 1904 [7] shows a young man intensely preoccupied with looking at a coin. But he has no story either. True, an expert observer like Poul Vad has claimed that the man's activity has "taken on a mysterious, almost furtive character, a strangely dramatic staging".[6] That is, there is a suggestion that the man could be a counterfeiter. But strictly speaking the picture tells us nothing of this. It reveals nothing about who he is, or what he is doing, apart from the fact that he is absorbed in looking at a coin.

The people in the pictures are all in a situation where there seem to be no options. Time is frozen, and their existence appears quite static – even though we know rationally that neither the reading nor the household chores could in reality be drawn out through all eternity.

Things are not quite that simple when it comes to the rooms they are in. Confined as these rooms may be physically, the pictures still often have the character of presenting the viewers with an existential choice. Very often we see that there is access through a doorway to one or more adjacent rooms. By definition, a door offers you a choice: you can choose to walk through the door, or you can choose not to, and from a closed room the door leads out into the open or to another room which will possibly offer other choices. The doors in Hammershøi's pictures may open into a space which from the standpoint of the viewer is difficult to take in – or they may block off the view and prevent us from getting out of the confined space we see in front of us. In reality there is no way out of the room. Nor do the people seem to notice the opening that the door – or the doors – might offer.

Through a doorway in the painting *Interior, Strandgade 30* from 1905 [8] we can see a woman who stands with her back to us, half hidden in the darkness of the passage. We can only just make her out and we are given no impression of what she is doing – if she is doing anything at all. Her presence raises more questions than it answers. Why is she standing there, and what is she doing? We get no answer.

In a couple of cases Hammershøi has placed his easel in the empty room [9]. In so doing he has suggested a depiction of one of two familiar subjects: "the artist in his studio" or "the artist and his subject". After all, the room was both his studio and his subject. But the painter himself is not present, and the easel has been positioned so we can only see the back of the painting. The suggested theme is therefore only hinted at, quite without any of the narratives that are normally associated with the two subjects. On the other hand, the picture has taken on an almost supernatural character thanks to the light that falls in from the window on the wall just where the artist must be conceived as standing. However, to speak of divine artistic inspiration in connection with Hammershøi's art is quite clearly to go too far.

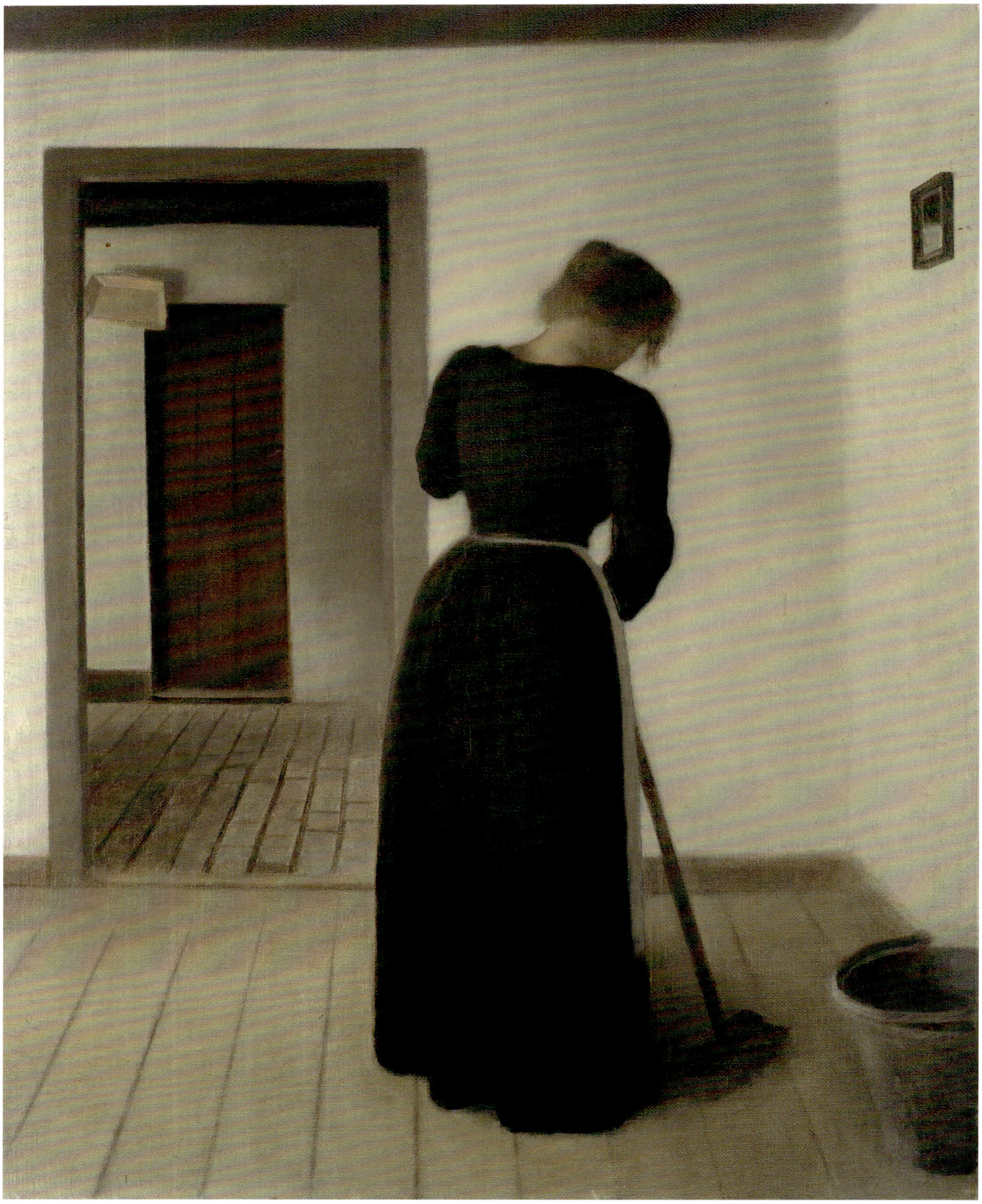

[5]
Vilhelm Hammershøi 1864-1916 Danish
Interior with a Young Woman Sweeping 1899
Oil on canvas 50.2 x 40.3 cm
The Hirschsprung Collection, Copenhagen

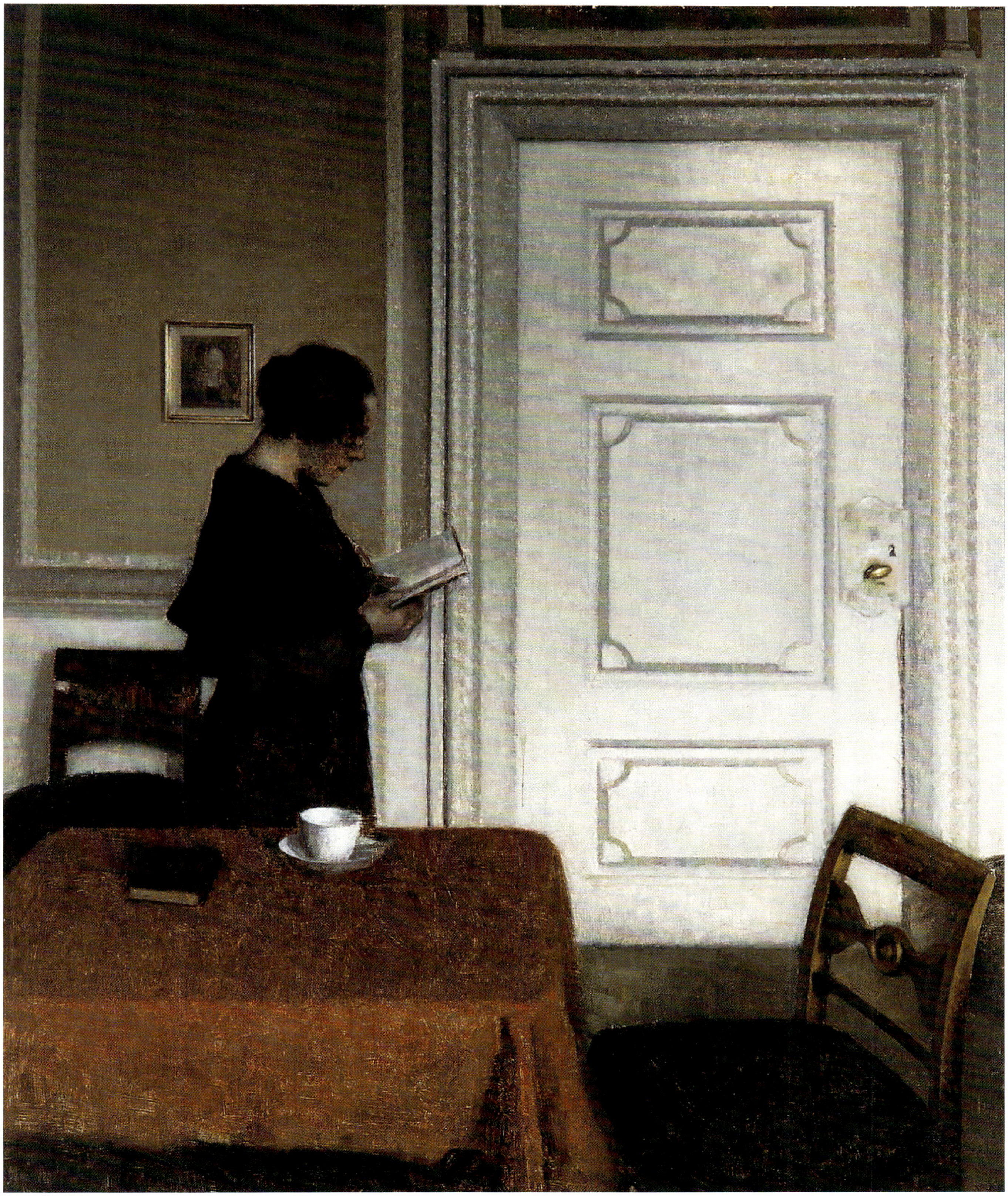

[6]
Vilhelm Hammershøi 1864-1916 Danish
Interior with a Woman Reading 1908
Oil on canvas 65.5 x 56 cm
Museum Sønderjylland – Kunstmuseet Brundlund Slot, Aabenraa

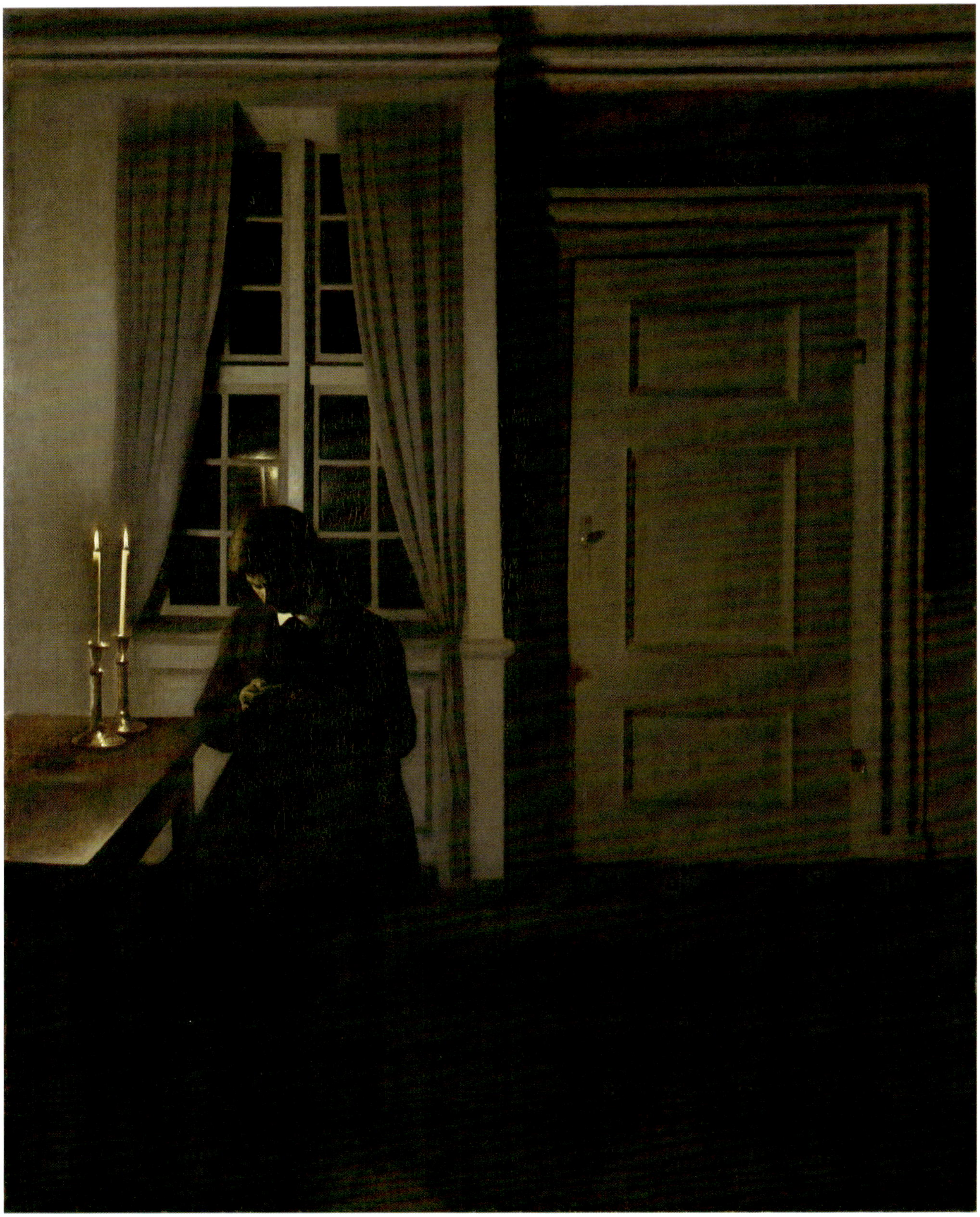

[7]
Vilhelm Hammershøi 1864-1916 Danish
The Coin Collector 1904
Oil on canvas 89 x 69.5 cm
The National Museum of Art, Architecture and Design, Oslo

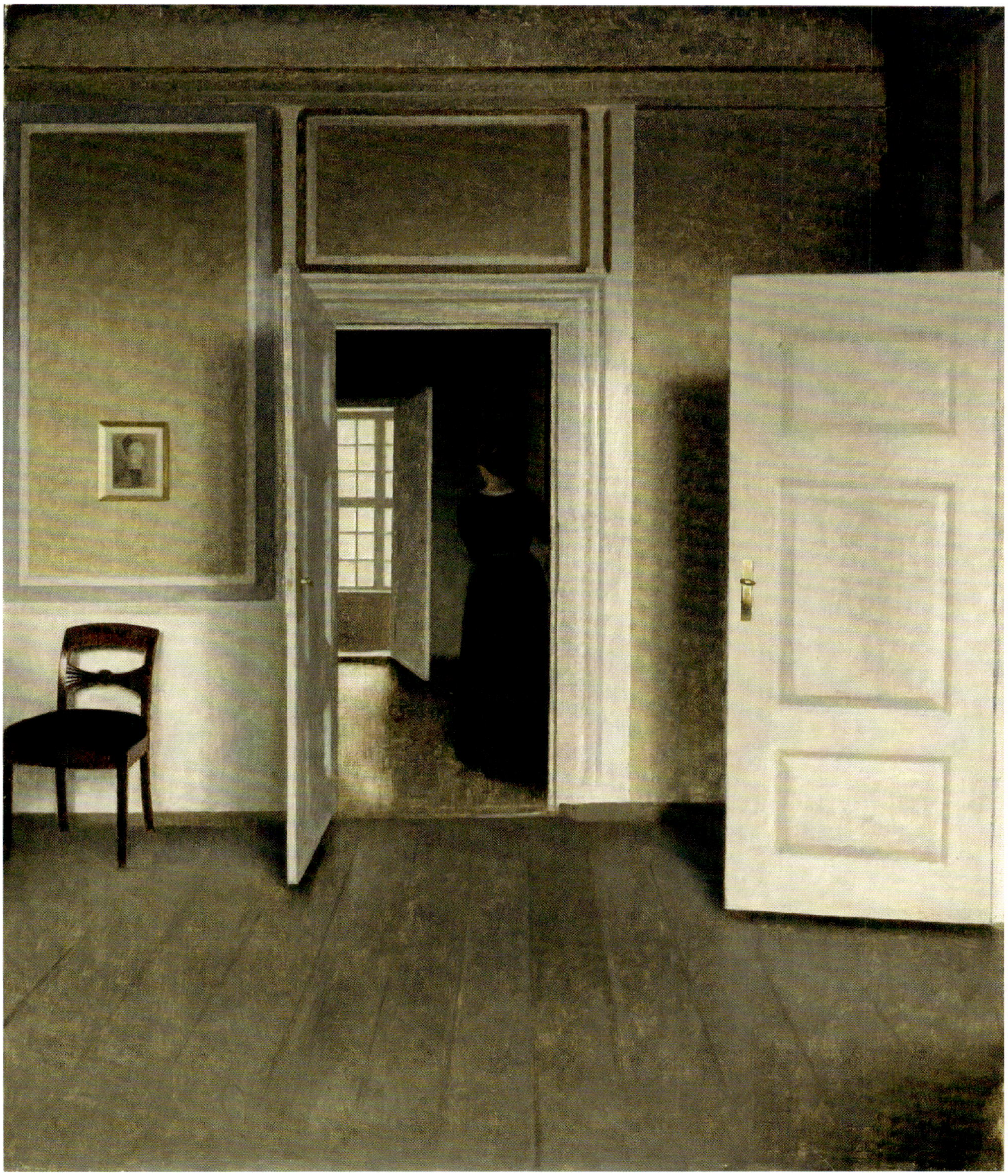

[8]
Vilhelm Hammershøi 1864-1916 Danish
Interior, Strandgade 30 1905
Oil on canvas 65.5 x 54.5 cm
Ateneum Art Museum, Finnish National Gallery, Helsinki

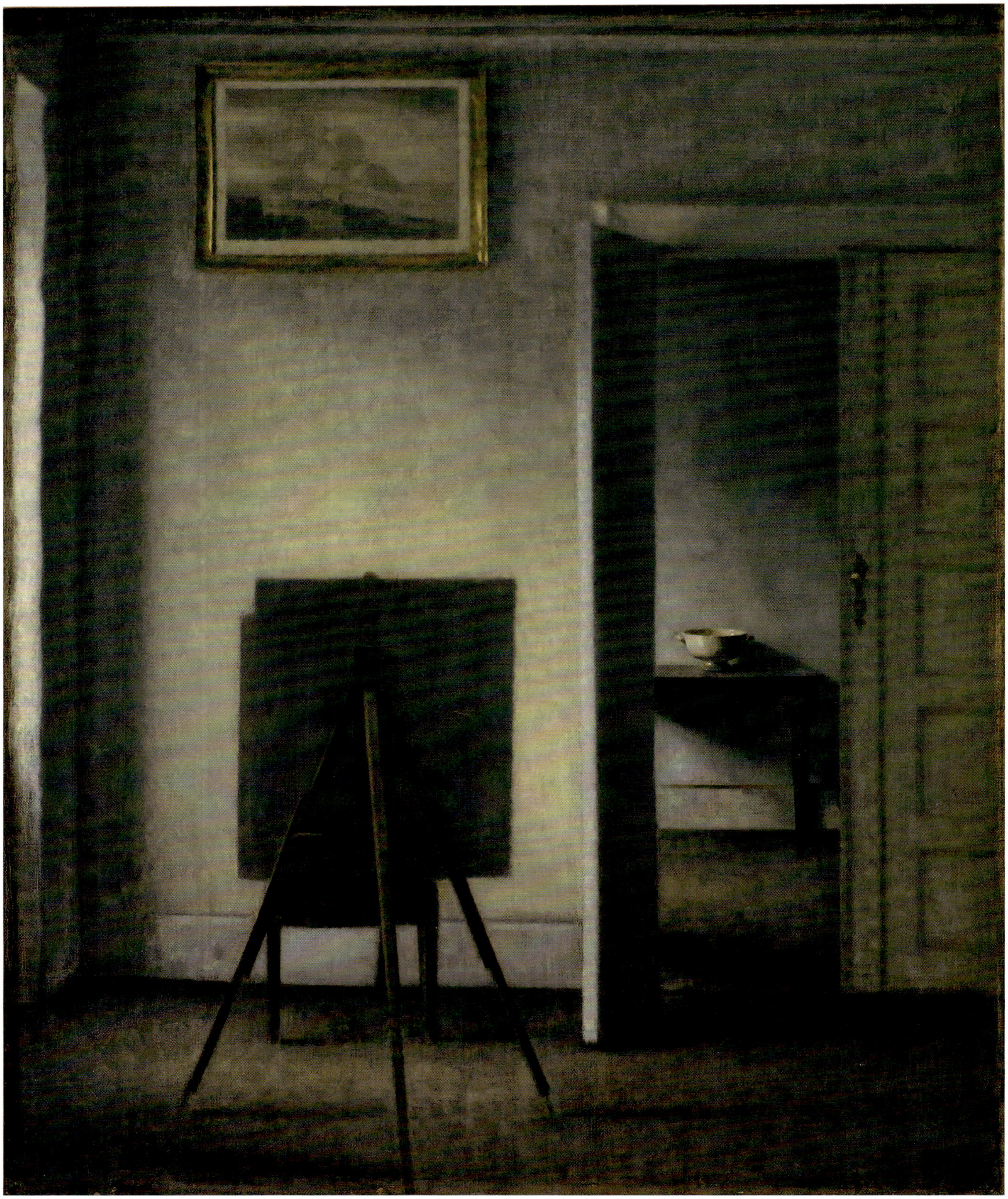

[9]
Vilhelm Hammershøi 1864-1916 Danish
Interior with the Artist's Easel 1910
Oil on canvas 84 x 69 cm
Statens Museum for Kunst

To choose or not to choose

For good reasons, the solitary women in the closed rooms are prevented from making contact with other people. But even when Hammershøi shows several people together, they are apparently isolated from one another. Yet it was not in an interior painting that he first attempted a complex figure composition; it was in the large painting with the mythological title *Artemis* [10]. This is an odd, closed-in picture that was immediately perceived as a Symbolist manifestation by the painter Mogens Ballin when he reviewed it at Den Frie Udstilling (The Independent Exhibition) in 1894: "Yet how delightfully beautiful these nude figures are, refreshingly distant from the body of the model; they are not cowed by the frailties and struggles of wretched life; freely they move in the pure world of the ideas; without words and almost without motion, they communicate their sublime thoughts: soul speaks to soul of the deepest mysteries of life, of the highest beauty, the purest harmony."[7] Despite the exalted style, which fails to capture the vague, ethereal aspect of the picture, Ballin does point to something essential; that its subject is intangible and can only be determined further with difficulty. The art critic and art historian Emil Hannover, who was extremely well informed about the discussions that went on among the artists, was able to state that the picture was only given its title when it was almost finished: "It is furthermore a picture which in ordinary terms represents nothing, and which yet bears the name *Artemis* in the catalogue. It is said only to have been given a title when it was almost finished. And asked about the meaning of its name, Hammershøi is said to have been disinclined to admit that it has only been given a name because such a thing is necessary to a picture."[8]

This means that the painting is unlikely to show a particular subject from antiquity; it is rather the painter's personal reworking of something from the ancient range of subjects. Although Hammershøi was apparently unable to indicate a specific action in the picture, he would hardly have agreed with Hannover that the painting shows nothing. With its three women and one man, the painting at first sight bears a certain resemblance to classical representations of *The Judgement of Paris*, but the women in his picture are not all identical to the goddesses in this traditional scene. As we know, Prince Paris chose Aphrodite (Venus in the Roman mythology), but here the divine huntress Artemis (Diana) is at the centre (she is not in the original Paris story). It would appear that a different scene is being played out.[9] The main figure in the picture, who has her status as moon goddess emphasised by the crescent moon above her head, is being accompanied forth by another woman who appears to be the harvest goddess Demeter (Ceres). The body language of the two women is ambivalent, but they seem to be on their way towards a man whose identity is uncertain. Is he Apollo, or is he Paris, now making a different choice? He is standing up leaning against a support that we cannot see and his look of introversion and his feminine appearance weaken any suggestion of the erotic in the picture.[10] The third woman stands with her back to us – perhaps she is Aphrodite turning away because she did not win the contest this time?

However, the connection between the women and the man is vague and indeterminate. Does the man stand contemplating which of the women he is to choose (like Paris in *The Judgement of Paris*)? Or is Artemis trying with her contact to arouse the man to life, purely sensually, and thus help him to find his masculine identity? Or is she not on her way towards him at all, but wants to walk past him, so they will never have any contact with each other?

Hammershøi himself would hardly have been able to answer these questions – he probably did not think so concretely about it. In this picture he seems to have carried out a

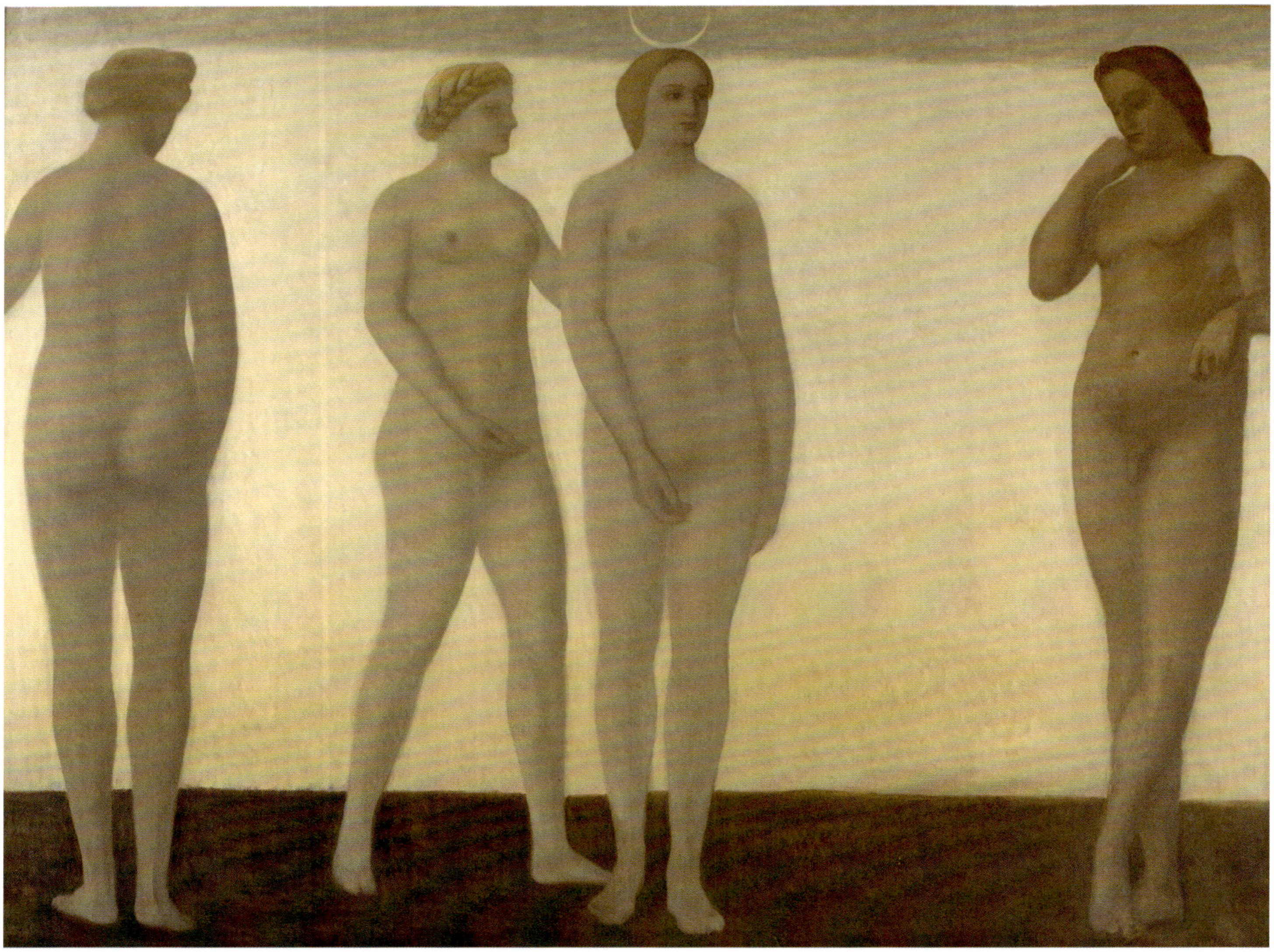

[10]
Vilhelm Hammershøi 1864-1916 Danish
Artemis 1893-94
Oil on canvas 193 x 251.5 cm
Statens Museum for Kunst

[11]
Vilhelm Hammershøi 1864-1916 Danish
Standing Female Nude 1909-10
Oil on canvas 205 x 153 cm
Statens Museum for Kunst

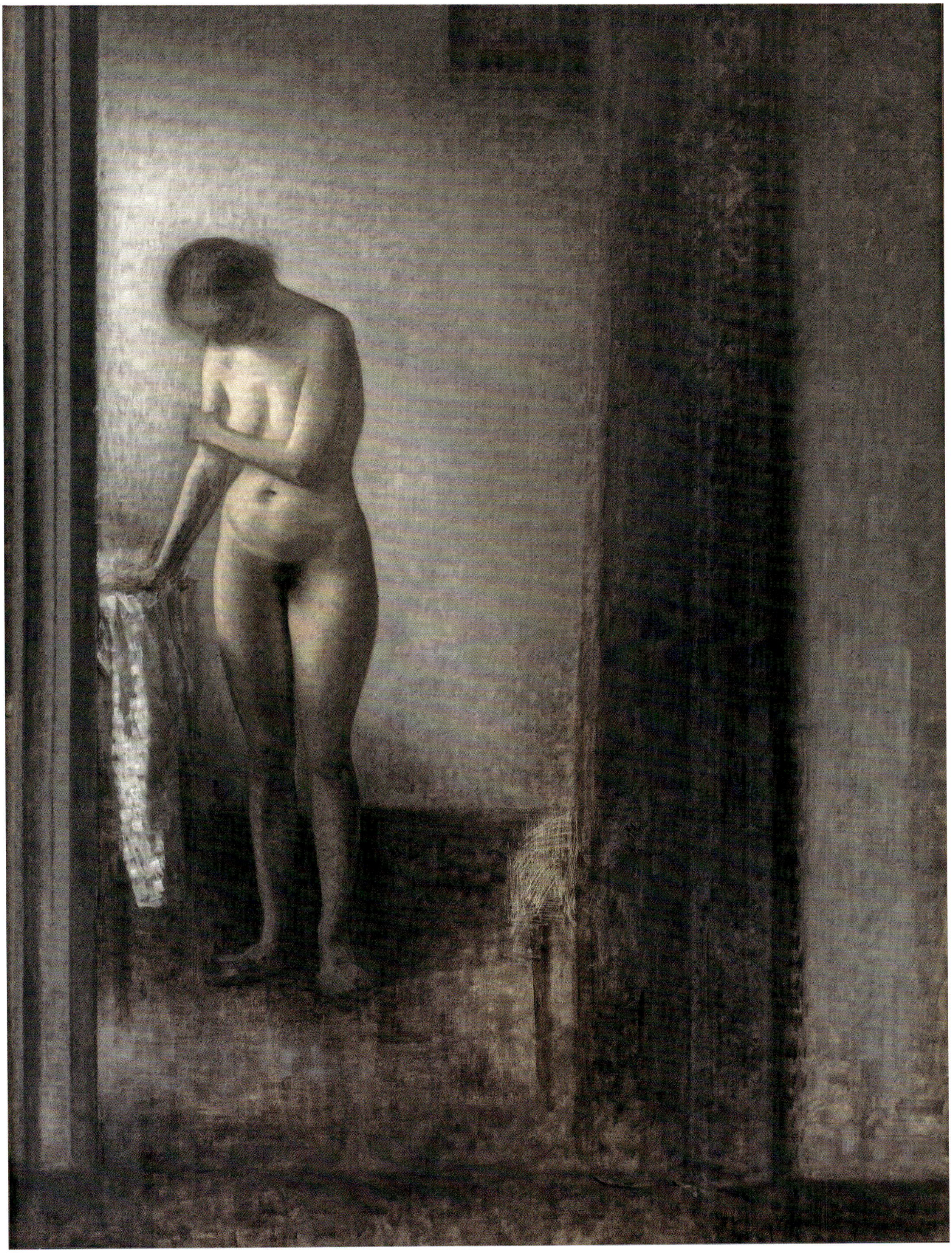

decoding of a traditional motif so that the figures have lost their original meaning; he also seems to have created his own contradiction-filled myth which consists more of hints than of specific narrative.

After *Artemis* Hammershøi never took up the thread of ancient mythology again, and more than ten years passed before he chose to paint another nude female figure. She was now placed in a contemporary setting, in a room in a private home. In the painting *Standing Female Nude* [11] we see a woman who at first sight seems to be about to get dressed. This is therefore not a picture of a model. Here Hammershøi adheres to a Danish tradition of nudes, a further development of the true life study that was created by C.W. Eckersberg around 80 years earlier.[11] But in reality the woman is detached from any such everyday situation. She has stopped in the midst of her movements, and we do not expect her to proceed to any sort of action. The woman's individual features appear to have been obscured by the painter at a late phase of the work. Since, presumably at the same time, the painter scraped the paint from the seat of the stool in the foreground, it might look as if the painting has not been completed. But it is more likely that Hammershøi simply decided to regard the painting as finished despite these unfinished areas. The absence of facial features, and not least of eyes, makes it look as if the woman has turned her gaze inward. This is reinforced by the way she stands with bowed head. The woman's nudity makes her look particularly exposed and vulnerable. There is no direct contact with the woman, and this helps greatly to suggest existential reflection. The statement of the picture is not unequivocal. But it is tempting to view the woman as an image of loneliness and doubt.

Together yet separate

In his compositions with several figures, Hammershøi stuck to the people of his own time after *Artemis*. In 1897-98 he painted a picture of a man and a woman seated facing each other at a table [12, 13, 14]. Here too there is no direct contact between the figures, and they seem to be in their own worlds. The models for the painting were the artist himself and his wife, but there is no question of a true portrait. The painter has given no sense of the closeness and intimacy that supposedly must exist between two spouses.[12] And it is evident that this was not his intention either from a letter dated 14 March 1898: "The one picture I am busy painting [...] is a kind of double portrait of Ida and myself; that is, I myself almost have my back turned; and they are not meant to be portraits in the strictest sense either."[13] This is underscored by the title he gave the picture when he exhibited it in 1908: *Two Figures*.[14] The picture must therefore be viewed at a more universal level. Here too there is no real story; rather, a situation is outlined – we see the essence of a narrative. The man appears as an anonymous, impersonal figure who seems to be intruding on the woman, but without being able to compel her attention. With her introversion and inner calm she rejects his approach. The picture is thus about modern human beings' opportunities to make contact with one another.

With his major work, the large painting *Five Portraits* from 1901-02 [15], Hammershøi embarked on a type of picture that had been cultivated frequently over the last couple of decades of the 19th century both in Denmark and abroad: the group portrait of artists. Danish artists like P.S. Krøyer and Viggo Johansen had painted occasional pictures where the artists were often captured in sociable gatherings and where it was more the conviviality than their artistic calling that was the theme of the pictures. A contrast with these was the homage pictures that several French painters did of a group of artists gathered to pay tribute to a shared mentor (see p. 74). However, Hammershøi's painting differs strikingly from both types of picture.

Quite predictably, the painting raised expectations in a reviewer of a story that could be retold when it was exhibited in 1902: "The situation is more or less this: there has been profound talk about something or other that has moved everyone deeply, and they are now waiting for a conclusive word from a sixth party" (i.e. from an observer outside the picture).[15] Such a conclusive word is of course unthinkable in Hammershøi's universe.

In the huge painting we see five men, all of whom were close to the artist: the architect Thorvald Bindesbøll; his brother, the painter Svend Hammershøi; the painter and art historian Karl Madsen; the painter and sculptor J.F. Willumsen; and the painter Carl Holsøe. Yet there is nothing private about the picture and no real interaction. The five men are gathered around a table in the dusk, but all seem to be more or less absorbed in their own thoughts. The only source of light is two candles, but in reality these would hardly shed as much light on the tabletop as they do. There is no visible action that might connect them, and no direct contact among them. Three of them gaze directly at the viewer, but this does not make them any more present. The picture has a monumentality and an earnestness that extend far beyond the traditional artists' gathering in this type of picture. No obvious artistic credo that might link the five comes to expression, and we do not know why they have gathered. Nevertheless the picture has a sense of intensity, and a strange kind of affinity prevails among them.

The frontal composition, the placing of the table parallel to the picture plane, and the grouping of the men all recall the depictions in earlier epochs of *The Last Supper.*[16] The back wall is moreover divided into dark and light areas by the black windows, which evoke associations with the windows and wall hangings in Leonardo da Vinci's famous version of this subject. Willumsen is viewed entirely frontally like Christ in paintings of The Last Supper (but displaced from the middle towards the right), and the artist's brother is isolated on the closer side of the table in the same way as Judas. But of course there is no hint of the Symbolism traditionally associated with the subject. Svend Hammershøi does not stand out from the company more than any of the others. And Carl Holsøe's large feet, which stick out right in the face of the viewer, effectively kick a hole in the hint of the devotional that suffuses the picture. Neither a cursory nor a detailed examination of Hammershøi's painting dispels the impression of a quite inscrutable picture.

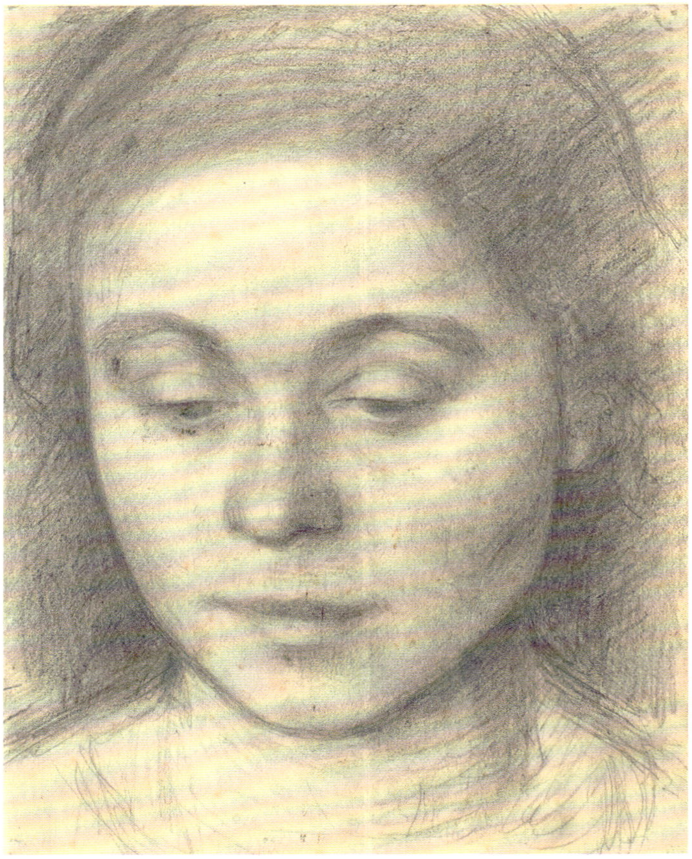

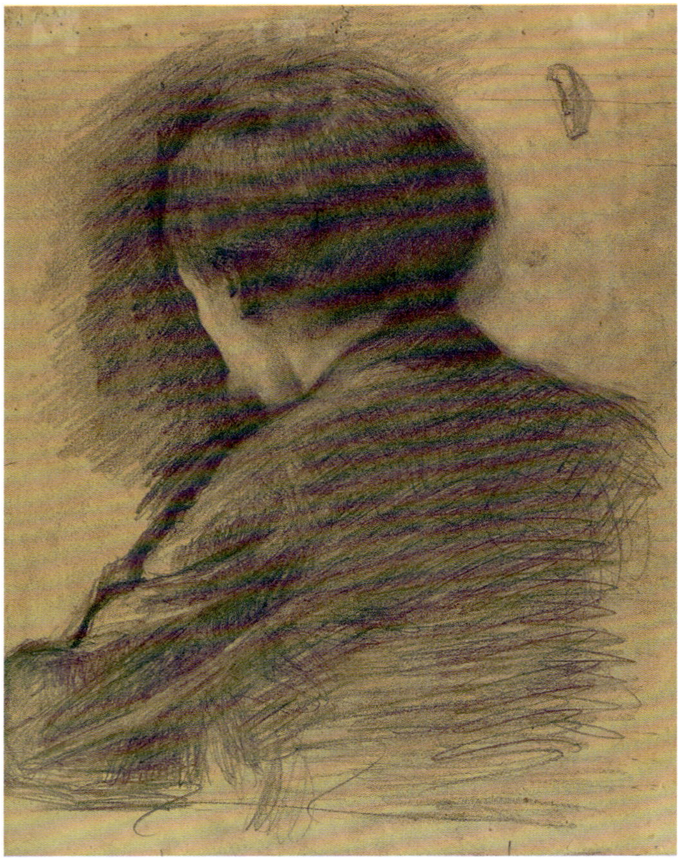

[12]
Vilhelm Hammershøi 1864-1916 Danish
Portrait of Ida, the Artist's Wife 1898
Drawing, Pencil 24.2 x 18.8 cm
Statens Museum for Kunst

[13]
Vilhelm Hammershøi 1864-1916 Danish
Self-portrait, seen from behind 1898
Drawing, Pencil 24.7 x 18.9 cm
Statens Museum for Kunst

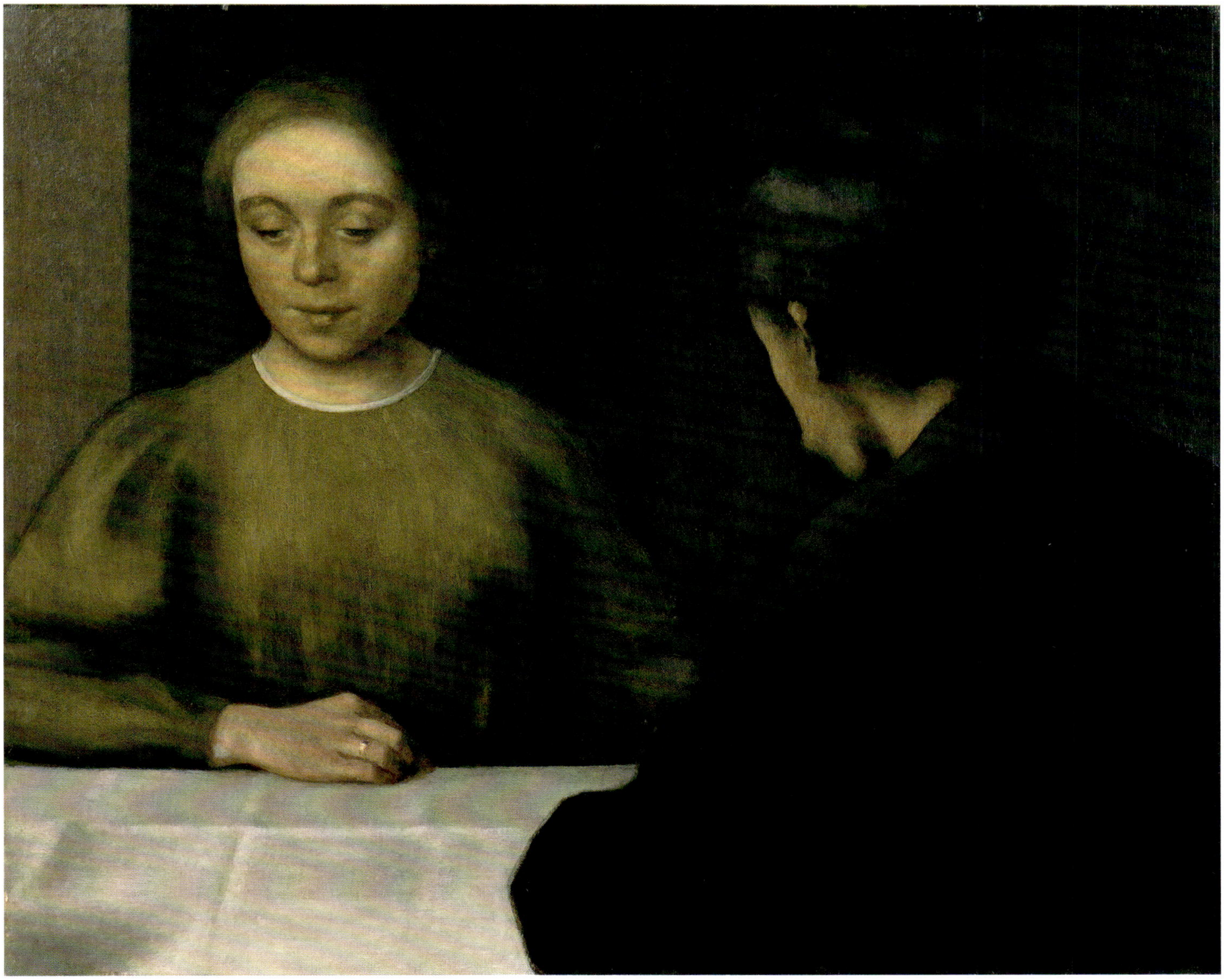

[14]
Vilhelm Hammershøi 1864-1916 Danish
Two Figures. The Artist and His Wife 1898
Oil on canvas 71.5 x 86 cm
ARoS Aarhus Kunstmuseum

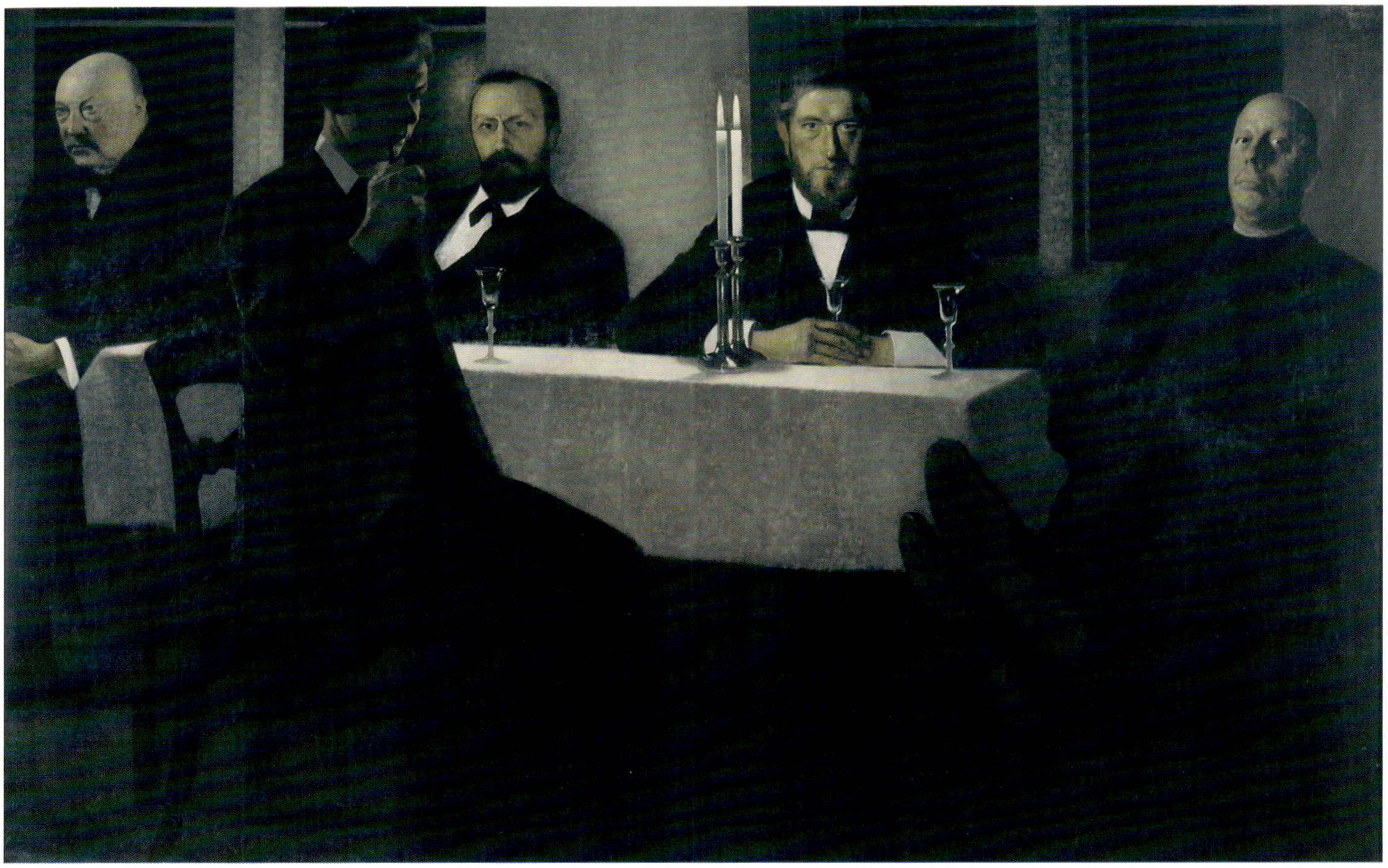

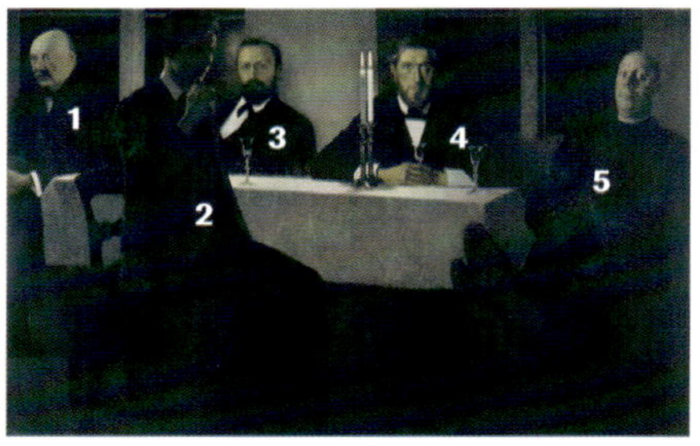

1 Thorvald Bindesbøll

2 Svend Hammershøi

3 Karl Madsen

4 J.F. Willumsen

5 Carl Holsøe

[15]
Vilhelm Hammershøi 1864-1916 Danish
Five Portraits 1901-02
Oil on canvas 190 x 340 cm
The Thielska Gallery, Stockholm

No sign of life

Hammershøi was equally unwilling to say anything about his subjects when his attention turned to some of the monumental buildings in Copenhagen. He painted a succession of monumental pictures of historic Danish architecture, always shown as if the buildings stood in a ghost town; that is, quite without the street life that had typified the many Danish urban pictures of the preceding decades, and without any hint of the social function the buildings had. In the painting of *St. Peter's Church, Copenhagen* [16] Hammershøi has chosen to disregard the surrounding houses in this densely populated old neighbourhood of the city, and the street that runs along outside the church is lost in mist and devoid of human beings. In the preceding decades the Danish painters had used the Copenhagen streets as the setting for large and small everyday scenes or even for personal and social dramas. But there is nothing of this in Hammershøi. An oddly silent mood prevails in the picture, and there are no people who could disturb it. The city was populated in the pictures of the Renaissance, and continued to be so in the subsequent centuries. Hammershøi emptied it of all life.

Hammershøi related to nature in the same way as to the city – with the same distance and without any suggestion of the life associated with the places he painted. This is very much the case in the painting *Landscape, From Lejre* [17]. In this subject – rolling Zealand fields – Hammershøi has chosen a type of landscape that had been associated for several decades with the efforts of the artists to profile a national Danish identity and at the same time to express an affinity between man and nature. All this Hammershøi has peeled away from the subject. You get no sense that this is a landscape that has been extensively reworked by man in recent times; nor is there any suggestion of the great forces of nature that created this rolling landscape in the Ice Age. The role of both nature and man is played down. The hills seem stylized, and the same goes for the three forest areas and the clouds in the sky. All forms have been given a look of regularity that distances them from a direct study of a specific subject. At the same time the landscape has lost the appearance of lushness that has normally been associated with the depictions of the Danish farming country. The picture gives the viewers a sense of a distant, alienated relationship with nature.

Even as a landscape painter, Hammershøi did not tell the "stories" suggested by the subjects.

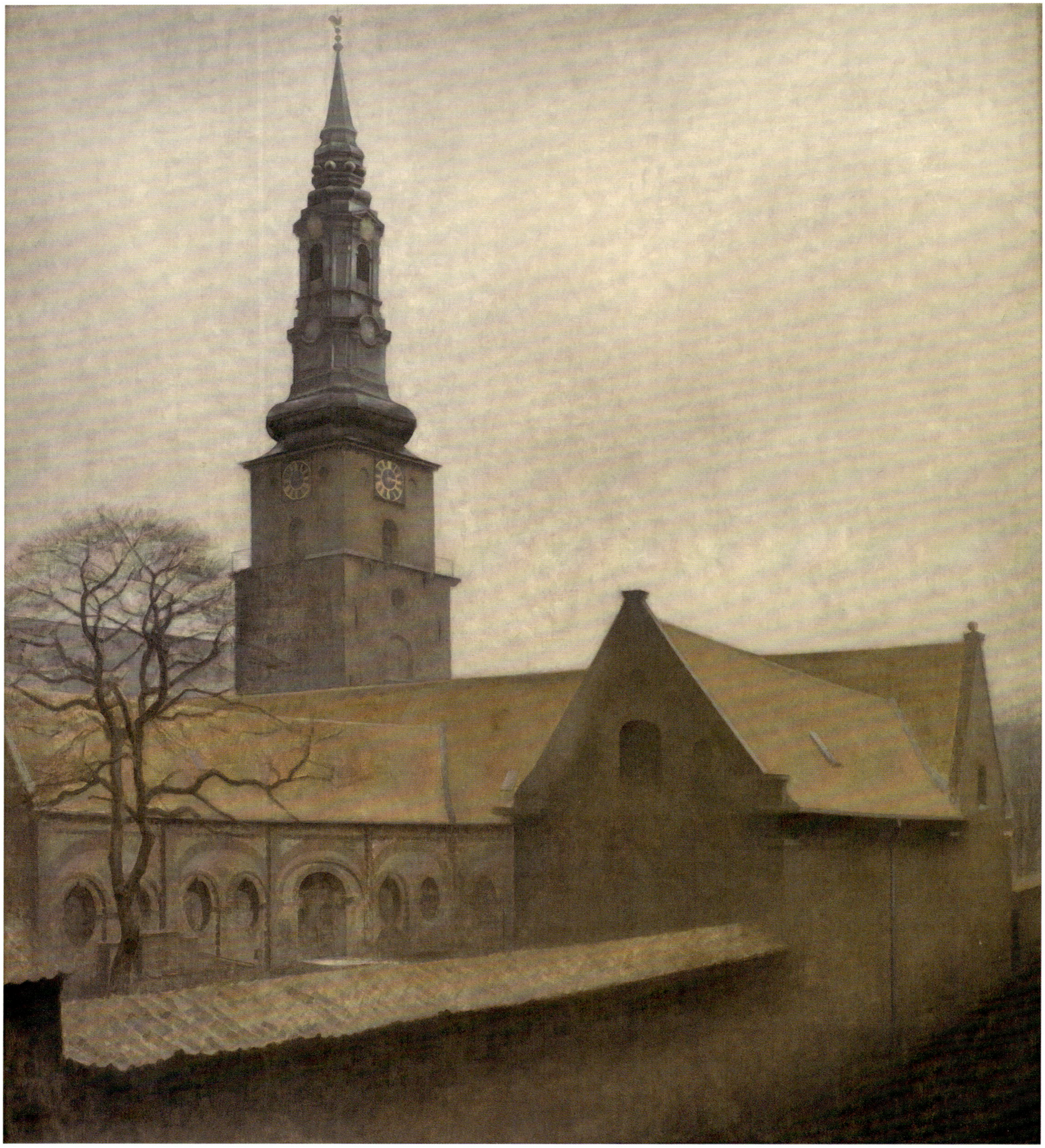

[16]
Vilhelm Hammershøi 1864-1916 Danish
St. Peter's Church, Copenhagen 1906
Oil on canvas 133 x 118 cm
Statens Museum for Kunst

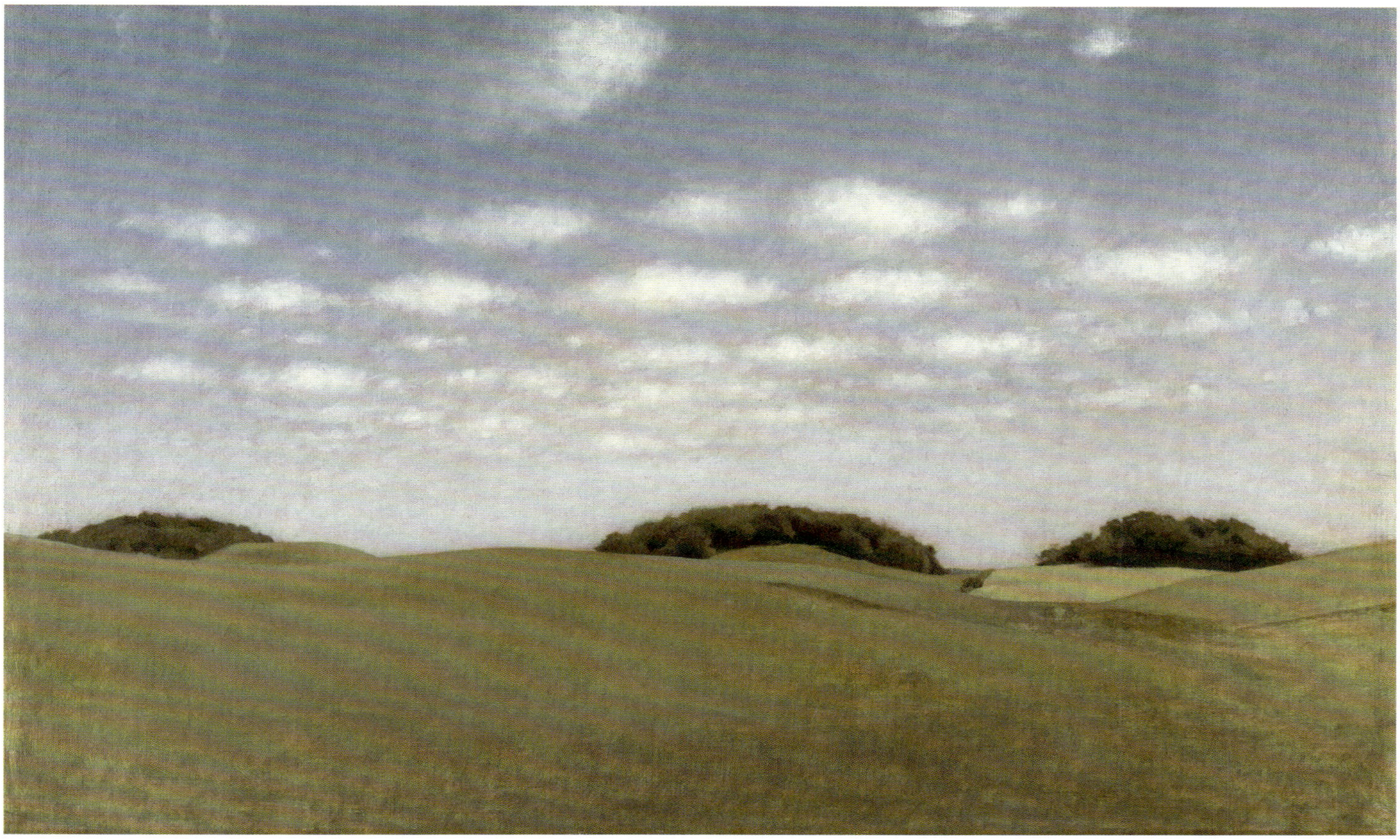

[17]
Vilhelm Hammershøi 1864-1916 Danish
Landscape, From Lejre 1905
Oil on canvas 41 x 68 cm
Nationalmuseum, Stockholm

HAMMERSHØI IN EUROPE

Hammershøi was a frequent traveller, but also an uncommunicative traveller. The preserved letters from himself and his wife Ida to his mother and siblings are mainly about the practicalities of the journey, and they rarely tell us what kind of art he was seeing on his travels. If nothing else, though, the letters can be used to determine where he was and when. In a few cases we know the specific purpose of his journey – as when he went to Paris in 1889 to see the Universal Exposition, in which he was himself participating with several works.[17]

In the nature of things it is difficult to tell which works by other artists Hammershøi may have seen, when he does not explicitly mention specific artworks. Even in the cases where he may have been actively interested in a particular artist, he was hampered by the limited possibilities for seeing both original works and reproductions. In this respect some remarks from his close acquaintance Johan Rohde are quite characteristic. When he had the chance, during his stay in Brussels in May 1892, to see a couple of works by "the much-discussed Belgian Symbolist" Fernand Khnopff, he studied them with great interest. All the same, he had to conclude: "But judging from these two things I am unable to have any opinion of the man, who it seems plays some role in young Belgium."[18]

We must be content to take our point of departure in Hammershøi's journeys in our attempt to pinpoint what he may have seen. To do so we can rely to some extent on the above-mentioned Rohde's travel account, which he drew up during his journey abroad in 1892. Already at the time Rohde was seen as the person who was reporting on the latest art abroad for his artist contemporaries.[19] But we can only rely on Rohde's words about Hammershøi to a limited extent, since the two quickly moved in widely different artistic directions, and they are unlikely to have taken the same view of the current art.

Hammershøi and photography

It was at this time that real distribution of reproductions of artworks began, at first in the form of line drawings or photogravures; but gradually photographs began to play a role in spreading familiarity with works of art.[20] In France, from 1887 on, illustrated versions of the Salon catalogues were issued. Characteristically, though, it was works by the well established artists that were reproduced. The art dealer and print maker Adolphe Goupil, for example, collaborated with the Salon artist Gérôme on the distribution of his works.[21] Naturally, there were exceptions, and some of the more innovative art also found its way to the reproductions. In the 1890s the photographer Eugène Druet began systematically photographing the works of many of the most important contemporary French artists – those artists, in fact, whom posterity has also chosen: the Impressionists, the Post-Impressionists and the Symbolists.[22] In other words the artists were given brand new, better opportunities to learn about one another's works. Yet there is no reliable information about how much the artists actually exploited these opportunities. In many cases we find information that artists owned collections of photographs, but we rarely hear what the collections contained.

The duplication of photographs had by no means been systematized. Johan Rohde regularly complained that he had no opportunities to buy photos of the particular works of art that interested ham. Hammershøi too collected photographs.[23] He frequently bought photos of subjects he saw on his travels, and later he began to buy postcards; but we do not know the original extent of his collection. Only the photographs from his honeymoon in 1891-92 and from the first journey to London in 1897-98 have been pasted on cardboard and therefore preserved together. Many of the other preserved photographs are thin and fragile, and several others may have been lost, so the original size of the collection is not known. That the collection contains more photos of older than of recent art does not necessarily reflect on Hammershøi's true interests. On the one hand it was easier to buy photos of old masters; on the other, later owners of his photographs may have scrapped poorly preserved photos of contemporary artworks which were perhaps less well known to his relatives who inherited the photos.

Hammershøi's collection of photographs of other artists' works raises the same issues as his statements about contemporary art. The collection comprises only photographs of paintings that he deliberately selected. Instances of unplanned inspiration are not reflected by the photographs. In other words the collection includes no photographs of artworks that Hammershøi saw more or less by accident – for example in the studios or homes of artist colleagues – and which may have made an impression, become stored in his memory and later have left traces in his art.

Apart from a few specific cases where Hammershøi has obviously used photographs – probably photos he himself took – as an aid during his work, the issue of his use of photography has not yet been dealt with in depth. One question in particular arises: to what extent was he inspired by the photographic aesthetic when he fixed on his own idiom? Gertrud Oelsner has discussed a number of paintings by Hammershøi in terms of the artistic effects of photography.[24] But no comparison has been made between his paintings and possible specific photographic originals; and perhaps this cannot be done to any adequate degree since it is difficult to tell which examples he may have seen. The preserved photographs from his collection are all highly traditional in their choice of subject and pictorial composition.

The aesthetic of photography has features in common with Hammershøi's in several respects, not least the limited colour scale (which after all at the time consisted for technical reasons of brownish or greyish tones), and in many cases the print-like effect of the pictures. But there are also crucial differences. In the first period of the lifetime of photography it registered all details without subtle shadings, and the pictures were reproduced unedited and unmanipulated – unless the photographers drew support from weather phenomena like fog, backlight and the darkness of night. By and large, photography therefore offered a view of the subject and a richness of detail that would not have appealed to Hammershøi.[25]

Both as an architectural and as a landscape painter, he was far more selective in his choice of details than the photographer could be. Moreover, photography's representative and documentary function undoubtedly repelled him – except when he bought photos of sights he had seen on journeys.

Among the innovative photographers who were active in Hammershøi's lifetime, a photographer like his contemporary, the German pioneer Heinrich Kühn, could presumably have attracted his interest.[26] But his idiom was generally more related to the French Impressionists' paintings than to Hammershøi's art. Photographers such as the Americans Alfred Stieglitz and Edward Steichen, who worked seriously with the aesthetic resources of photography, only appeared on the scene after the turn of the century; that is, too late for their works to have influenced Hammershøi in the formative years.

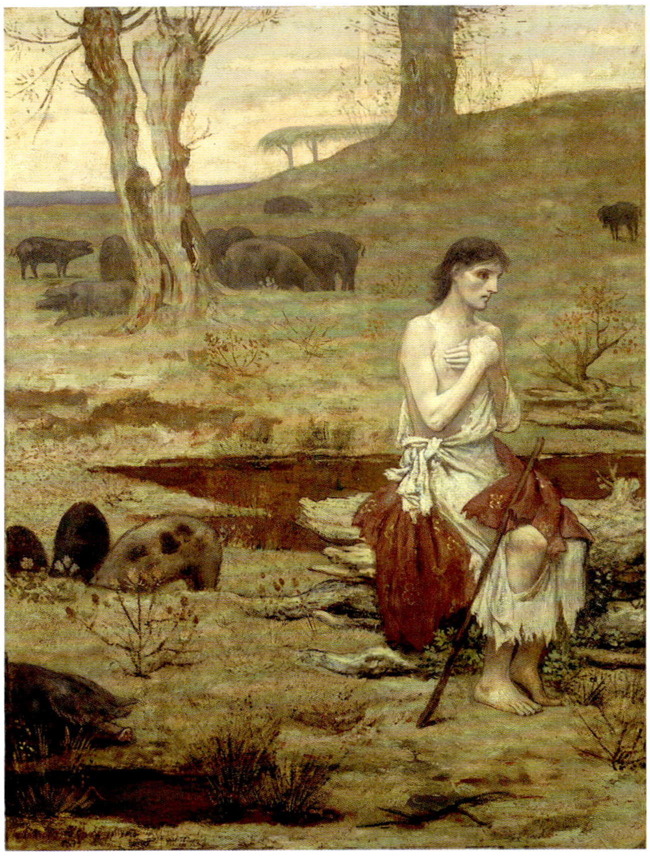

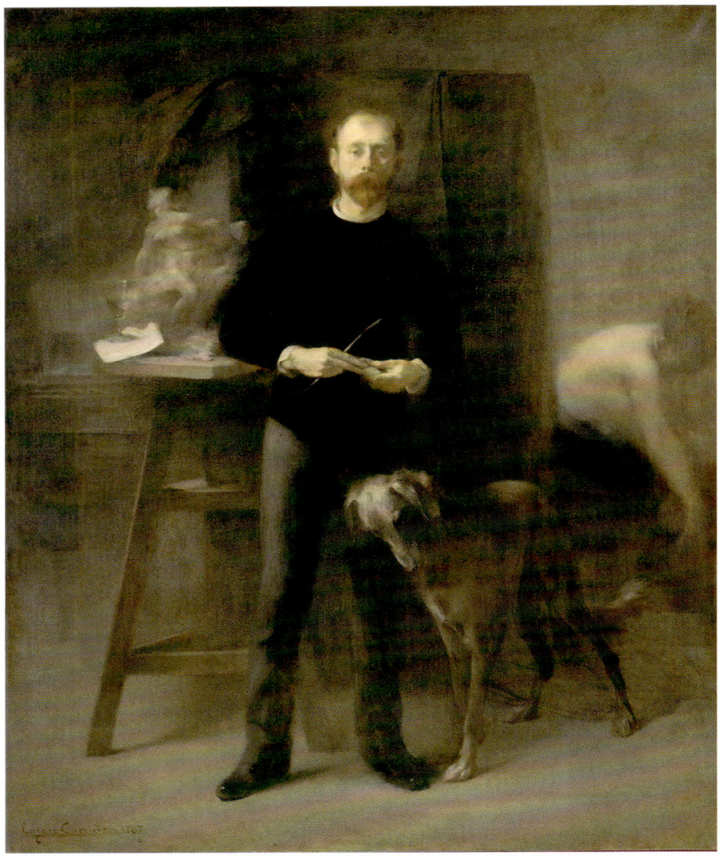

[18]
Pierre Puvis de Chavannes 1824-98 French
The Prodigal Son c. 1879
Oil on canvas 130 x 96 cm
Stiftung Sammlung E.G. Bührle, Zürich

[19]
Eugène Carrière 1849-1906 French
The Sculptor Louis-Henri Devillez in his Studio 1887
Oil on canvas 220.5 x 181 cm
Musée d'Orsay, Paris

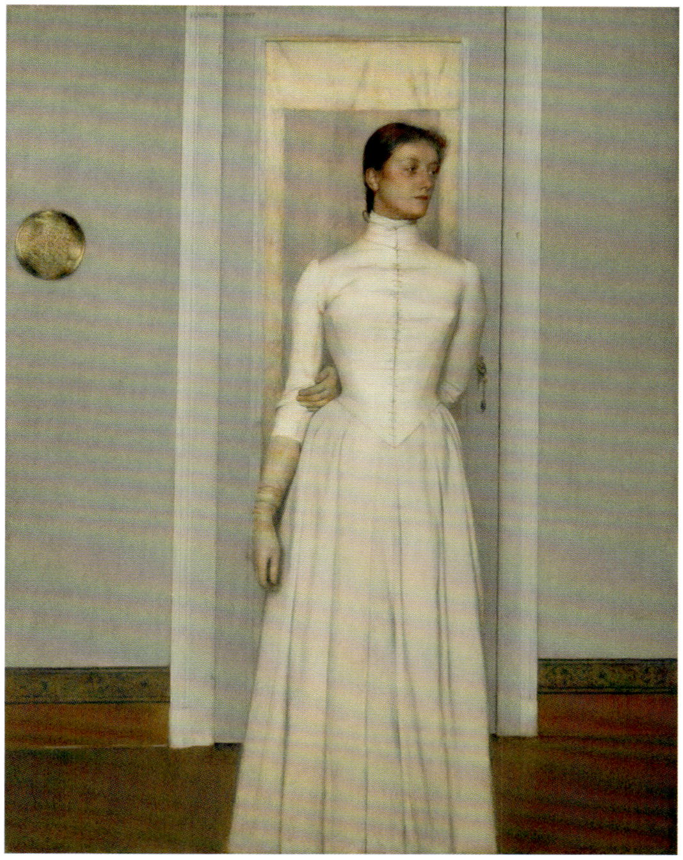

Paris

Hammershøi went to Paris in 1889 with the clear aim of seeing the Universal Exposition, where he was himself represented by four paintings. He would undoubtedly have seized the opportunity to see as many as possible of the huge number of artworks exhibited. However, we do not know whether he also tried to see exhibitions of current art elsewhere in the city.

Besides the contributions of the individual countries, the Universal Exposition included two special exhibitions of French art. One was an anniversary exhibition marking the centenary of the French Revolution, and thus comprised French art from the period 1789-1889; the second showed the art of the preceding decade.[27] The two French sections alone exhibited more than 2000 paintings, and it would have been a quite insurmountable task to try to form a general overview or impression of the individual artists.

Hammershøi undoubtedly made a highly selective choice from the overwhelming quantity of works he could see. The French Impressionists had by now won so much official recognition that a few of them were represented at the centenary exhibition. But while several of his fellow-countrymen, after a delay of many years, had opened their eyes to the qualities of the Impressionists, he is unlikely to have paused very long before their works. We must suppose that he was primarily interested in artists who demonstrated aims that were in some way related to his own.

[20]
Fernand Khnopff 1858-1921 Belgian
Portrait of Marguerite Khnopff c. 1887
Oil on canvas 96 x 74.5 cm
Fondation Roi Baudouin
(Dep. Musées Royaux des Beaux-Arts de Belgique, Brussels)

In the historic French exhibition, Hammershøi probably noticed the painter Pierre Puvis de Chavannes. At the time he enjoyed great recognition among the Danish artists, and he was a hot topic of conversation among the Danes who had gone to Paris in the spring of 1889, many of them for the sake of the Universal Exposition. Willumsen, for example, had declared that this was the year when Puvis de Chavannes was "the big artist"; Krøyer portrayed him in the large painting *The Committee for the French Art Exhibition in Copenhagen, 1888*, which he painted that spring in Paris,[28] and Anna Ancher was a pupil of his at the same time.[29] During his stay in Paris a few years later, in 1892, Rohde too singled out the French painter at an exhibition: "Tallest among the exhibitors stands Puvis de Chavannes."[30]

Among the exhibited paintings by Puvis de Chavannes was a painting, *The Beheading of John the Baptist*, which had in fact already been exhibited the previous year at the large French exhibition in Copenhagen.[31] It is evident that Hammershøi really paid attention to the art of the French painter because a couple of years later – during his second stay in Paris – he speaks of Puvis de Chavannes in a letter to his mother with no further presentation.[32] He assumes that the recipient has also heard of the Frenchman. At the Universal Exposition Hammershøi himself showed a painting with a subject from the Biblical story of Job, who endures the trials to which God subjects him in silent, painful resignation.[33] It therefore seems reasonable to assume that he must have noted Puvis de Chavannes' painting *The Prodigal Son* [18], which also shows a tormented Biblical figure who, with a dull, despondent gaze, resigns himself to his humiliation.[34] The figure actually sits in almost the same position as Job[35] and has the same faraway, contemplative aura as several of the people in Hammershøi's paintings. The use of a very limited colour scale must also have interested him. On the same occasion the Dane must also have had the opportunity to see the Frenchman's major work, *Young Women by the Sea*, which may well have inspired him in his later work [38, p. 60].

Among the French painters, Hammershøi presumably also studied Henri Fantin-Latour's group portrait *Homage to Delacroix*.[36] The picture type as such – a group portrait where a single person is acclaimed – lies very far from Hammershøi's own efforts, and the same is true of the direct contact with the viewers of the picture that is created by the gazes of the figures. But as a group portrait of a number of artists, the painting may have captured his attention and led to a general interest in the painter. He had previously had the opportunity to see a couple of portraits by Fantin-Latour that had been shown the preceding year at the large French exhibition in Copenhagen.[37]

Even if Hammershøi himself did not notice the French painter Eugène Carrière, it seems reasonable to assume that one of the other Danes in Paris drew his attention to his paintings. For it must have interested him to see paintings by an artist who in several respects used clearly related devices. In his figure paintings Carrière often obscured the surroundings, just as Hammershøi did in a number of his early paintings; and he also let a single colour – brown, in a wide variety of shades – dominate his pictures. At the exhibition Hammershøi would however also have been able to see an aspect of Carrière's art for which he probably did not care much: a pronounced sentimentality in the painting *The Sick Child*.[38] But the painting *The Sculptor Louis-Henri Devillez in his Studio* [19] would have been all the more interesting to him.[39] This is a far more sober picture with no infusion of narrative or romanticizing. Nor had the painter made any attempt to associate the subject with the artist myths of the age, or to give the picture the impression of the momentary of which the Naturalists of the

1880s were so fond. The man just stands there with an erect posture – apparently interrupted in his work, but this is not narrated specifically.

If Hammershøi had expected to familiarize himself with the latest currents in French painting at the Universal Exposition, he would have been disappointed. Apart from a single painting by Paul Cézanne, there were no works by the young artists who were well on their way to blazing the trail for the new departures in French art in the 1890s, such as Georges Seurat, Paul Signac and Paul Gauguin. The selection of French artists was far more conservative, for example, than that of Danish artists, among whom a number of the young innovators had been invited to participate.

Hammershøi probably also took the opportunity to see the two paintings that the American James McNeill Whistler was exhibiting in the British section. One was a figure painting of some women on a balcony, and the other was a large half-length portrait of a standing woman.[40] Both paintings revealed aspirations that were rather far from Hammershøi's own. But at an early stage the Dane had taken an interest in Whistler's art (see p. 63), and this appears to have been the first time he had occasion to see original paintings by the American artist,[41] so it must have been a welcome opportunity to study Whistler's paintings at last with his own eyes.

Given his great interest in Whistler, it must have been obvious for Hammershøi to stop before the Belgian painter Fernand Khnopff's paintings in the Belgian section. With his four paintings, Khnopff showed the range of his art – from portraits in the Realist tradition through a mood landscape to a mythological subject in the Symbolist vein. Hammershøi must have paid particular note to *Portrait of Marguerite Khnopff* [20],[42] where the Belgian continued to develop and vary the techniques Whistler had used in his major work *Arrangement in Grey and Black No. 1. Portrait of the Painter's Mother* [40, p. 62]. As with the American, the subject of the portrait interacts with the background's meticulously built-up geometrical composition created by the wall areas, the panels, the door and the gilt metal dish on the wall.

As we know, Hammershøi did not write down his opinions of the art he saw at the Universal Exposition. But during his second stay in Paris in 1891-92 he also tried to form an impression of the contemporary art he was able to see. In January 1892 he commented on an exhibition in a letter to his close acquaintance Johan Rohde: "There is a small Impressionist and Symbolist exhibition here at the moment, which is rather poor. I would hope for the Symbolists that it is a very poor exhibition. Most of the paintings look like jokes. There is one with a chequered lady in it, where the blades of grass and the leaves on the trees are square, and then there is one by the same painter – I do not know what he is called – of a lady who has round coins on her dress, and where the leaves and the grass and everything are round – even if there's a little doggy, it's round. They certainly have a style! There are also paintings with stirring content, for example one showing a man who is hurrying into a public convenience. That appealed to me greatly."[43]

In all probability this was an exhibition of Impressionist and Symbolist art that was shown at Galerie Le Barc de Bouteville from December 1891 until February 1892. There has been some doubt about which artist and which painting Hammershøi is talking about, but Felix Krämer has pointed convincingly to Pierre Bonnard's painting *Women in the Garden* from 1891 [21].[44]

Apart from the fact that the Danish painter, in his account of the French exhibition, revealed a well developed sense of both humour and irony, the statement may also easily

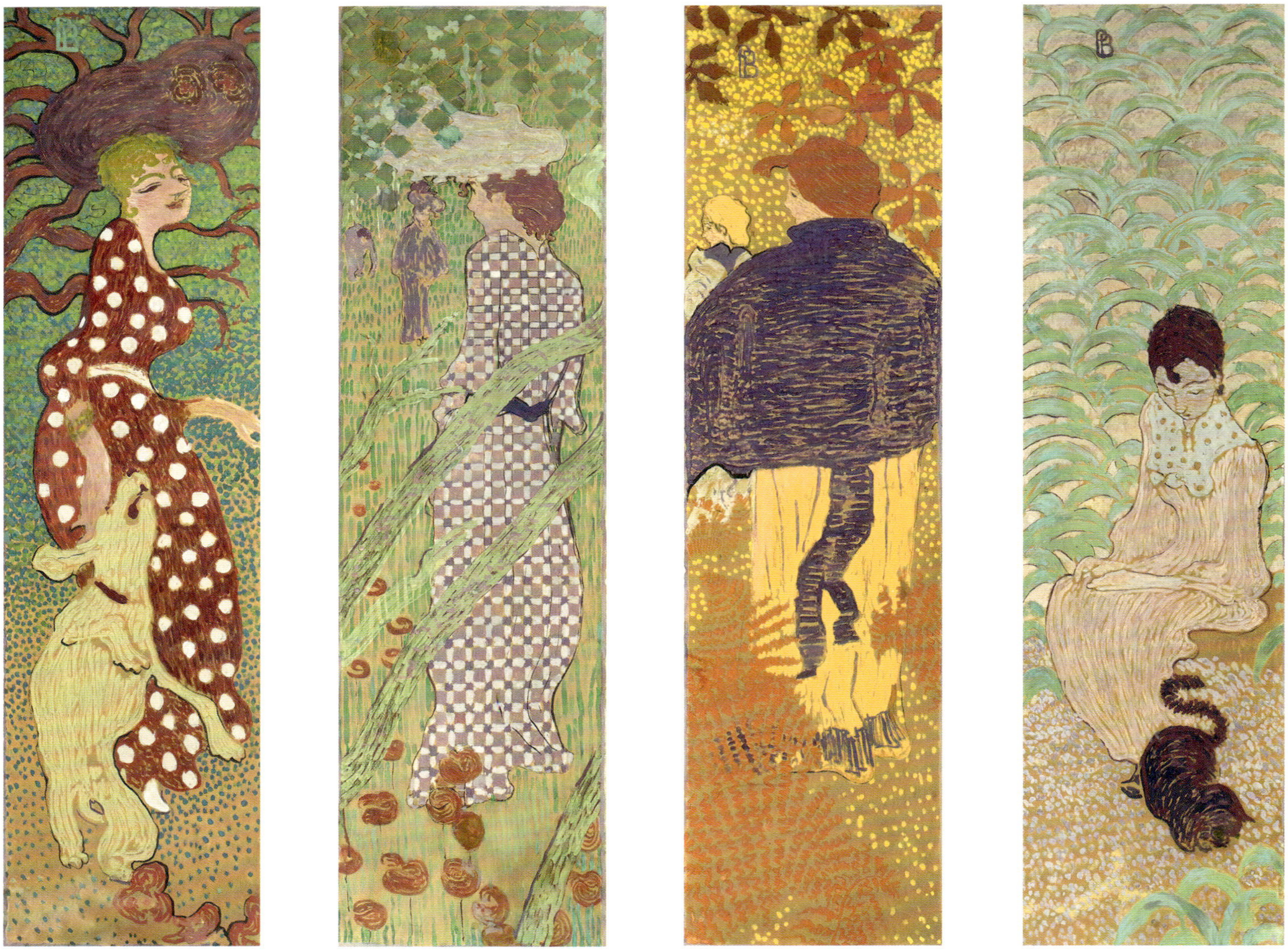

[21]
Pierre Bonnard 1867-1947 French
Women in the Garden 1891
Tempera on four canvases each 160 x 48 cm
Musée d'Orsay, Paris

give the impression of strong reservations – if not direct animosity – towards the latest international artistic currents of the age. With an idiom that placed the main emphasis on line and surface, Bonnard was in a quite different place with his art from Hammershøi, and the Dane spontaneously rejected what he saw. However, one must be cautious about drawing far-reaching conclusions from Hammershøi's remarks – for example that he was totally dismissive of French Symbolism. We cannot know whether he expressed a more subtle view of the current French art later, in conversation.

In 1891 Hammershøi had come too late to Paris to see the annual Salon, and the next spring he went too early to see the next one. But this does not rule out the possibility that during this stay, or later, by leafing through the illustrated editions of the exhibition catalogues, he may have tried to form an impression of the art that was shown at the Salons. True, he would on the whole only have been confirmed there in his view that the officially recognized academic painting had nothing whatsoever to offer him, nothing that could challenge or stimulate his artistic ideas. But Hammershøi had not necessarily searched entirely in vain. In 1893, in the illustrated Salon catalogue for that year, he may for example have come upon a reproduction of Eugène Carrière's central work, *The Painter's Family* [55, p. 73].

During his stay in Paris Hammershøi spent a considerable amount of time copying an antique Greek relief in the Louvre [p. 244], which underlines his great interest in the "old art". In December 1891 he had an opportunity to show *Portrait of Ida Ilsted* [50, p. 69] to the prominent art dealer Paul Durand-Ruel, who had promoted the art of the French Impressionists.[45] This seems to have been done at the urging of the French critic Théodore Duret, who had with great interest seen a number of Hammershøi's paintings during a stay in Copenhagen the previous year. The Danish painter met the two Frenchmen, but nothing concrete came out of the visits, and neither of the parties followed up on them later. Hammershøi thus missed out on a more targeted presentation of his art in Paris.

Holland and Belgium

On several of his journeys Hammershøi stopped off in cities in Holland and Belgium on his way to both Paris and London. Especially on his honeymoon trip in 1891-92 we can follow his route thanks to the photographs he bought. Johan Rohde's travel accounts from 1892 suggest what Hammershøi may possibly have seen or tried to see. Rohde noted among other things paintings by the Dutchman Johan Eduard Karsen. In addition a painter like Willem Arnold Witsen may have aroused his interest (see p. 114 for more detail).

During their stay in Amsterdam Ida Hammershøi wrote to her mother-in-law: "We have [...] taken long walks out into the countryside and photographed mills."[46] The photos in question do not seem to be known today, but the statement clearly shows that the painter was using photographs in his work.

The photographs from the honeymoon journey all seem to have been taken by professional photographers and bought by Hammershøi. Most of them were meant to capture impressions of the places he had seen. In the majority of cases no parallels can be drawn between the subjects and his own art. But a few of them perhaps reflect some of his deliberations. This is true of a photograph of Rotterdam Harbour [23]. A few years later Hammershøi chose to paint similar scenes from Copenhagen Harbour,[47] and at one point he even considered painting subjects from the Thames in London (see page 114).

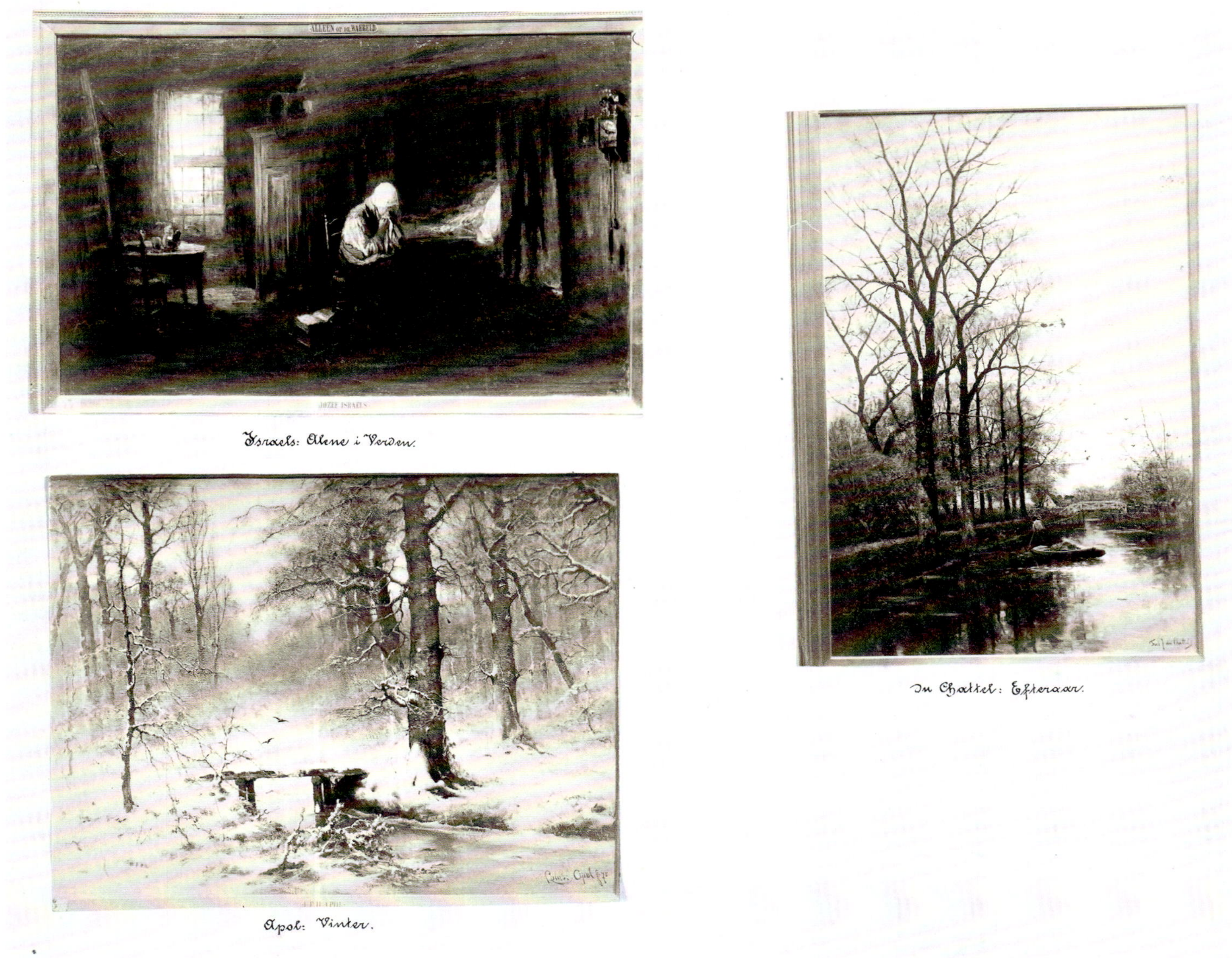

[22]
Unknown photographers
Carton mounted with three photos of paintings
by Israëls, Apol and Du Chattel
Hammershøi's scrapbook with photographs
The Hirschsprung Collection, Copenhagen

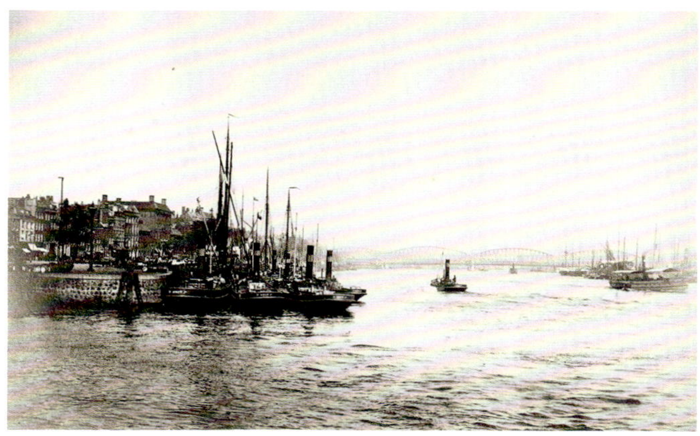

[23]
Unknown photographer
The Harbour of Rotterdam
Photograph from Hammershøi's archive
The Hirschsprung Collection, Copenhagen

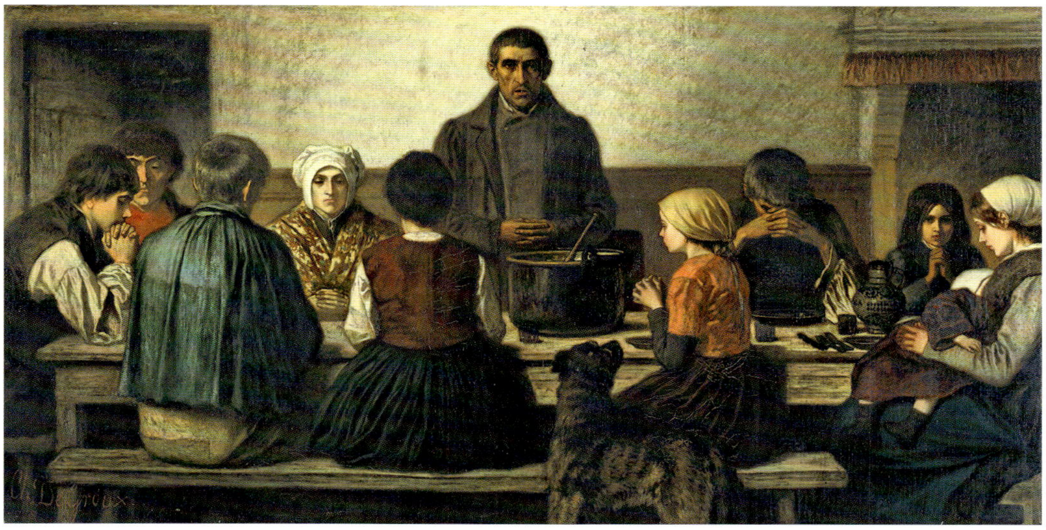

Most of the photographs of artworks show important works by the Dutch painters of the 17th century, especially Rembrandt. However, they also include three photographs of paintings by contemporary Dutch artists [22]. One of these, *Alone in the World* (1878; Rijksmuseum, Amsterdam), is by the prominent social realist painter Jozef Israëls, while the other two are by artists who specialized as landscape painters: a winter landscape by Louis Apol, *January A January Evening in the Park "Haagse Bos", The Hague* (1875; Rijksmuseum, Amsterdam), and a river landscape by Fredericus Jacobus van Rossum du Chattel, *Autumn* (owner unknown). In all probability these are artworks he had seen in the original. While the choice of Israëls' painting presumably reflects the fact that he was one of the most highly esteemed Dutch artists at the time, Hammershøi probably bought the photographs of the landscapes because he was interested in the artists' use of mood-evoking effects in them.

We do not know what choices he had when he bought these photos, so we do not know either what others he could have chosen instead. But the photographs that he did in fact buy reveal a very important aspect of Hammershøi's approach to art on his journeys: already then the paintings by Israëls and Apol belonged to the Rijksmuseum in Amsterdam, and we can therefore calculate that at the museum he not only looked at the old masters, but also tried to form an impression of current Dutch art. We can undoubtedly also conclude that the same was the case with the other European national galleries he visited. He did not content himself with seeking out "the old art".

The stays in Belgium are also surrounded with uncertainty. In his travel account Rohde mentions several Belgian artists in whom his friend is unlikely to have been interested. Yet it is worth noting that Rohde singles out Khnopff. On the other hand he makes no mention at all of Xavier Mellery, but his art too may have attracted Hammershøi's interest – if he had the opportunity to see his pictures.

At the Belgian Royal Art Museum in Brussels, Hammershøi could have seen a greatly admired painting by the Belgian Charles de Groux, *Saying Grace* from 1861 [24].[48] It is unlikely to have been the theme itself that appealed to him, rather the artistic seriousness. It is an everyday subject that has been elevated beyond the everyday and given a touch of

[24]
Charles de Groux 1825-70 Belgian
Saying Grace 1861
Oil on canvas 80 x 154 cm
Musées Royaux des Beaux-Arts de Belgique, Brussels

sublimity. This is due not least to the absolutely frozen, motionless figures, but also to the rigorously frontal composition, which recalls the older Christian Last Supper pictures. The painting may very well have helped to inform Hammershøi's ideas when he worked several years later on the large painting *Five Portraits* [15, p. 32].

Germany

Hammershøi travelled several times in Germany and visited a number of cities there throughout his life. But apart from the first journey – his very first tour abroad, which went to Berlin and Dresden in 1885 – this consisted of short stops he made on his way to and from Italy. On his first trip he was probably interested in the works of the old masters in the collections of paintings in the two cities, and the same was presumably the case in 1903 when he spent a few days in Berlin with Karl Madsen. The art historian had gradually turned more and more to the older art, and this was probably what they looked for when they are said to have been at the museum together from morning to evening.

By contrast there is not much to indicate that Hammershøi showed any special interest in contemporary German art. The dominant currents in German art at the time were flowing in other directions than the one he sought. He surely felt no close affinities with either Realist painters like Wilhelm Leibl and Hans Thoma, or Naturalists and Impressionists like Max Liebermann and Max Slovogt. He probably therefore accepted very quickly that he would not find crucial inspiration in current German painting.

Hammershøi exhibited more in Germany than in any other country apart from Denmark. But he did not follow up on these exhibitions by travelling personally to the cities in question. Most remarkably, he did not travel to Berlin in connection with the big retrospective exhibition that was shown, first at Galerie Eduard Schulte and later in Düsseldorf, Cologne and Hamburg. This exhibition led to sales of several paintings, including *Interior. (The Old Cabinet Sofa)* [25], which had been donated to the National Gallery in Berlin by a German collector as early as 1906. At the same time he also sold *Drawing Room. The Four Copper Prints* [78, p. 102] which was at the exhibition in 1905 and was until recently in a German private collection.[49]

Italy

Hammershøi went on a total of three journeys to Italy.[50] The first was in the autumn of 1893. In September he travelled via Munich and Verona and made a stop in Venice before he arrived at his destination, Florence. There he stayed for a couple of months and went on excursions to the surrounding cities. At the beginning of December he stayed for a few days in Padua before he travelled home. The second journey was to Rome. On the way down there he apparently travelled through Germany and Austria without extended stays. The period in Rome lasted from October 1902 to February 1903 and ended with a visit of a few days to Naples. From this stay comes his painting *Interior of the Church of Santo Rotondo in Rome* [26]. The journey home was probably also via Verona and Munich. The third and last trip once more took in Florence, in the autumn of 1907, but it was abruptly broken off when the painter and his wife were arrested as counterfeiters, because they had unknowingly paid with some forged notes to which they had changed their money back in Copenhagen. Although the misunderstanding was quickly cleared up, and they were then released, they immediately travelled home to Denmark.

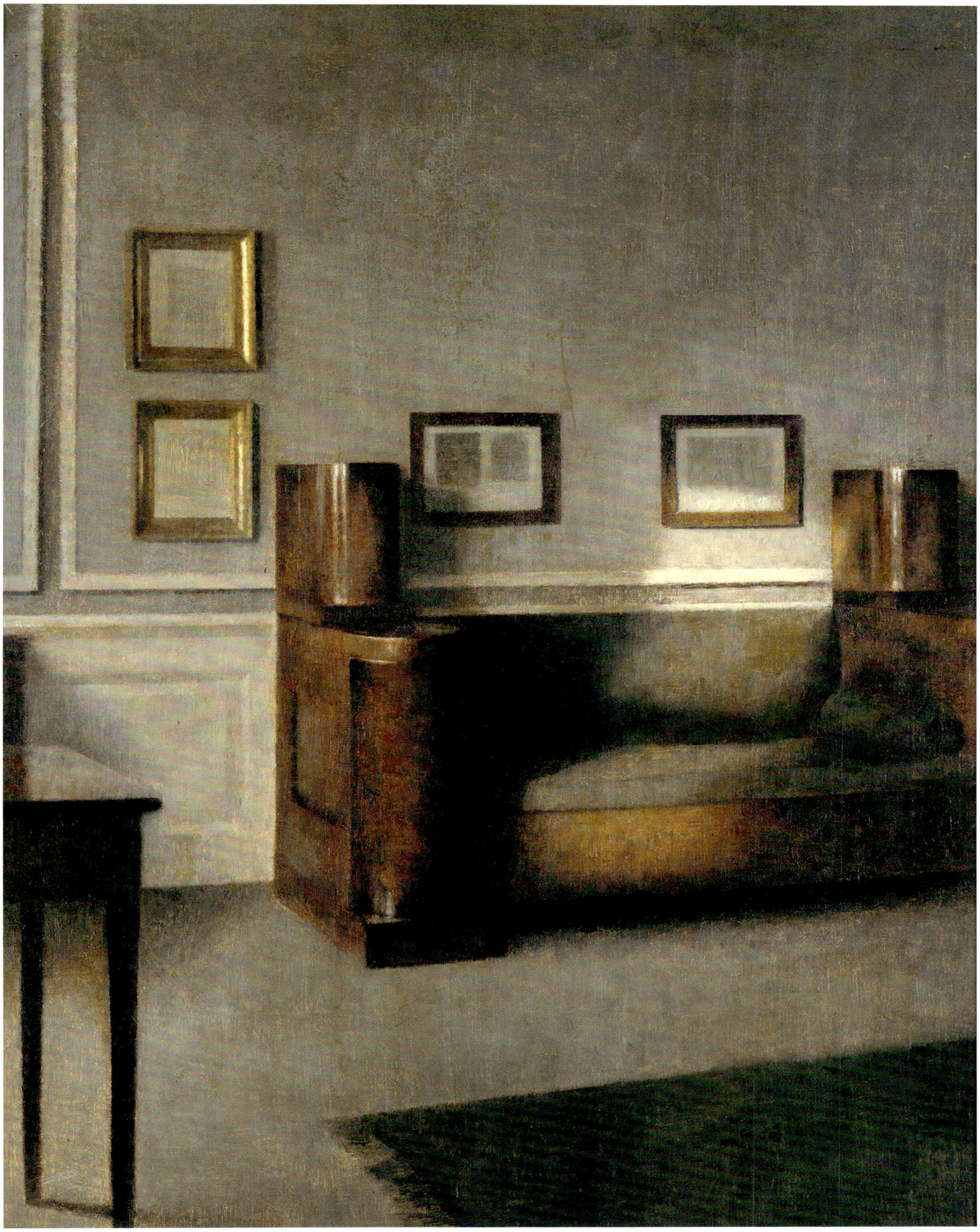

[25]
Vilhelm Hammershøi 1864-1916 Danish
Interior (The Old Cabinet Sofa) 1905
Oil on canvas 49.7 x 40 cm
Staatliche Museen zu Berlin, Nationalgalerie

Hammershøi's chances of seeing examples of contemporary Italian painting seem to have been rather limited. But during the stay in Rome in 1902-03 it was at the Galleria Nazionale d'Arte Moderna that he had the best opportunities to see current Italian art.[51] Established in 1881, this was one of the very few galleries and museums in Europe at the time that was wholly devoted to contemporary art (i.e. art from after 1800), and we must assume that the Danish painter did not neglect to visit it. But if he went there to seek inspiration, it would have been a doubtful pleasure for him to see the exhibited works. There were few paintings by the artists who had been responsible for the renewal of Italian art in the 1890s. The Symbolists were hardly represented, as were the so-called Divisionists.

All the same, Hammershøi probably found occasion to pause before some of the paintings in the gallery. One of those that must have caught the Danish painter's eye is Luigi Selvatico's *Morning Departure* from 1899 [27].[52] In painterly terms the picture is a study in changing grey shades in a room, and is thus related to a long succession of Hammershøi's central works. Its basic theme – solitude and isolation – was also treated again and again by Hammershøi, similarly with a lone female figure, although it is undeniably handled here in a far more sentimental and theatrical way than the Dane would have dreamt of. However, the actual spatial construction of the picture also exhibits parallels with the Danish painter. About the same time as Selvatico was painting his picture, Hammershøi painted a picture of the back yard of the apartment building where he lived [29].[53] Apart from the fact that the Danish painter depicted a closed, clearly delimited space, and the Italian a relatively open, diffuse one, the two pictures are similar in the way they show wall surfaces and windows seen from different angles in non-uniform lighting, with the resulting differences in light, shade, reflections and colour shades.

Perhaps Selvatico's painting, despite the differences, prompted Hammershøi to return to the subject again a few years later, when he painted the back yard with a solitary figure looking out of the window [28].

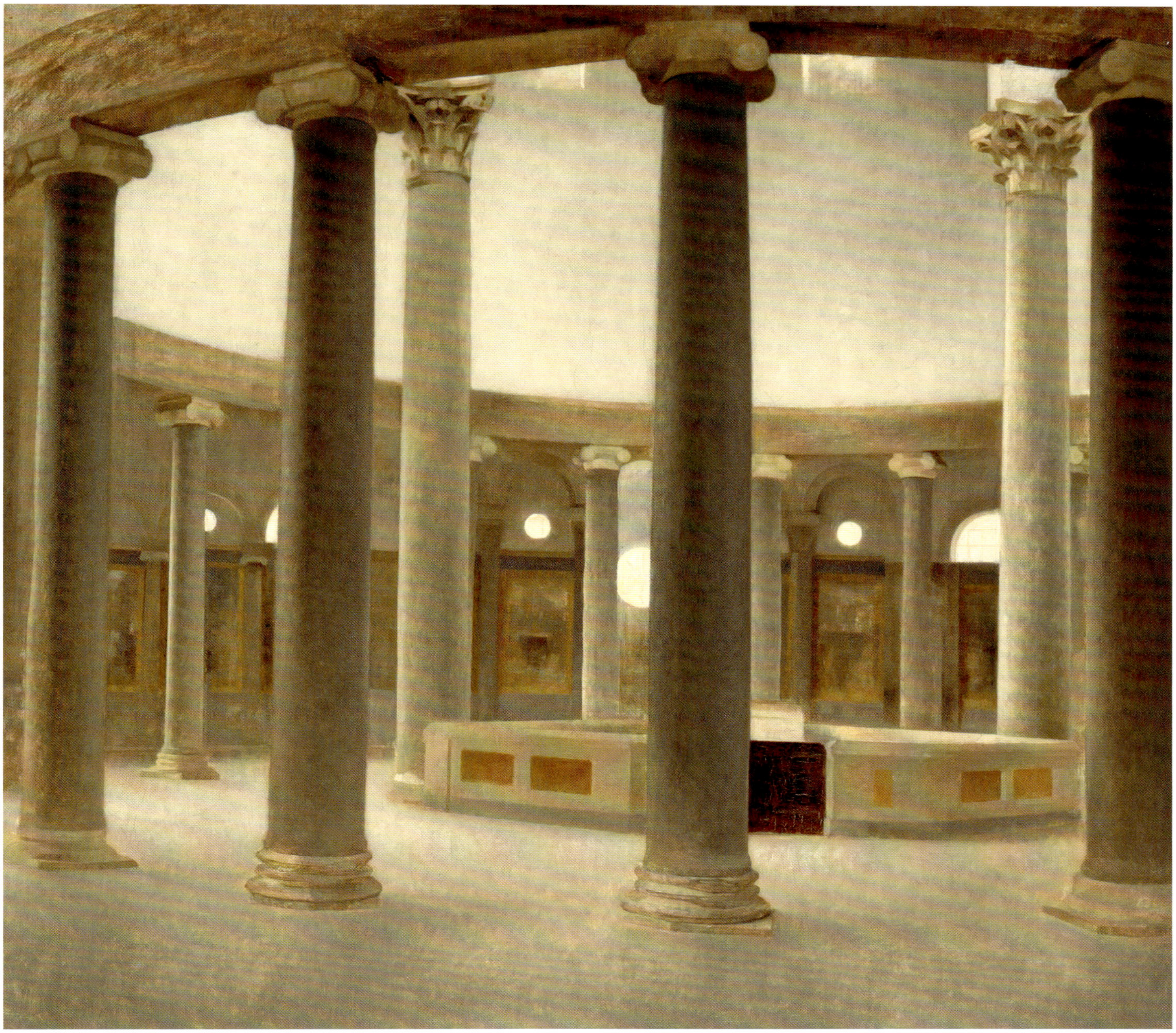

[26]
Vilhelm Hammershøi 1864-1916 Danish
Interior of the Church of Santo Rotondo in Rome 1905
Oil on canvas 67.3 x 72.8 cm
Fyns Kunstmuseum, Odense City Museums

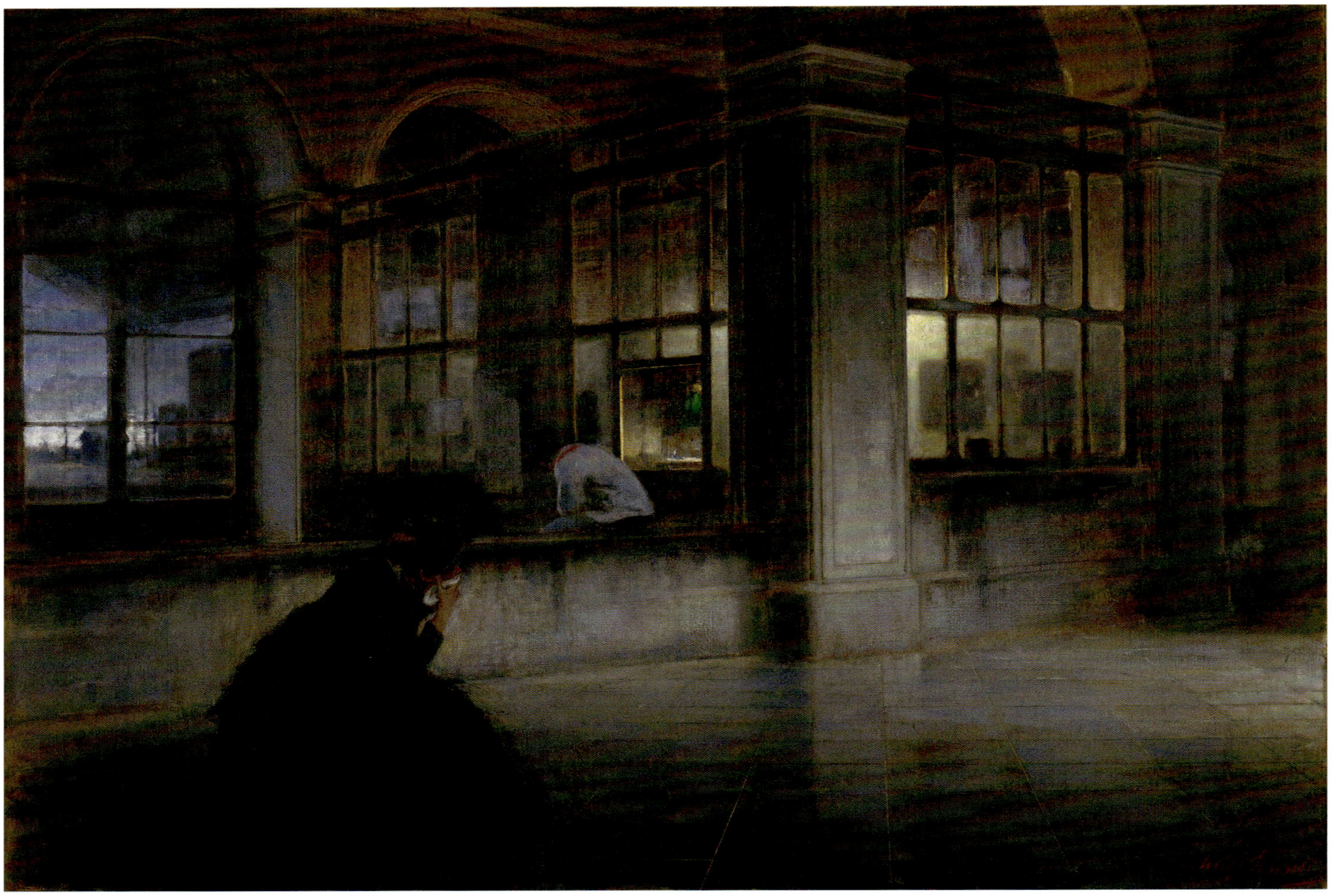

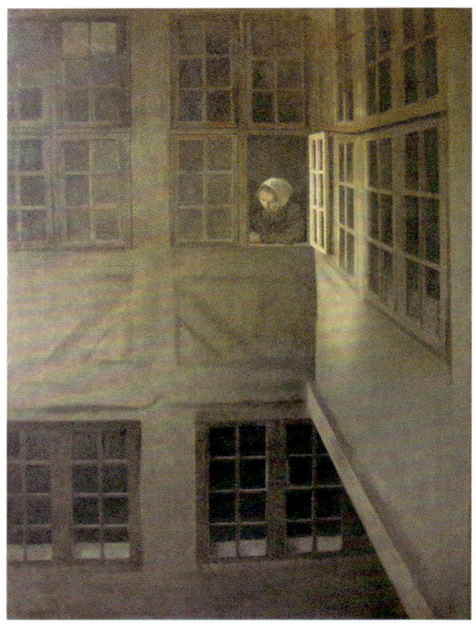

[27]
Luigi Selvatico 1873-1938 Italian
Morning Departure 1899
Oil on canvas 116 x 169 cm
Galleria Nazionale d'Arte Moderna e Contemporanea, Rome

[28]
Vilhelm Hammershøi 1864-1916 Danish
Interior courtyard c. 1905
Oil on canvas 80 x 60 cm
Private collection

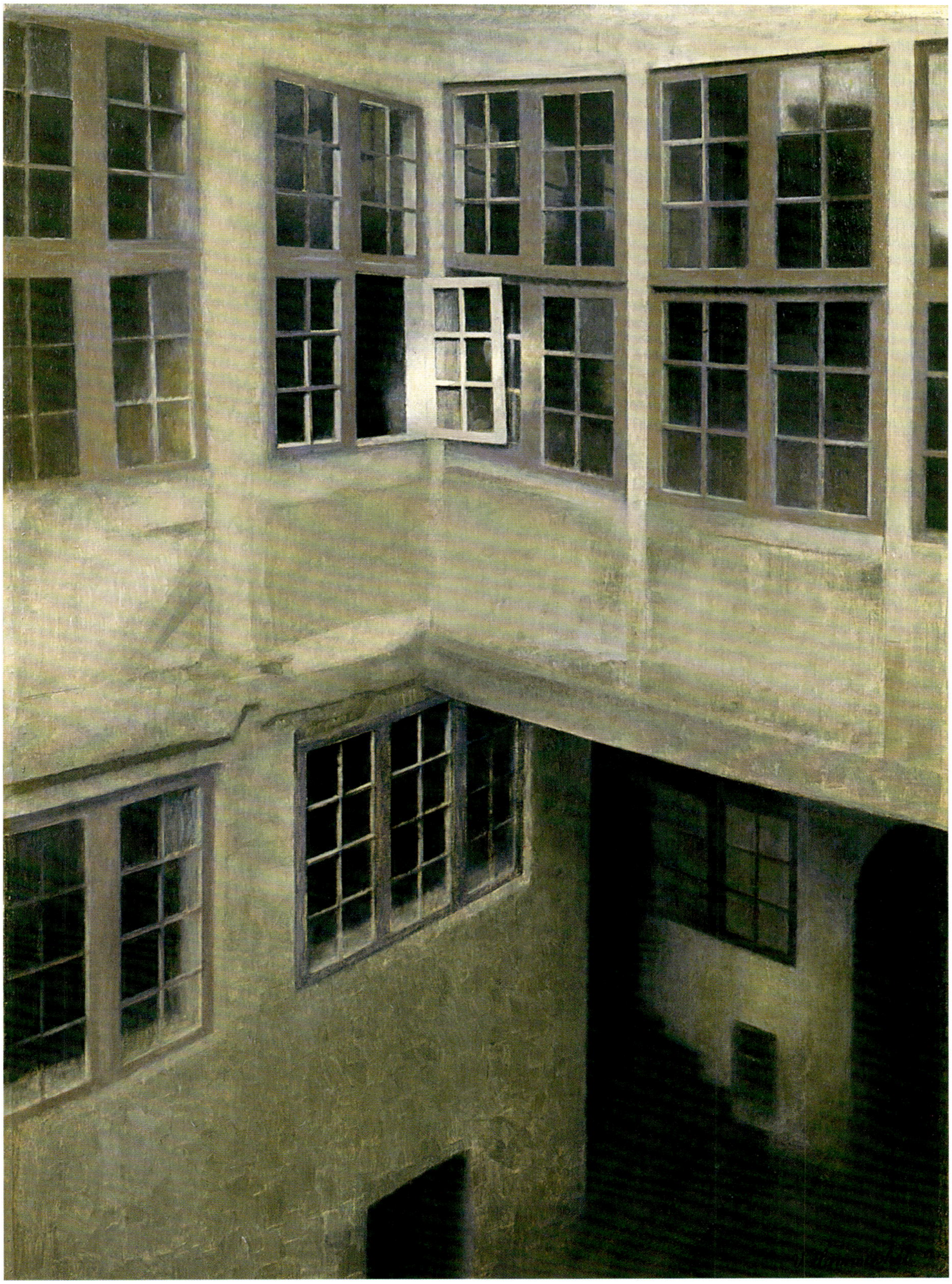

[29]
Vilhelm Hammershøi 1864-1916 Danish
Interior of Courtyard, Strandgade 30 1899
Oil on canvas 65.7 x 47.3 cm
Toledo Museum of Art, Ohio (Gift of the Apollo Society)

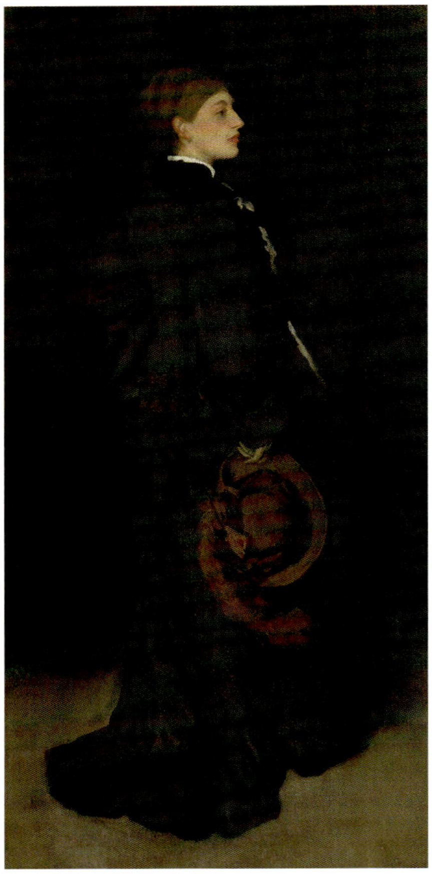

[30]
James McNeill Whistler 1834-1903 American
Arrangement in Brown and Black: Portrait of Miss Rosa Corder 1876-78
Oil on canvas 192.4 x 92.4 cm
The Frick Collection, New York

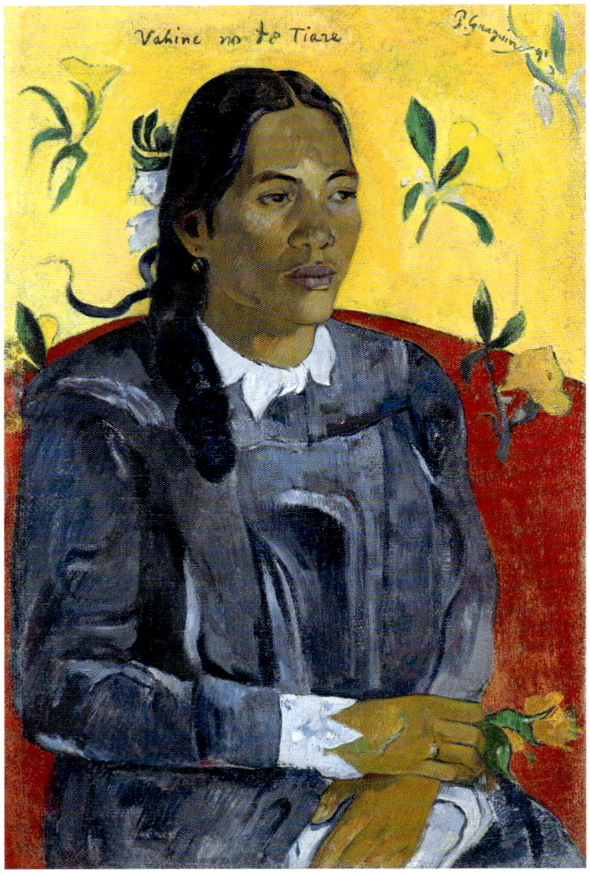

[31]
Paul Gauguin 1848-1903 French
Woman with a Flower 1891
Oil on canvas 70.5 x 46.5 cm
Ny Carlsberg Glyptotek, Copenhagen

Copenhagen

For several decades the Danish art world had lived in self-elected isolation from the surrounding world. In particular, the two Danish-German wars in 1848 and 1864 had effectively broken off the formerly close links between Danish and German artists. But a brand new openness towards art from abroad arose. This began on the small scale in the 1870s, when several young artists once more went to Paris to further their training – after an interval of several decades. They brought this new international perspective back with them to Denmark, which meant not only that more artists now began to travel abroad and have their art exhibited there more often; in the 1880s and 1890s Copenhagen also formed the setting for a large number of international art exhibitions.

The first result of the resurgence of Nordic solidarity among the artists was that large pan-Nordic art exhibitions were held in 1883 and 1888. In the latter year, too, the largest exhibition so far of French art on Danish soil, "The Exhibition of French Art in Copenhagen" was held.[54] The man behind the exhibition was the brewer Carl Jacobsen, and it bore strong marks of his artistic preferences. He appreciated the French Realists and Naturalists more than the Impressionists, and only a few of the latter group's artists were represented at the exhibition. On the other hand, painters like Fantin-Latour, Carrière and Puvis de Chavannes participated with one or more works.

The downplaying of the Impressionists at the "French Exhibition" provoked a smaller yet important exhibition the same year in Copenhagen: "Nordic and French Impressionists", which was shown at the Fine Arts Society (Kunstforeningen).

Viewed with the eyes of posterity, however, the most spectacular event took place in 1893 when the newly founded Den Frie Udstilling (The Independent Exhibition) was able to present two of the most controversial innovative artists of the time – Paul Gauguin and Vincent van Gogh – and display a wide range of their works (51 and 29 works respectively).[55] Gauguin was not an unknown name in Denmark, since he had lived in Copenhagen for a short period in the mid-1880s with his Danish wife. But the exhibition gave the Danish public the opportunity to see some of his wholly up-to-date paintings from Tahiti.

For Hammershøi the encounter with van Gogh's art is unlikely to have led to any reflections on the aims of his own art. Nor would the use of colour in Gauguin's paintings have appealed to Hammershøi. But the pictures may well have opened his eyes in other ways to new artistic perspectives that he could relate to his own art. The French painter consistently detached his subjects from observed reality and incorporated his own personal myths in them.[56] This is very much the case with his figural compositions, but also with a painting like *Woman with a Flower* [31], which is formally a portrait, but where the woman's self-absorbed appearance takes on a character both remote from reality and mysterious.

The presentation on the grandest scale of contemporary foreign art was the large international exhibition at the Ny Carlsberg Glyptotek in 1897.[57] This too had the founder of the Glyptotek, Carl Jacobsen, as its artistic backer; and again it was coloured by his view of art. Once more the focus was very much on the French Realists and Naturalists, and this time the Impressionists were conspicuous by their total absence. On the other hand, Jacobsen appears to have been more open to the Symbolists. At all events an artist like Puvis de Chavannes was well represented, with several paintings,[58] and the Belgian Khnopff contributed a single painting.[59] So did the Dutchman Karsen.[60] Most notable, viewed with the eyes of posterity, is the fact that it had been possible to procure a single painting by Whistler for the exhibition at the Glyptotek. This was *Arrangement in Brown and Black: Portrait of Miss Rosa Corder* from 1876-78 [30], one of his favourite portrait types, showing a monumental standing woman.

THE SOLITARY HUMAN BEING

In 1885 Hammershøi aroused a great deal of attention at the annual exhibition at Charlottenborg in Copenhagen with his debut work, *Portrait of Young Woman. The Artist's Sister, Anna Hammershøi* [32].[61] In many ways the picture represents a striking departure from the dominant Naturalist tendencies in the Danish art of the time. The clearly defined light of Naturalism has been replaced by a more diffuse light whose source is difficult to determine. Instead of clear, bright colours, the picture is dominated by grey, brown and black tones. In addition, all the lines are obscured and none of the contours are sharp. As the title of the picture suggests, it was intended as a portrait. But there is no direct contact between the viewer and the woman in the picture. The painter has not attempted a psychological characterization of the woman or indicated her social position, nor is there any approach to a genre-like narrative in the portrait. On the contrary, the young woman sits gazing ahead with a faraway, ethereal look. One could justifiably say that Hammershøi here ushered into Danish art the Symbolist and anti-Naturalist currents of the period to come – although it should be emphasized that Hammershøi never became a pure Symbolist, but always stuck to his own highly personal mode of expression.

Without contact

In this painting Hammershøi plays through one of the most important themes in his art, the solitary human being depicted isolated in her own world, alone or together with others. If there are others present, there is no real contact. This certainly reflects important factual conditions of life in the modern society of the time, where the collective lifestyle of former times had been abandoned. But it can undoubtedly also be interpreted existentially as a reflection on the situation of modern man – apart from the cases where Hammershøi was primarily concerned with trying out aesthetic devices.

Irrespective of the fact that in many ways Hammershøi had no counterpart in Danish art, there are still clear parallels in contemporary international art. The fundamental theme of his art links him with a number of the period's most significant artists. A good twenty years before the Danish artist, the Frenchman Henri Fantin-Latour painted a picture of his sister, who is sitting down reading a book [33].[62] Viewed as a portrait, the painting is as ambivalent as Hammershøi's. The young woman is wholly absorbed in herself and seems unaware that she is being watched. She is sufficient unto herself, and there is no contact whatsoever between her and the viewer of the picture.

Hammershøi had not yet had the opportunity to see original paintings by Fantin-Latour when he painted the picture of his sister. So the parallels are due not to influence, but to similarity of intentions. The shared expression may serve to explain why Hammershøi probably developed an interest in Fantin-Latour's paintings later, when he saw some of them at the French Exhibition in Copenhagen in 1888 and at the Universal Exposition the following year.

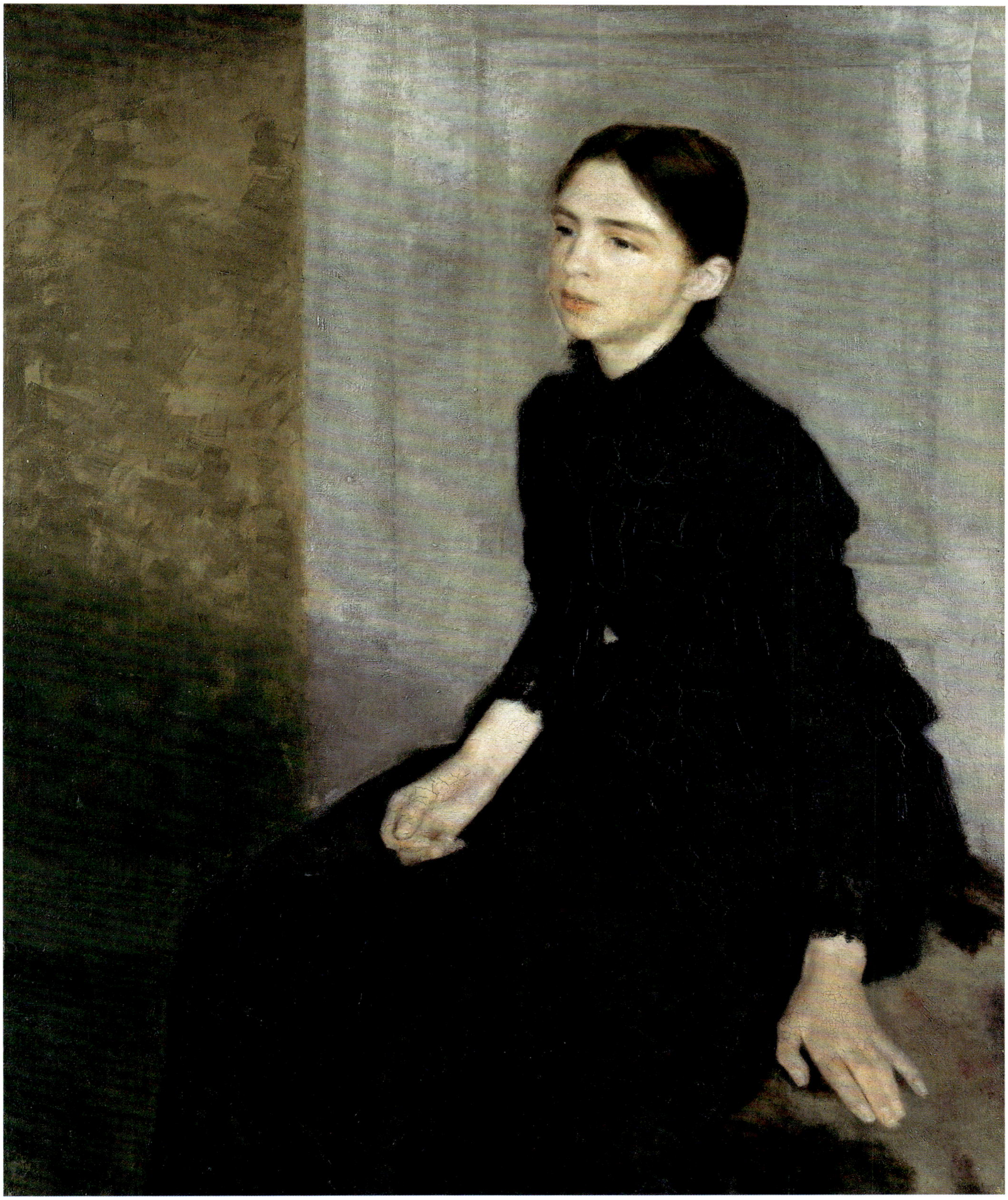

[32]
Vilhelm Hammershøi 1864-1916 Danish
Portrait of Young Woman. The Artist's Sister, Anna Hammershøi 1885
Oil on canvas 112.4 x 91.3 cm
The Hirschsprung Collection, Copenhagen

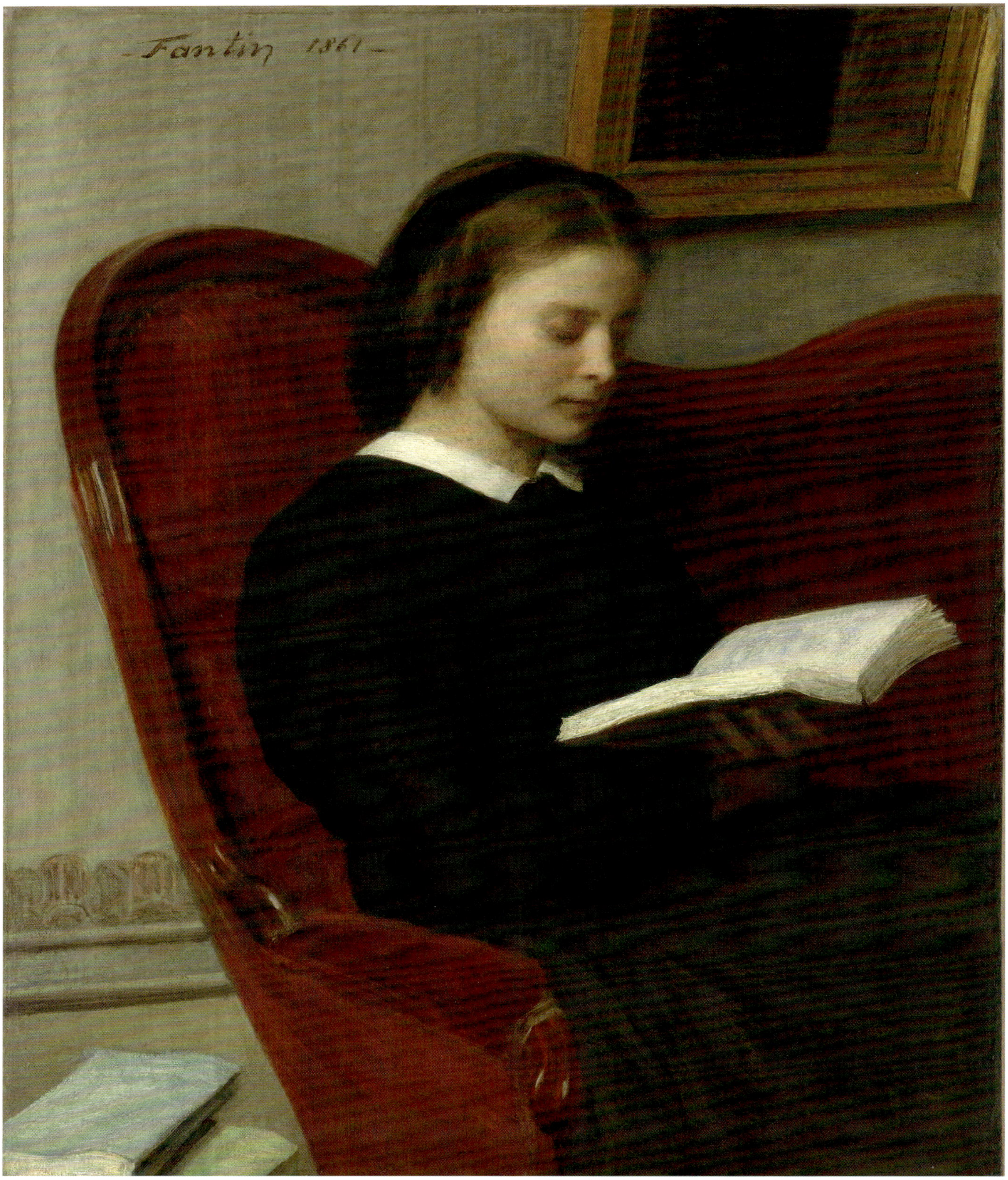

[33]
Henri Fantin-Latour 1836-1904 French
Reading (Marie Fantin-Latour) 1861
Oil on canvas 100 x 83 cm
Musée d'Orsay, Paris

Separately absorbed

In 1891 Hammershøi painted a picture of his mother and his wife, sitting together in the evening in a dimly lit room [34, 35, 36]. The painting is dominated by the soft contours that arise because of the half-light in the room. Each of the two women is absorbed in her own task – the wife in her knitting, and the mother in her reading. This is an everyday situation, but without any action and without the contact that normally connects the people in a narrative genre painting. In terms of the narrative content the picture is thus related to several other pictures that Hammershøi painted at this time.

In both subject and execution the painting bears a striking resemblance to a picture that the Frenchman Carrière had painted four years earlier, *Winding Wool*, which shows the artist's wife and daughter [37].[63] Here too we have an everyday situation in the bosom of the family, and although the mother and daughter are busy with the same task, there is as little contact between them as in Hammershøi's painting. The similarity between the two pictures is so striking that it is hard to believe that it is due solely to coincidence. The obscured contours and the greatly reduced colour scale reinforce a conjecture that the Danish painter must have seen Carrière's painting before he went to work on his own.

However, it is hard to explain how this could have happened quite practically. Carrière exhibited his painting at the Salon in Paris immediately after it was finished in 1887, but it was not reproduced in the exhibition catalogue, and was only exhibited again and reproduced in a periodical twenty years later. The most likely explanation is therefore that during his stay in Paris in 1889 Hammershøi took an interest in Carrière's paintings at the Universal Exposition and subsequently saw a photograph of this picture, inasmuch as even a black-and-white reproduction would give an impression of the distinctiveness of the painting.[64] But this remains conjecture. It could simply be a question of very similar intentions.

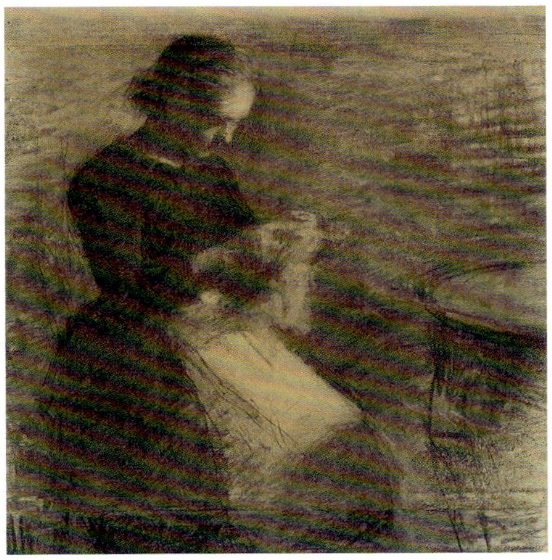

[35]
Vilhelm Hammershøi 1864-1916 Danish
Portrait of Ida Hammershøi with Needlework 891
Drawing, black chalk 43,4 x 41,3 cm
Statens Museum for Kunst

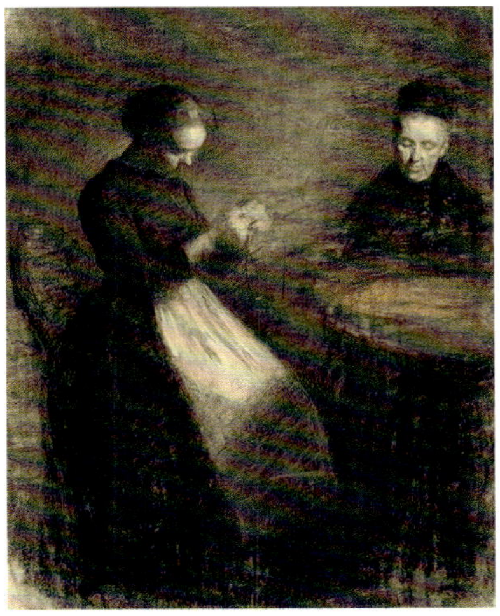

[34]
Vilhelm Hammershøi 1864-1916 Danish
Evening in the Drawing-Room 1891
Charcoal and chalk on paper 57,2 x 44,3 cm
The David Collection, Copenhagen

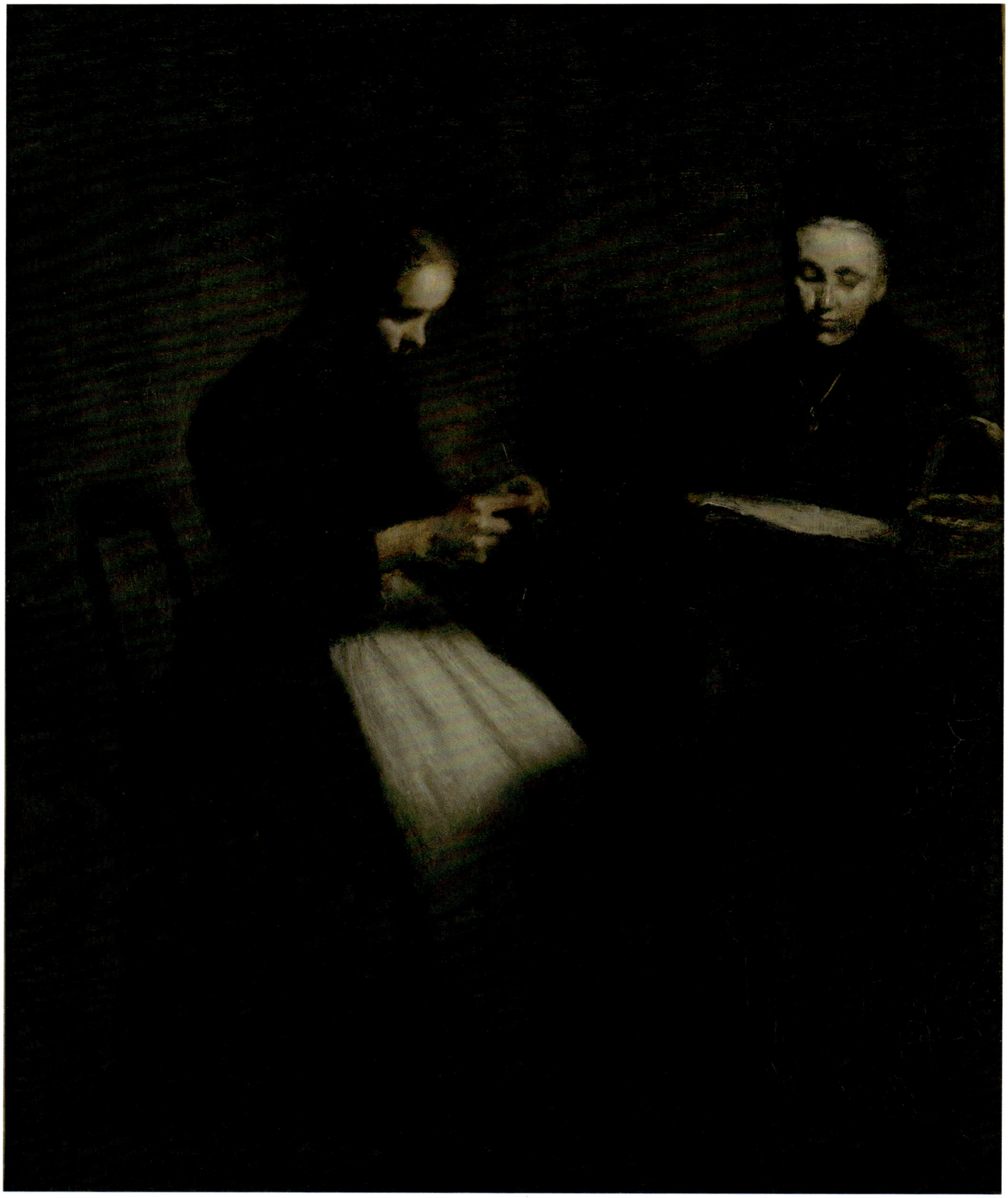

[36]
Vilhelm Hammershøi 1864-1916 Danish
Evening in the Drawing Room. The Artist's Mother and Wife 1891
Oil on canvas 63 x 49.5 cm
Statens Museum for Kunst

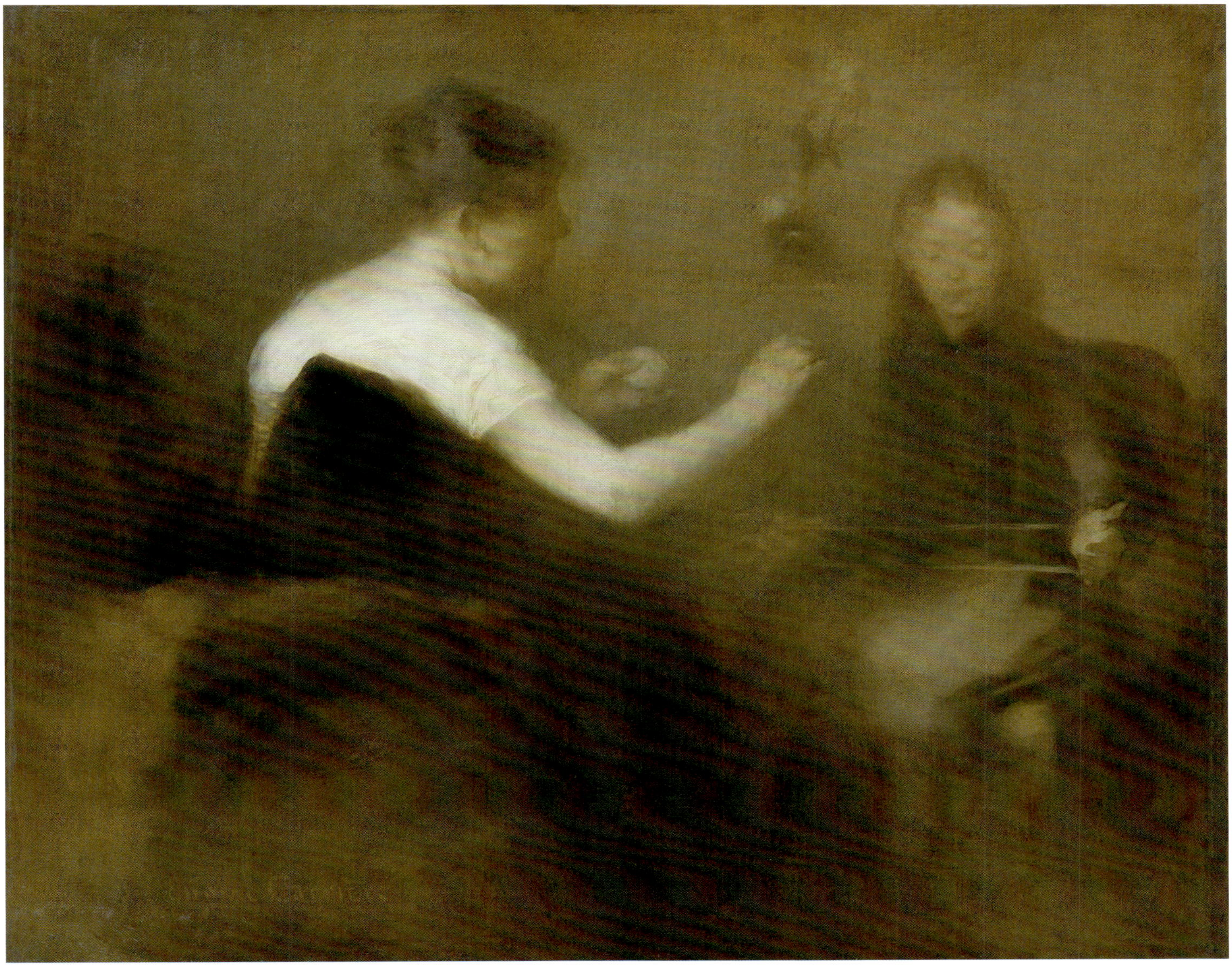

[37]
Eugène Carrière 1849-1906 French
Winding Wool. The Artist's Wife and Daughter 1887
Oil on canvas 60 x 73 cm
Tate, London. Presented by Mrs R.M. Dunlop 1927

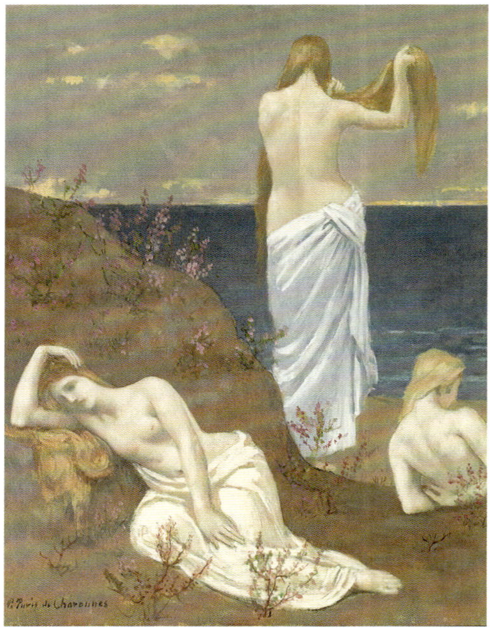

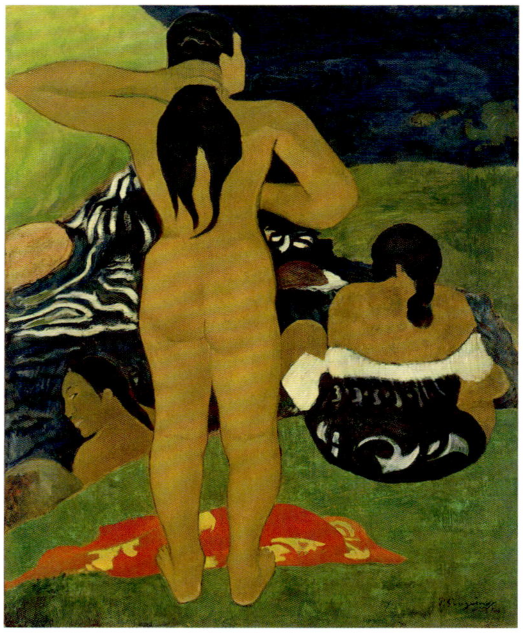

Private mythology

Among the four figures in Hammershøi's large painting *Artemis* there is strictly speaking no contact either [10]. It is very important to the understanding of the picture that there seems to be no question of a specific mythological subject; this is a highly personal interpretation of the mythological universe of antiquity, and there is no predetermined action in the picture (see p. 25).

The question as to where Hammershøi may have drawn his inspiration for the picture has long been discussed, and the interest of the art historians has mainly been directed towards the older art he had just seen in Italy – and with good reason, for several of the figures seem to have been taken over from older models. But the actual idea of the picture should rather be viewed in the context of the art of his own time. At the Universal Exposition in Paris in 1889 Hammershøi undoubtedly saw one of the French painter Puvis de Chavannes' major works, *Young Women by the Sea* [38]. In the picture of the three women on the beach one can find not only obvious parallels with Hammershøi's painting in the whole atmosphere, in the colour scheme and in the subject with its three separate figures who appear to have no contact with one another; the woman with her back to us, who is about to braid her hair, can also be said to be related to the woman with her back to us in Hammershøi's picture.[65]

Another possible antecedent is the Frenchman Paul Gauguin. A few months before Hammershøi started work on *Artemis*, he could see an extensive selection of Gauguin's paintings exhibited at Den Frie Udstilling in Copenhagen, including several brand new pictures from Tahiti (see p. 53).[66] The Dane did not of course attempt to imitate the French painter's intense colours. On the other hand he may have felt attracted to the highly personal, myth-like motivic content in Gauguin's work and to the strange inexplicable interrelations of the figures that is so characteristic of many of the Tahiti pictures.[67]

[38]
Pierre Puvis De Chavannes 1824-98 French
Young Women by the Sea (small version) c. 1879
Oil on canvas 61 x 47 cm
Musée d'Orsay, Paris

[39]
Paul Gauguin 1848-1903 French
Tahitian Women Bathing 1892
Oil on canvas 109.9 x 89.5 cm
Metropolitan Museum of Art, New York (Lehman Collection)

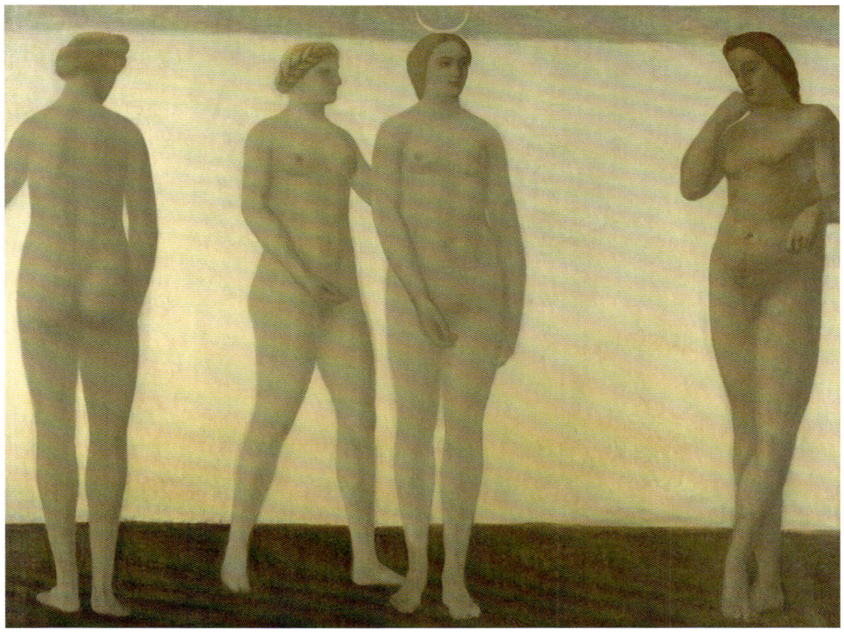

A striking parallel that Hammershøi is unlikely to have known in the original is Gauguin's *Tahitian Women Bathing* from 1892 [39].[68] At first glance the subject simply looks like an everyday scene. But the figures seem to have stiffened in their movements, and the standing woman has been given a monumentality that cannot be directly explained in terms of the subject. Both elements help to elevate the scene above the everyday and add an element of something exalted, but also self-contradictory and indefinable. The subject thus comes to appear inscrutable, like *Artemis*. The affinity with Hammershøi's painting is no less when we consider that Gauguin probably also made a thorough examination of Puvis de Chavannes' *Young Women by the Sea* before he started on his painting.[69]

Tahitian Women Bathing was not shown at Den Frie Udstilling in 1893, but Hammershøi could see several paintings with related subjects where the Frenchman had added a mythical and mystical dimension to everyday scenes.

Arrangement with a woman in a room

There is one particular painting that must have meant more than any other to Hammershøi. It is Whistler's *Arrangement in Grey and Black No. 1. Portrait of the Painter's Mother* from 1871 [40].[70] The painting shows the black-clad woman seated in profile against a uniformly grey wall. The first part of the title of the painting is very telling, for the picture is an "arrangement" rather than a portrait. The painter has placed the figure in a tight composition in a meticulously calculated interplay with the wall area, a hanging and one of his own etchings on the wall. The elderly woman sits quite motionless, apparently completely closed in on herself. The subject is fixed and reveals nothing of the passing moment.

After Whistler had exhibited the painting in 1883 at the Salon in Paris, it had become one of modern art's most famous and controversial paintings, and it was among the artworks

[10]
Vilhelm Hammershøi 1864-1916 Danish
Artemis 1893-94
Oil on canvas 193 x 251.5 cm
Statens Museum for Kunst

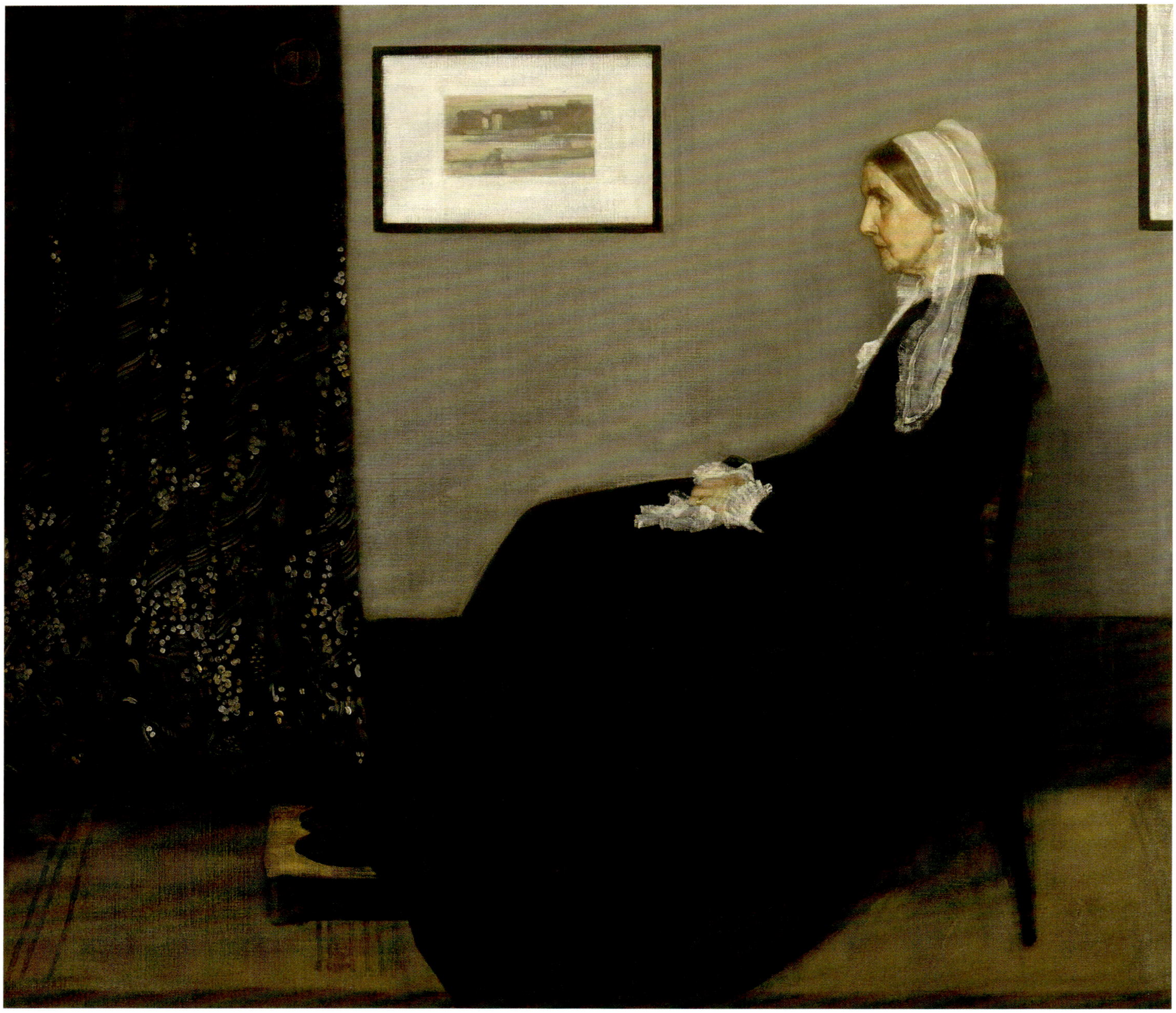

[40]
James McNeill Whistler 1834-1903 American
Arrangement in Grey and Black No. 1.
Portrait of the Painter's Mother 1871
Oil on canvas 144.3 x 162.5 cm
Musée d'Orsay, Paris

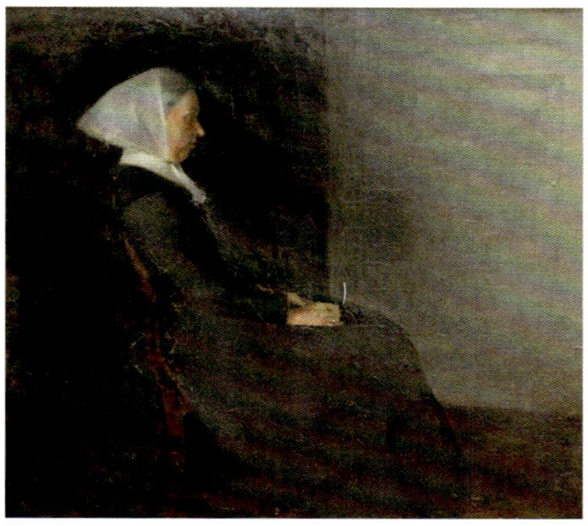

that exerted the greatest influence on other artists in the period. The same year it was reproduced as a print in the highly esteemed French art periodical *Gazette des beaux-arts*, and Hammershøi appears to have seen this.[71] At all events, in 1886 he painted a small picture of his own mother, who is also seen seated in profile in a dark dress against a neutral wall [41].[72] The picture appears to be a reversed paraphrase of Whistler's painting. However, it is only the postural motif that he has adopted, not the American's sophisticated effects.

Hammershøi later had the opportunity to see the painting in the original in November 1891 – during his second stay in Paris – when it was bought by the French State to great media attention and transferred to the Musée du Luxembourg.[73] This gave him the chance to make an in-depth study of the painting, and it soon left its mark on his art.

In 1893 Hammershøi painted *Interior* [42], where a woman, sitting with her back to us at a semicircular mahogany table, is reading a letter. She is almost squeezed into one corner of the room. The placing of the woman in the space as well as the other elements in the composition emphasize that the painting is not to be seen as an interior in the normal sense, but as an "arrangement" in Whistler's sense. Hammershøi has attempted to create a similar interaction among the components of the picture – besides the woman and the table also an open door, a hanging and a print on the wall – and has carefully balanced the individual elements against one another.

Two years later, in 1895, he painted a large group picture of three young women sitting together in a room [43].[74] The models for the three women were the painter's wife Ida, seen flanked by Ingeborg Ilsted (married to Ida's brother, the painter Peter Ilsted) and Anna Hammershøi. The three women are sitting down in almost the same position, quite erect, and each is portrayed from a different angle. There is no contact at all among them and they are all absorbed in their own inner worlds. The picture is hardly to be viewed as a social situation with interaction among people. It is rather about shared yet separate existences.

Strictly speaking, these are variations on a theme, and here Hammershøi seems to have been trying to further develop the motif from the American's painting, since each of the three women can be seen as a transformation of Whistler's mother.[75] Yet the picture seems unresolved. It offers no explanation of why the three women are sitting together. In the structure of the picture there is moreover an inner conflict, since different composition principles clash. The women are seated so far forward in the room that it can almost be called a frieze, but at the same time a table has been pushed in front of the woman on the right so that she is nevertheless drawn back in the space, which counteracts the frieze effect. This displacement means that the attempted symmetrical structure is broken down. The explanation must undoubtedly be sought in the painter's wish to engage the women in an interplay with the background – the three women set against a neutral wall, a door and a drawing or print on the wall.

The painting of the three women also shows how selective Hammershøi could be when he was inspired by other art. He could pick out individual pictorial elements such as a posture from a particular artist and at the same time disregard very important aspects of the artist's distinctiveness. Ida Hammershøi's figure, for example, seems to be indebted to one of Paul Gauguin's paintings, *Woman with a Flower* [31, p. 52], but without adopting the Frenchman's colour scheme or symbolism.[76]

[41]
Vilhelm Hammershøi 1864-1916 Danish
The Artist's Mother, Frederikke Hammershøi 1886
Oil on canvas 34 x 37 cm
Private collection

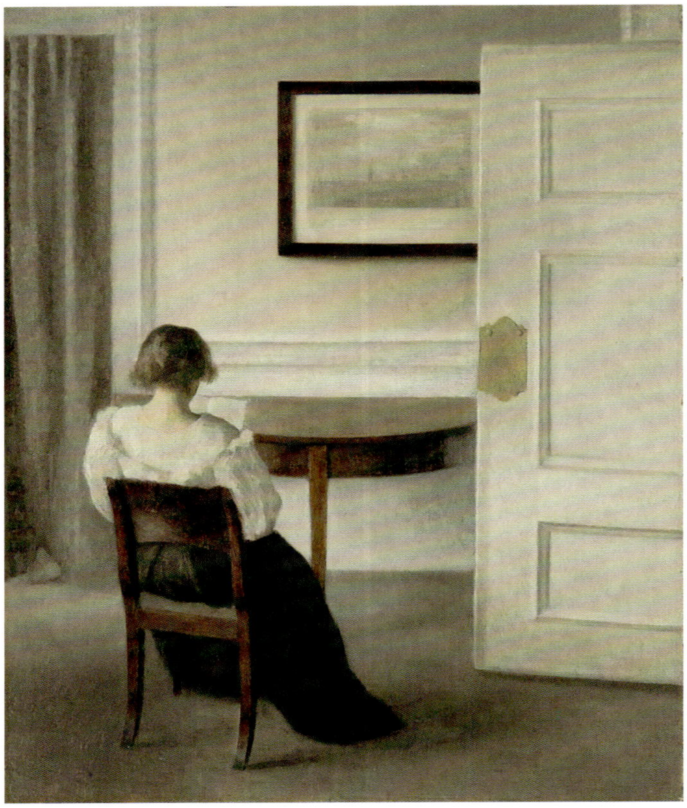

More arrangements with women

Hammershøi was by no means alone in being inspired by Whistler's painting. Fernand Khnopff took an interest in the picture at more or less the same time, and this came to expression for the first time in 1887 in *Portrait of Marie Monnom* [44].[77] The young woman sits in a position just like Whistler's mother, and like the American the Belgian painter has structured the picture surface with the aid of the areas in the background. Khnopff was undoubtedly aiming at a portrait likeness in the picture, but the woman looks straight ahead with a faraway gaze, in rather the same way as Hammershøi's sister Anna in the painting from 1885 [32, p. 55].

The English painter William Nicholson was also profoundly influenced by Whistler's painting and by his art in general. His painting *Lady in Yellow* [45][78] takes its point of departure very directly in the American painter's subject and composition, inasmuch as the woman is seen entirely in profile and sits in a quite identical way in a chair with her feet on a footstool. This woman too is absorbed in her own universe. But Nicholson shows an understanding of the picture in a quite different way from both the Belgian and the Dane. He has not sought a tight geometrical composition and has omitted the details of the background. On the other hand he has carefully balanced the colours of the picture within a very limited scale of yellow shades.

At the same time the Danish painter Anna Ancher was painting her mother, also seen in profile and sitting with joined hands [46]. But she has taken a much more concrete approach to her subject. She undoubtedly knew Whistler's painting, but she neither adopted

[42]
Vilhelm Hammershøi 1864-1916 Danish
Interior 1893
Oil on canvas 56.5 x 46.5 cm
The Gothenburg Museum of Art

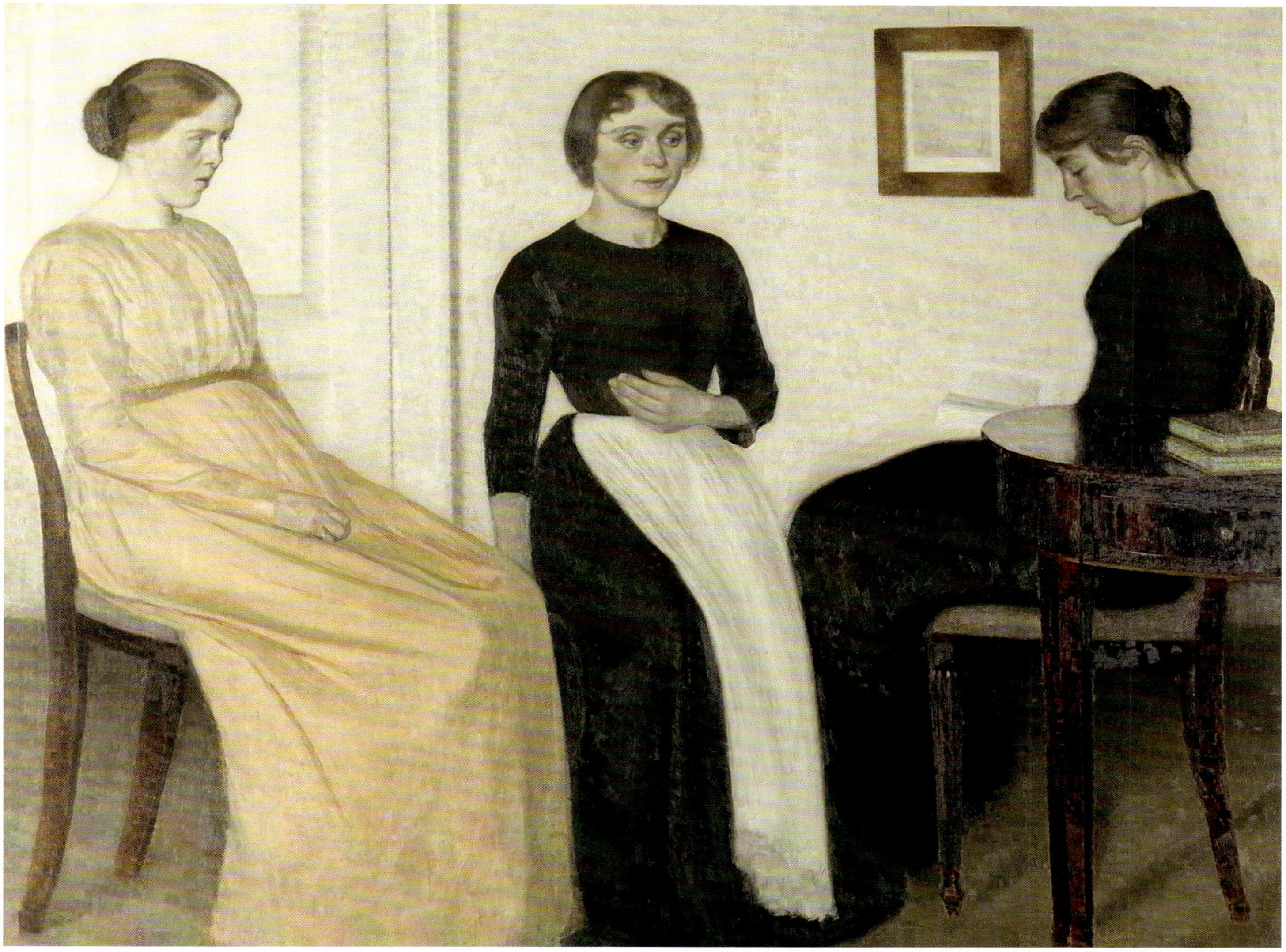

[43]
Vilhelm Hammershøi 1864-1916 Danish
Three Young Women 1895
Oil on canvas 128 x 167 cm
Ribe Art Museum

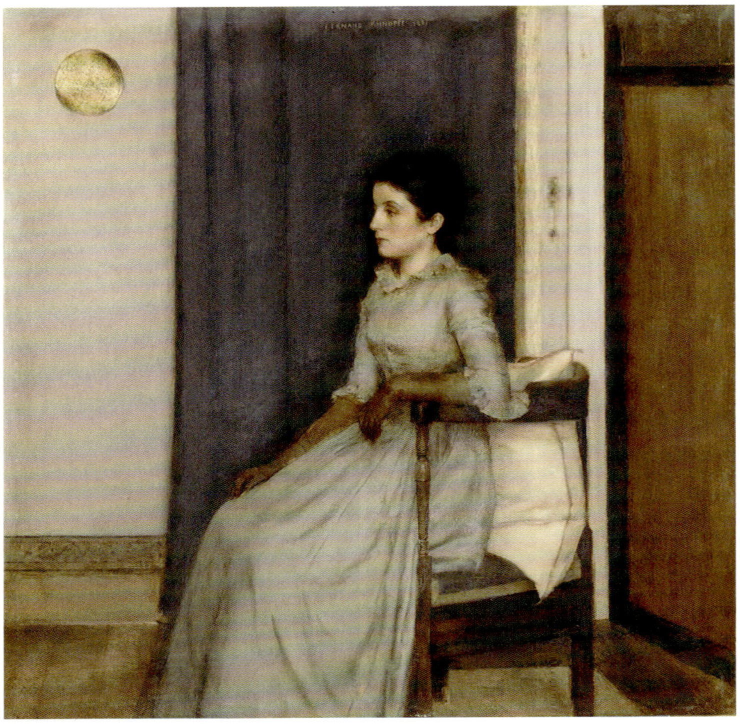

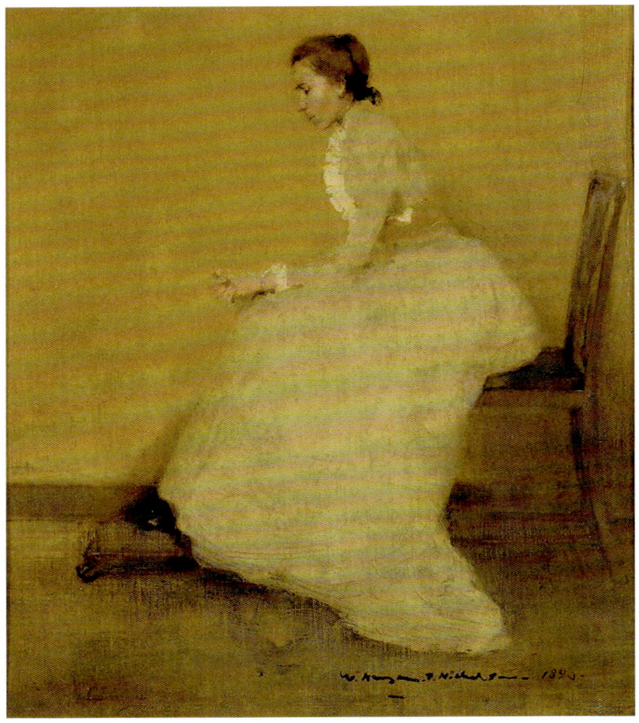

his painterly devices nor wished to quote directly from it. Anna Ancher's mother also seems more present than the other women. True to her own artistic temperament the painter has worked with the colouristic resources and played on the contrast between the black of the dress and the blue background.[79]

The Finnish painter Helene Schjerfbeck also seems to have been fascinated by Whistler's famous picture – although grudgingly, it is said. In her painting *The Seamstress* from 1903-05 [47] the main figure, like the other female figures, is seated in profile, and the picture has been kept in grey shades like Whistler's painting.[80] But Schjerfbeck has radically simplified the subject. All details have been omitted, and the background is quite neutral. The woman is entirely calm and self-absorbed, although the slightly tilted rocking chair does introduce an element of potential unrest into the picture. It remains no more than a hint, though, and nothing in the woman's body shows signs of motion. As for the colour scheme, there are obvious parallels between Schjerfbeck's and Hammershøi's art. At the Universal Exposition in 1889, where the Finnish painter showed pictures in the Nordic Naturalist tradition, she may have drawn inspiration from the Dane. He is unlikely, however, to have been influenced by her mature style. By the time she painted *The Seamstress*, she lived in isolation, and Hammershøi had no opportunity to see her works.

Arrangement with standing woman

Among the painters of the English-speaking world at the time, one particular type of portrait was especially favoured: the full-length portrait of a person standing.[81] This is a type that Whistler cultivated greatly, mainly with women as the subjects. But he liked to give the por-

[44]
Fernand Khnopff 1858-1921 Belgian
Portrait of Marie Monnom 1887
Oil on canvas 49.5 x 50 cm
Musée d'Orsay, Paris

[45]
William Nicholson 1872-1949 British
Lady in Yellow 1893
Oil on canvas 72.4 x 62.3 cm
Private collection, London

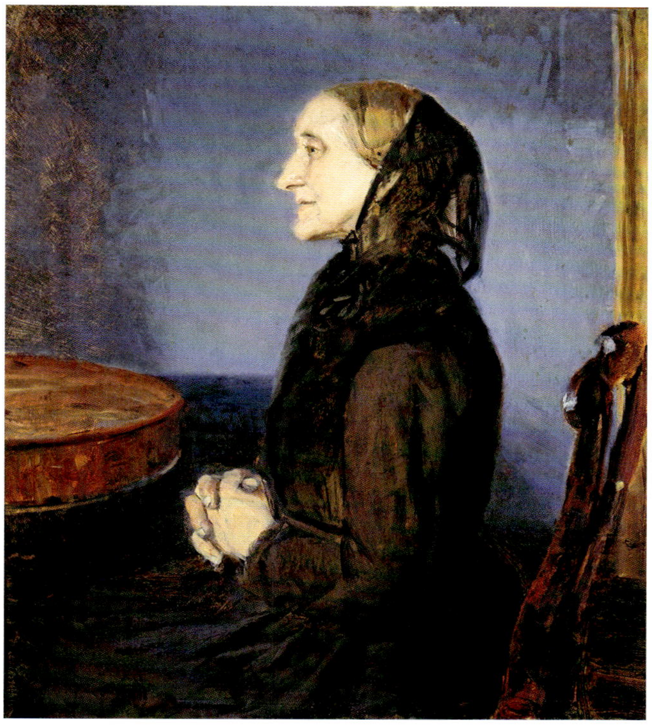

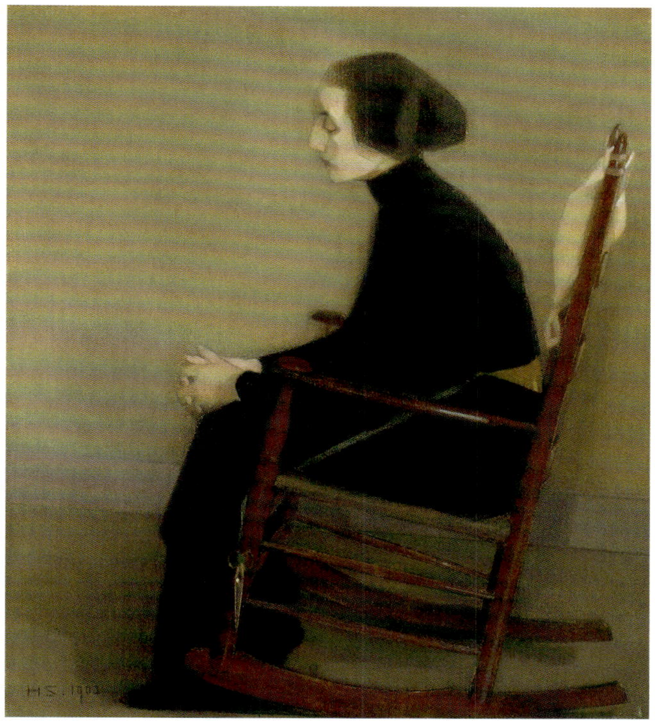

trait a twist – quite literally. The woman portrayed is often turning partly away from the viewers, so that the representative function associated with portrait painting is played down. Whistler furthermore added something indeterminate to the subject.

Whistler's painting *Arrangement in Yellow and Grey: Effie Deans* from 1876-78 [48] belongs to this group of ambivalent portraits.[82] The picture shows the painter's mistress, Maud Franklin, ostensibly acting in the role of Effie Deans, a character taken from one of Sir Walter Scott's historical novels. But he only added the name of the character in the novel to the canvas at a late stage, so the picture was perhaps not at all intended from the outset as a literary-historical portrait, but as a true portrait. It is, however, no ordinary portrait. The woman has turned her head so her face is partly veiled in shadow. In other words there is no direct contact between her and the viewer, and she appears remote and aloof. Moreover, her figure seems to merge with the diffuse, obscure surroundings.

Hammershøi did not paint portraits of standing figures in the same way. But in his *Portrait of Ida Ilsted*, his later wife [50], the female figure has been given the same monumentality as if she had been portrayed standing. Hammershøi has adhered to the formal ground rules of portrait painting and maintained direct eye contact with the portrait subject. But there is something distant and dreaming about the young woman's facial expression, and one does not feel one has real contact with her.

Hammershøi made use of a photograph that he squared off carefully before laying the portrait out on the canvas.[83] The practical reason for this was undoubtedly that he was not yet married to Ida and therefore did not have the model in front of him every day. But there is no doubt that in the crucial phase when the portrait was to take its final form, he painted

[46]
Anna Ancher 1859-1935 Danish
Portrait of the Artist's Mother, Ane Hedvig Brøndum c. 1893
Oil on canvas 67.8 x 59.8 cm
The Helga Ancher Foundation, Michael & Anna Ancher's House, Skagen

[47]
Helene Schjerfbeck 1862-1946 Finnish
The Seamstress 1903-05
Oil on canvas 95.5 x 84.5 cm
Ateneum Art Museum, Finnish National Gallery, Helsinki

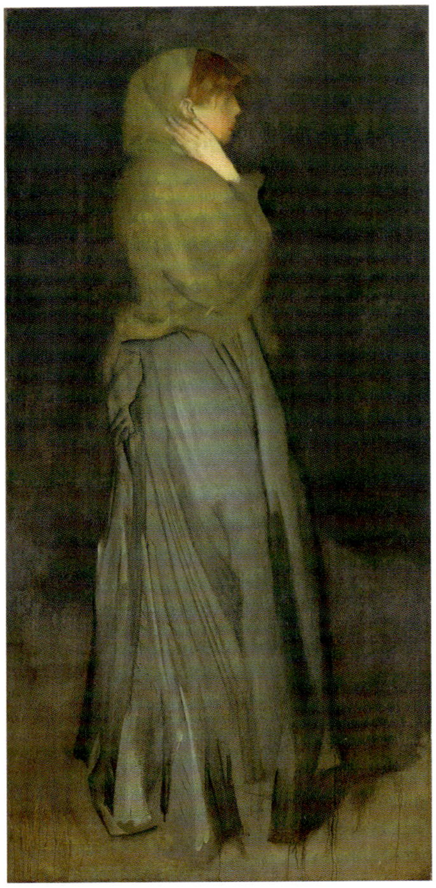

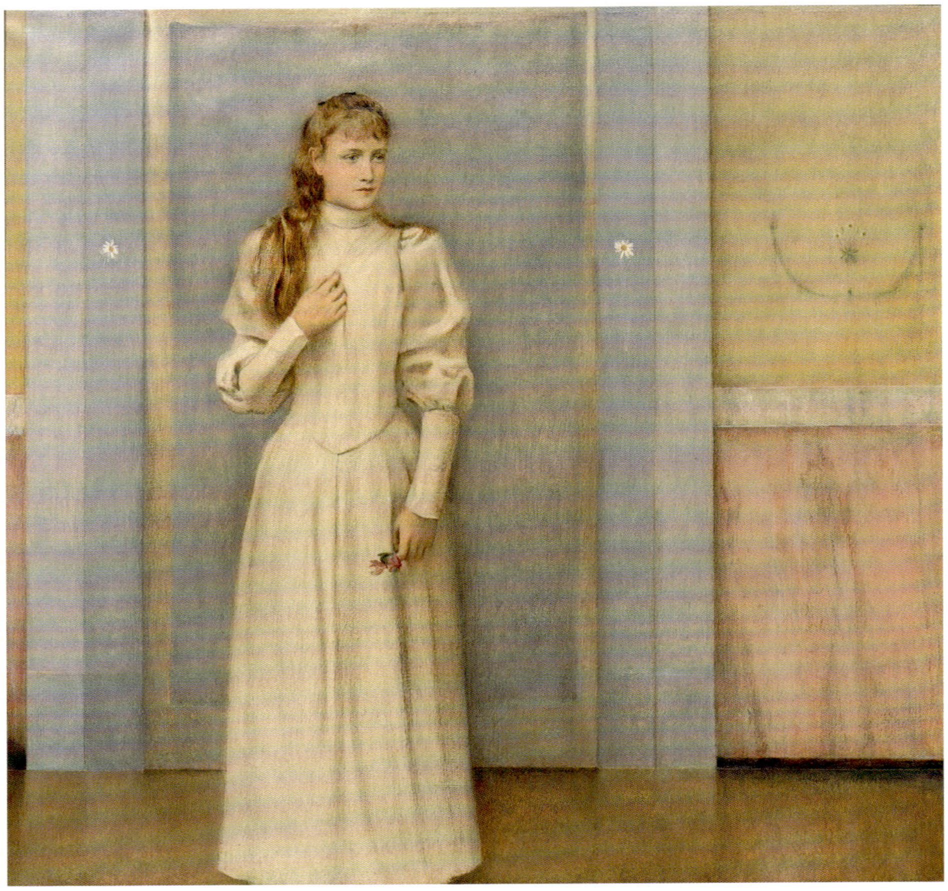

directly in front of Ida. In the photograph there is eye contact with her, so the dreaming expression in the painting emerged while the painter looked at his fiancée face to face. The rendering of the woman's hands – which perhaps a little unusually had to rest idly in her lap – also testifies to first-hand observation. The result is a both penetrating and delicate depiction of the young woman.

Fernand Khnopff's *Posthumous Portrait of Marguerite Landuyt* from 1896 [49] is more obviously related to Whistler.[84] The actual arrangement of the model – standing in front of a door opening that frames her, and surrounded by decorative wall panels – is something the Belgian has taken over from Whistler's portrait of his mother [40, p. 62]. But she is seen standing with her face turned a little to one side and a slightly preoccupied gaze, and in that respect she evokes reminiscences of Whistler's portraits of standing women. The woman's distant expression can perhaps be explained by the fact that this is a posthumous portrait – the painter was only given the commission after Marguerite Landuyt had died. Still, the same absent-minded gaze can be found in the portrait of his sister, Marguerite Khnopff, and she stood in front of the painter in flesh and blood when he painted her [20, p. 39].

[48]
James McNeill Whistler 1834-1903 American
Arrangement in Yellow and Grey: Effie Deans c. 1876-78
Oil on canvas 194 x 93 cm
Rijksmuseum, Amsterdam (Dep. Van Gogh Museum, Amsterdam)

[49]
Fernand Khnopff 1858-1921 Belgian
Posthumous Portrait of Marguerite Landuyt 1896
Oil on canvas 75.2 x 74.5 cm
Musées Royaux des Beaux-Arts, Brussels

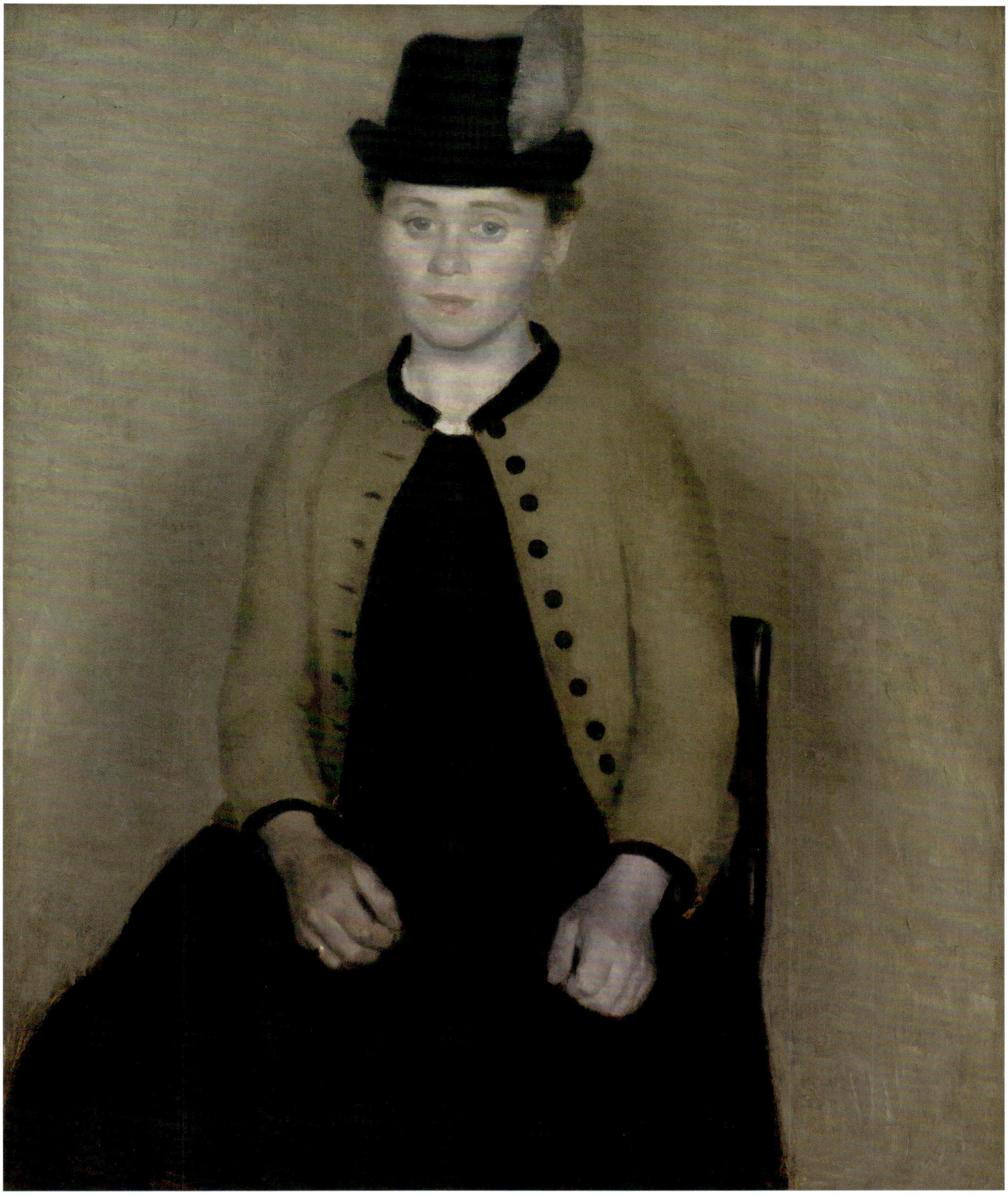

[50]
Vilhelm Hammershøi 1864-1916 Danish
Portrait of Ida Ilsted 1890
Oil on canvas 106.5 x 86 cm
Statens Museum for Kunst

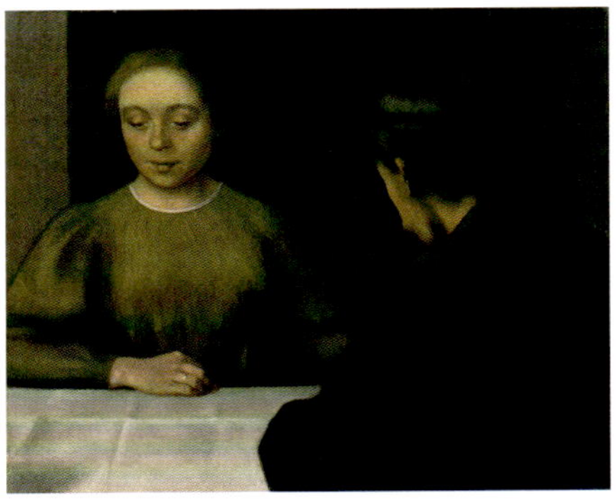

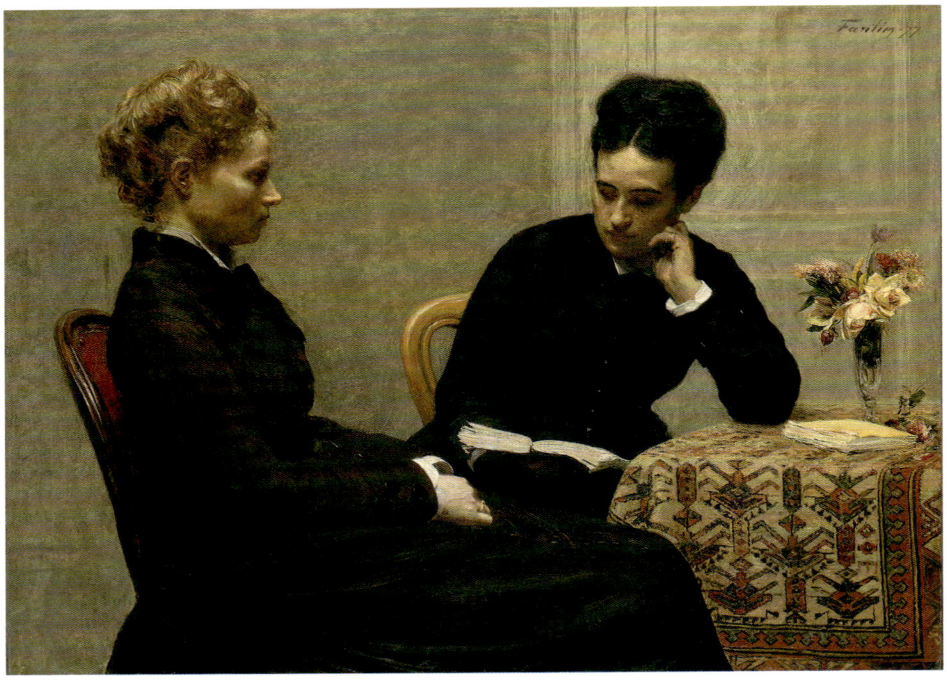

Each in a world apart

Hammershøi's painting *Two Figures* [12] is about two people who are together without apparently having any contact with each other (see p. 28). But any elements that could explain the relationship between them or place them in a social context have been peeled away.

The picture has no direct parallels in Danish art. But there is an obvious parallel that may well have been a direct model. Some twenty years previously the French painter Fantin-Latour had painted the picture *The Reading* [51], where two people are also seen together without really communicating with each other. Neither the reader nor the listener seems to be interested in what is going on between them. The listening woman looks as though she is sitting lost in her own thoughts, and the reader has perhaps come to a halt in the reading. Hammershøi had the opportunity to see the painting at the Universal Exposition in 1889,[85] and it may therefore have played a role for him when he conceived his subject. But the lack of human contact is a recurrent theme in Fantin-Latour,[86] and the Danish painter may therefore also have drawn inspiration from other paintings by him.

Pablo Picasso took up the same theme in his so-called blue period in the early years of the 20th century. In the painting *Poor Couple in a Cafe* [52] we see two wretched people huddled together in a café, apparently linked by a shared fate. Despite the physical proximity, the two do not seem to have any close relationship with each other. In other words, it is a subject that is related to Hammershøi's. However, it should be added that the Spanish painter has turned both figures' faces towards the viewer, and has thus achieved a confrontation that neither his French nor his Danish colleague wished to create. Picasso has also added an element of sentimentality that Hammershøi would have none of.

[12]
Vilhelm Hammershøi 1864-1916 Danish
Two Figures. The Artist and His Wife 1898
Oil on canvas 71.5 x 86 cm
ARoS Aarhus Kunstmuseum

[51]
Henri Fantin-Latour 1836-1904 French
The Reading 1877
Oil on canvas 97 x 130 cm
Musées des Beaux-Arts, Lyon

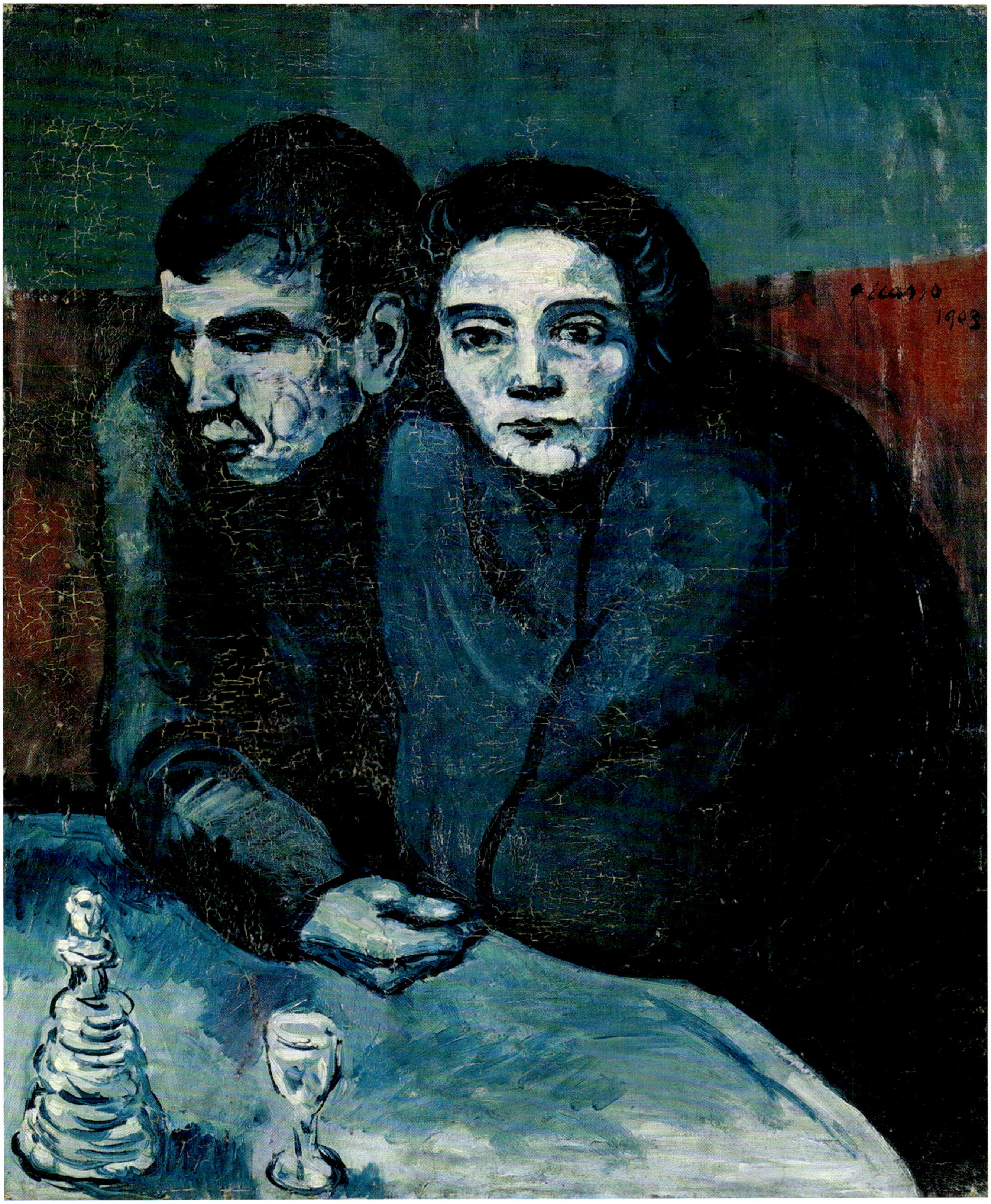

[52]
Pablo Picasso 1881-1973 Spanish
Poor Couple in a Cafe 1903
Oil on canvas 81.5 x 65.5 cm
The National Museum of Art, Architecture and Design, Oslo

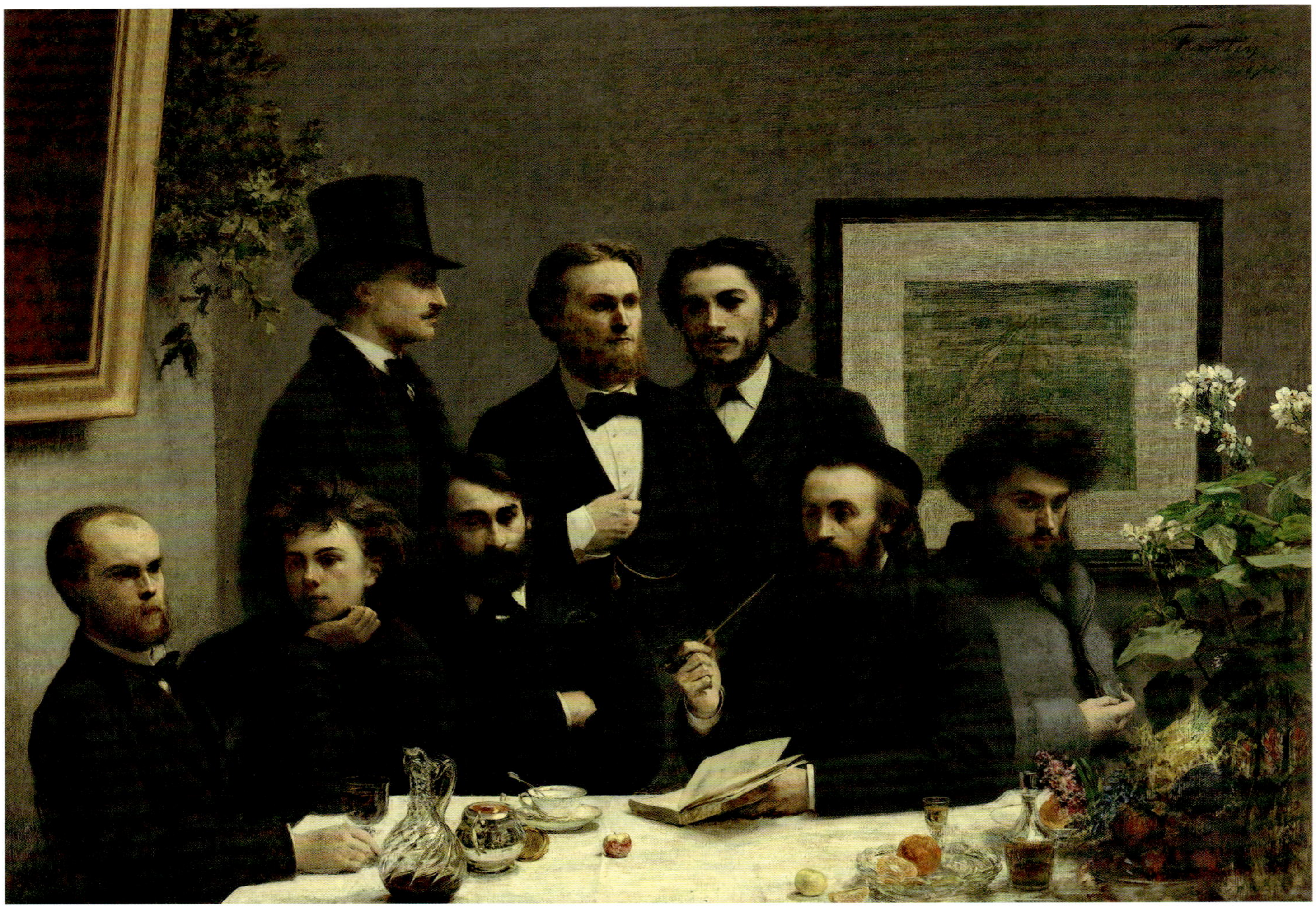

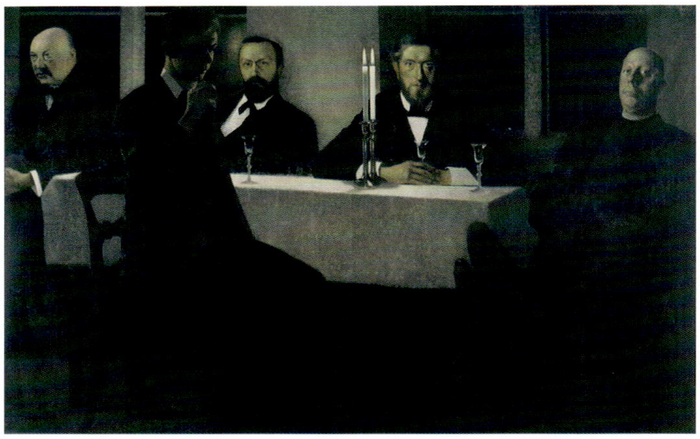

[53]
Henri Fantin-Latour 1836-1904 French
A Corner of the Table 1872
Oil on canvas 160 x 225 cm
Musée d'Orsay, Paris

[15]
Vilhelm Hammershøi 1864-1916 Danish
Five Portraits 1901-02
Oil on canvas 190 x 340 cm
The Thielska Gallery, Stockholm

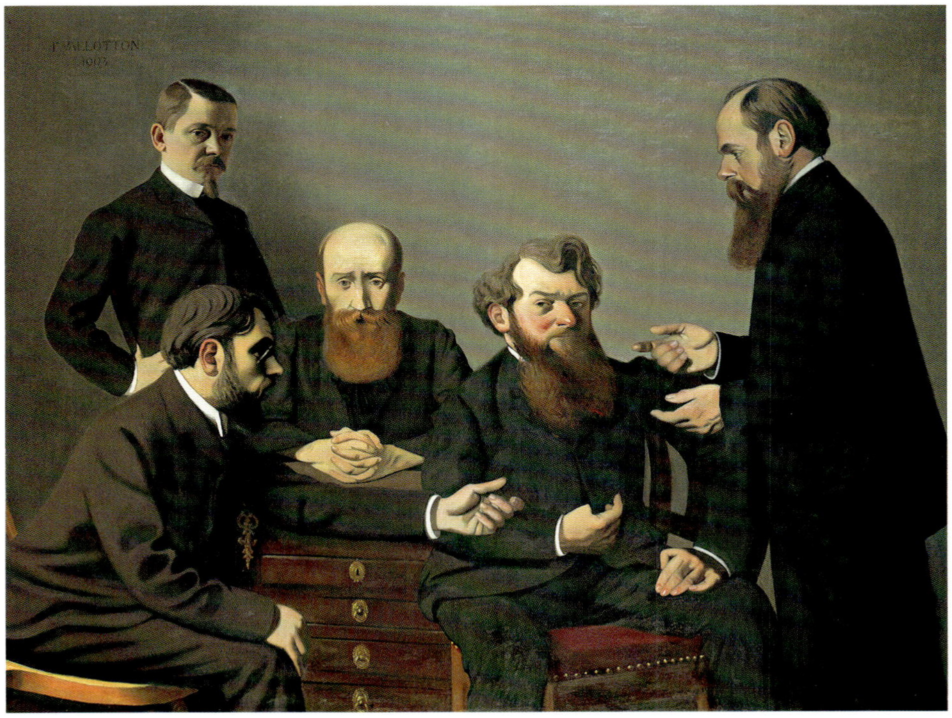

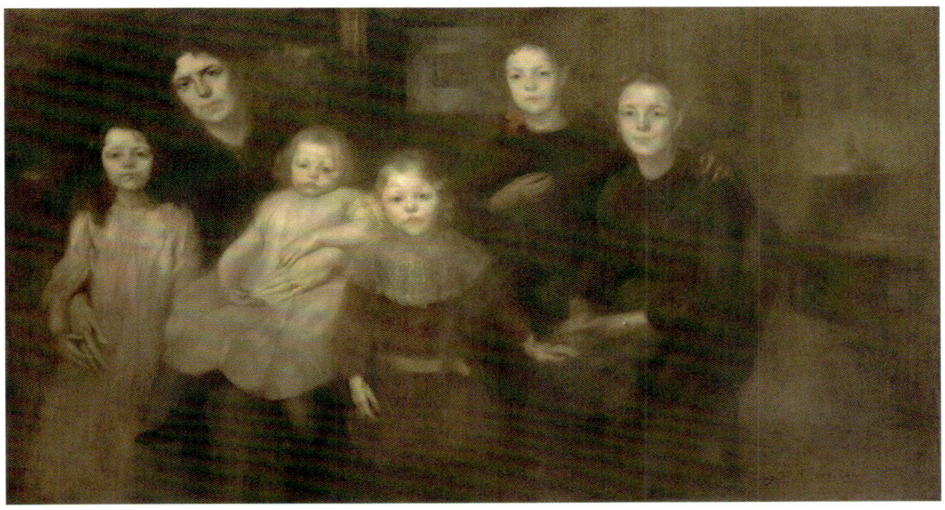

[54]
Felix Vallotton 1865-1925 Swiss
The Five Painters 1902-03
Oil on canvas 145 x 187 cm
The Winterthur Museum of Art

[55]
Eugène Carrière 1849-1906 French
The Painter's Family 1893
Oil on canvas 125.5 x 221.5 cm
Musée d'Orsay, Paris

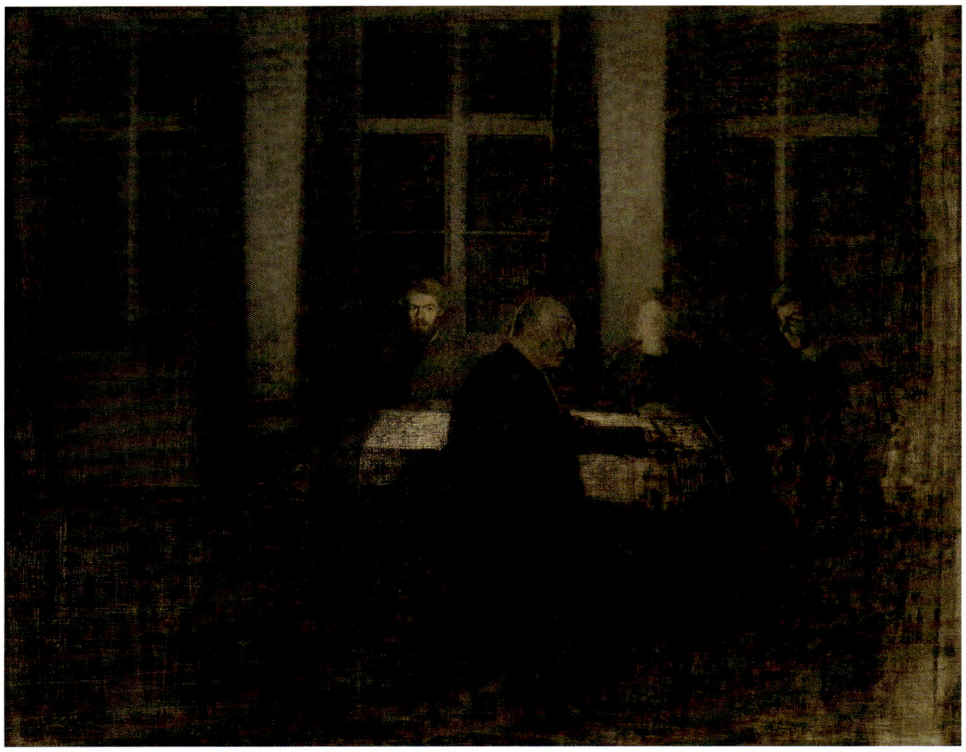

Together without contact

Hammershøi developed and transformed the theme that underlies *Two Figures* in the monumental painting *Five Portraits* [15, p. 32]. Here the figures are linked in a collective identity of whose significance both they and the viewers of the picture were aware – their activity as artists. But this shared identity apparently creates no bond among the figures, and each seems to exist in a world of his own (see p. 28).

An important antecedent of Hammershøi's painting is the group portraits of artists that were assiduously cultivated in France in the final decades of the 19th century. In the French pictures the artists are often gathered around a common mentor, if they do not actually constitute a unified artist group. As mentioned (p. 40) Hammershøi must have seen Fantin-Latour's *Homage to Delacroix* at the Universal Exposition in 1889. There is a crucial difference from this picture, inasmuch as Hammershøi's painting does not take the form of a tribute or an artistic manifesto. There is however a certain affinity between the two artists, and this becomes even more pronounced if one compares Hammershøi's picture with another of Fantin-Latour's group pictures, *A Corner of the Table* from 1872 [53], where a number of prominent Parisian writers are gathered.[87] Here too there is no unifying idea that binds the men together and the writers are by and large just as isolated from one another as Hammershøi's men. Moreover, something of the same mood prevails in the picture.

However, Hammershøi's figure group in the dim room also has a parallel in Carrière's painting *The Painter's Family* [55].[88] The painter's wife and children are assembled without really having any contact with one another, and they are in a diffuse, obscure space, so that

[56]
Vilhelm Hammershøi 1864-1916 Danish
Evening in the Drawing Room 1904
Oil on canvas 101 x 123.5 cm
Statens Museum for Kunst

we are as unclear about the surroundings as in Hammershøi's picture. There is a definite similarity both in the grouping of the figures parallel to the picture plane and in the colour scheme. But Hammershøi's art does stand out from the Frenchman's painting in crucial respects. It is characterized by rigour and simplicity, just as he economizes with his artistic resources. The Dane may have seen paintings by the Frenchman on several occasions, and this very painting was reproduced in the illustrated edition of the catalogue of the Salon in Paris in 1893.

Another artistic affinity is evident, one that is more difficult to pin down with any certainty – the relationship with the Swiss Félix Vallotton's art. In a number of ways there are striking parallels between the group of men in *Five Portraits* and the group of artists in Félix Vallotton's painting *The Five Painters* [54]. Vallotton's picture, it should be noted, was painted the year after Hammershøi's picture and could have been inspired by it.[89] The parallels are however unlikely to be due to direct influence; they are rather related solutions to the same artistic challenge. But there was in fact some Danish awareness of Vallotton's art at the time. Johan Rohde held the Swiss artist in great esteem, especially his prints. And he shared this admiration with the painter Kristian Zahrtmann, who met Vallotton in Saint Trojan in 1894.[90] Perhaps these contacts aroused the interest of the Swiss in Danish art? The painter and artist-craftsman Mogens Ballin also knew and socialized with Vallotton, and in 1899 the Swiss artist executed a double portrait of Ballin and his wife as a woodcut, presumably when the couple spent some time in Paris on their honeymoon.[91] Perhaps these contacts aroused Vallotton's interest in Danish art? However, when it comes to artistic expression, there are definite differences between the two artists – in particular the emphatic drawing of the figures distinguishes Vallotton from Hammershøi.[92]

Immediately after the completion of *Five Portraits,* Hammershøi went to work on another group picture, *Evening in the Drawing Room*, but he never finished this painting [56]. He may have broken off the work in his disappointment that *Five Portraits* was not bought by Statens Museum for Kunst, as he had hoped. He considered *Five Portraits* one of his most important works and would have liked to see the painting in the country's national gallery.

Alone in the room

The motif of the solitary human being comes to expression in earnest in Hammershøi's interior pictures. He created so many paintings of this type that in his time and for posterity it became his hallmark. Although he settled on his mode of painterly expression at an early stage, a relatively long time passed before he distilled out the interior painting as his most frequent subject. In the early years he often depicted people indoors, but he did not give any clear account of the space they were in. Neither the indication of the character of the interior nor the fine rendering of the light was yet a regular concern in his art. In the first paintings the people are therefore placed in diffuse, unspecified surroundings that cannot be localized.

This aroused considerable surprise in Hammershøi's day. In his review of his works at Charlottenborg in 1886 Karl Madsen emphasized a "peculiarity" in Hammershøi: "There is an extremely vague indication of the localities in which the figures find themselves. One does not know where the figures sit, nor does one really know where the light comes from."[93]

It was only gradually that Hammershøi began to detail the people's surroundings. It is possible that in this area he drew some inspiration from his contemporary Danish colleague Carl Holsøe. The review of the latter's debut work at the Charlottenborg December exhibition in 1886 strongly suggests that already then he had settled firmly on features that later became highly characteristic of Hammershøi. The critic Carl Hartmann singled out Holsøe's "talent for rendering the diffraction of the light through hazy air in a home-like space", but at the same time Hartmann mentioned that "the objects almost appear as if they are seen through half-closed eyes".[94]

Hammershøi's wife Ida soon exclusively became the model in his interior pictures, yet she remains precisely that – a model. One must not view the pictures as portraits of her in their home. However, Hammershøi constantly assigned changing roles to the solitary woman. In many cases he emphasized her loneliness, while in others he placed the female figure in an arrangement with the space and the furnishings – that is, in an alternation between a symbolic narrative and an aesthetic exploration of the subject. There are of course fluid boundaries between the two types, and one should speak rather of a both-and than an either-or.

Hammershøi first began to cultivate the subject in the 1890s. But an important step along the way was *Interior with the Artist's Mother* from 1889 [57], where he began to home in on the two themes that became central to his interior pictures: the solitary woman in a room and the delicately graduated light that comes from a window outside the picture, falls in on the wall and helps to define the space. However, the room in which we see the woman is not clearly defined in the painting.

Hammershøi did not yet fully exploit the potential interplay between figure and space. But he went to work exploring it in the interiors he painted in his childhood home in an apartment on Frederiksberg Allé and his own apartment in the Frederiksberg neighbourhood in the 1890s. In a couple of paintings he exploited the two windows of the apartments as sources of light and as unifying elements in the composition. In one of the paintings he appears to have done first, he has not yet settled on the subject [58]. Here two women stand with their backs turned at one window. It is not clear what relationship and what kind of contact exist between them, and they do not seem to be preoccupied with the view from the window. Hammershøi has deliberately chosen not to indicate this in any detail, so we do not know what they may have been looking at. The soft contours of the figures give them an

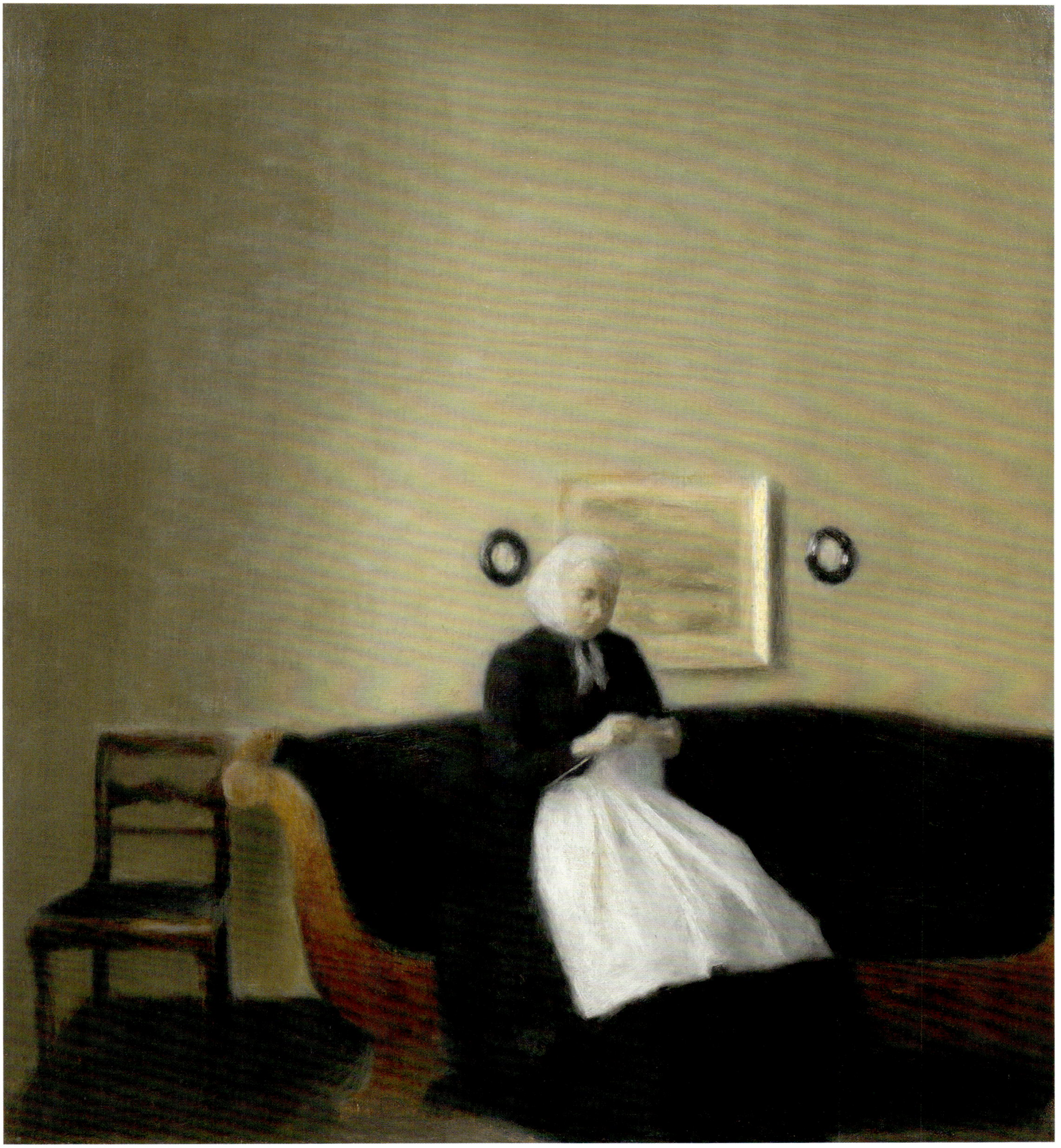

[57]
Vilhelm Hammershøi 1864-1916 Danish
Interior with the Artist's Mother 1889
Oil on canvas 55 x 51 cm
Nationalmuseum, Stockholm

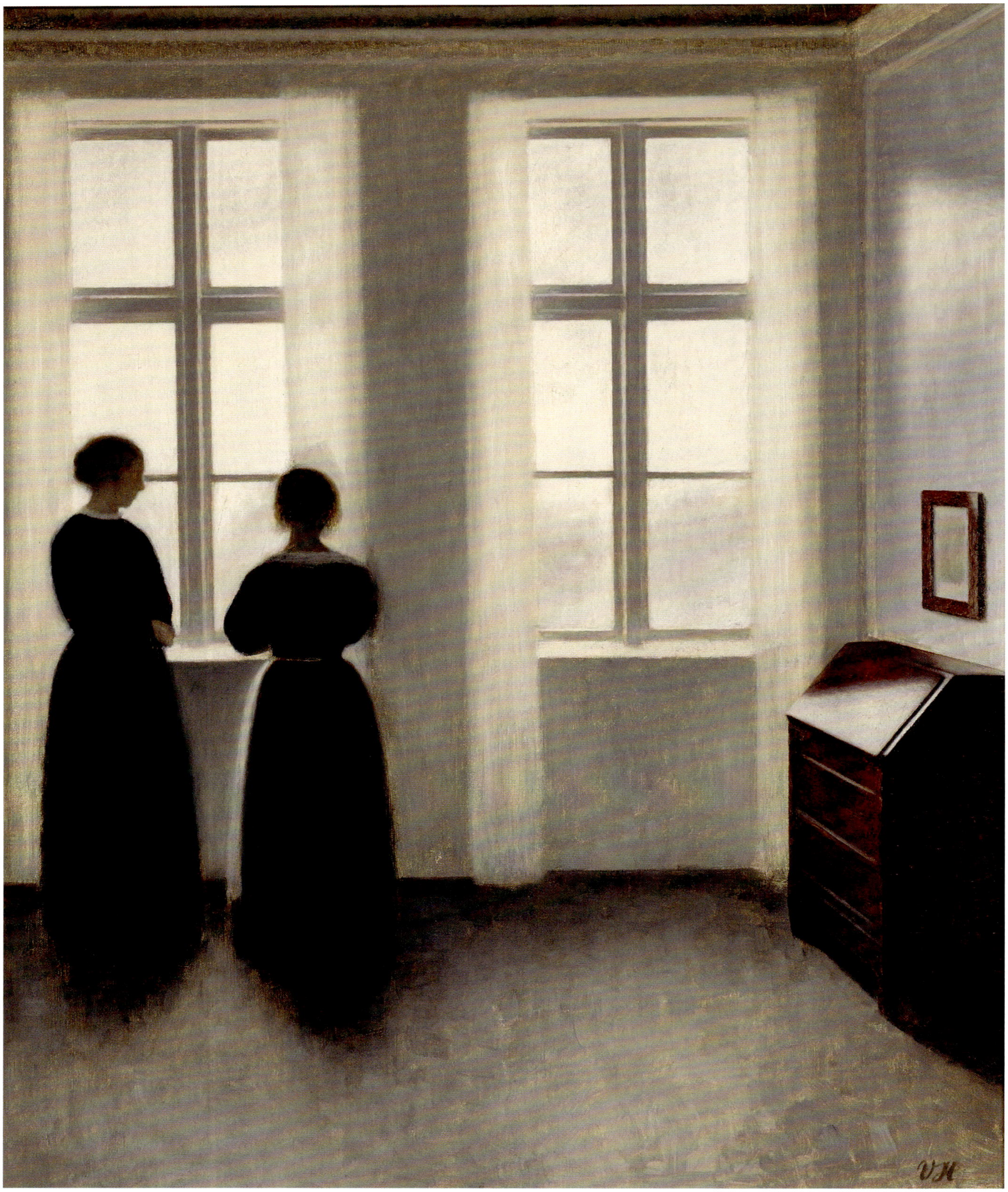

[58]
Vilhelm Hammershøi 1864-1916 Danish
Figures by the Window c. 1895
Oil on canvas 55 x 46 cm
Private collection

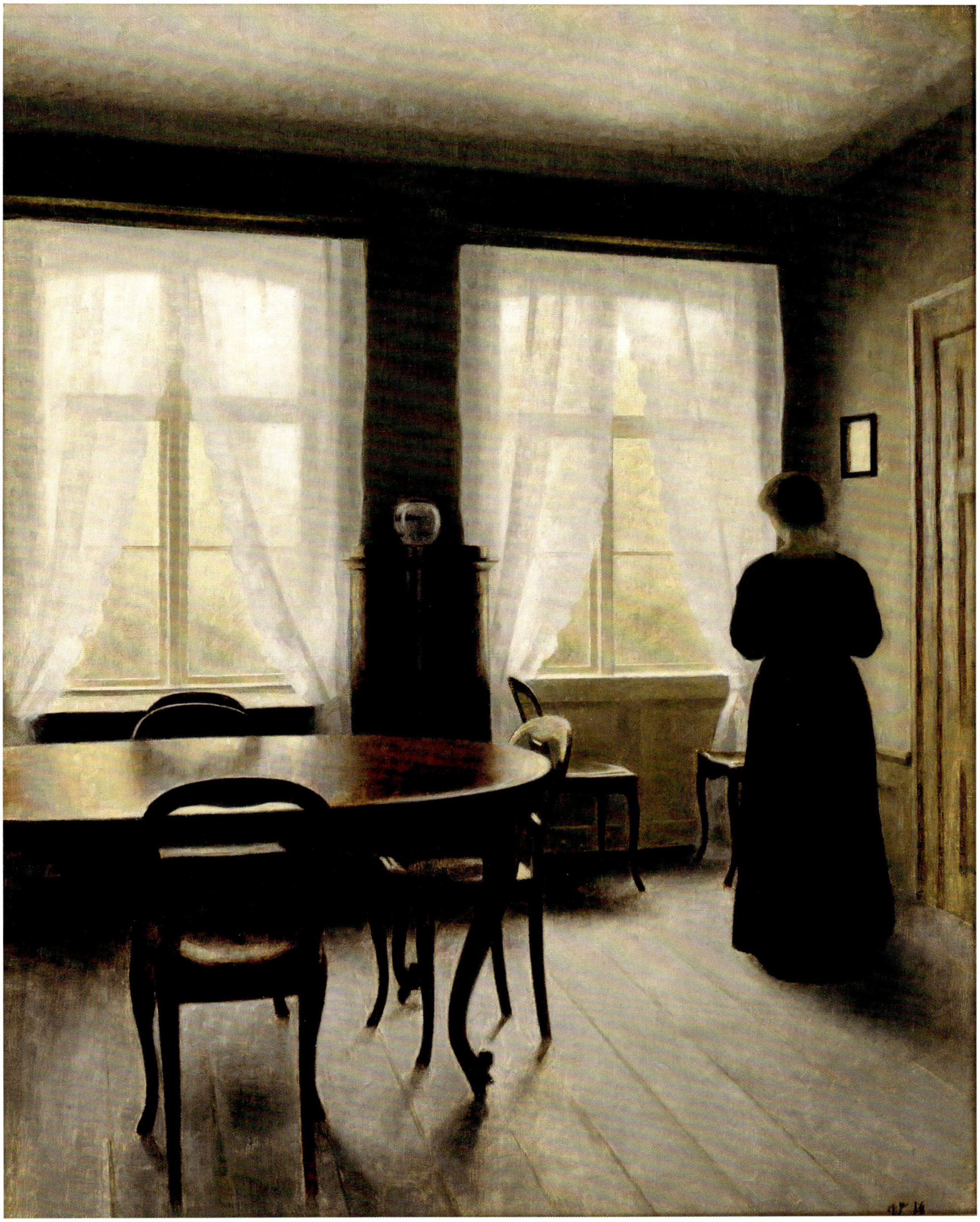

[59]
Vilhelm Hammershøi 1864-1916 Danish
Interior, Frederiksberg Allé 1900
Oil on canvas 56 x 44.5 cm
Private collection, United Kingdom

oddly ghostly appearance, and this gives the picture its defining character. The scene seems indeterminate and inexplicable.

The second painting is characterized by much greater precision in the details [59]. Here he appears to have drawn support from a photograph of the room, possibly taken by his friend, the painter Valdemar Schønheyder Møller.[95] In that case it was undoubtedly taken in consultation with Hammershøi. All the furnishings and their placing recur in the photograph and in the painting, but the painter has omitted the chandelier in the room, presumably to create a simpler and more compact spatial effect. There is however one crucial difference: while the photographer's lens has only been able to register the windows as vague openings with light, the eye of the painter, as is only natural, has been able to adjust the light in the various parts of the room so that the windows have the same distinctness in the details as the rest of the painting. If he did indeed use the photograph as a support, in this important respect he must have laid it aside and made his own necessary observations. In this picture we see a single woman from behind, standing in a sparsely furnished room. She is so far from the window that she can hardly be observing something outside. Nor is there any account here of the surroundings outside the windows. In front of her the woman has a pair of chairs, and since she seems wholly frozen into her position, her presence in the room makes no logical sense. Perhaps the painter simply regarded the woman as part of a painterly composition.

However, Hammershøi only really took up the theme "solitary woman in a room" after he had moved in 1898 to an apartment in a 17th-century house in Strandgade, in the Christianshavn neighbourhood of Copenhagen. One of the first pictures he painted in his new home was *Interior* from 1899 [60], where he has cultivated the forms created by the doors, the wall panels, the table and the figure of the black-clad woman with great consistency. But at the same time he has played on the decided sense of claustrophobia evoked by the limited space. The woman almost seems forced into a corner.

In the painting *Interior, Strandgade 30* from 1901 [61] the solitary woman has for once gone over to one of the windows and is looking down at the street outside. But we are not told what she is looking at, and the building on the other side of the street effectively blocks off the view. The painter has directed all attention to the shape of the room, and this makes it rather conspicuous that the woman's back is turned to the essential features of the picture.

The room is dominated by a table that has been set up for the occasion in the middle of the floor, and a piano standing against the wall. Felix Krämer has pointed out several contradictory details in the presentation and placing of the furniture.[96] The table, which is not surrounded by chairs, has no function in the middle of the room, just in front of the piano, and the two legs of the piano closest to the wall are missing. Krämer tries to give these logical flaws a symbolic meaning, as if the painter had wanted to create a sense of the unreal in the room. But Hammershøi was trying neither to depict the actual furnishings of his home nor to furnish the rooms out of logical or functional considerations. His wish was to create a formally harmonious interplay of space and furniture and in this case also the solitary figure. Omissions and adjustments were subordinated to this wish, and in many cases this leads to the omission of details such as door hinges and handles, table legs and even a wrought-iron stove that can be seen in other paintings. In such cases aesthetic considerations played in – that is, the wish for more simplification and rigour in the details. One should therefore not evaluate the changes and simplification in the subjects in the light of factual reality, nor is there any likelihood that they should be interpreted symbolically. The symbolism in Hammershøi should be sought at the overall level, not in the details.

Hammershøi used the different rooms in the apartment to vary the interplay between the woman's figure and the room in which she is shown. In particular he liked to use the room where a window had been placed right beside a door [62]. There he could exploit the window as a source of light, while playing on the contrast between the view of a world outside that the window, at least in theory, could offer, and the door, which is effectively closed against this world. The woman's motionlessness in the almost entirely bare room thus signals that she has no other choice than to remain seated. In several paintings Hammershøi varied the motif by having the woman sitting or standing in front of the open door. Formally, this presents an opportunity for a choice, but the woman seems unwilling to accept this choice.

Only in rare cases did Hammershøi choose to paint a single man alone in a room. In *Interior with a Young Man Reading* from 1898 [63] he used his younger brother Svend as his model. He stands leaning against the windowsill – to use the daylight for his reading – and can be regarded as a study in absorption. But as a counterweight to the young man Hammershøi has painted an assemblage with a chest of drawers, a chair and some drawings that seem to be atop a chest of drawers leaning against the wall; that is, a decidedly aesthetic arrangement. The emphasis in the picture is thus not unequivocal.

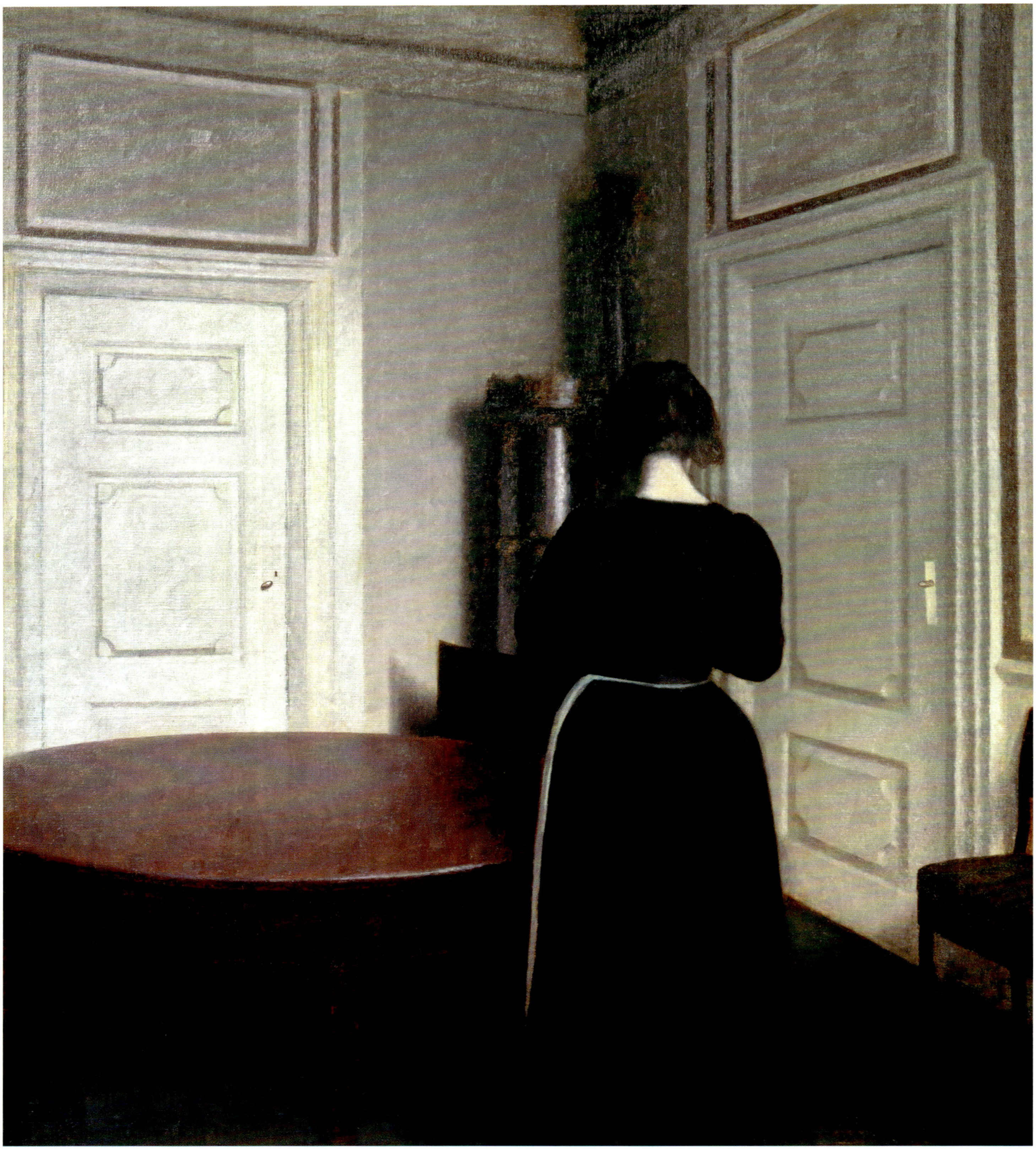

[60]
Vilhelm Hammershøi 1864-1916 Danish
Interior 1899
Oil on canvas 64.5 x 58.1 cm
Tate, London. Presented in memory of Leonard Borwick
by his friends through the Art Fund 1926

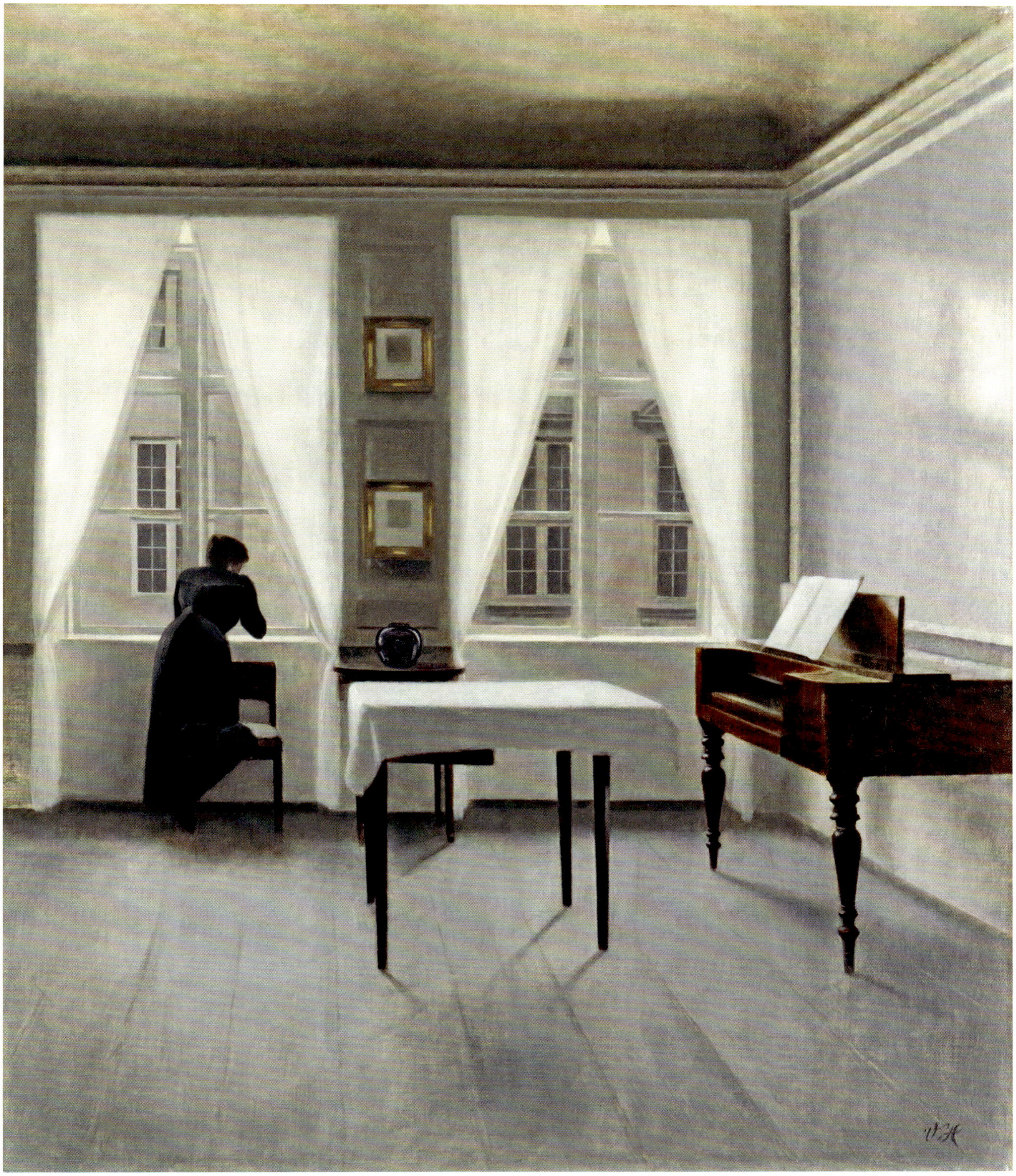

[61]
Vilhelm Hammershøi 1864-1916 Danish
Interior, Strandgade 30 1901
Oil on canvas 62.4 x 52.5 cm
Niedersächsisches Landesmuseum, Hannover

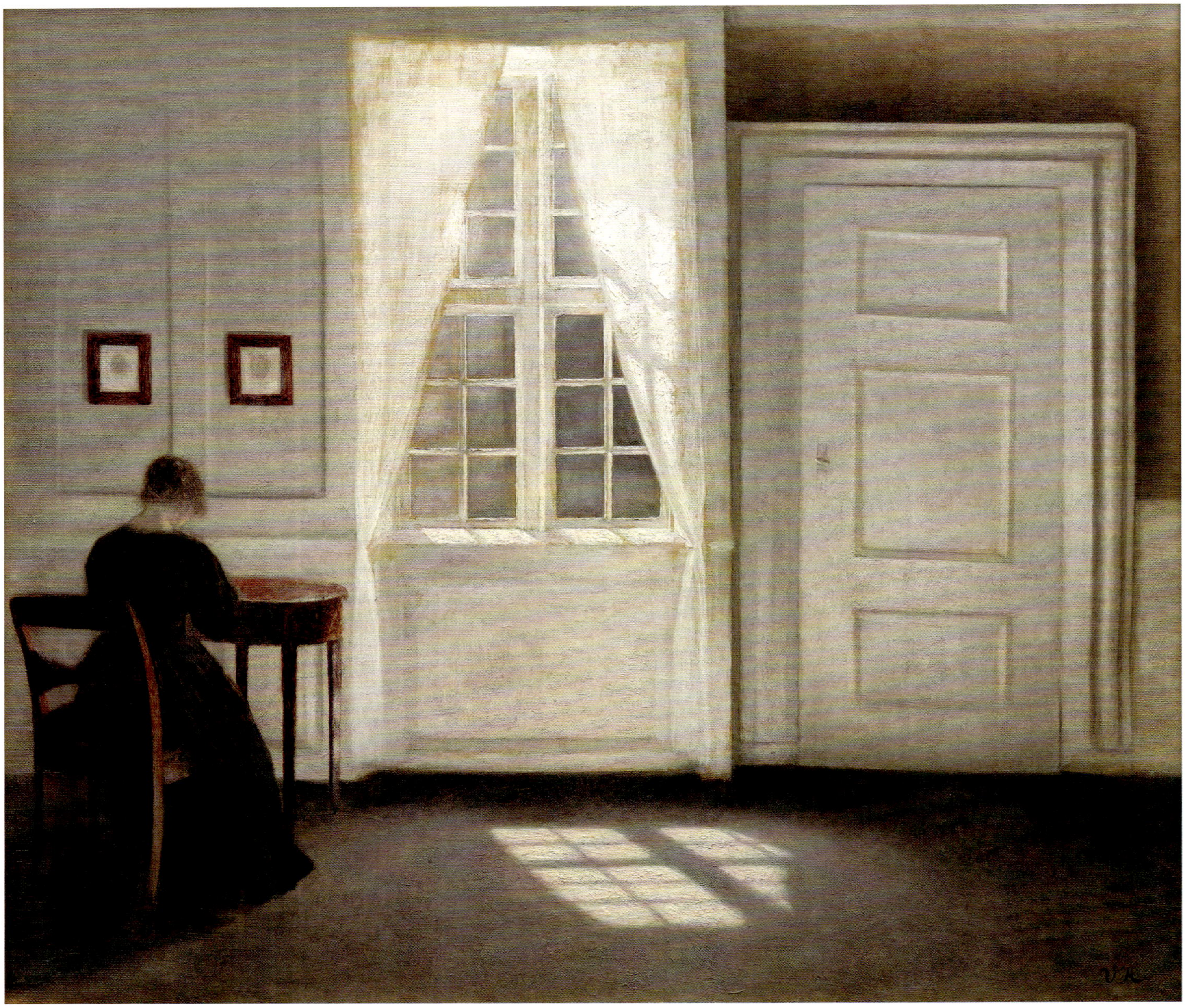

[62]
Vilhelm Hammershøi 1864-1916 Danish
Interior from Strandgade with Sunlight on the Floor 1901
Oil on canvas 46.5 x 52 cm
Statens Museum for Kunst

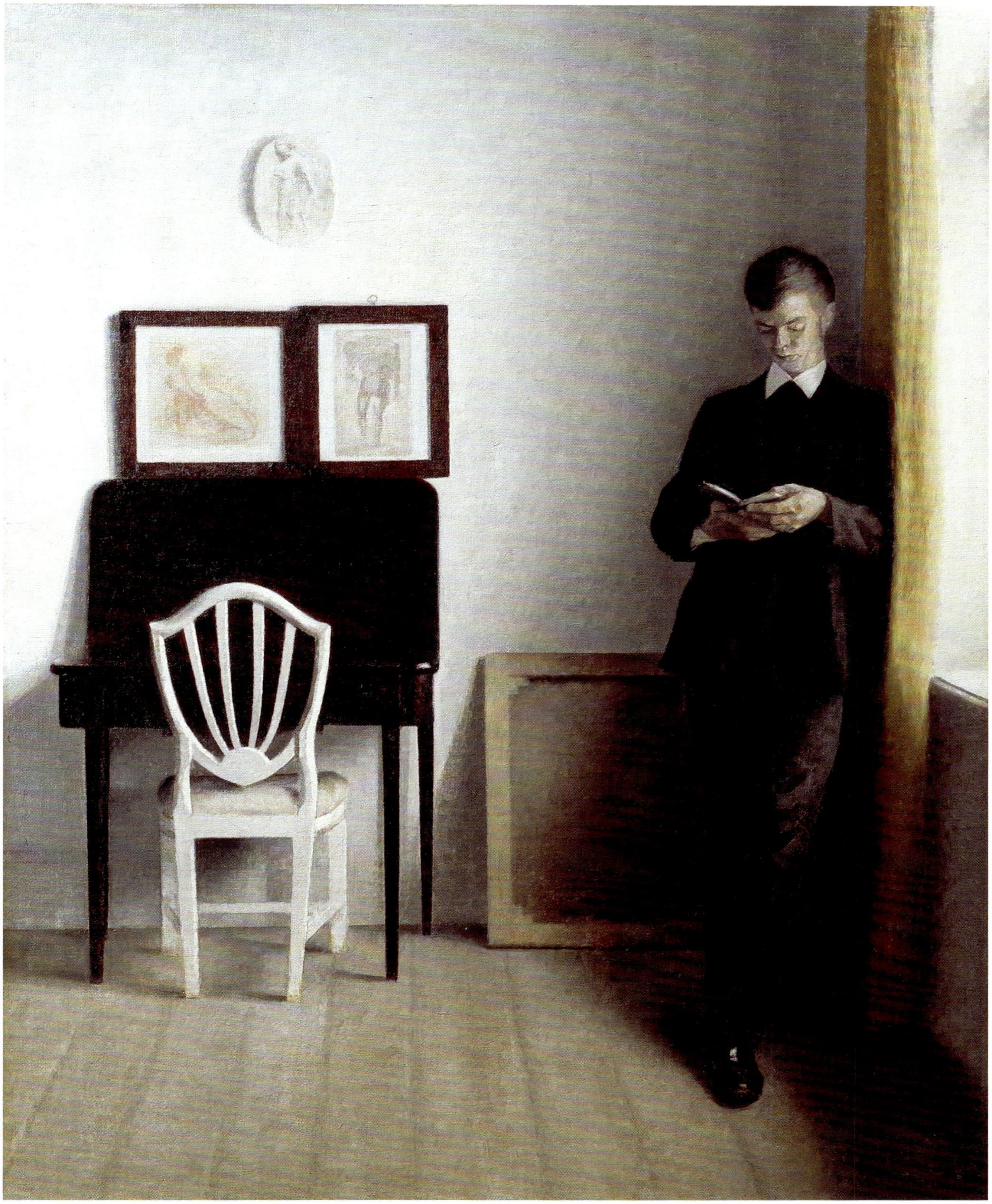

[63]
Vilhelm Hammershøi 1864-1916 Danish
Interior with a Young Man Reading 1898
Oil on canvas 64.4 x 51.8 cm
The Hirschsprung Collection, Copenhagen

Still life with woman

In a number of paintings Hammershøi has shifted the emphasis in the picture so that it lies entirely on the meticulous arrangement of furnishings and pictures on the wall, and here the woman does not play a role as a solitary person. She becomes so to speak part of a still life. In this he is associating himself with a firmly rooted classic picture type, but he appears to have totally disregarded the traditional meaning assigned to the things in the older still lifes. In these paintings Hammershøi could simplify all the forms in the picture so that the individual character of the objects recedes into the background [64]. The clear lines and rigorous forms were the main issue for him, and the figure of the black-clad woman becomes part of the overall ensemble – with the fine graduation of the light from the window as the prime determining factor.

But he could also place greater emphasis on the individual objects and give a precise, very detailed characterization of each of them – still with the woman as an unbudgeable part of the composition [65]. Even though the elements in the individual pictures are by and large the same – a table covered by a white cloth, an item of furniture against the wall, a mirror or some prints and the lone female figure – the overall effect varies greatly in the paintings. When he moves in close to the subject in the painting *Interior with Woman at Piano, Strandgade 30* from 1901 [65] and at the same time crops the table in the foreground, he achieves an element of intimacy that is not present in *Interior* from 1898 [64], where he seems to be at an aloof distance from everything.

In both paintings the woman with her back to us and her exposed neck play a major role. This neck has in fact become the main issue in the painting *Young Lady* with the subtitle *Resting* [66]. For once Hammershøi has gone up close to the woman and looked at her at close quarters. Here he has almost completely banished all other references, so there is no explanatory context the woman can be placed in. The subtitle of the picture makes no real sense, since strictly speaking this is not a resting situation. It is the woman alone who is in focus. But despite all this it is no study of a clothed model, since the woman is in a room in real surroundings.

One of Hammershøi's most radical works is the painting *Interior with Woman Sitting at a Table* from around 1910 [67].[97] In this picture he has removed the last trace of an everyday situation that could justify the woman's presence in the room. She sits leaning forward with no connection with the assemblage of two bottles and a book placed on a table beside her. The table is placed in a diagonal position in the room, quite obviously not in the place it would normally occupy. In other words it has been set up in the middle of the floor for the occasion. The placing of the print on the absolutely bare wall is adapted to the assemblage on the table, but would make no sense if one imagined it as part of any true furnishing of the room.

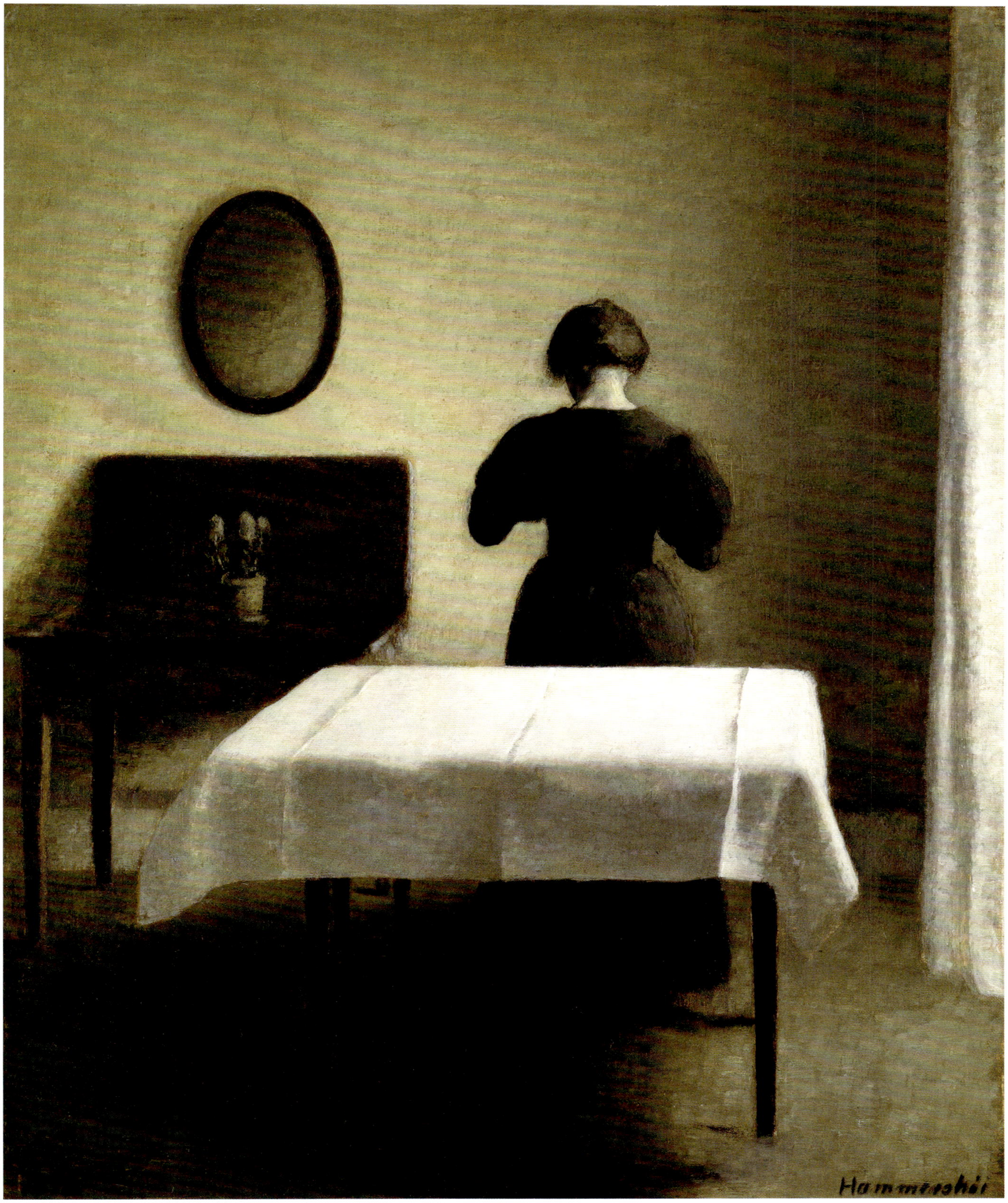

[64]
Vilhelm Hammershøi 1864-1916 Danish
Interior 1898
Oil on canvas 51.5 x 46 cm
Nationalmuseum, Stockholm

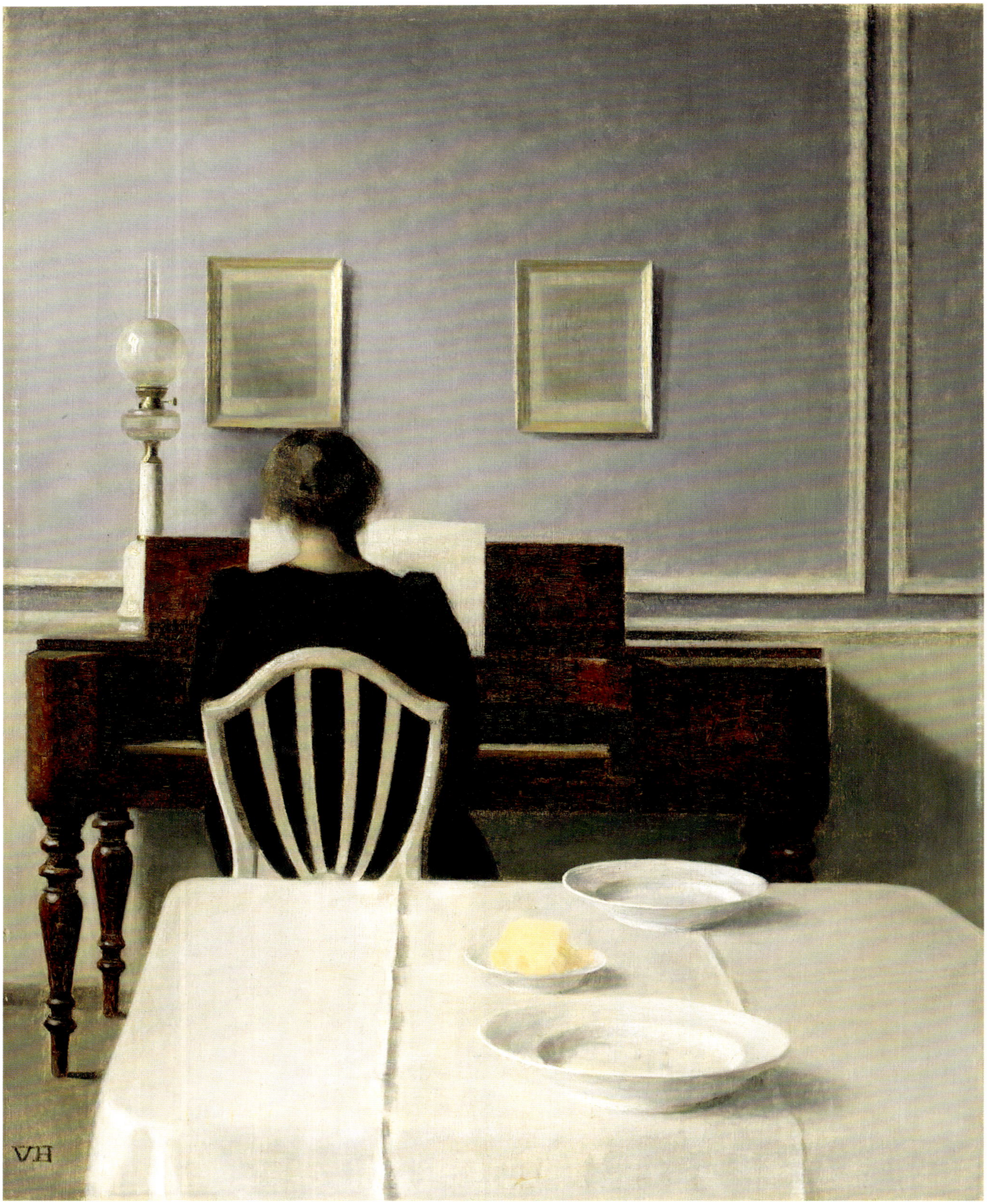

[65]
Vilhelm Hammershøi 1864-1916 Danish
Interior with Woman at Piano, Strandgade 30 1901
Oil on canvas 55.9 x 45.1 cm
Private collection

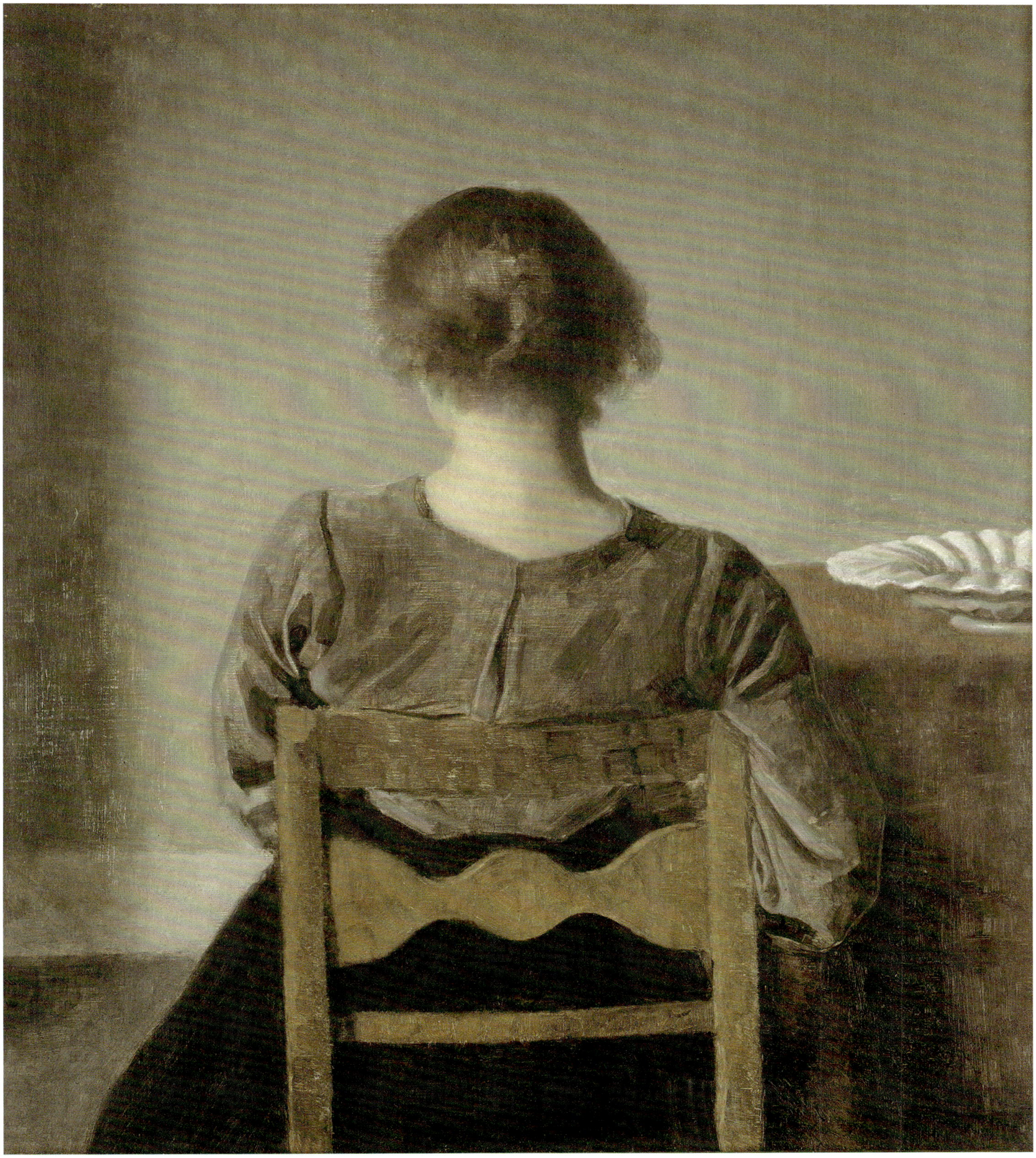

[66]
Vilhelm Hammershøi 1864-1916 Danish
Young Lady. "Resting" 1905
Oil on canvas 49.5 x 46.5 cm
Musée d'Orsay, Paris

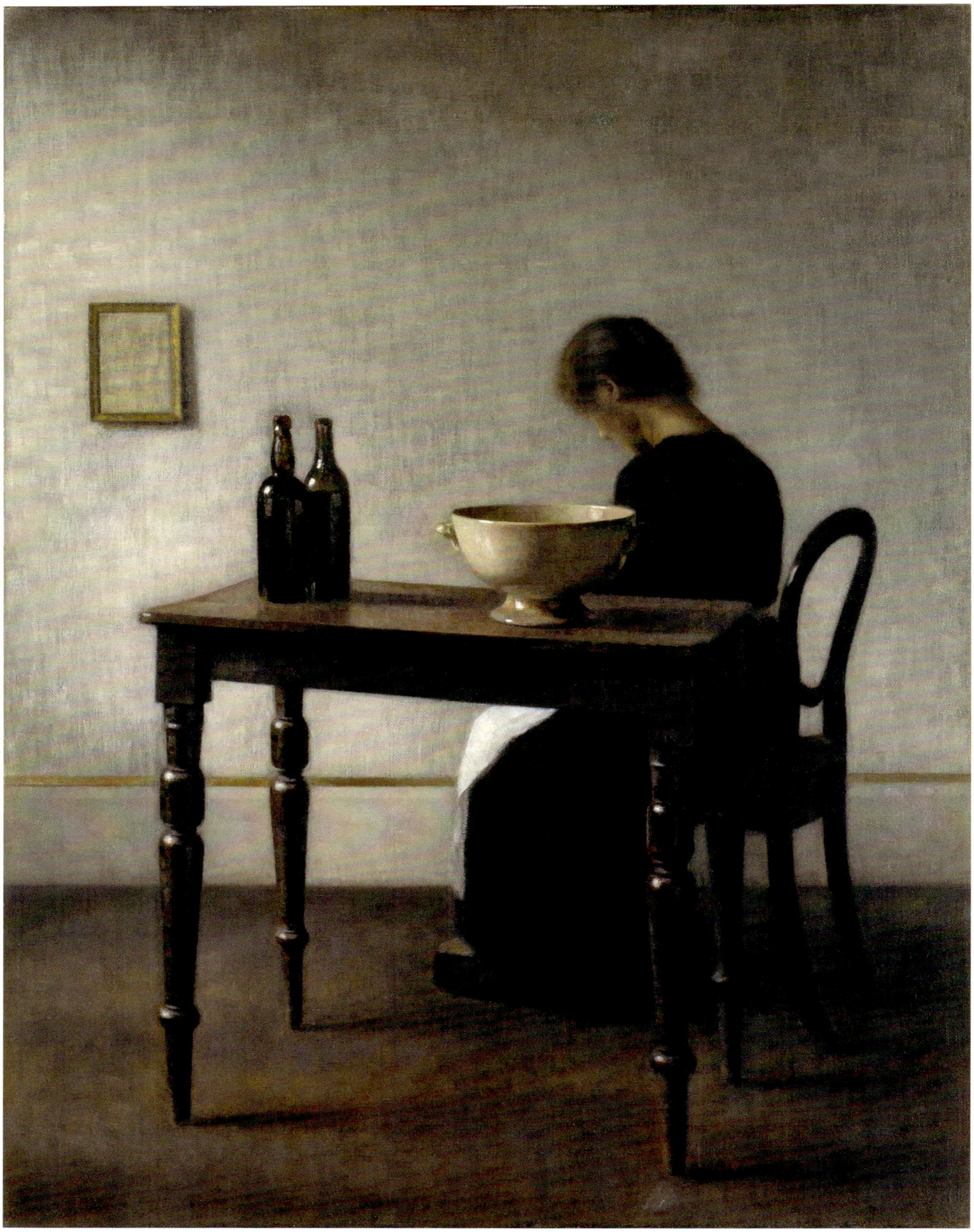

[67]
Vilhelm Hammershøi 1864-1916 Danish
Interior with Woman Sitting at a Table c. 1910
Oil on canvas 82.5 x 64 cm
Ordrupgaard, Copenhagen

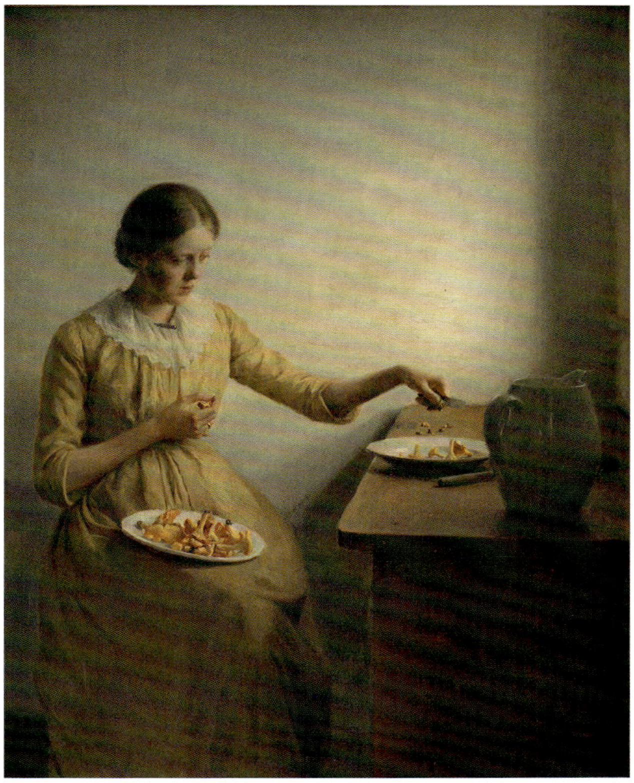

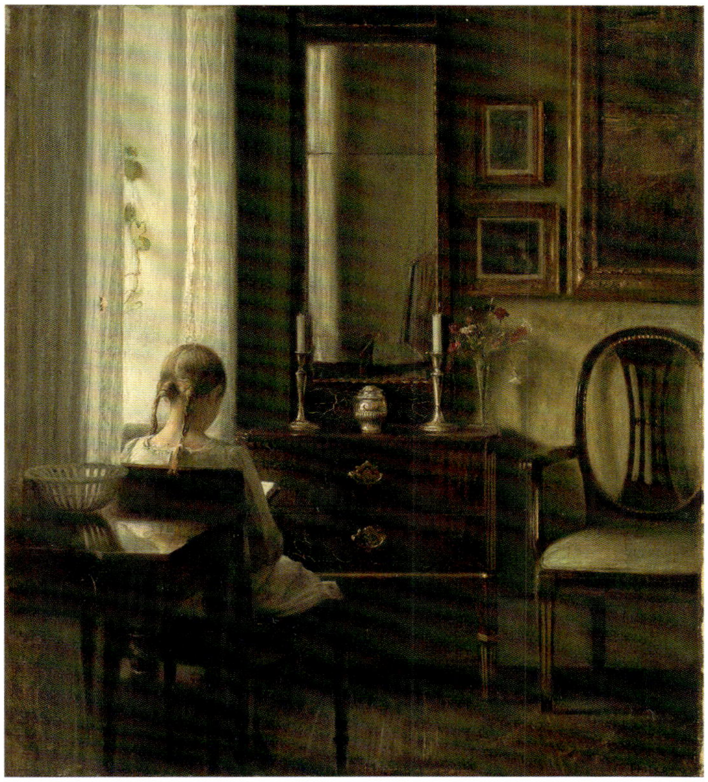

Everyday situations without action

Formally speaking, Hammershøi continued with the motifs of the narrative genre painting, but removed any narrative (see the section "Stories that are not told", p. 14). When he paints his mother on a sofa knitting, what she is doing is in reality without meaning [57, p. 77]. Hammershøi was not alone in playing down the narrative in the picture. Several other painters showed related aspirations, although each artist gave a different emphasis to the context of the subjects. Among the Danish painters it was primarily Peter Ilsted and Carl Holsøe who drew inspiration from Hammershøi and took over his range of subjects; still, in crucial ways they followed their own paths.

In 1892 Hammershøi's brother-in-law, Peter Ilsted, painted *A Young Girl Preparing Chanterelles* [68]. To the superficial gaze the motif is close to Hammershøi's pictorial world: a woman sitting alone in a sparsely furnished room where the light falling in on the wall constitutes the unifying element in the picture. But Ilsted takes a much more concrete approach to his subject than Hammershøi does. Although there is not much narrative in his painting, we do get an impression of a tangible action: the cleaning of the mushrooms. Not only motivically, but also in painterly terms, the picture is an example of the lifelong inspiration Ilsted drew from his brother-in-law Hammershøi.

Hammershøi's distinctiveness becomes even more obvious from a comparison with a painting by his friend Holsøe, *Interior with a Girl Reading* [69]. Here he shows a bourgeois home of more or less the same type as we find in Hammershøi. But the differences are quite

[68]
Peter Ilsted 1861-1933 Danish
A Young Girl Preparing Chantarelles 1892
Oil on canvas 66 x 51.5 cm
Statens Museum for Kunst

[69]
Carl Holsøe 1863-1935 Danish
Interior with a Girl Reading 1903
Oil on canvas 53 x 46 cm
Statens Museum for Kunst

plain to the eye. The room is much more densely furnished, and there is not the same simplicity and clarity (as in his friend's pictures). On the contrary the room is so overfilled that it seems almost claustrophobic. Holsøe has moreover focused in a quite different way on the specific character of the objects, so that the subject appears very concrete and present. The young girl almost disappears into the totality, and we are given no hint of her inner life.

We find a closer affinity on the other hand in the work of Anna Ancher, although here too there are conspicuous differences. Her painting *Sunshine in the Blind Woman's Room* from 1885 [71] shows a simply furnished room that corresponds to Hammershøi's interiors.[68] The quite dominant element in the picture is the sunlight falling into the room and creating some yellowish areas on the wall beside the blind woman. She cannot see the light we see, but can presumably feel the warmth from the light – as, for good reasons, we cannot. The sunlight thus becomes not only a source of light, but a meaning-bearing factor in the picture. Perhaps the woman sees something with her mind's eye that we cannot share with her either. This very aspect – the suggestion of an inner life that is not directly evident from the painting – can be said to accord with the recurrent theme of Hammershøi's pictures of women seen alone in a room.

We find a more direct parallel in Ancher's *Interior with Red Poppies* from 1905 [70]. The motif of a woman sitting immersed in the reading of a book is the same as in several of

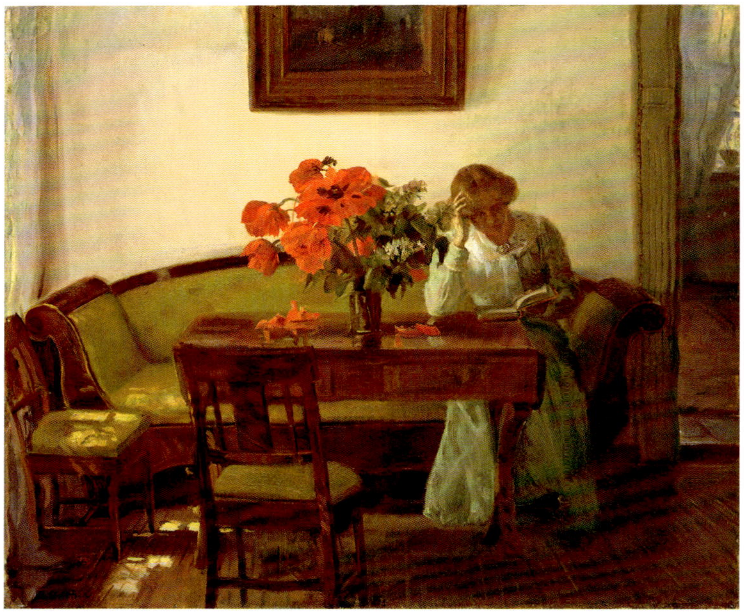

[70]
Anna Ancher 1859-1935 Danish
Interior with Red Poppies 1905
Oil on canvas 56.2 x 65 cm
Skagens Museum

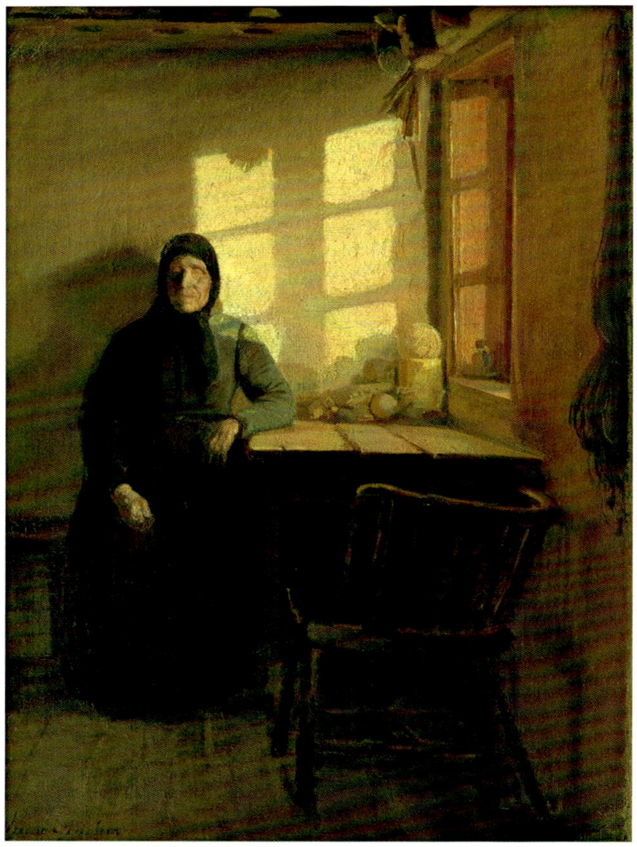

[71]
Anna Ancher 1859-1935 Danish
Sunshine in the Blind Woman's Room 1885
Oil on canvas 58.5 x 43.3 cm
The Hirschsprung Collection, Copenhagen

Hammershøi's paintings, and a related introverted, almost contemplative mood prevails. The interest in the light is also something the two artists have in common. But here too there are pronounced differences. The slightly random placing of some of the furniture shows that Ancher was not at all aiming at the same tight composition, and with her warm, glowing colours she achieves a unifying totality that is far from the one Hammershøi sought.

Beyond the borders of Denmark there were many painters at the time who were cultivating subjects with a person seen alone in a room and apparently preoccupied with everyday pursuits. But in most cases their intention was quite different from Hammershøi's – even those painters who in other respects are related to the Dane. For example the Swiss Félix Vallotton almost always added a strong element of narrative – often with erotic content – to his pictures,[99] while a painter like the Belgian Xavier Mellery often suffused his interiors with a mystical dimension.

Around 1877 the German artist Louis Eysen painted a picture of his mother sitting crocheting [72].[100] The picture has something of the same introverted atmosphere as we find in Hammershøi. The meticulous rendering of the details such as the books on the shelf reveals the artist's firm roots in the Realism of the preceding epoch. However, he has simplified the forms in the picture. In addition he has cropped the woman's dress and chair in an unexpected way for the period. All this points forward to the final years of the 19th century. Eysen

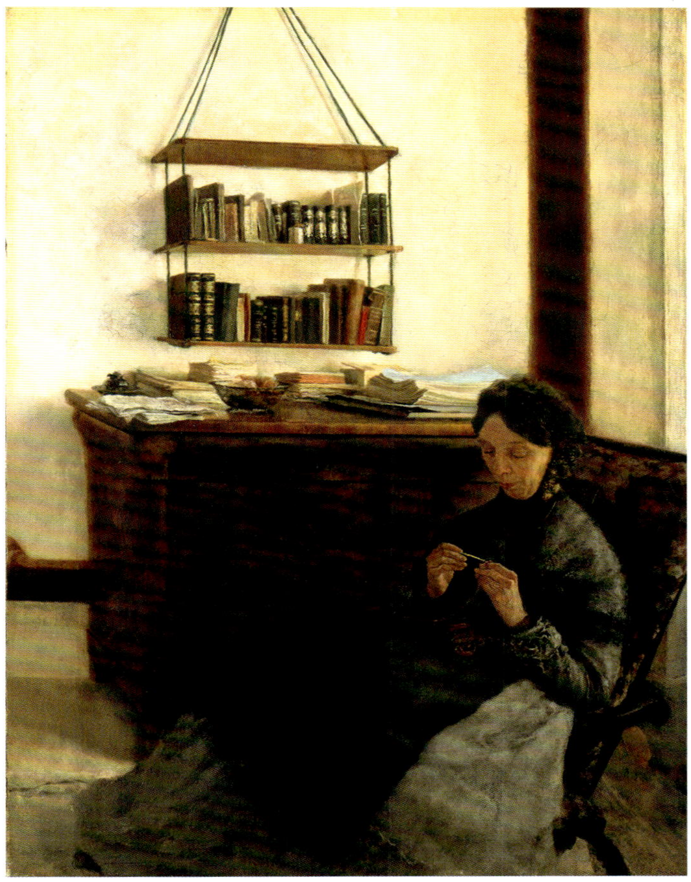

[72]
Louis Eysen 1843-1899 German
The Artist's Mother c. 1877
Oil on canvas 54 x 42 cm
Staatliche Museum zu Berlin, Nationalgalerie

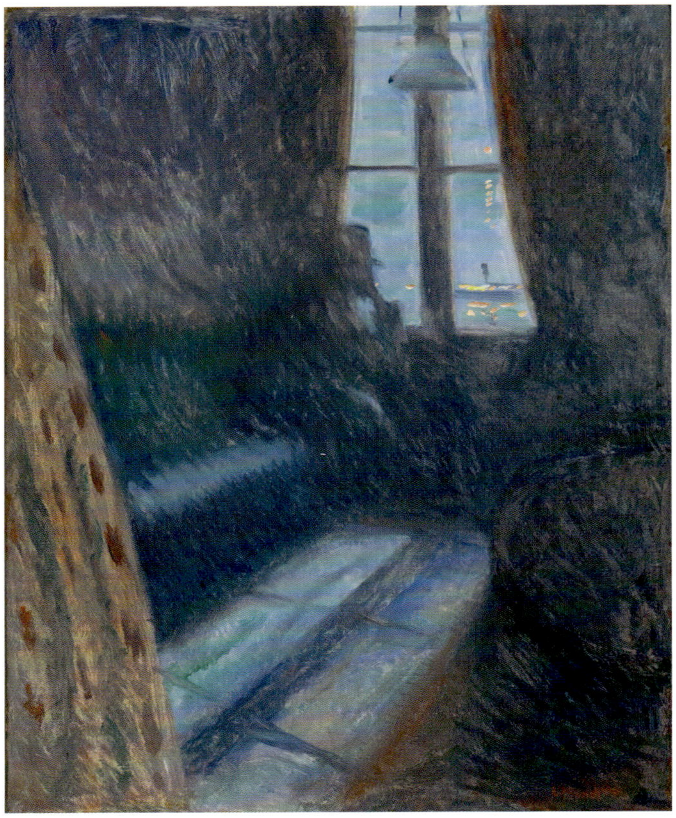

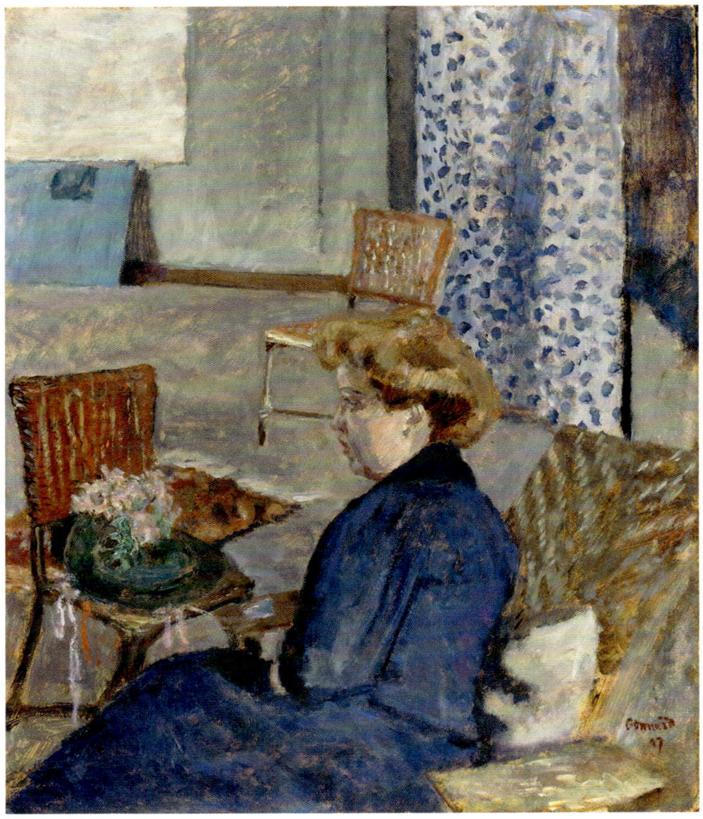

[73]
Edvard Munch 1863-1944 Norwegian
Night in Saint Cloud 1893
Oil on canvas 70 x 56.5 cm
Private collection (Dep. Metropolitan Museum of Art, New York)

[74]
Pierre Bonnard 1867-1947 French
The Milliner 1907
Oil on cardboard 68.5 x 59 cm
Statens Museum for Kunst (Dep. Ny Carlsberg Glyptotek, Copenhagen)

lived greatly withdrawn from the rest of the German art world, and there is nothing to suggest that Hammershøi had any opportunity to see his painting.

In comparison there is no trace of external action in Edvard Munch's painting *Night in Saint Cloud* [73]. The picture most of all depicts a mental state.[101] Around 1890, when he painted the first version of this subject, he jotted down some notes that have afterwards been interpreted as his artistic manifesto: "Interiors should no longer be painted. People reading and women knitting. It should be living people who pant and feel, suffer and love."[102] The subject of the painting – a solitary man seated in a dark room at a window on a moonlit night – functions in reality at three levels. Munch himself indicated that the painting was done as a reaction to his father's death, and the lone figure is a reminiscence of his father. In reality it was a friend who posed as the man in the picture. But deepest down the painting reflects Munch's own state of mind: it can be interpreted as an image of grief, loneliness and melancholy. The painting can justifiably be regarded as a self-portrait.[103] Despite the great differences in the method of painting and other artistic devices in Munch's and Hammershøi's pictures, they both used the interior motif here in a closely related way. But there may in fact have been a certain influence. The Norwegian probably had the opportunity to see paintings by Hammershøi during his stays in Copenhagen in the summer of 1888 and the autumn of 1891, thanks to their shared acquaintance Johan Rohde.[104]

In 1911 Hammershøi had an opportunity to form a new impression of Pierre Bonnard's art. At that time the French painter had put his surface- and line-oriented Symbolist idiom behind him and had turned to a mode of painterly expression that can almost be described as late Impressionism. At the premises of the Danish art dealer Valdemar Kleis, Hammershøi could for example see the painting *The Milliner* from 1907 [74]. He would certainly have noticed the picture when it was bought at the exhibition by Statens Museum for Kunst at the urging of his friend Karl Madsen, who had just been appointed director of the museum. We must suppose that he now viewed the Frenchman's art with greater interest than at the first encounter in Paris almost twenty years before (see p. 41). The woman sits and looks straight ahead, perhaps lost in thought, and absolute calm reigns in the locality. In this respect the painting is a direct parallel to Hammershøi's interiors. But the differences are also obvious. Whereas Hammershøi aimed at simplicity and clarity, Bonnard has rather filled his space with so many details – fragments of furnishings, curtains and things that cannot be identified specifically – that it is difficult to get an overall view of the space the woman is in. All these details are of such great diversity and are shown in such a wide spectrum of colours that the overall effect he has created is complex and richly faceted – and very far from Hammershøi's artistic ideals.

THE EMPTY ROOM

For a long time Hammershøi's primary concern was the interplay of the figures and the space in his interiors. But in time he became interested in exploring the spaces themselves without the involvement of the human figure. He said himself that he painted his first interior in 1888 – *Interior. An Old Stove. Albertines Lyst, Lyngby* – which very much has the character of an exercise [75].[105] In the time that followed he further developed and refined the interior motif, at first in connection with figure motifs. He expanded the field of vision so that the neutral background wall gradually became part of a well defined space. He continued to develop the motif well into the 1890s [42, 58], without however settling on any particular room type or artistic effects. He experimented with pictorial structure, spatial effects and light. While he lived in Frederiksberg, he made use of the two windows of the drawing room in several compositions, but primarily as sources of light. What he could see through the windows he seems to have veiled deliberately.

It was only after Hammershøi had moved to the apartment in Strandgade, Christianshavn, in 1898 that he chose to focus on the room alone and reached a first culmination with the subject.[106] The apartment consisted of a number of rooms of different sizes and with different orientations, which afforded the painter the opportunity to work with varied spatial sequences and in changing light. He used the simple, classical-looking room and the sparse furnishings to give the pictures a tight composition. The empty rooms with their bare walls are permeated by a static, almost oppressive atmosphere, and whether or not we see a single female figure, all life seems to have come to a halt. Although it was his own home he painted, the rooms do not have a private or intimate character, but have taken on a universality.

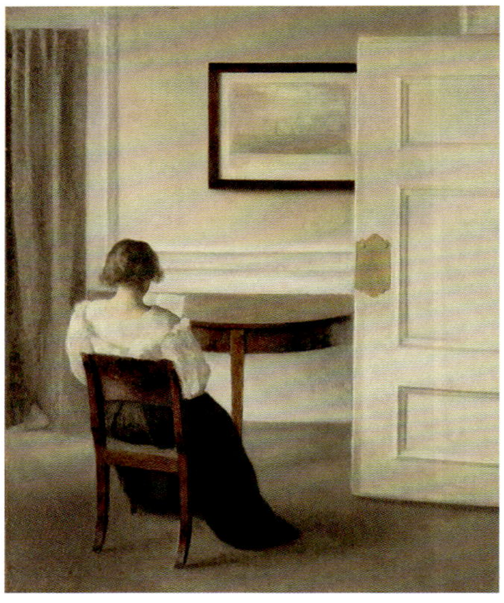

[42]
Vilhelm Hammershøi 1864-1916 Danish
Interior 1893
Oil on canvas 56.5 x 46.5 cm
The Gothenburg Museum of Art

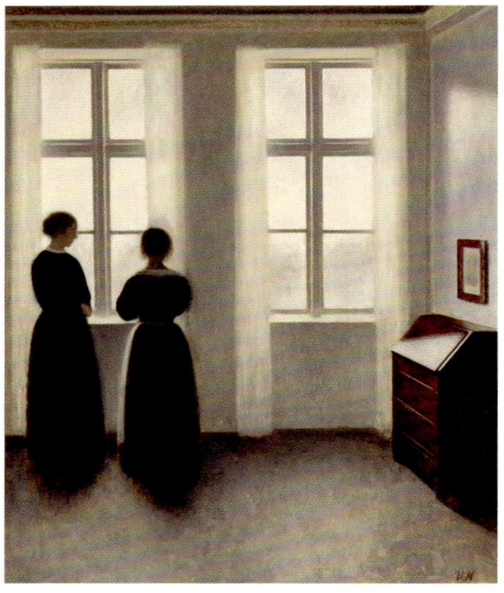

[58]
Vilhelm Hammershøi 1864-1916 Danish
Figures by the Window c. 1895
Oil on canvas 55 x 46 cm
Private collection

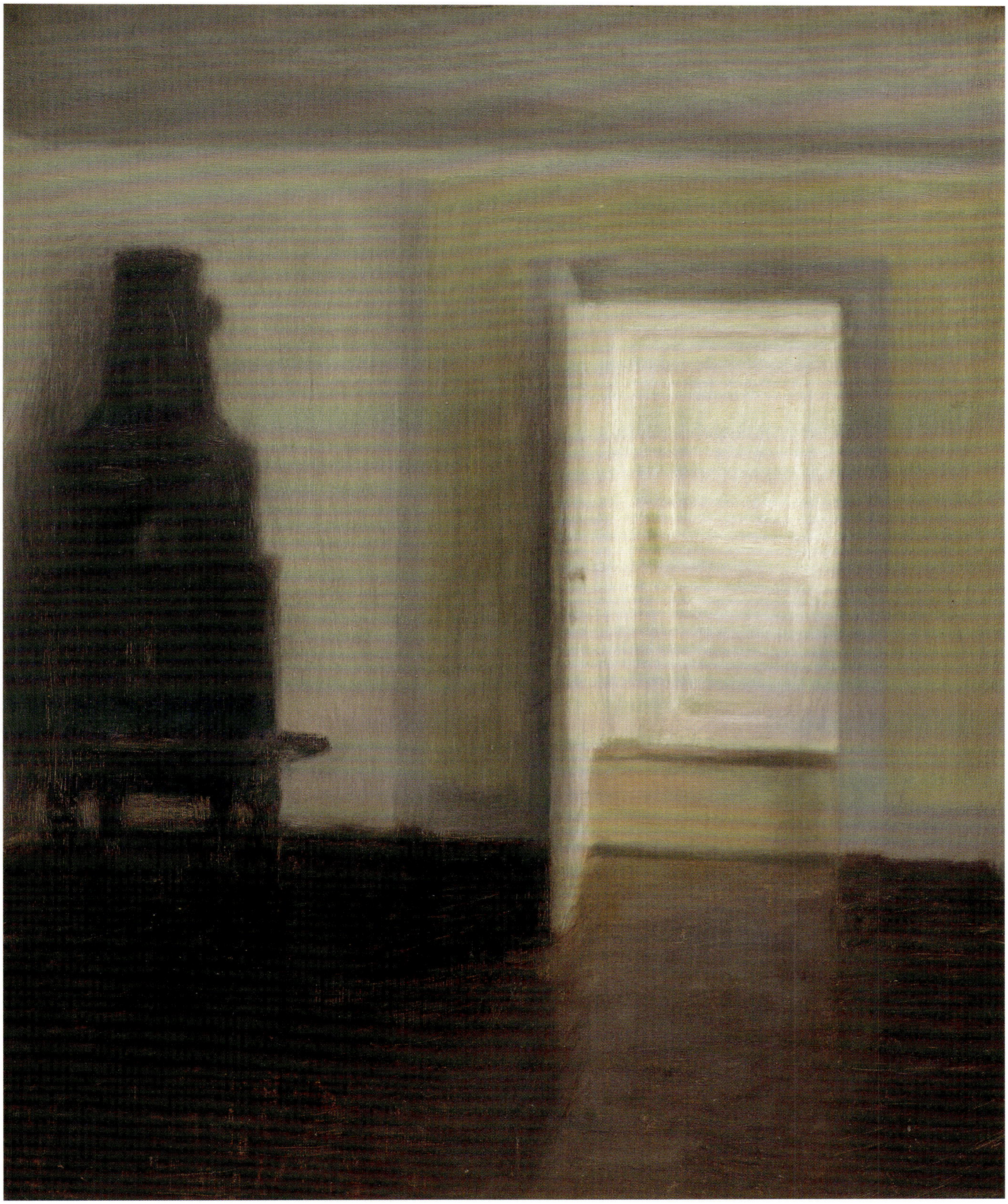

[75]
Vilhelm Hammershøi 1864-1916 Danish
Interior. An Old Stove. Albertines Lyst, Lyngby 1888
Oil on canvas 61 x 51 cm
Statens Museum for Kunst

In 1900 he painted the masterpiece *Sunbeams* or *Sunshine. Dust Motes Dancing in the Sunbeams* [76], which is a high point of his art, but which is in fact atypical of his interiors. The intense rendering of the light that falls in through the window, and the reflection on the door and the panels, capture all one's attention. The room has been purged of disturbing elements and does not really appear as a place frequented by people. Here a single figure would have seemed quite out of place, from the point of view of both form and content.

Hammershøi varied this interior in a succession of pictures where he constantly changed the fall of the light and the character of the room. At times he placed emphasis on details in the room – such as door handles and hinges – and at other times he omitted them entirely. In several paintings walls and floor were almost dissolved and took on a non-material character, as in the painting *Interior. Strandgade 30* from 1906 [77]. Here we do not see the same firmness and stringency as in *Sunbeams* or *Sunshine Dust Motes Dancing in the Sunbeams*, and the reflection of the light on the panels and the door makes all the forms appear vibrant. The focus is unconditionally on the room itself, not on the building that can be seen through the windows.[107]

Contrasting with this we have the clearly defined interior in the painting with the subtitle *The Four Copper Prints* from 1905 [78]. Here he has turned his gaze to the windows that face the street. But the picture gives us no opening towards the world outside. Through the windows we do see the house on the other side of the street, the Asiatisk Kompagni (Asiatic Company) building, but there is no sign of life, nor is one given any hint of what is happening in the street below. The four round prints almost look like dark eyes gazing back at the viewer

The effect of the painting *Interior with a View of an Exterior Gallery* from 1903 [79] is quite claustrophobic.[108] Although there is a view from the room from which the subject is observed, the windows of the gallery block it, so that the gaze is effectively stopped. The distinctive atmosphere of the painting is reinforced by the strange lighting that has arisen because the light from an open door illuminates part of the room and leaves the rest in semi-darkness. It is hard to imagine that one could live in this room. Hammershøi has thus completely detached the interior from its function as a place frequented by people.

Only a few artists worked with the empty room in a way that can be compared to Hammershøi's – if we disregard his two Danish successors Peter Ilsted and Carl Holsøe. Still, both painters related very concretely to the rooms they depicted (cf. [68, p. 91] & [69, p. 91]), and compared with Hammershøi they lack an existential dimension in their pictures. An important parallel can be found, on the other hand, in the work of the Belgian painter Xavier Mellery. His use of the room as an expression of fundamental aspects of existence greatly recalls Hammershøi's.[109] In the painting *The Doors* [80] Mellery has two open doors leading from one room through a passage to another room.[110] But one gets no impression of where the doors lead, and any further view is blocked. Strictly speaking the doors give us no options. In that respect the Belgian's painting has a counterpart in Hammershøi's picture *Open Doors* from 1905 [81]. In the nature of things, the two open doors should lead out of the room, but the view is blocked, nor can the viewer in this case see where the doors lead. A related ambivalent mood prevails in the two paintings. But with his dark, sombre colours the Belgian has given his interior a far more solid look than Hammershøi did. Moreover, his interior has not been dated with certainty, which makes it rather unsafe to link the two more closely artistically. We do not know whether Hammershøi saw works by Mellery during his stays in Belgium in 1887 and 1891.

In the later years of his artistic activity Hammershøi continued to explore the room in the pure interior pictures. In his new home in Bredgade, where Hammershøi lived from 1910 until 1913, he exploited the fact that the apartment had a different partitioning, and made a double door between a large drawing room and a smaller room a fixed element in several paintings. Equally important is the light from the window that can be glimpsed to the left of the doors in several paintings. In these pictures he varies the roles that the two rooms play in relation to each other. In some pictures the furniture in the adjacent room attracts almost all the viewers' attention, while in others he gives the furniture in the front room the main role. This is the case in *Interior with the Artist's Easel* [9, p. 24] and even more so in *Interior with Potted Plant on Card Table* from 1910-11 [82]. Here the door opens on a quite empty room, and the card table in the middle of the front room effectively blocks access to the adjacent room. The open double door thus gives the viewer no real choices. For once we see a potted plant – that is, a living organism – in the room, but this does nothing to change the closed, static atmosphere of the room.

In 1913, when Hammershøi moved back to Christianshavn, he had the possibility of varying his preferred subject, and he took this opportunity in one of his very last paintings, *The Four Rooms. Interior from the Artist's Home, Strandgade 25* from 1914 [83].[111] It shows a very complex spatial sequence: from the room in the foreground we look through two rooms *en suite* towards a third room where the gaze is stopped by a sofa standing up against the back wall. However, we are given no impression of the rooms we look through, and despite the expansion of the field of vision the picture space seems almost as restricted and closed-off as in the pictures where a door obstructs the view. The open doors do not lead us out of the room we are in.

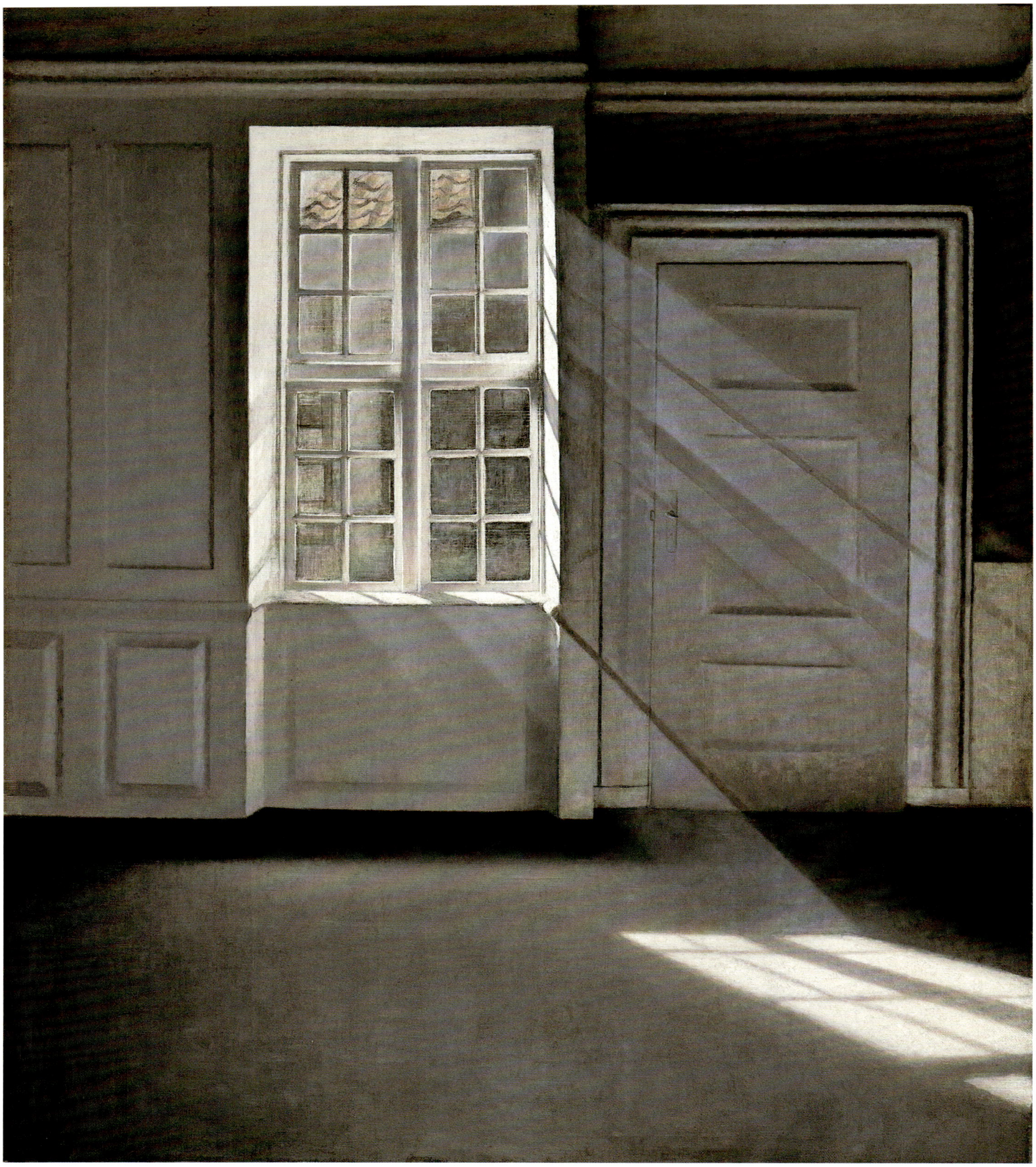

[76]
Vilhelm Hammershøi 1864-1916 Danish
Sunbeams or **Sunshine. Dust Motes Dancing in the Sunbeams** 1900
Oil on canvas 70 x 59 cm
Ordrupgaard, Copenhagen

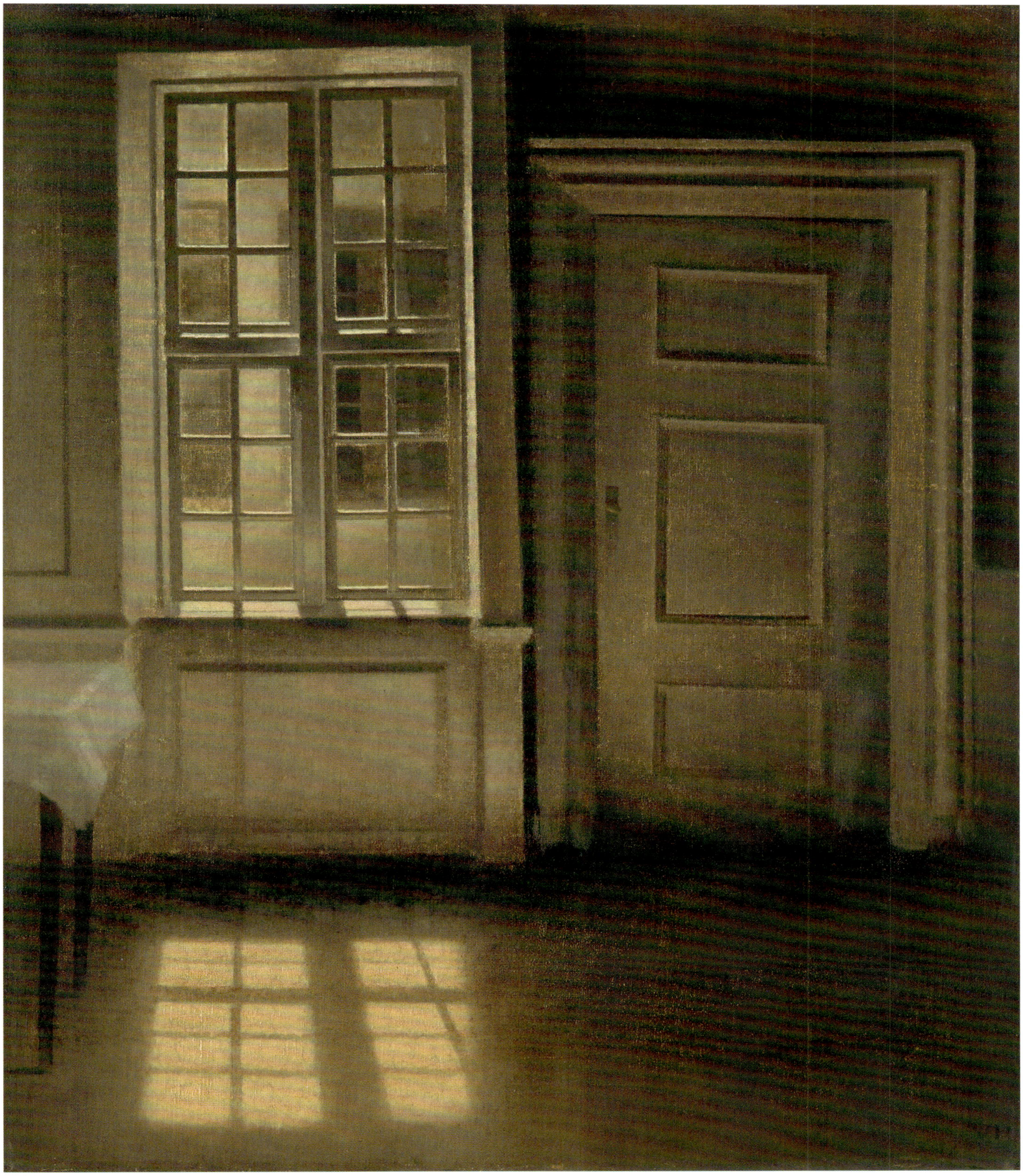

[77]
Vilhelm Hammershøi 1864-1916 Danish
Interior. Strandgade 30 1906
Oil on canvas 51.8 x 44 cm
Tate: Purchased 1930

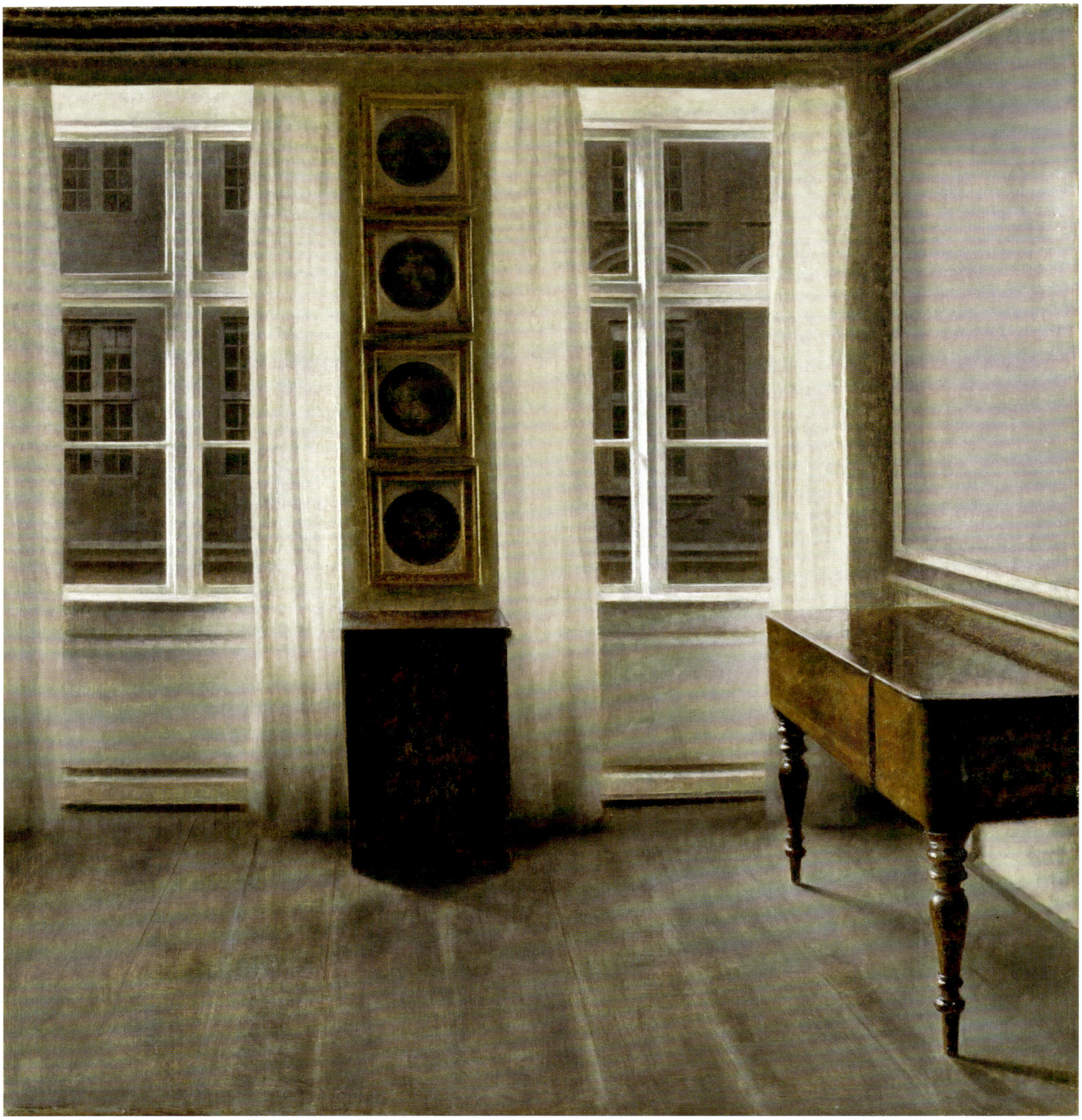

[78]
Vilhelm Hammershøi 1864-1916 Danish
Drawing Room. The Four Copper Prints 1905
Oil on canvas 64 x 61 cm
Private collection, Belgium

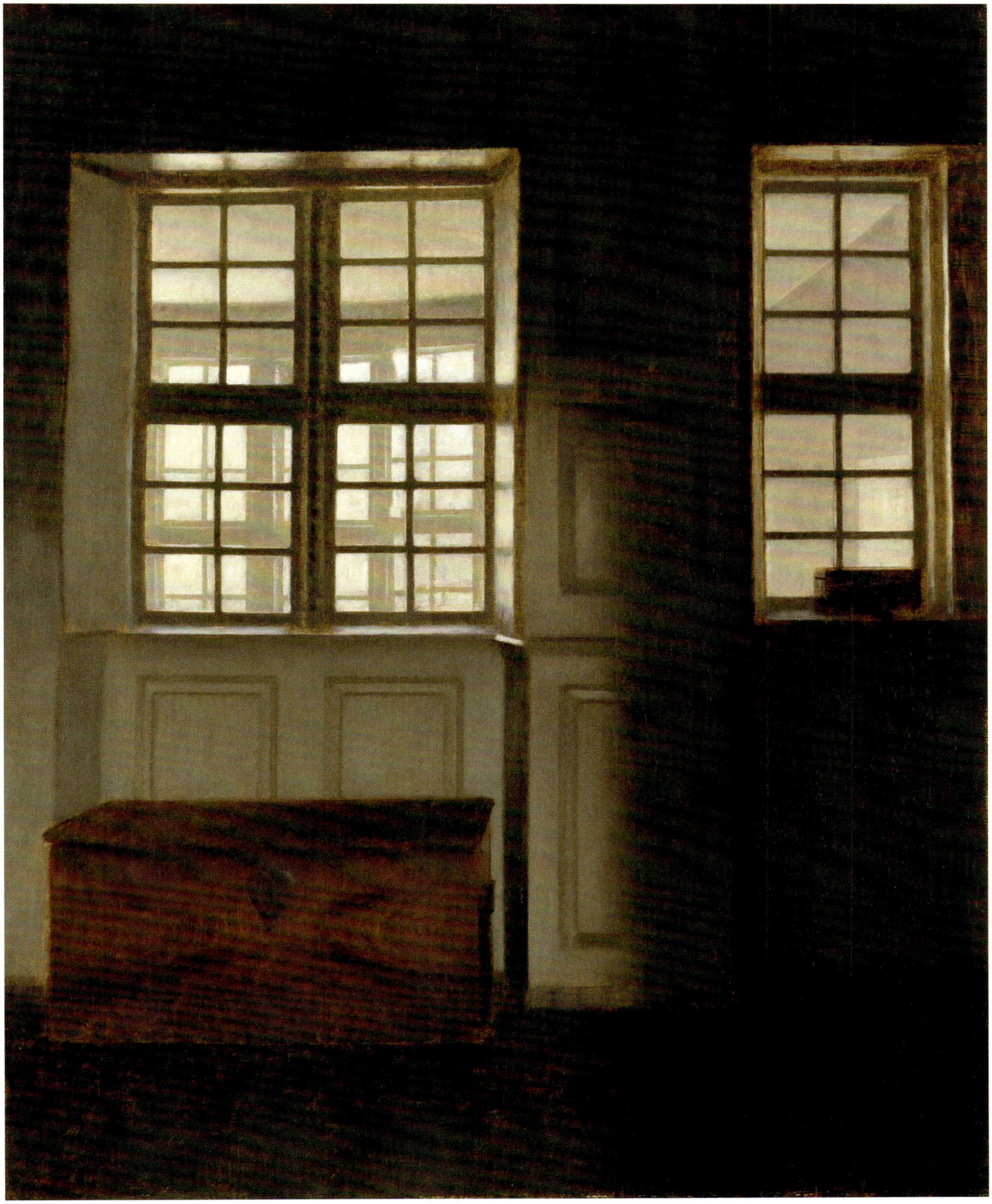

[79]
Vilhelm Hammershøi 1864-1916 Danish
Interior with a View of an Exterior Gallery 1903
Oil on canvas 72 x 58 cm
The David Collection, Copenhagen

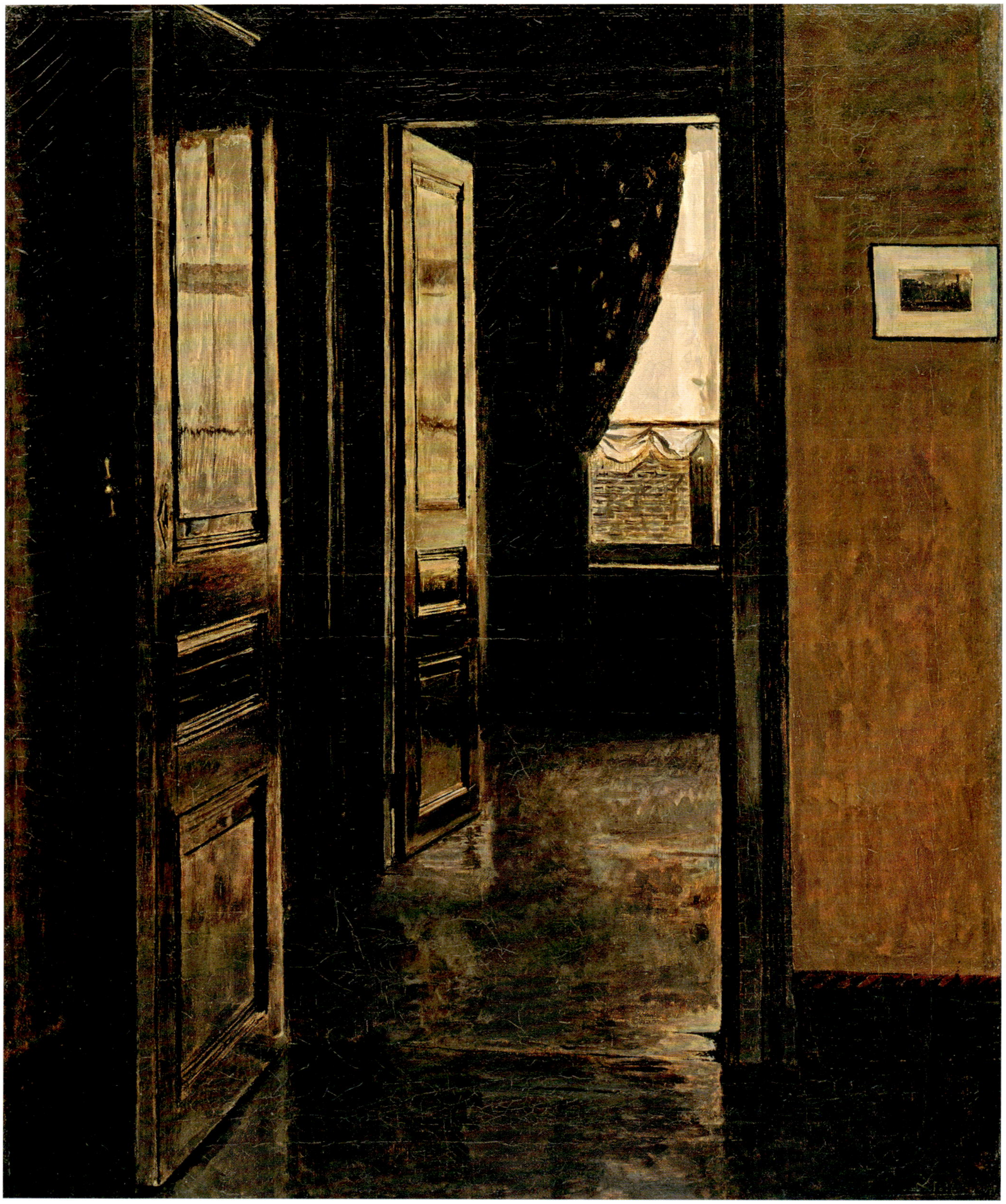

[80]
Xavier Mellery 1845-1921 Belgian
The Doors undated
Oil on canvas 72.5 x 58 cm
The Hearn Family Trust, New York

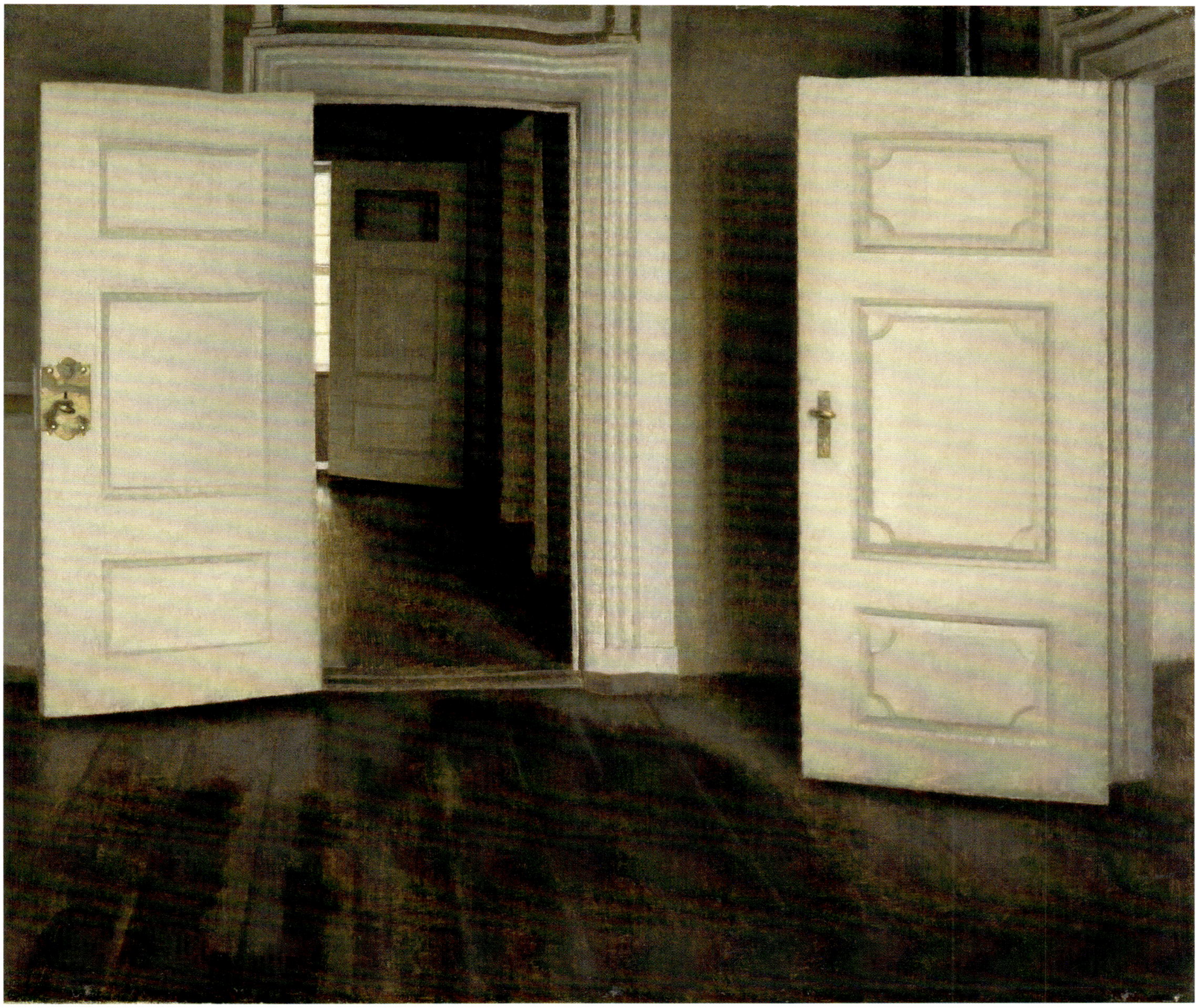

[81]
Vilhelm Hammershøi 1864-1916 Danish
Open Doors 1905
Oil on canvas 52.5 x 60 cm
The David Collection, Copenhagen

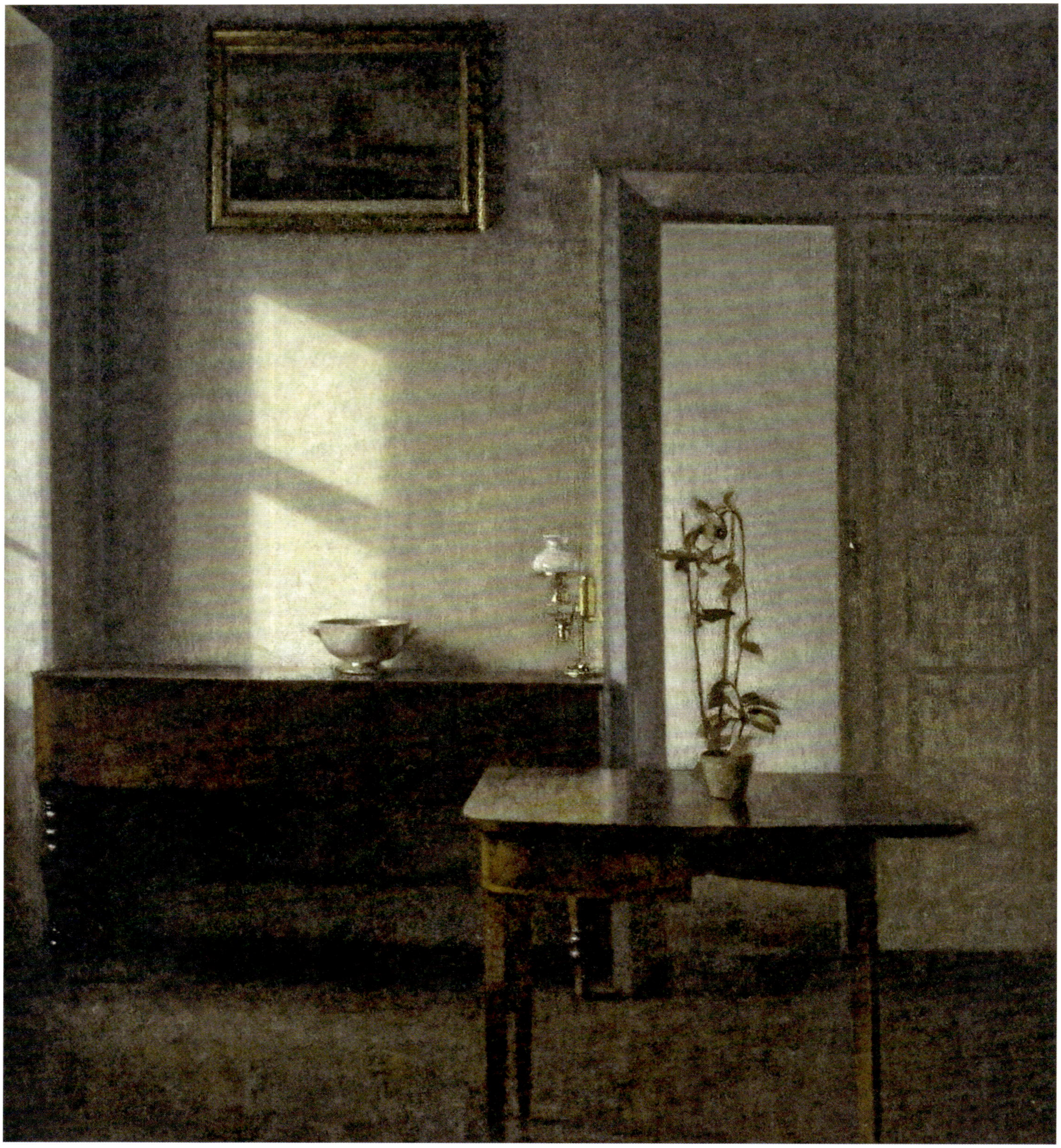

[82]
Vilhelm Hammershøi 1864-1916 Danish
Interior with Potted Plant on Card Table, Bredgade 25 1910-11
Oil on canvas 78.5 x 71 cm
Malmö Museum

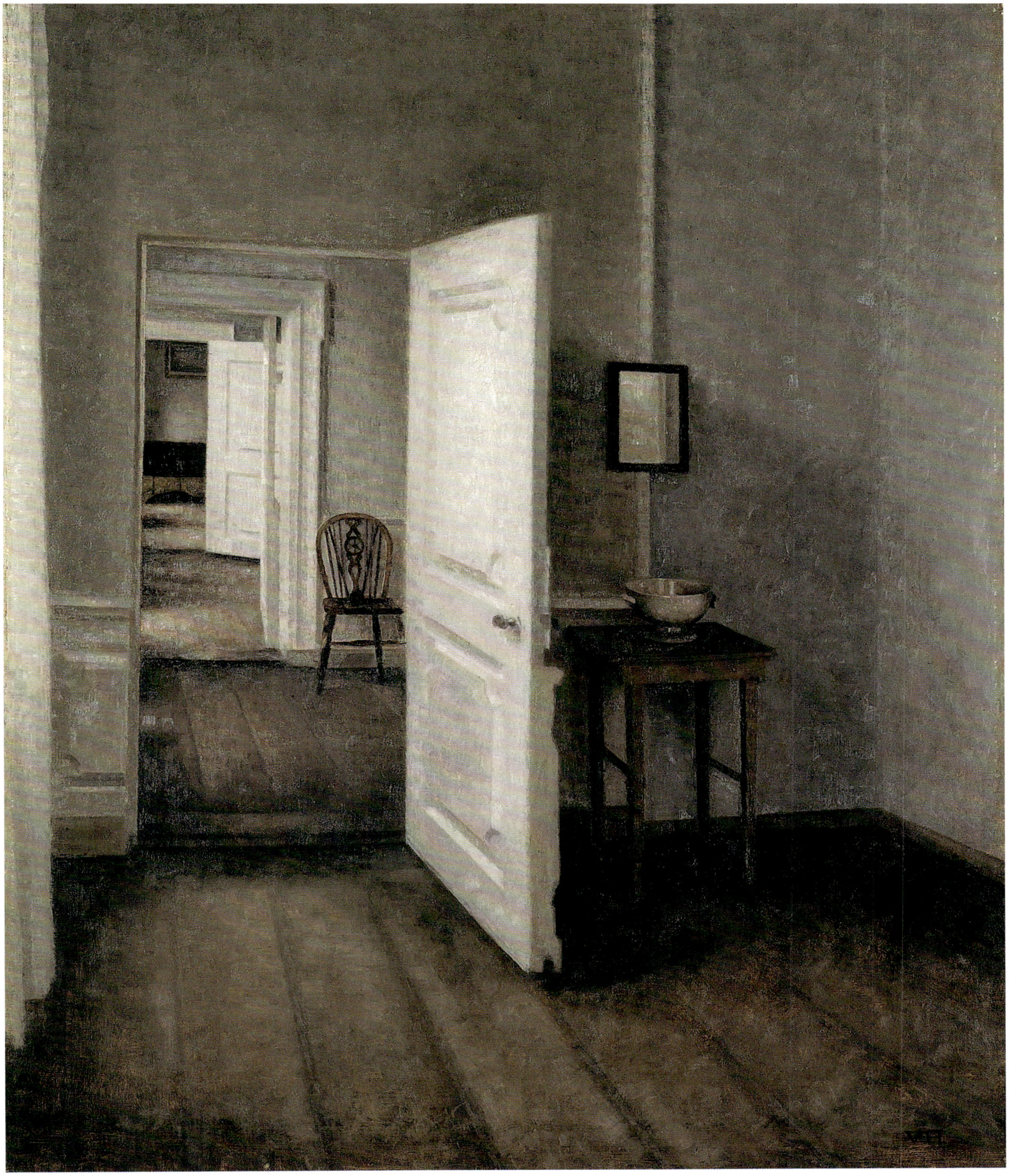

[83]
Vilhelm Hammershøi 1864-1916 Danish
The Four Rooms. Interior from the Artist's Home, Strandgade 25 1914
Oil on canvas 85 x 70.5 cm
Ordrupgaard, Copenhagen

THE DESERTED CITY

From Hammershøi's perspective the city is a silent, static world abandoned by humanity. He painted a succession of pictures both of monumental historic buildings, especially in Copenhagen, and of more anonymous houses in Christianshavn. But none of them is frequented by human beings.

Hammershøi's first large architectural picture shows the western part of the parliament building Christiansborg Castle [84].[112] The subject has been viewed from an apartment that belonged to his great supporter, the dentist Alfred Bramsen. Here he has disregarded the life that is played out in the streets around the castle, and avoided the ruins of the main building of the castle, which had burned down in 1884. Only the preserved monumental Baroque sections of the building are in focus. If we consider it as a purely architectural painting, the absence of life can in a certain sense be explained. But the painting is not a normal architectural picture. The dense, slightly oppressive atmosphere in the picture weighs heavier than the depiction of the architectural details and gives the castle a slightly melancholy, almost extinct look.

The absence of life is even more pronounced in the painting *The Buildings of the Asiatic Company, seen from St. Annæ Street* from 1902 [86], which shows a Late Baroque mansion and a related warehouse, built around a gateway and viewed frontally.[113] Considering that Christianshavn then too was a lively part of Copenhagen, it is even more remarkable that one sees no people.

While painting the picture Hammershøi drew support from a photograph of the subject that was undoubtedly taken at his request.[114] He has worked with the same strict symmetry as the German Romantic painter Caspar David Friedrich did in his visionary representations of Gothic cathedrals, but in a complete inversion: the German Romantic concentrates all attention on a central, symbolically charged building, whereas the Dane has made the space between the buildings the centre of the picture.

In this empty space we see hints of the masts of ships in the harbour; they were possibly, possibly not, meant to be pointed up more clearly – that is, if the artist at all wished to finish the painting. Through the gateway, however, Hammershøi could also look past the ships and across the harbour towards Copenhagen proper. But in the painting the view is much reduced because of the fog – which is rarely the case in reality! So we look straight into emptiness.

The strong focus on an empty centre in Hammershøi's painting is quite unusual in Danish – and in Nordic – art from the period. One does however find a similar effect in the work of the Dutch painter Johann Eduard Karsen, especially in the picture *View of the Port of Amsterdam* from c. 1895 [85], where a few ships frame a quite neutral, greyish water surface.[115] Karsen worked moreover with the same very limited colour scale of grey shades and also used photographs to support his work. The question is whether Hammershøi knew the Dutch painter's works. He could have seen them on one of his trips to Holland; moreover, Karsen was represented at the large international exhibition at the New Carlsberg Glyptotek in Copenhagen in 1897.[116] We also know that Johan Rohde noticed some of his works at an exhibition in Hoorn in July 1892,[117] and may have drawn his friend's attention to the Dutch painter's pictures.

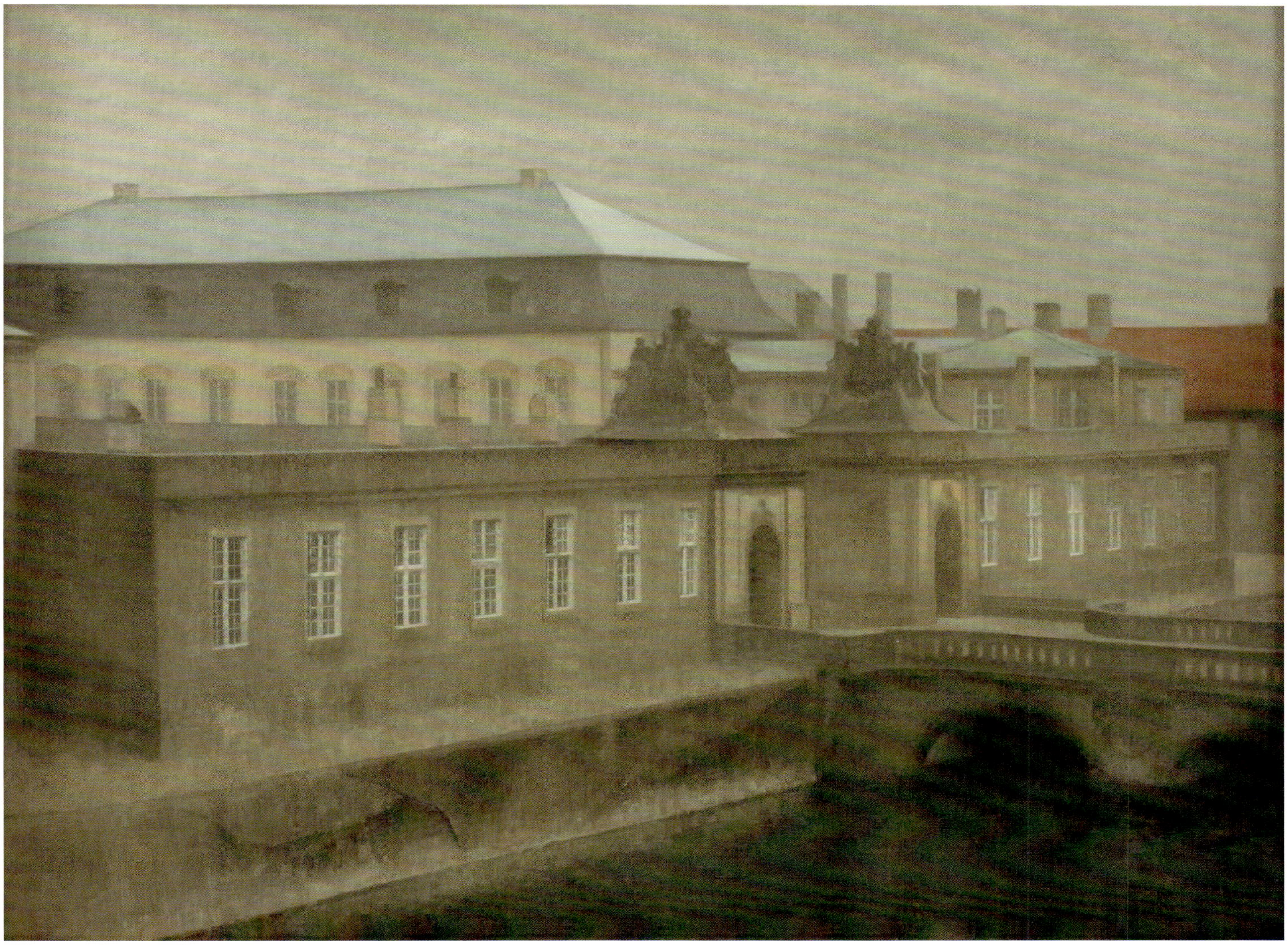

[84]
Vilhelm Hammershøi 1864-1916 Danish
View of Christiansborg Castle. Late Autumn 1890-92
Oil on canvas 115.5 x 147.5 cm
Statens Museum for Kunst

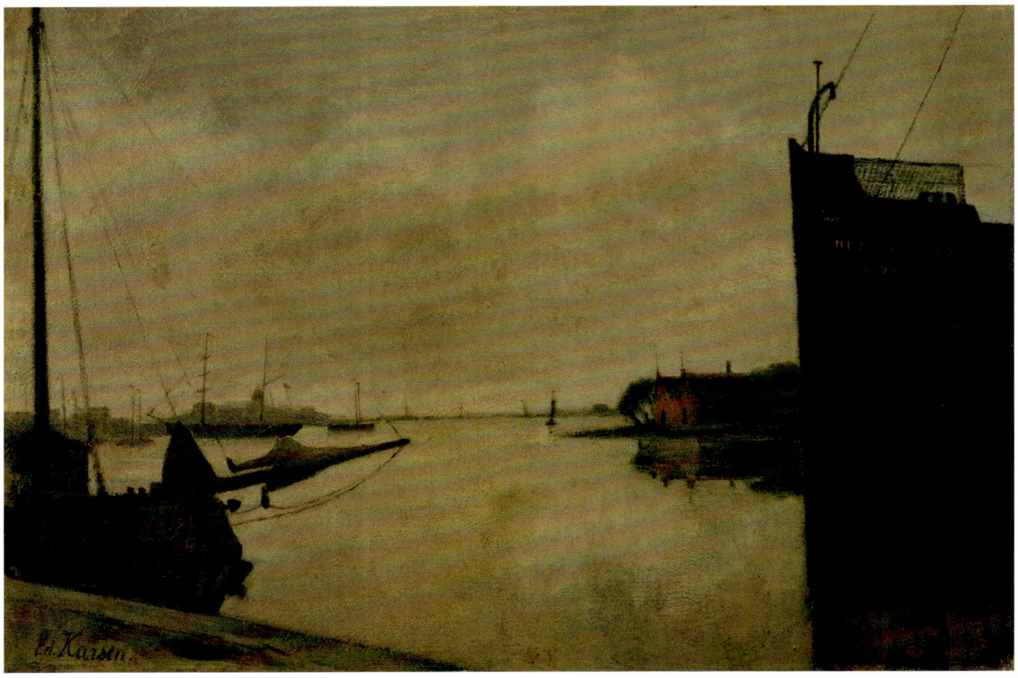

It was only during his many stays in London that Hammershøi painted pictures from the streets of a foreign city; in 1906 he painted *Montague Street in London* with the British Museum as the dominant building [87]. In the slightly foggy scenery the street looks completely purged of life. The fog further means that all the buildings have lost their solid, rooted look, and one has difficulty imagining that people could come out of the houses. The street seems almost ghostly.

The most direct parallel to this painting can be found among the Belgian Symbolist Khnopff's paintings. At more or less the same time he painted *In Bruges. A Portal* [88]. Here he has depicted a subject otherwise traditionally associated with colourful everyday life, the square in front of a church, more specifically the Gothic Church of Our Lady. But in his painting the square is deserted, and there is no indication that it will be populated. While Hammershøi has built his street scene up on classic principles, with a clear overview of the street as the result, Khnopff has come so close to the subject that it is cropped, and the detail is not even representative of the building; this further underscores the strange mood of the picture.

Even more unorthodox are the angle and cropping of the subject in the Polish painter Józef Pankiewicz' painting *Warsaw Cab at Night* from 1893 [89].[118] He has chosen the city's central square as his subject, but instead of showing it bustling and full of life, he has painted it at a peaceful moment of the night. He has also directed attention to the wet cobblestones, has frozen all life on the square and has thus transformed the busy market-place into a silent, melancholy and dream-like urban space. You do not expect the cab to leave the spot, and the painter has achieved a quite special night mood. Pankiewicz created the picture against the background of his impressions of contemporary French art, and not least of

[85]
Eduard Karsen 1860-1941 Dutch
View of the Port of Amsterdam c. 1895
Oil on canvas 30 x 44 cm
The Kröller-Müller Museum, Otterlo

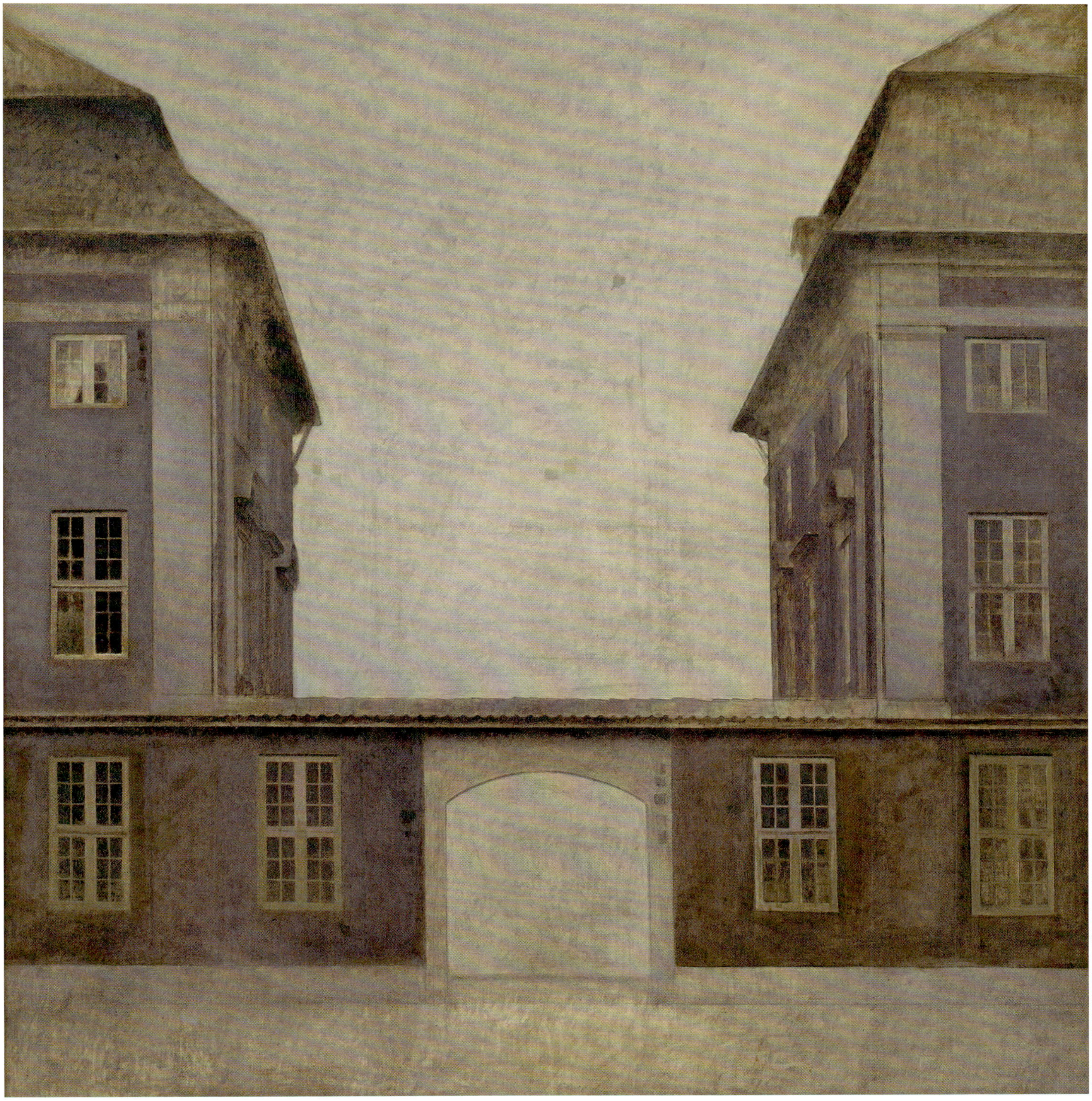

[86]
Vilhelm Hammershøi 1864-1916 Danish
The Buildings of the Asiatic Company, seen from St. Annæ Street 1902
Oil on canvas 146.5 x 140.5 cm
Statens Museum for Kunst

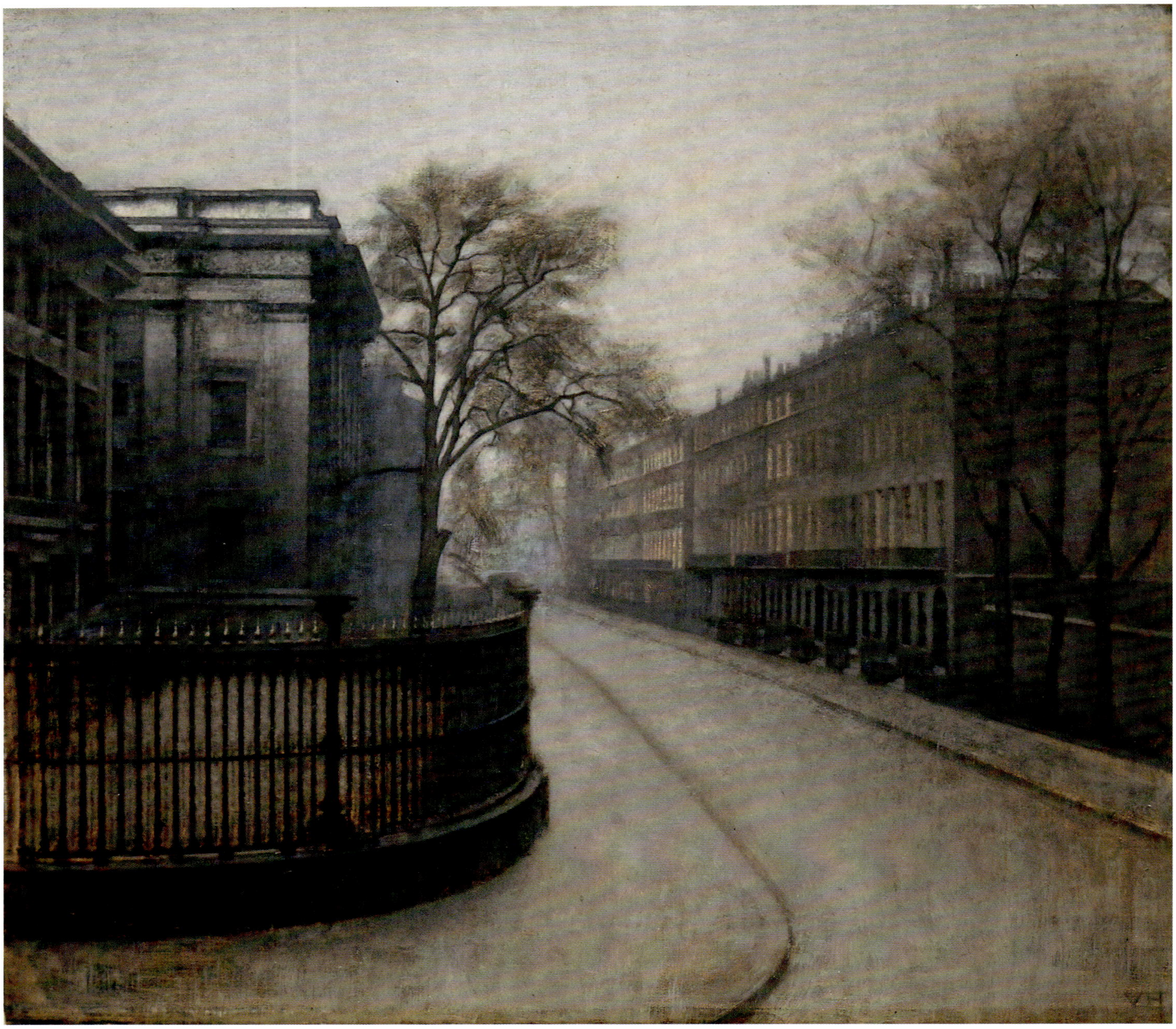

[87]
Vilhelm Hammershøi 1864-1916 Danish
Montague Street in London 1906
Oil on canvas 57 x 64 cm
Ny Carlsberg Glyptotek, Copenhagen

[88]
Fernand Khnopff 1858-1921 Belgian
In Bruges. A Portal c. 1904
Oil on canvas 44 x 87 cm
Clemens-Sels-Museum, Neuss

[89]
Józef Pankiewicz 1866-1940 Polish
Warsaw Cab at Night 1893
Oil on canvas 72 x 70.5 cm
The National Museum, Cracow

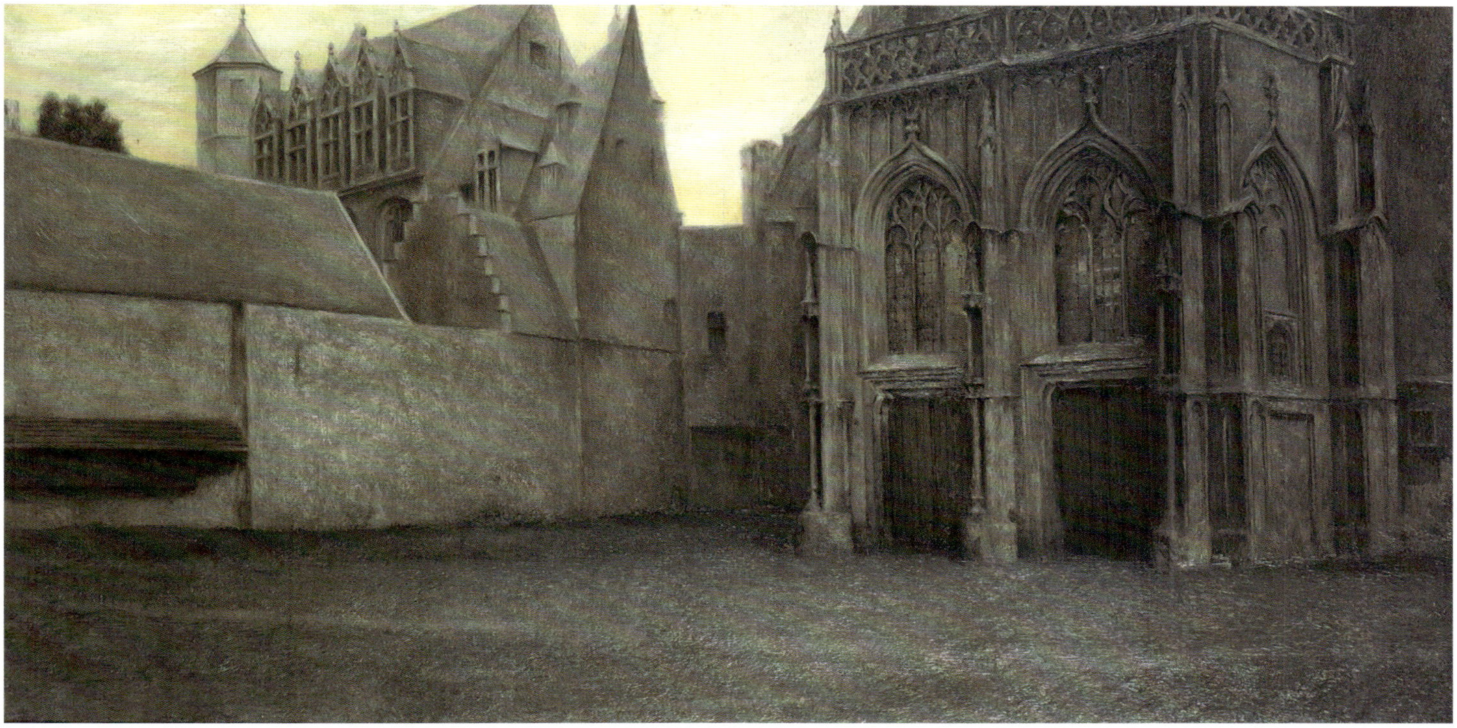

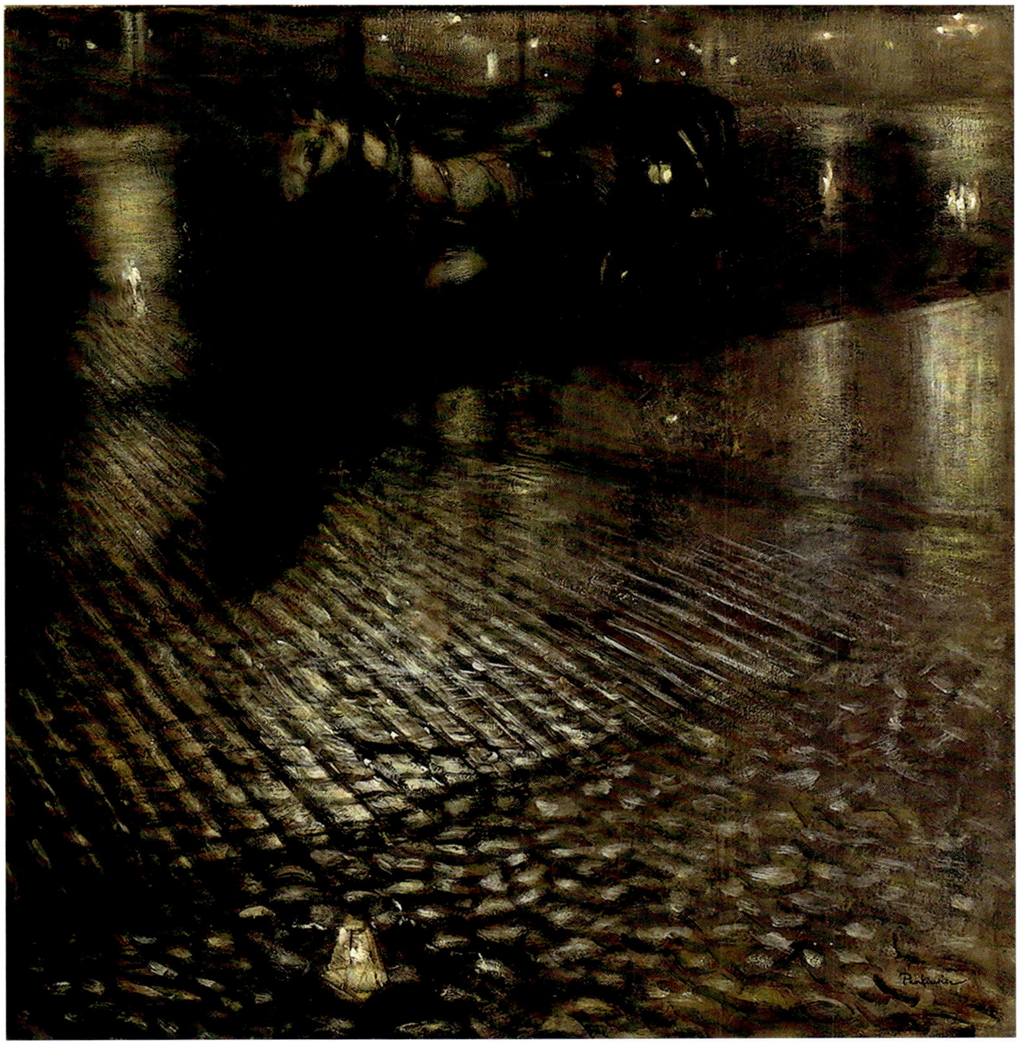

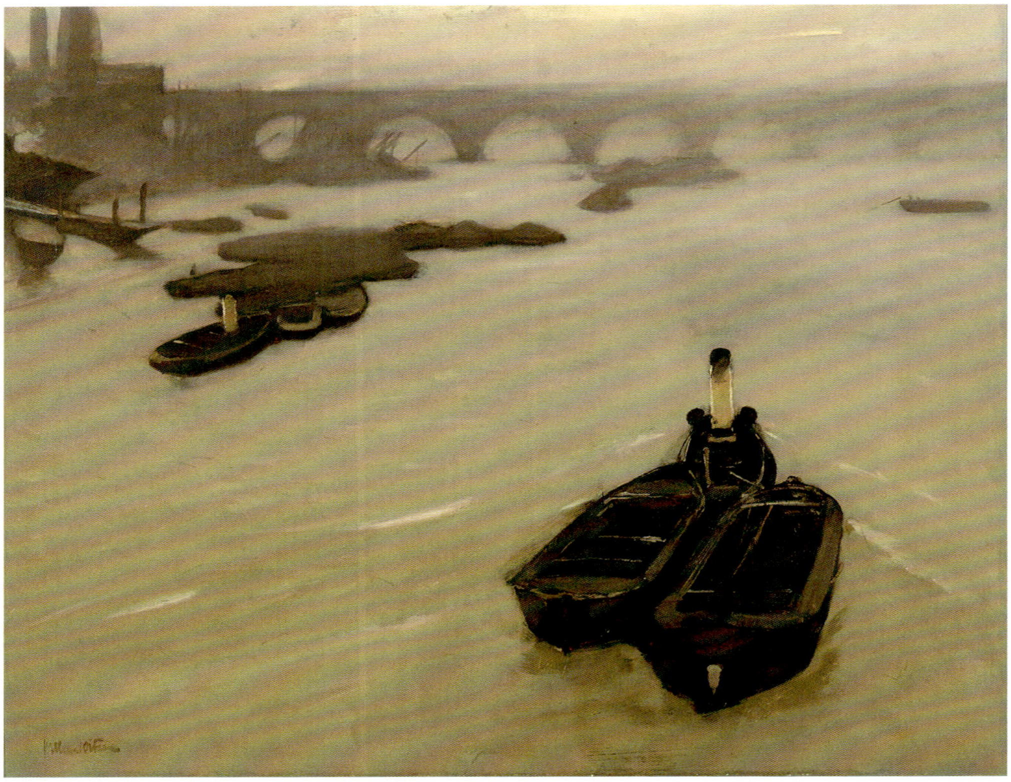

Whistler. His and Hammershøi's paths may have crossed during the Universal Exposition in Paris in 1889, but they are unlikely to have known each other; each reacted in his own way to the same artistic impulses.

The Dutch painter Willem Arnold Witsen used a similarly skewed angle when he painted *The Thames in London* [90].[119] He has turned his gaze down towards the water of the river and has left out the banks of the river on both sides of the painting, so that only the bridge in the background localizes the subject. The scene is enveloped in a light mist like several of Hammershøi's paintings from London and, like the Dane, Witsen has kept the colouring of the picture within a very limited scale, in this case especially brownish tones. As a source of inspiration for Witsen's painting one senses first and foremost Whistler's *Nocturnes* from the Thames.[120] Perhaps Hammershøi intended to paint similar pictures. At any rate, in November 1905, the Danish newspaper *Politiken* was able to write about his current plans: "As for Hammershøi himself, he has furnished a studio in south London, where he intends to paint pictures from the Thames. His stay in England, it seems, will be of some duration."[121] These plans were apparently never realized. But it undoubtedly occurred to Hammershøi that he should paint pictures from the Thames of the same type as those that Whistler and Witsen painted.

On the other hand, Hammershøi did paint several pictures from Copenhagen Harbour. But they are probably of quite another character than any river pictures from London would have been. He stuck to the narrow canals of Christianshavn, which in the nature of

[90]
Willem Arnold Witsen 1860-1923 Dutch
The Thames in London c. 1895
Oil on canvas 79 x 100 cm
The Kröller-Müller Museum, Otterlo

things presented opportunities for another type of subject than the wide Thames. One of these is *From Christianshavn's Canal, Copenhagen* which was done the same year, that is in 1905 [91]. In this painting, which is a study for a larger picture,[122] Hammershøi was interested in the compact pictorial structure created by the many lines in the rigging of the ships.

A similarly solid composition achieved by analogous means can be found in a closely related picture by Georges Seurat, *The Maria at Honfleur* from 1886 [93]. Both painters have used a tight geometrical composition to structure the reality they saw, and both achieved a solidly constructed, almost indissoluble totality where a network of horizontal, vertical and diagonal lines binds all the parts of the composition together. In the painting of the harbour in Honfleur the French painter has also maintained a greatly reduced colour scale not far from the one Hammershøi cultivated – an affinity that is even more marked in Seurat's drawings. Whether the Dane can have seen original works by the Frenchman is not clear. But photographs of his paintings may also have attracted the Dane's interest.[123]

A quite different type of source of inspiration for Hammershøi – and perhaps also for Seurat – could be a reportage photograph from a harbour. The silhouette effect created by masts and ropes in Hammershøi's painting recurs in many photos of related subjects taken by several of the photographers of the time. One example is *Ships in a Harbour* [92], which the photographer Henri Lemoine took around 1900.[124] The print-like effect produced by the monochrome photograph undoubtedly appealed to the painter, who after all himself worked with a very limited colour scale.

In Hammershøi's city pictures we see hardly any traces of nature, and only in exceptional cases are there trees, bushes or other plants. Occasionally he let tall trees play against buildings, as during his stay in London in 1912-13 when he painted *The Jews' College "Rabbinical Seminary" in Guilford Street, London* [94].[125] In the mist the buildings lose their solid appearance, and they seem almost as airy as the crowns of the trees. Both the houses and the trees appear almost non-material.

Perhaps Hammershøi drew inspiration for the painting from elsewhere. In 1893 the Dutchman Karsen painted a street scene, *Beguinage in Amsterdam* [96], where a similar play of trees and houses was the painter's most important concern, and where he did not make a point of giving an account of the design of the buildings.[126] Whether Hammershøi could have seen a painting like this is uncertain, but it is not inconceivable. In 1897 a now unknown painting by Karsen, possibly with a related subject, was shown at the international exhibition in Copenhagen.[127]

A more likely model is in fact more surprising. It is possible that for once he was influenced to some extent by his younger brother, Svend Hammershøi. In 1906 the latter painted *The Garden of Prinsens Palæ, Copenhagen* [95], in which the trees in the garden are given an absolutely dominant role compared with the surrounding houses.[128] But here too the light mist obscures the distinction between the trees and the buildings – with a rather unreal atmosphere as a result. His elder brother would not have sought such an effect at this time. Vilhelm must have noted the painting when Svend sold it to Statens Museum for Kunst the same year.

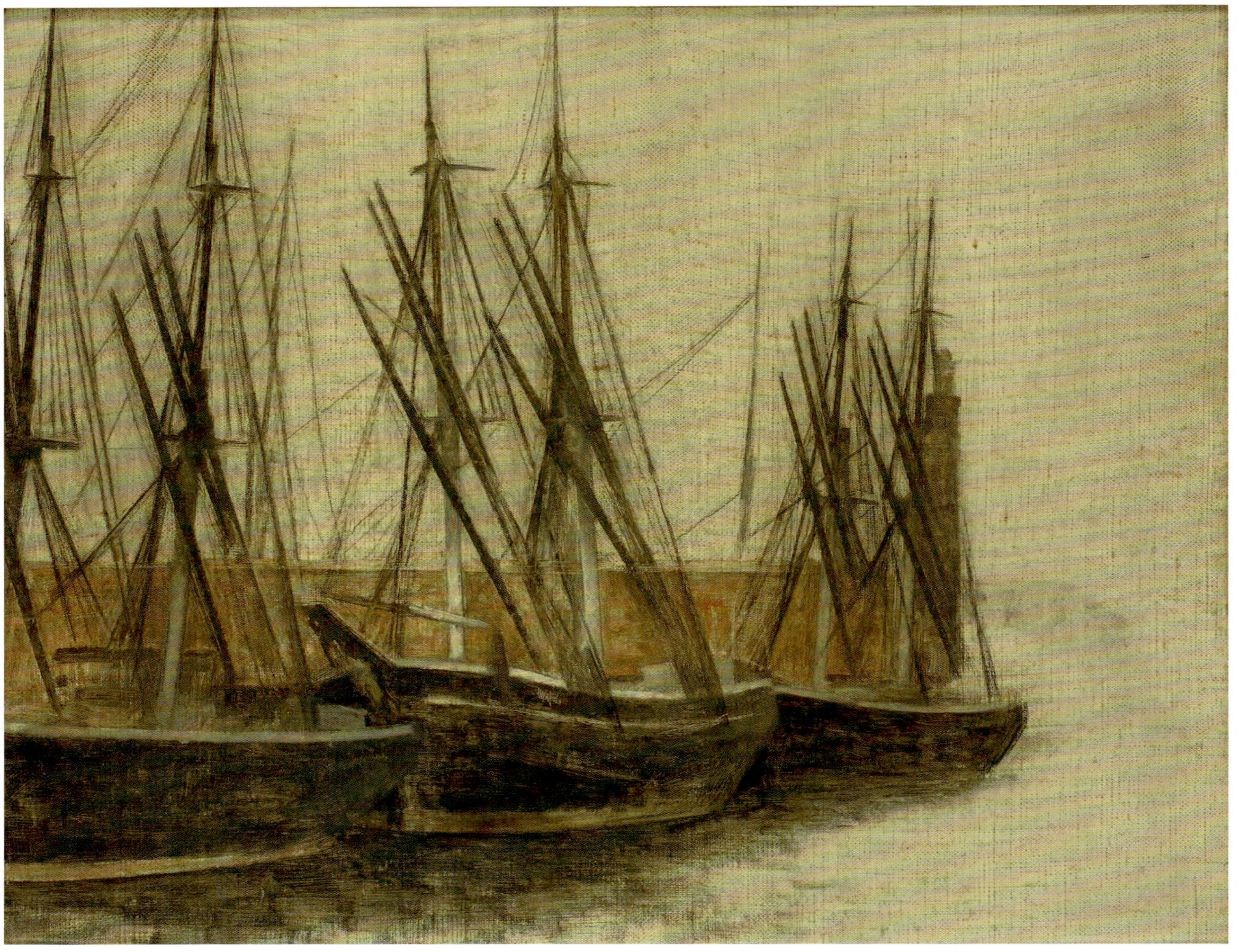

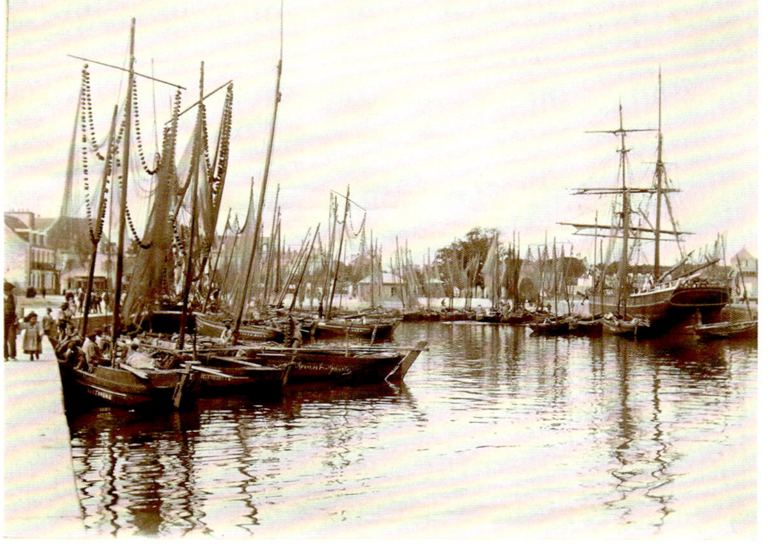

[91]
Vilhelm Hammershøi 1864-1916 Danish
From Christianshavn's Canal, Copenhagen 1905
Oil on canvas 33.1 x 40.8 cm
Statens Museum for Kunst

[92]
Henri Lemoine 1848-1924 French
Ships in a Harbour c. 1900
Photograph 7.8 x 10.5 cm
Musée d'Orsay, Paris

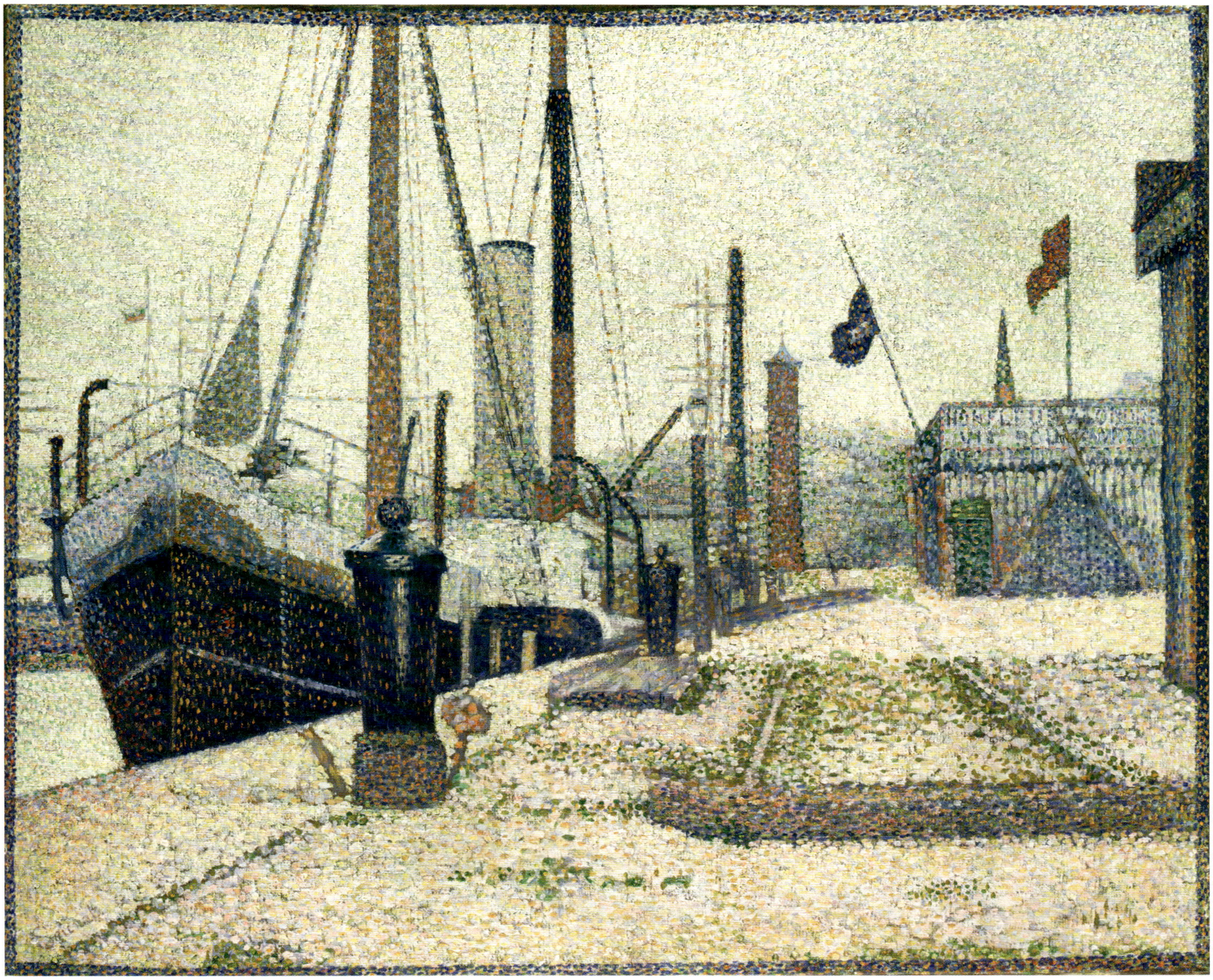

[93]
Georges Seurat 1859-91 French
The Maria at Honfleur 1886
Oil on canvas 54.5 x 65.5 cm
Národní Galerie, Prague

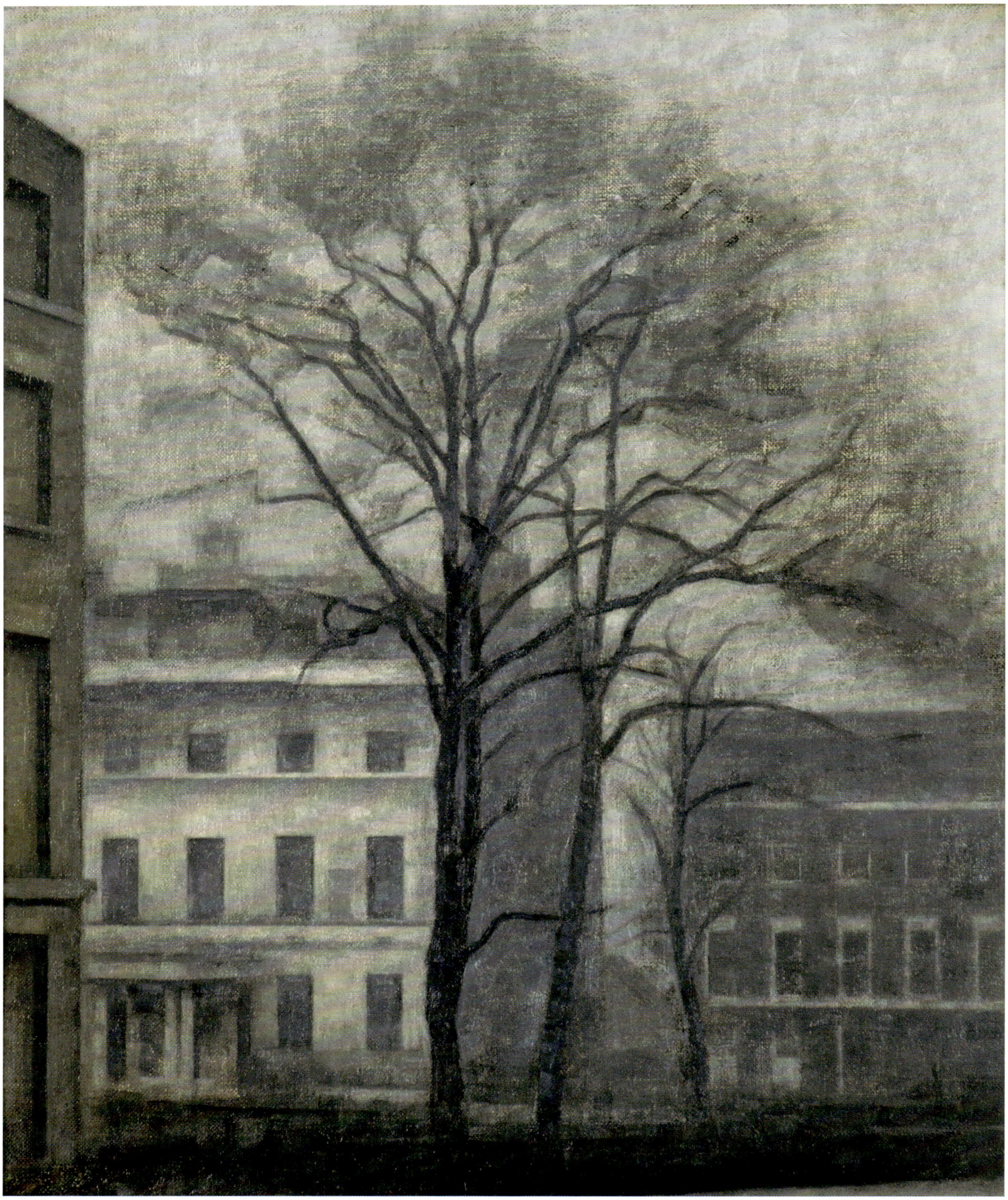

[94]
Vilhelm Hammershøi 1864-1916 Danish
The Jews' College "Rabbinical Seminary" in Guilford Street, London 1912-13
Oil on canvas 51 x 41.5 cm
Schleswig-Holsteinisches Landesmuseum, Schleswig

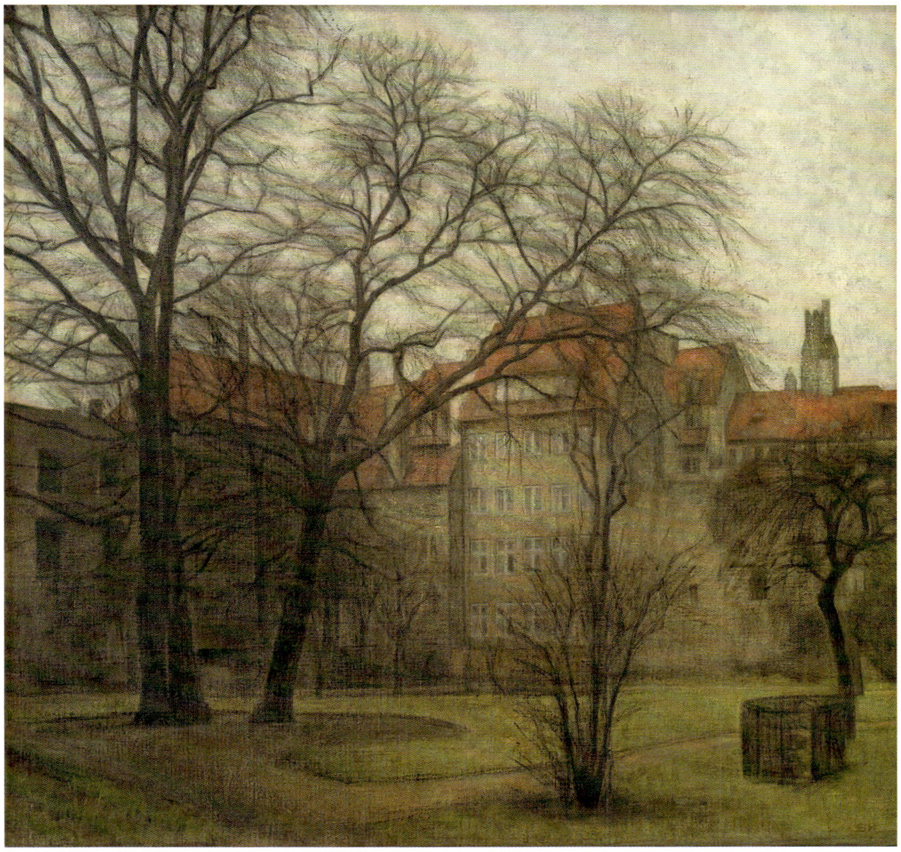

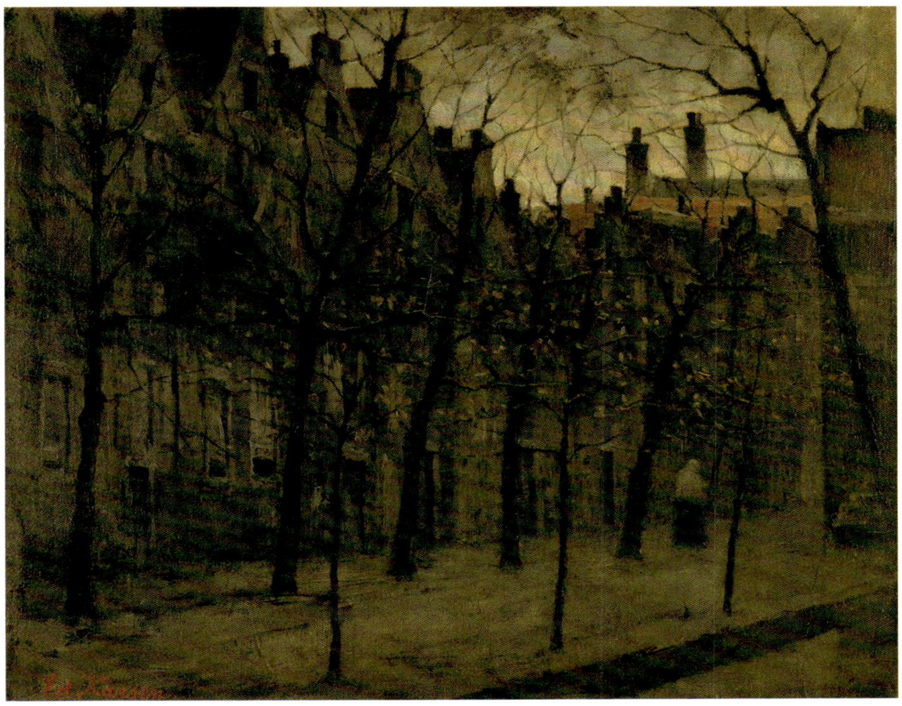

[95]
Svend Hammershøi 1873-1948 Danish
The Garden of Prinsens Palæ, Copenhagen c. 1906
Oil on canvas 63 x 65.5 cm
Statens Museum for Kunst

[96]
Eduard Karsen 1860-1941 Dutch
Beguinage in Amsterdam 1893
Oil on canvas 36.5 x 45 cm
The Kröller-Müller Museum, Otterlo

THE DEROMANTICIZED LANDSCAPE[129]

Unlike most other Nordic painters of the period, Hammershøi did not travel far from the capital to remote regions of his country to paint.[130] He had in other words no wish to discover unnoticed landscapes that had not been painted by other artists before him.

Nevertheless, landscape painting played a central role in his art. Throughout most of his career he painted a few landscapes at regular intervals. Yet there was no yearning for remote, virgin nature behind his choice of subjects. On the contrary, the pictures were always painted near settled areas, and they show places that were in fact regularly frequented by people – and yet we never see people in the pictures. He refused to be carried away by the Late Romantic wave of the period, so he did not share the wish of his Nordic contemporaries to create "mood-pictures" of the landscape or to express an interconnectedness with it. Nor do we find any approach to actual Symbolism in Hammershøi's landscapes. Against this background his landscapes seem typified by objectivity and sobriety. All the same it is hard to imagine a landscape art more remote from the Nordic Naturalism of the 1880s than his.

Hammershøi's first attempts at landscape painting from the beginning of the 1880s are quite unlike his later landscapes. These are small paintings showing narrow sections of farmhouses, a corner of a farmyard or a single wing of a farm [98, 99].[131] The subjects can be said to be related to the enduring tradition of Romantic folklife painting that had dominated Danish art from around 1850 until well into the 1870s, and which focused on the life of the rural population. But as in so many other cases Hammershøi removed all life and reduced the subjects to the depiction of some buildings without function and context. He has reproduced all the details strikingly blurred, as if viewed through a lens that is not in focus. This is quite surprising in view of the time at which they were painted, but it points forward to his endeavours in many later paintings.

A few years later Khnopff painted several small landscapes which are in various respects related to these pictures, including *In Fosset, Rain* from 1890 [97].[132] Here he has painted a farmhouse in a landscape, and the painting thus shows a far wider view than Hammershøi did in his earlier paintings. But the representation of the farm itself is to a striking degree related to Hammershøi's farmhouses. Khnopff has even blurred the focus in the picture in quite the same way. But he had no opportunity to know the Dane's landscapes at this time, and the parallels only testify that these were two artists who to a great extent viewed their surroundings in the same way.

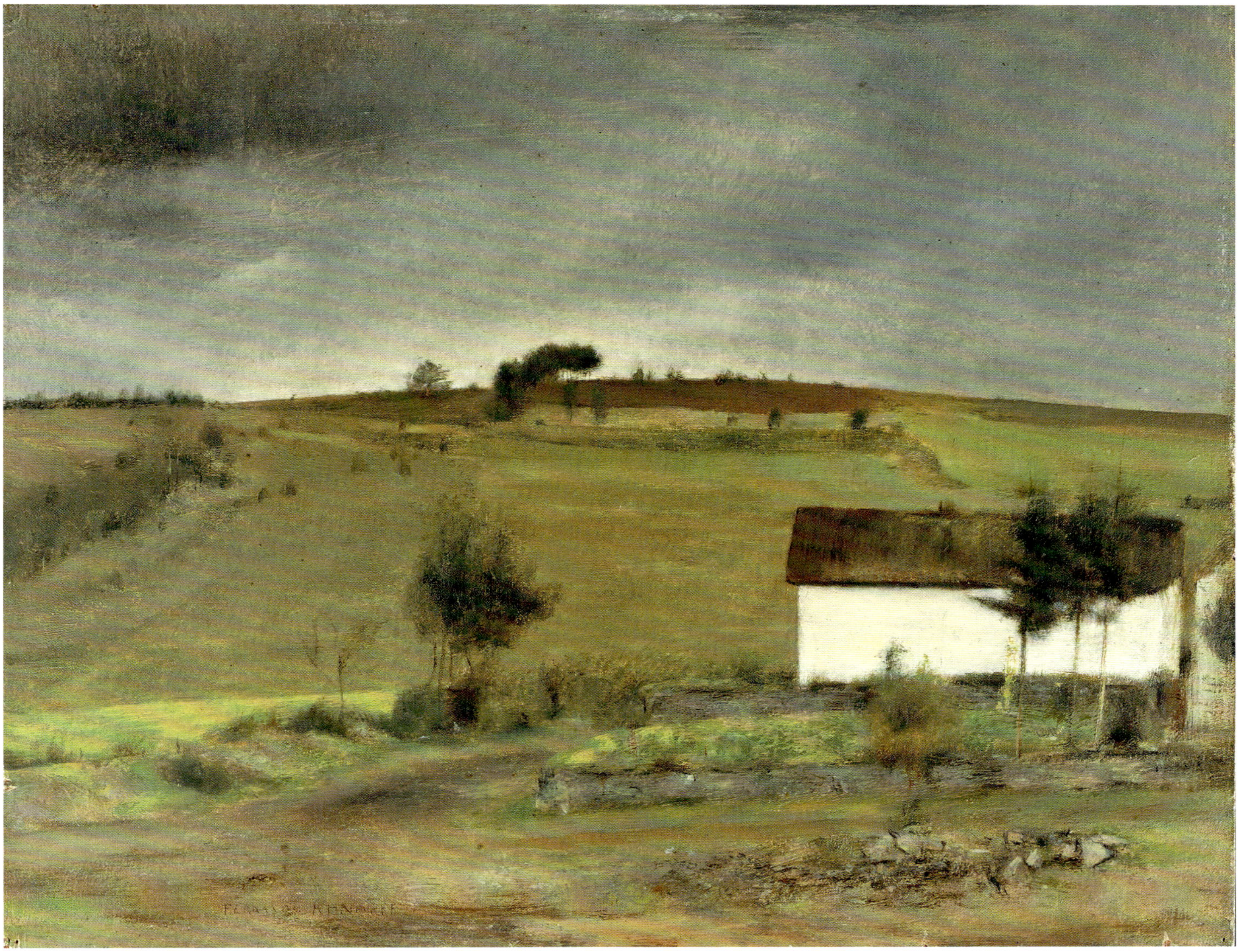

[97]
Fernand Khnopff 1858-1921 Belgian
In Fosset, Rain 1890
Oil on panel 19 x 23.5 cm
The Hearn Family Trust, New York

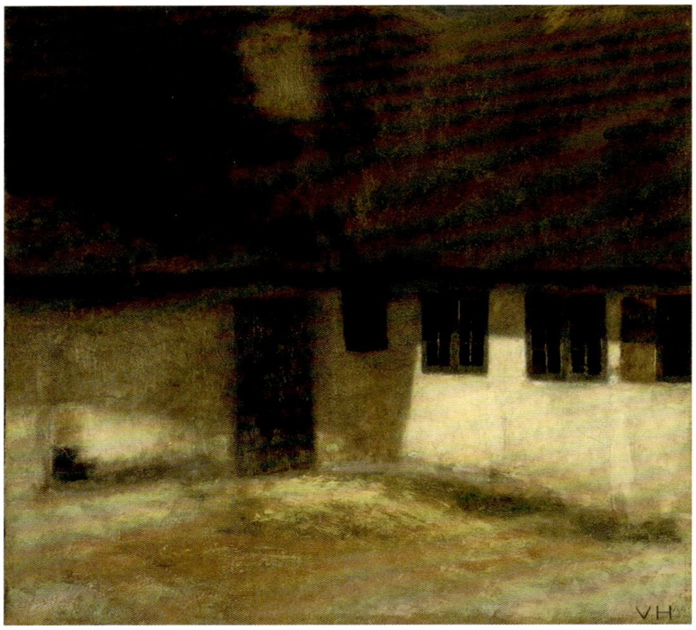

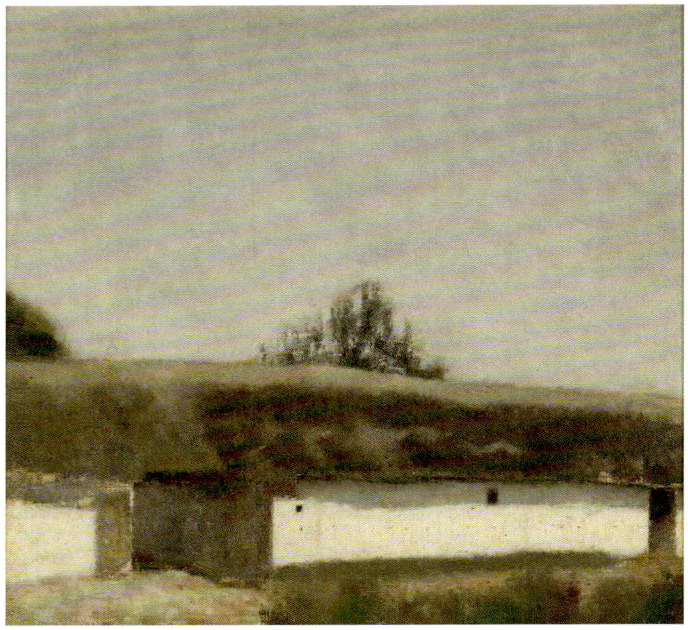

The depopulated landscape

Paradoxically, the point of departure for Hammershøi's true landscapes seems to have been the Danish landscape painting of Romanticism from the 1830s and 1840s, especially the works of Johan Thomas Lundbye.[133] Like Lundbye he painted a number of pictures of the open Zealand landscape; these were panoramic pictures of gently hilly terrain, often covered by cornfields and a few groups of trees, but otherwise without any element of the striking or dramatic, and viewed against a high sky that arches over the landscape. But Lundbye's aim was to capture the national distinctiveness of the Danish landscape, and nothing could have been further from Hammershøi's mind. The tenacious Danish Romantic landscape tradition was still alive in the 1880s, and Hammershøi put a firm distance between himself and it, like so many other Danish painters from the same generation. It was therefore essential for him to take an approach that was not obviously emotional. In many ways Hammershøi's landscapes become a negation of Lundbye's.

At the end of the 1880s he embarked on the depiction of the open Zealand landscape, at first in some small pictures [101]; but in the course of the 1890s he perfected his subject and painted several large, monumental pictures including *View of Gentofte Lake. Sunshower* from 1903 [100].[134] He found the subject a few kilometres north of Copenhagen, in rural surroundings near an old village that still only had scattered farmhouses among the fields. At this time Gentofte was being transformed from a village to a suburb, and the present-day residential neighbourhoods were just being built. The painter stood by Gentofte Lake, so he had the village and the new suburban homes behind him and the nearest farms were not far away. But he chose his angle with great care, so that he would neither paint the farms nor the houses of Gentofte. The high road, Kongevejen, which can be seen on the other side of the lake, is also entirely without traffic, and the painter has deliberately omitted any suggestion that it was one of the most important exit roads from Copenhagen.

[98]
Vilhelm Hammershøi 1864-1916 Danish
Farmhouse 1883
Oil on canvas 34.7 x 36.7 cm
Private collection, Professor Günther Fielmann – Schierensee Manor

[99]
Vilhelm Hammershøi 1864-1916 Danish
Landscape with a Barn 1883
Oil on canvas 34 x 36.5 cm
Private collection, Professor Günther Fielmann – Schierensee Manor

The scene that Hammershøi has shown was in reality a gently rolling landscape with no large hills. But he has levelled out any differences in the terrain so that the landscape has become quite flat. He has thus achieved a strictly geometrical structuring of the picture with a very low horizon and a resulting high sky. Hammershøi has not painted a foreground that could lead gradually into the picture and link the viewer with the subject itself, but has effectively let the water of the lake divide the main subject from the viewer. The road runs parallel with the picture surface and wholly cuts off the view towards a background farther off. An insurmountable distance from the landscape of the picture has arisen. This is put further in relief by the total absence of air or atmosphere. One gets a strange feeling of standing in front of a space empty of air into which no life can penetrate.

Out into the countryside

As an extension of this and other pictures from Gentofte, he also painted landscapes that were farther away from the city, and thus even closer to Lundbye's subjects. These were pictures of the slightly hilly Zealand farming land with ripe cornfields and scattered groups of trees. In a few cases he even chose subjects on the peninsula Refsnæs, where Lundbye had also painted [102].[135] Although Hammershøi has depicted the fields at the height of summer, it is not lushness and growth that typify his picture. On the contrary, the landscape seems as barren and inhospitable as if it were a desert he had painted. The subject itself – ripe cornfields – was not unfamiliar to Hammershøi's contemporaries. Since Lundbye and several other landscape painters from his generation had taken it up and perfected it in the 1840s, it had been treated regularly by the Danish painters. In the decades after 1850 – and well into the 1880s – the national genre painters had often populated the fields with harvesters who did not however seem overburdened by their work. In the 1890s painters like Harald Slott-Møller and Ejnar Nielsen had returned to pure landscape painting; but they had added an animistic, supernatural dimension to the subject. No other Danish painters both depopulated the subject and gave it an appearance of unreality and alienation the way Hammershøi did. The mill that can only just be made out in the distance does not add a human dimension to the landscape; it only underscores how insignificantly small mankind is in the context. Compositionally, the picture seems to have no points of reference. It is a strikingly decentral composition. Although it is a moraine landscape Hammershøi has depicted, the hills have been almost flattened out, so they do not contribute to a rhythmic division of the subject.

Of these landscapes Robert Rosenblum has said that Hammershøi chose "the most unpopulated, barren territories that elicit stillness and reverie".[136] This is a truth that requires a clarificatory remark. There can be no doubt about the effect of the pictures, but in actual fact it was populated areas that the painter depicted, although he made them appear desolate and abandoned by humanity. Rosenblum is therefore right in stating that the pictures "defy our sense of scale, time, and space [...]. For all their expansive spaces, these landscapes are ultimately as imprisoning as the rectangular enclosures of the artist's rooms or, for that matter, of his views of Copenhagen's buildings."

The same tendency to make the landscape appear less built-up and thus less populated than it was in reality can be observed in contemporary French landscape painting.[137]

Only a few other contemporary artists looked at the landscape with the same eyes as Hammershøi in his open landscapes. At one point in the 1890s his friend Valdemar Schønheyder Møller painted a narrow section of the beach at Skagen [103]. Several other painters

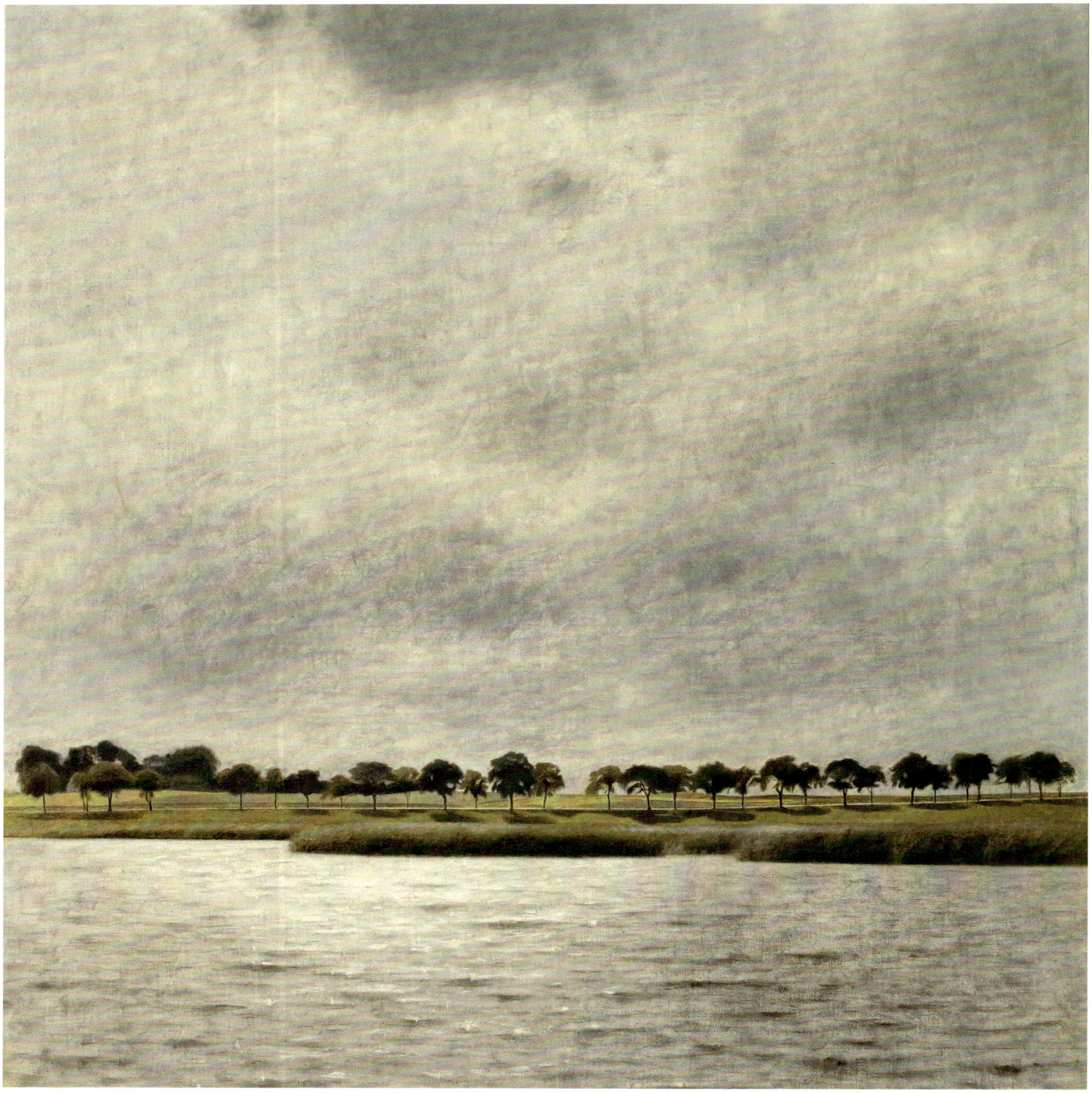

[100]
Vilhelm Hammershøi 1864-1916 Danish
View of Gentofte Lake. Sunshower 1903
Oil on canvas 83 x 78 cm
Private collection

had shown this very beach full of bathers, but here it is devoid of human presence. The subject has furthermore been purged of details, and the black boat that lies on the beach seems reduced to an abstract form. Nor does the intense sunlight that strikes the sea help to create any atmosphere in the picture.

One finds great motivic correspondences with Hammershøi's landscapes in the German painter Hans am Ende's *Weyerberg with Summer Clouds* [104]. He too has painted some fields where any differences in level have been neutralized so that the landscape in the picture looks quite flat. The fields are divided into a number of smaller areas, and this produces more variety than in Hammershøi's landscape, although the German painter has used the same limited colour scale. He too gives no impression of the fertility of nature, and despite the clouds in the sky one senses no motion and no life.

Am Ende and Hammershøi are unlikely to have known each other personally. But one possible link between them is the poet Rainer Maria Rilke, who published a book about the painters from the artists' colony at Worpswede in northern Germany, including am Ende, in 1903, and who met Hammershøi in Copenhagen in 1904. Am Ende's painting was done in 1899, that is five years before this meeting (see Anne Hemkendreis' article, p. 166). It can thus only be a matter of parallel aims, not of mutual influence.

On the other hand it is far more likely that Hammershøi at some point met the English painter William Nicholson and saw his paintings during his stays in London. With Alfred Bramsen's contacts in London and especially his interest in Nicholson's art, it would be odd if the two artists had never met. But we have no firm evidence (see MaryAnne Stevens' article, p. 152).

Nicholson painted a series of landscapes from the South Downs in England, where he stayed regularly in the years after 1909.[138] In several of the paintings he looked at the rolling landscape with rather the same eyes as Hammershøi looking at the Danish landscapes. The hills there were rounded in a special way, so that the landscape offered neither contrasts nor great differences. A striking work in this context is the painting *Viola on the Downs* from 1909 [105].[139] The picture is dominated by the gentle curves of the landscape. Like Schønheyder Møller, Nicholson liked to view his subjects facing the sun, and he too exploited the sunlight glittering on the water. The tone of the painting is thus utterly different from Hammershøi's landscapes, and neither here nor in his other landscape pictures did Nicholson try to remove the impression of people's movements in the landscapes. On the contrary, the woman who has given the painting its title is strolling in the foreground of the landscape.

Hammershøi may very well have seen landscape paintings like this one by Nicholson during his stays in London in 1912 and 1913. In that case he would have viewed them with great interest, but he would hardly have felt the urge to change his own artistic idiom.

[101]
Vilhelm Hammershøi 1864-1916 Danish
View of Jægersborg Allé, North of Copenhagen 1892
Oil on canvas 35.3 x 41.8 cm
Statens Museum for Kunst

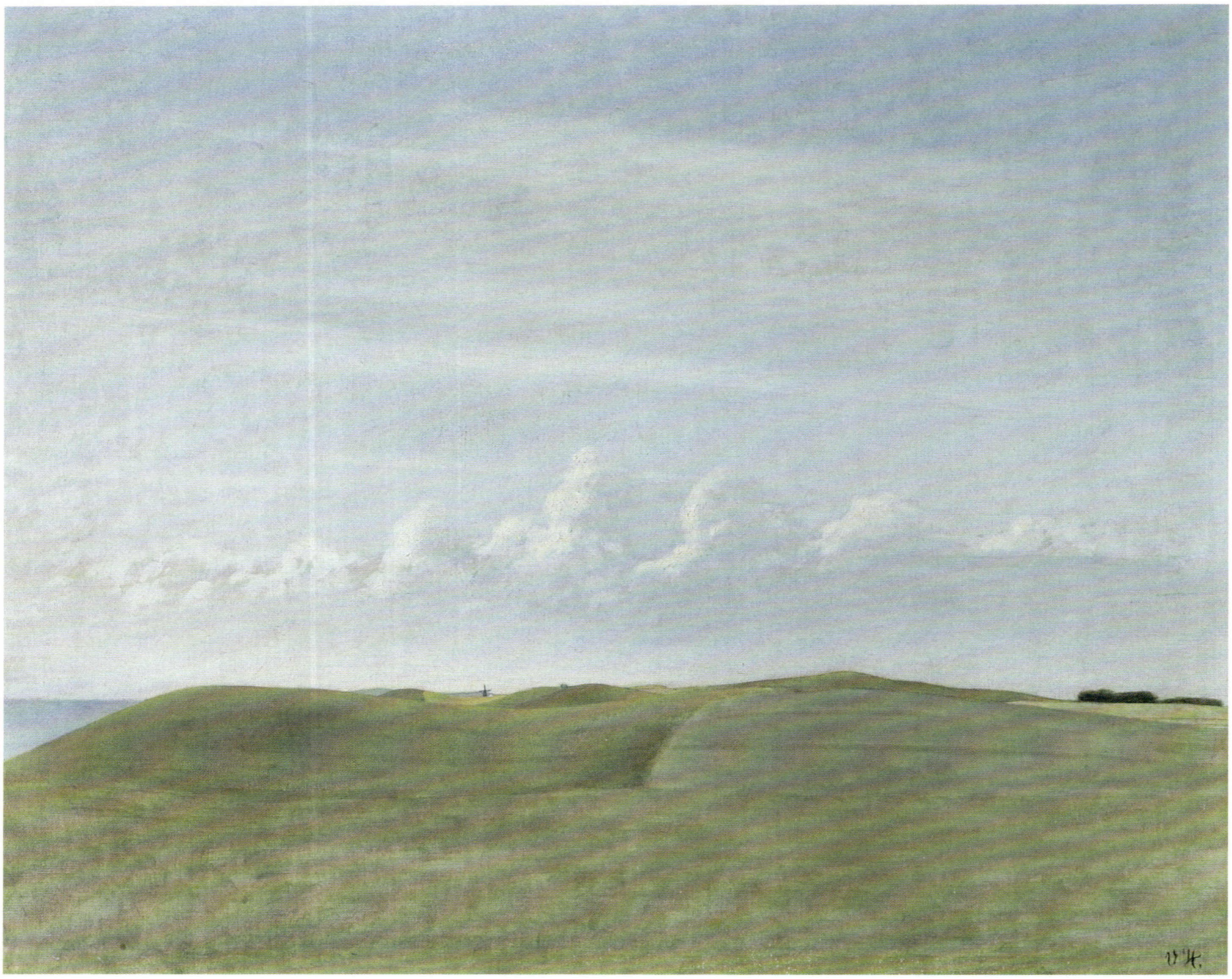

[102]
Vilhelm Hammershøi 1864-1916 Danish
View of Refsnæs 1900
Oil on canvas 63 x 78 cm
The Thielska Gallery, Stockholm

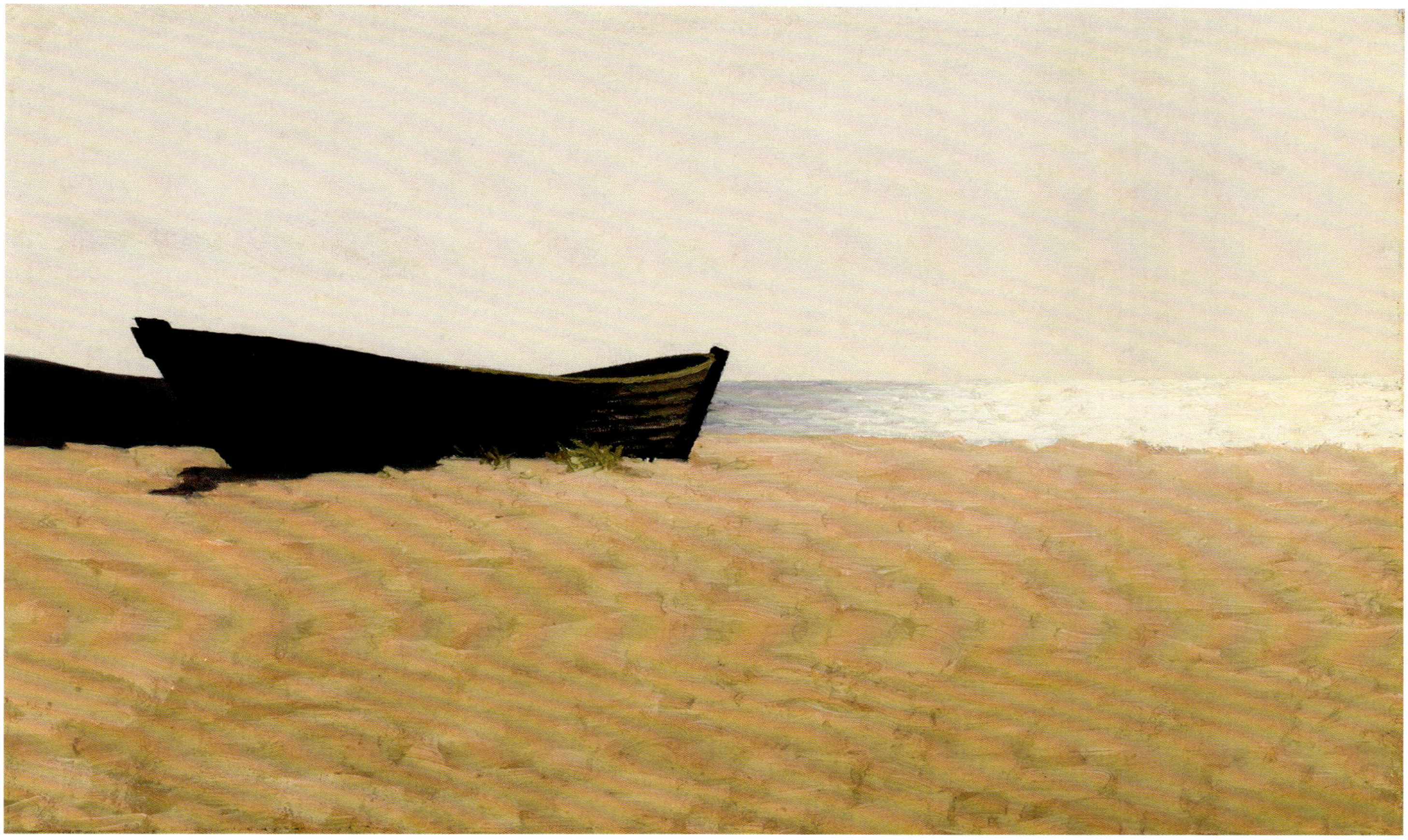

[103]
Valdemar Schønheyder Møller 1864-1905 Danish
Two Boats on the Beach.
The Sun Glittering over the Sea beg. of the 1890s
Oil on canvas 29 x 46.5 cm
Skagens Museum

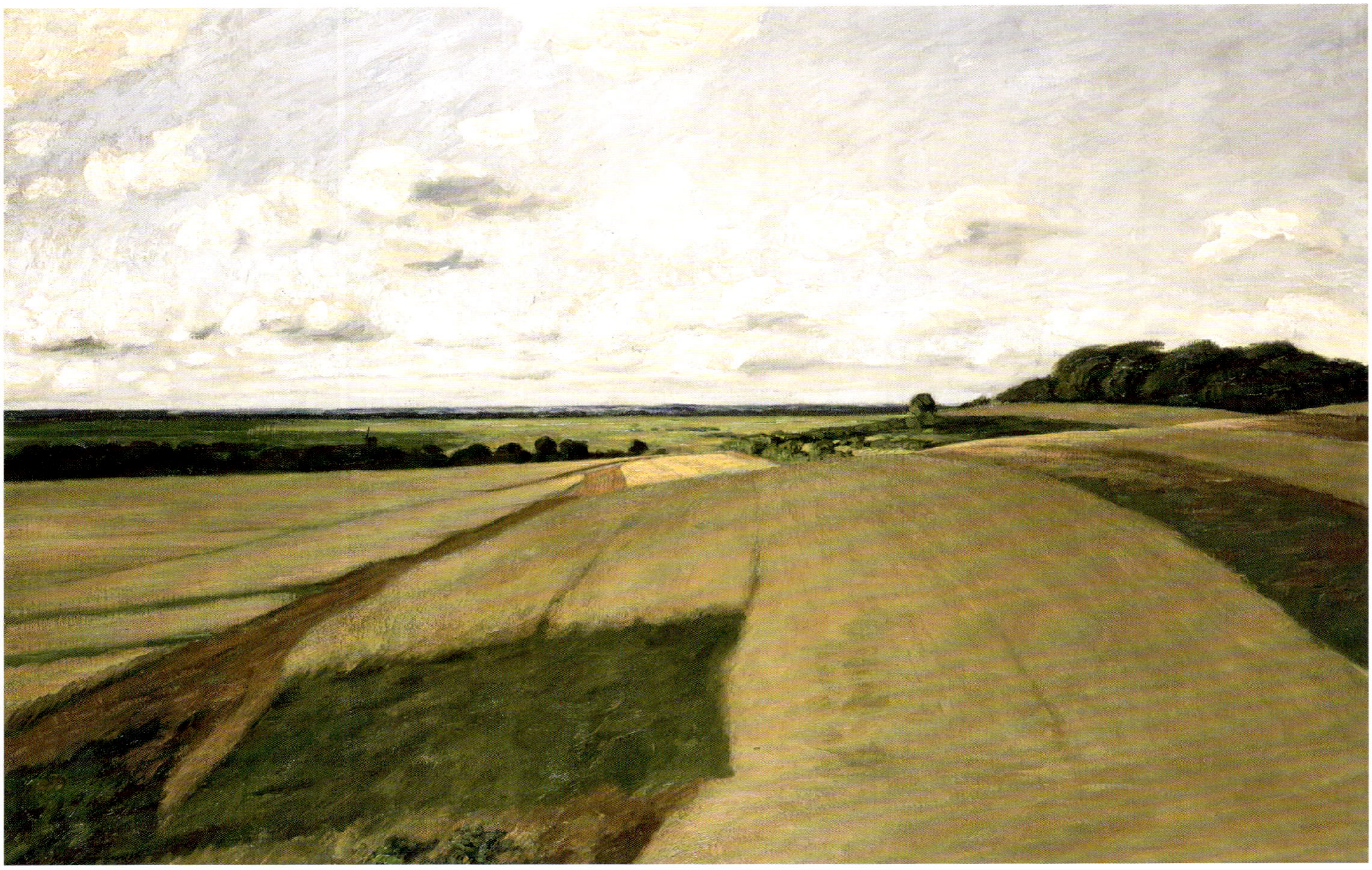

[104]
Hans am Ende 1864-1918 German
Weyerberg with Summer Clouds 1899
Oil on canvas 87.5 x 129.5 cm
Staatliche Museen zu Berlin, Nationalgalerie

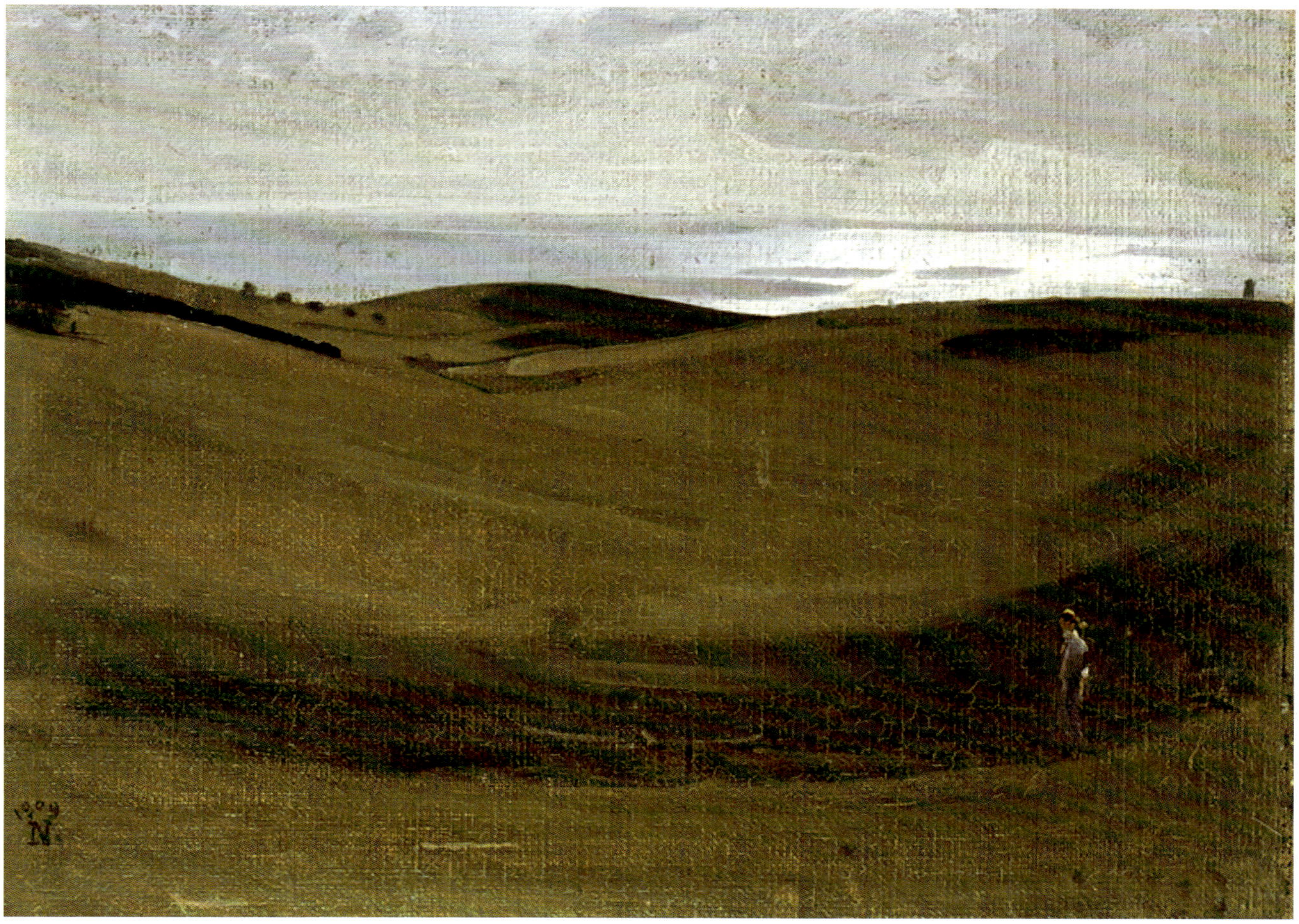

[105]
William Nicholson 1872-1949 British
Viola on the Downs 1909
Oil on canvas board 28.5 x 40 cm
Private collection

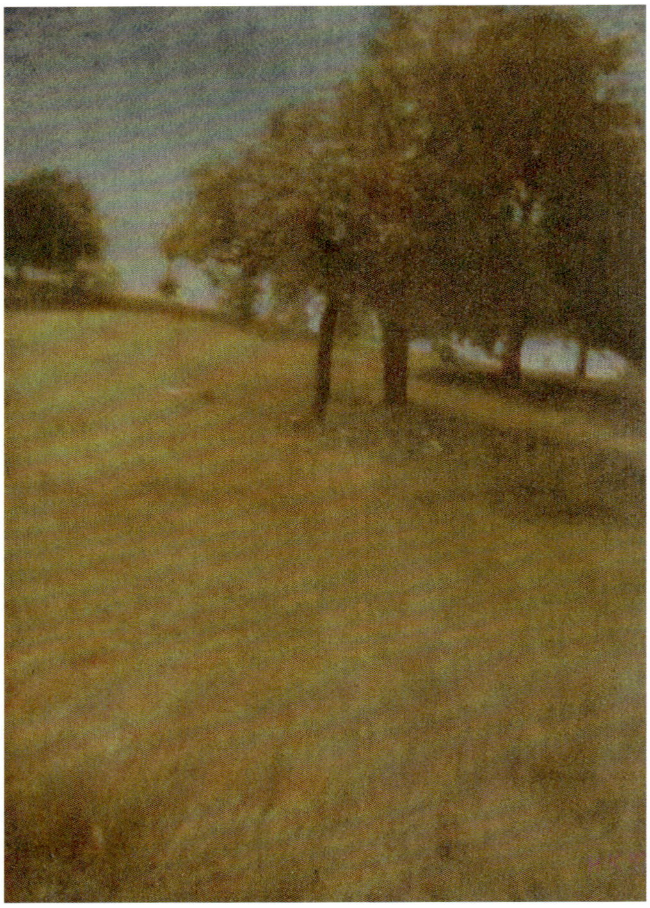

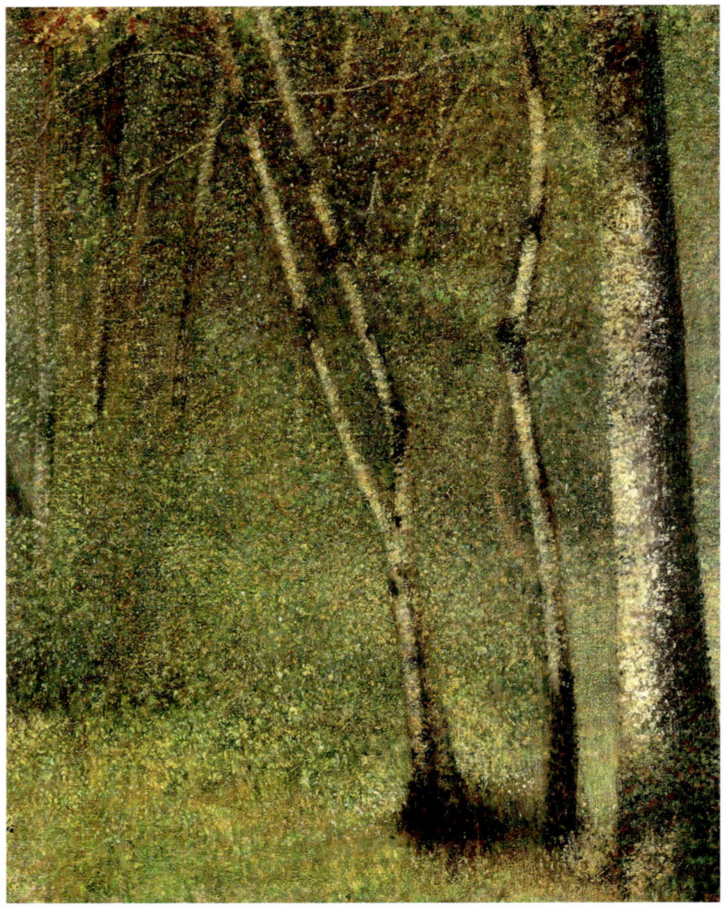

Among the trees

Alongside the pictures of the open countryside, Hammershøi also turned to another type of landscape, the forest scene. In these pictures he was more than usually open to departures from the classic compositional principles and experiments with unconventional points of view. In the painting *Landscape in Snow, Søndermarken* [108], he has looked at a park on the outskirts of Copenhagen from a high point, so he could direct his gaze down towards the trees.[140] The naked crowns of the trees overshadow one another from this point of view, and each does not have its own individual appearance. But the foremost tree trunks do, as they stand in dark silhouette against the white snow, and thus attract the main attention. The positioning of the trees in the picture causes the viewer's gaze to be directed from the front tree almost in a fan shape out to the sides. The subject is in all respects unusual for Hammershøi, also because with the reddish evening sky he suggests a mood of nature which he however does not stress as strongly as the contemporary Nordic practitioners of the special "mood-paintings" did.

The strong focus on the tree trunks in the foreground is something the painting shares with one of Seurat's early paintings, *The Forest at Pontaubert* from 1881 [107].[141] Seurat has merged the forest floor, scrub and tree crowns so that only the illuminated trunks

[106]
Heinrich Kühn 1866-1944 German
Meadow with Trees 1897
Tri-color gum bichromate print 37.9 x 27.8 cm
Museum für Kunst und Gewerbe, Hamburg

[107]
Georges Seurat 1859-91 French
The Forest at Pontaubert 1881
Oil on canvas 79.1 x 62.5 cm
Metropolitan Museum of Art, New York

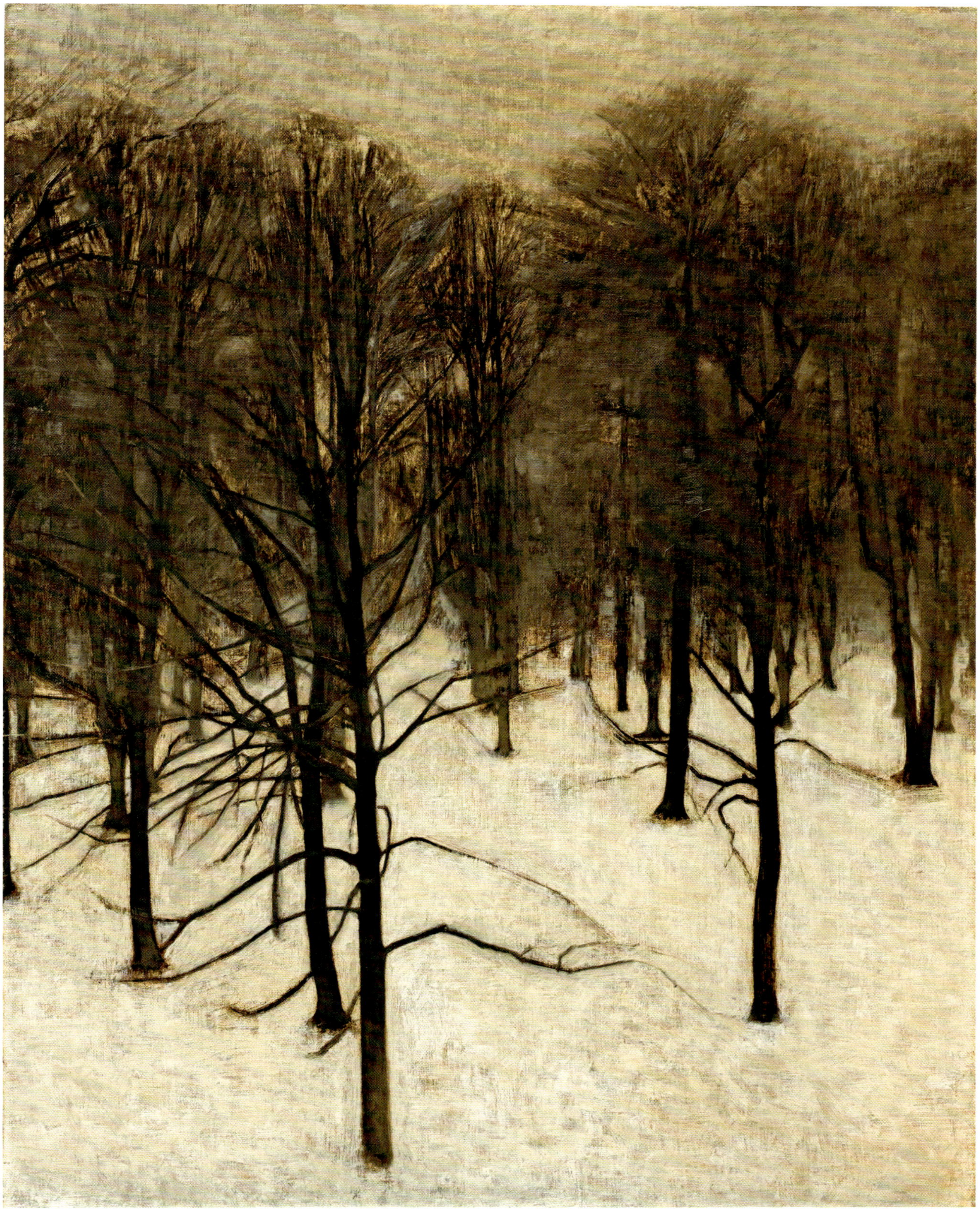

[108]
Vilhelm Hammershøi 1864-1916 Danish
Landscape in Snow, Søndermarken 1895-96
Oil on canvas 83.2 x 64.8 cm
The Hirschsprung Collection, Copenhagen

stand out. The way of seeing the subject is thus related in the two paintings, just as the two painters share the slightly blurred view of the subject. But in his experiments with the painting method which in the end would lead to Pointillism, Seurat has arrived at a painterly expression that is strikingly different from Hammershøi's.

A related veiled view of a similar subject is rather surprisingly also characteristic of a contemporary photograph, the German photographer Heinrich Kühn's *Meadow with Trees* from 1897 [106], one of the earliest attempts at colour photography.[142] Here too the main subject of the picture is a group of trees placed such that the tree trunks are seen in silhouette against a neutral foreground. But for Kühn the yellow meadow of the foreground is even more conspicuous than the snow in Hammershøi's picture. By placing the group of trees right out to one side the photographer has moreover achieved a strikingly skewed composition that we do not find in the works of the Danish painter. In that respect Kühn's photograph is therefore more closely related to the idiom of the Impressionists.

None of the three artists had heard of the others when their pictures were painted. Hammershøi and Kühn may later have become aware of each other's works, but in general Kühn worked with quite different resources from Hammershøi.

In a number of paintings Hammershøi chose to make a forest his main subject. He liked to depict the forest while standing in the midst of the trees, and had no wish to give an impression of the forest as such, but focused on a restricted segment of it. In the painting *Tree Trunks. Arresødal, Frederiksværk* from 1904 [109], whose subject Hammershøi found in northern Zealand, he has also isolated the trees from one another, so that the context the forest would otherwise create has entirely disappeared. Nor do we get a full impression of the individual trees, since the crowns are cut off by the top edge of the picture. Between the trees we see only a dense mist, and the viewer is given a view neither of the rest of the forest nor of landscapes farther off. We look into the same kind of emptiness in the painting as in *The Buildings of the Asiatic Company, seen from St. Annæ Street* [86, p. 111]. The forest is no longer a peaceful place where man can be in harmony with nature, as was the case in the Danish landscape painting of the preceding decades, particularly as cultivated by Peter Christian Skovgaard. In the forest, on the contrary, one is isolated from any meaningful context. Peter Nørgaard Larsen has viewed the subject as an image of the individual isolated human being and stated that "the trees live their own lives like a kind of allegory of human life. Some isolated in pairs, some stand on their own, but of all the trees it is true that they are depicted in a dark, almost black silhouette against a radiant sky in the background."[143] In this context he has pointed to other Nordic painters who have used the trees symbolically in similar ways.

There are however no other artists who have quite so consistently reduced the meaning of the interplay of the trees with the surroundings. Svend Hammershøi painted a number of pictures of free-standing trees, first and foremost *Landscape 1901* [112].[144] Unlike his brother, he was careful to make the one large oak in the picture fill out the whole composition and to give it an all-dominating role. He also gave a very careful account of every single branch and twig. His version of the powerful, isolated tree has more in common with a traditional interpretation of the solitary tree – alone and strong. Only a limited colour scale with grey and brown as the most important colours really links the two artist brothers.

However, the strong veiling of the details in the foliage is something Vilhelm Hammershøi has in common with the Danish painter Julius Paulsen. In the painting *Summer Landscape at Dusk, Horneby* [110], painted in northern Zealand in 1894, Paulsen has

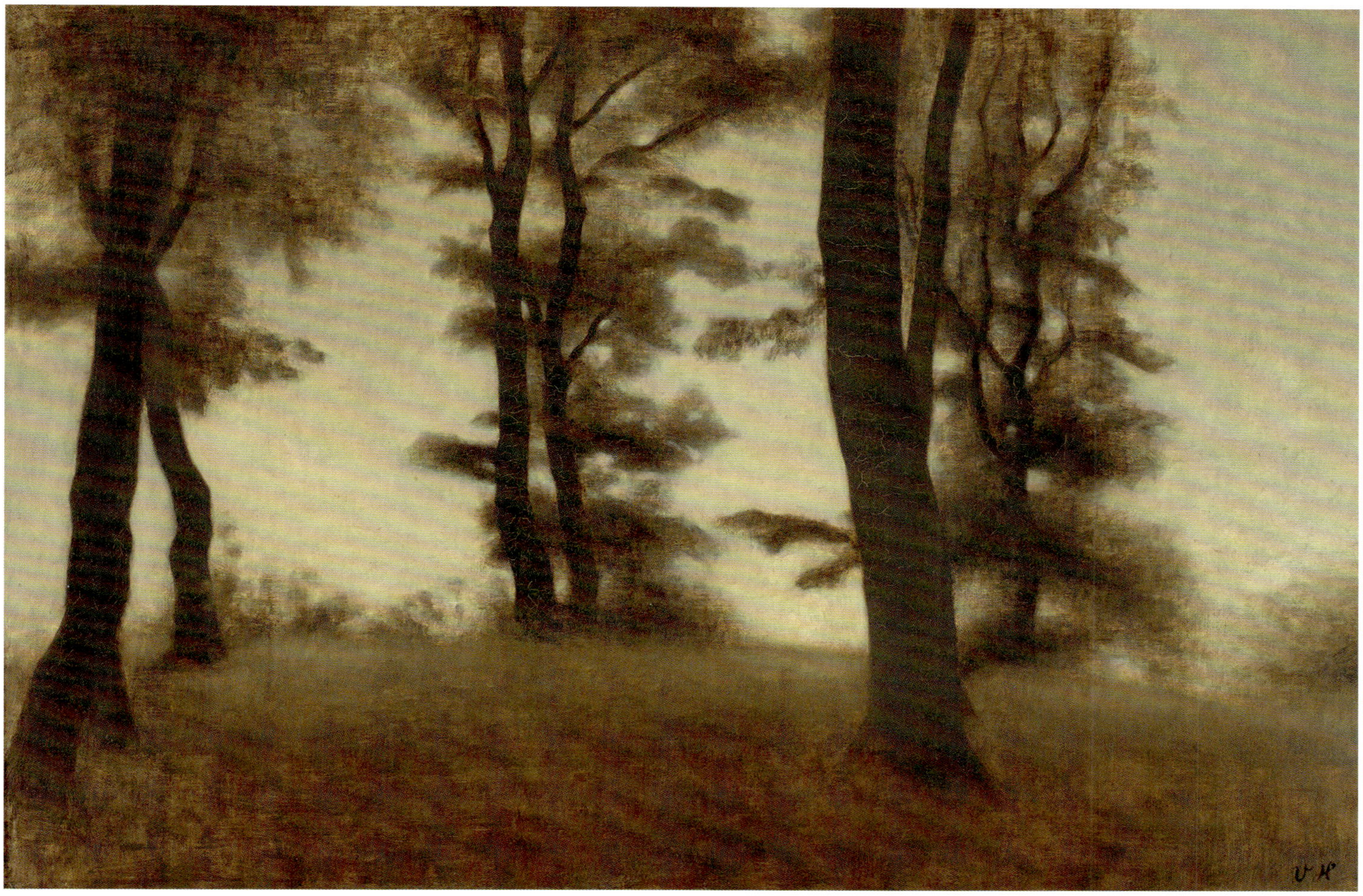

[109]
Vilhelm Hammershøi 1864-1916 Danish
Tree Trunks. Arresødal, Frederiksværk 1904
Oil on canvas 45.5 x 68.5 cm
Statens Museum for Kunst

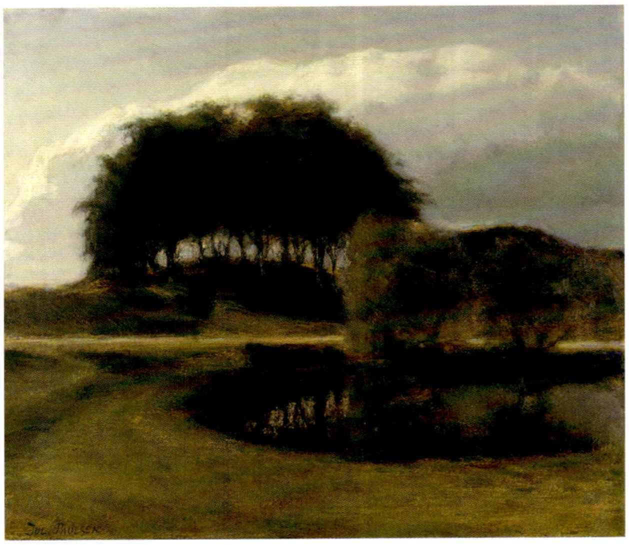

merged a group of trees into a totality where the individual tree is not profiled. He has made the trees the central point in the middle ground of the picture, and created a quite traditional composition. His fondness for evening moods after sunset brings his paintings far closer to the Neo-Romantic landscape painting that was especially prevalent in the other Nordic countries around the turn of the century.[145] But Hammershøi's paintings do not belong in that context.

Quite in keeping with Paulsen's painting is Józef Pankiewicz' *The Park in Dubój* from 1897 [111].[146] Like so many other European painters he has drawn crucial inspiration from Whistler's *Nocturnes*, and transformed it in several urban pictures in night lighting [89, p. 113], but also in a landscape like this one. The Polish painter has looked at the trees in the park in dark silhouette against the light evening sky and achieved a strong atmospheric effect in the picture. He has given his subject a slightly blurred appearance in the twilight, like Hammershøi's tree trunk and Paulsen's summer landscape. This gives the scene a slightly unreal look, which is reinforced by the reflection of the trees in the lake in the foreground. In other words the mood is different from Hammershøi's, but the slightly intangible character of the subject is something the two painters have in common.

Against the light

Quite unique in Hammershøi's art is the painting *Near Fortunen, Jægersborg Deer Park North of Copenhagen* from 1901 [113],[147] where he has looked through the crowns of the trees up towards the sun and where he has extremely effectively let the light penetrate down among the branches and strike the forest floor. He found the subject in the Royal Deer Park, a few kilometres north of Copenhagen. On a summer's day he has experienced a quite special, almost unreal lighting where the sunlight has completely enveloped the trees and cancelled out their material appearance. The yellowish sunlight and the shadows on the grass make the ground seem to dissolve, so it takes on the same airy consistency as the crowns of the trees. Through the thinly painted sky we can in several places make out the underlying

[110]
Julius Paulsen 1860-1940 Danish
Summer Landscape at Dusk, Horneby 1894
Oil on canvas 56 x 62 cm
Ordrupgaard, Copenhagen

[111]
Jósef Pankiewicz 1866-1940 Polish
The Park in Dubój 1897
Oil on canvas 96 x 130.5 cm
The National Museum, Warsaw

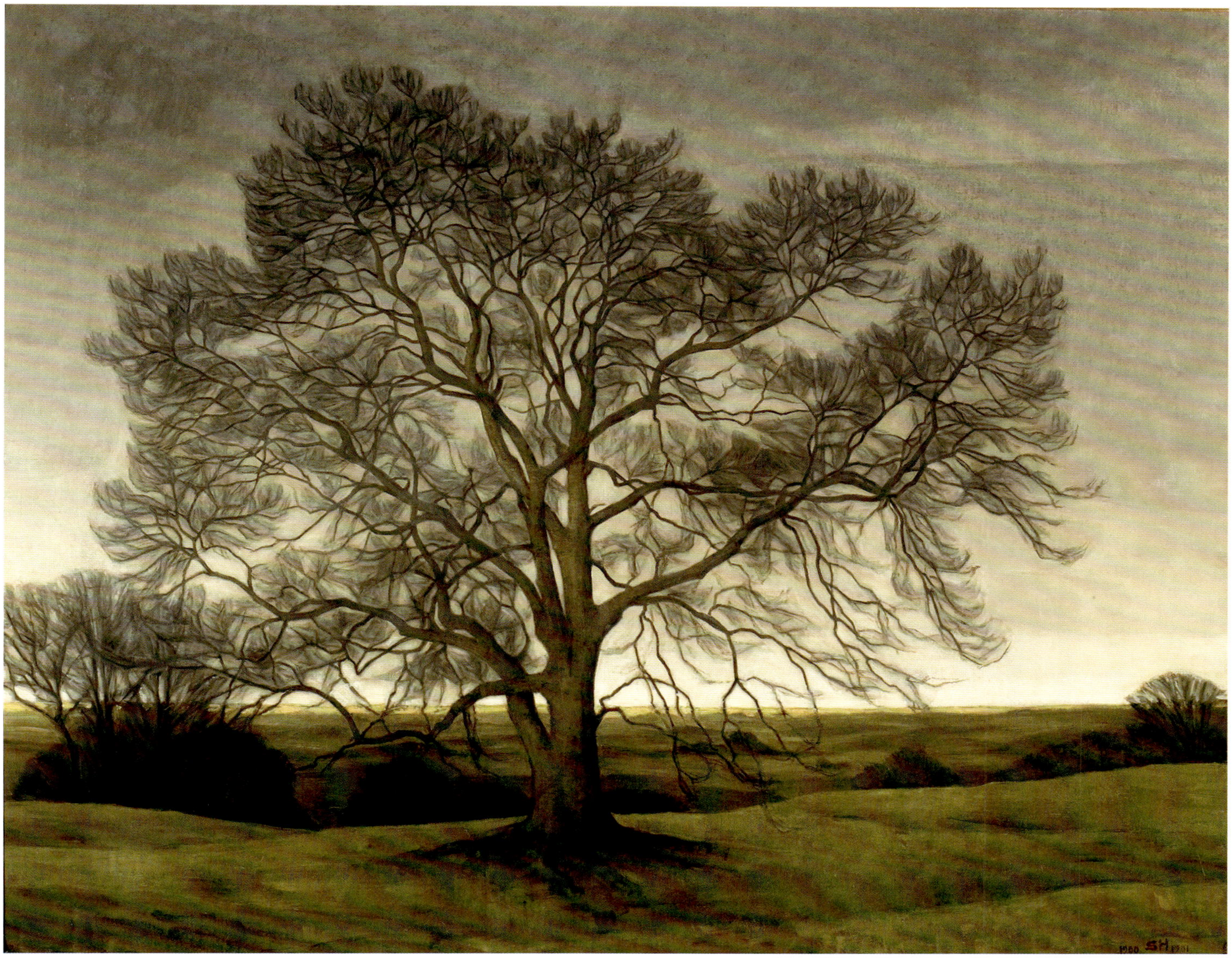

[112]
Svend Hammershøi 1873-1948 Danish
Landscape 1901 1901
Oil on canvas 118 x 144 cm
The Skovgaard Museum, Viborg

squaring-off in pencil. The painter first did a drawn sketch with identical squaring-off but this sketch looks more like a compositional draft than a study of nature. On the whole we know very little about Hammershøi's working method. We do know, however, that other landscape paintings by Hammershøi were done outdoors in front of the subject.[148]

The picture, with its effects, is almost completely unparalleled in Danish art. A single significant exception does come to mind, however. It is Schønheyder Møller's *Sunset. Fontainebleau* from 1900 [114].[149] During his stay in Paris around the turn of the century he experimented with painting landscapes viewed directly against the sun. In the forest view from Fontainebleau he appears to have gone further than in any other painting. He has looked towards the sun between the trees, but the sunlight has taken on such brightness that the lowest parts of the tree trunks appear to dissolve in a sea of fire and lose all their material substance. Similar attempts to capture the intense, almost destructive sunlight were made by a number of other European painters at the same time, especially by the Italian Giuseppe Pellizza and the Pole Wojciech Weiss.[150]

No such destructive forces were ever unleashed by Hammershøi. But he made a single attempt to paint directly against the sunlight in the apparently unfinished painting *Sun over the Sea* [115].[151] Here too he has looked directly at the sun, but has enveloped it in a haze, so it does not have the same intensity as in Schønheyder Møller. The subject itself – a seascape – is likewise unusual for Hammershøi. The sea and the sky take up almost the whole picture surface; only a single ship on the right offers a fixed point of reference in the composition. In the present form of the picture it is difficult to get an accurate impression of how Hammershøi had conceived the finished painting, so it is open to interpretation.[152]

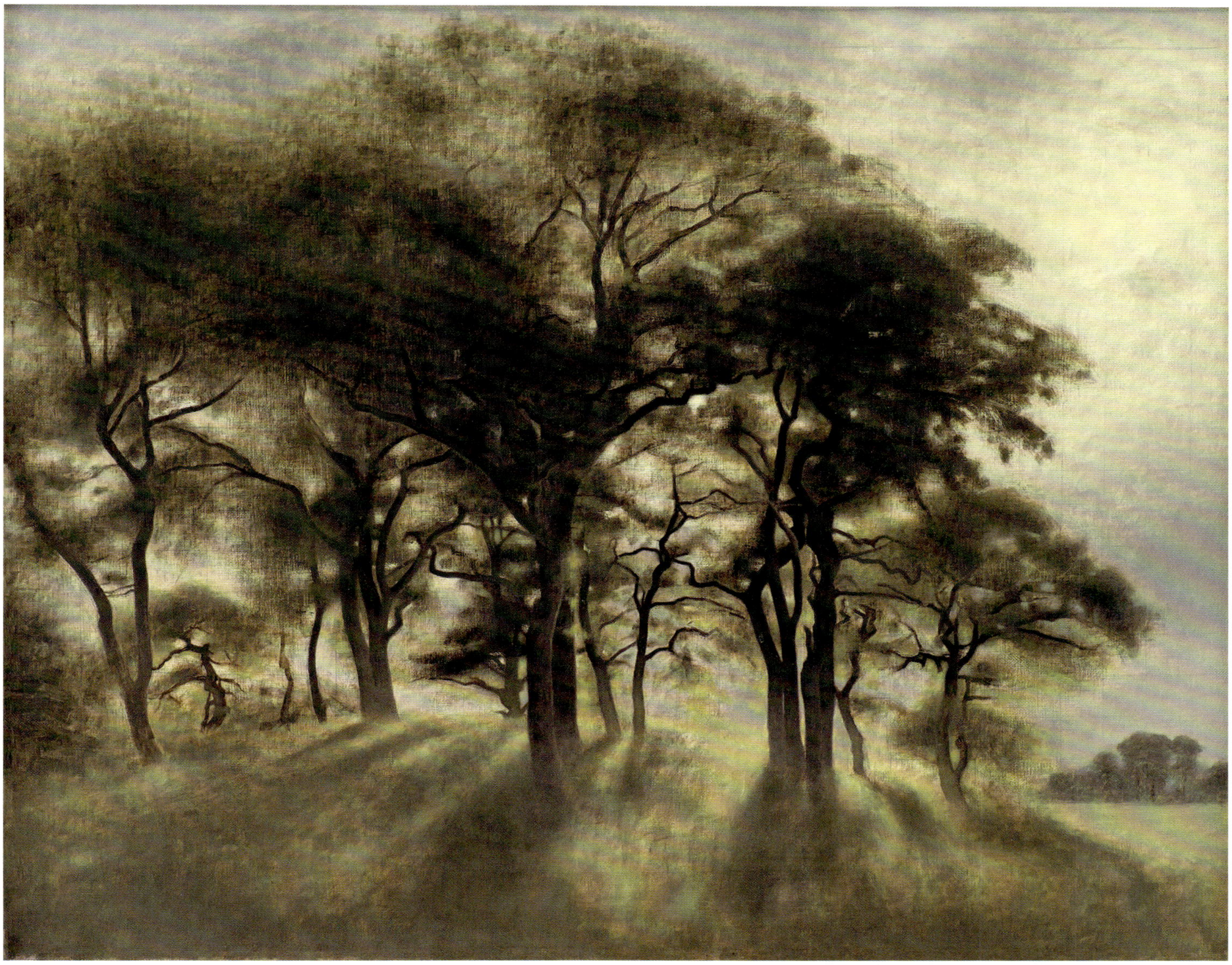

[113]
Vilhelm Hammershøi 1864-1916 Danish
Near Fortunen, Jægersborg Deer Park
North of Copenhagen 1901
Oil on canvas 55 x 66.5 cm
Statens Museum for Kunst

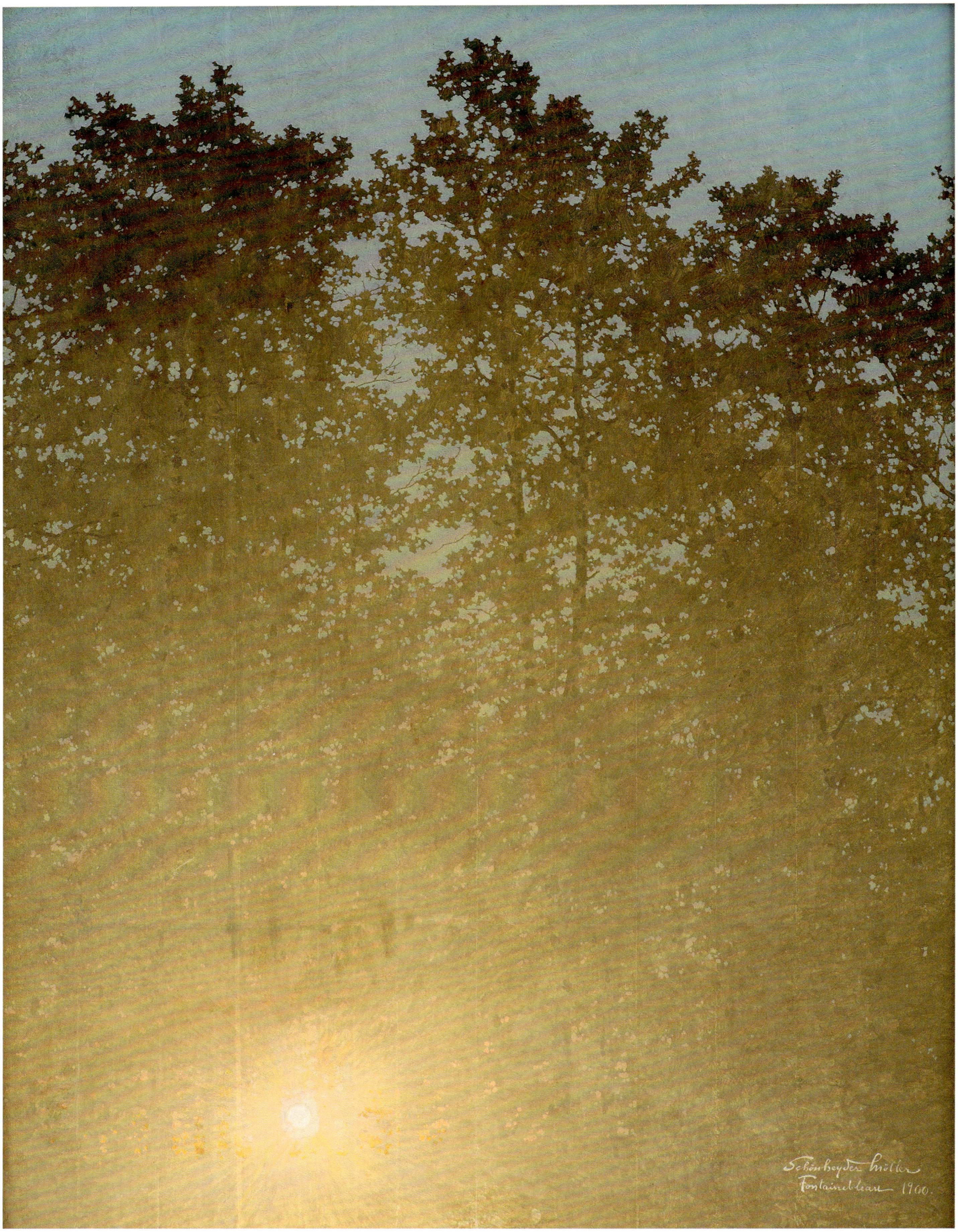
Schönheyder Møller
Fontainebleau 1900.

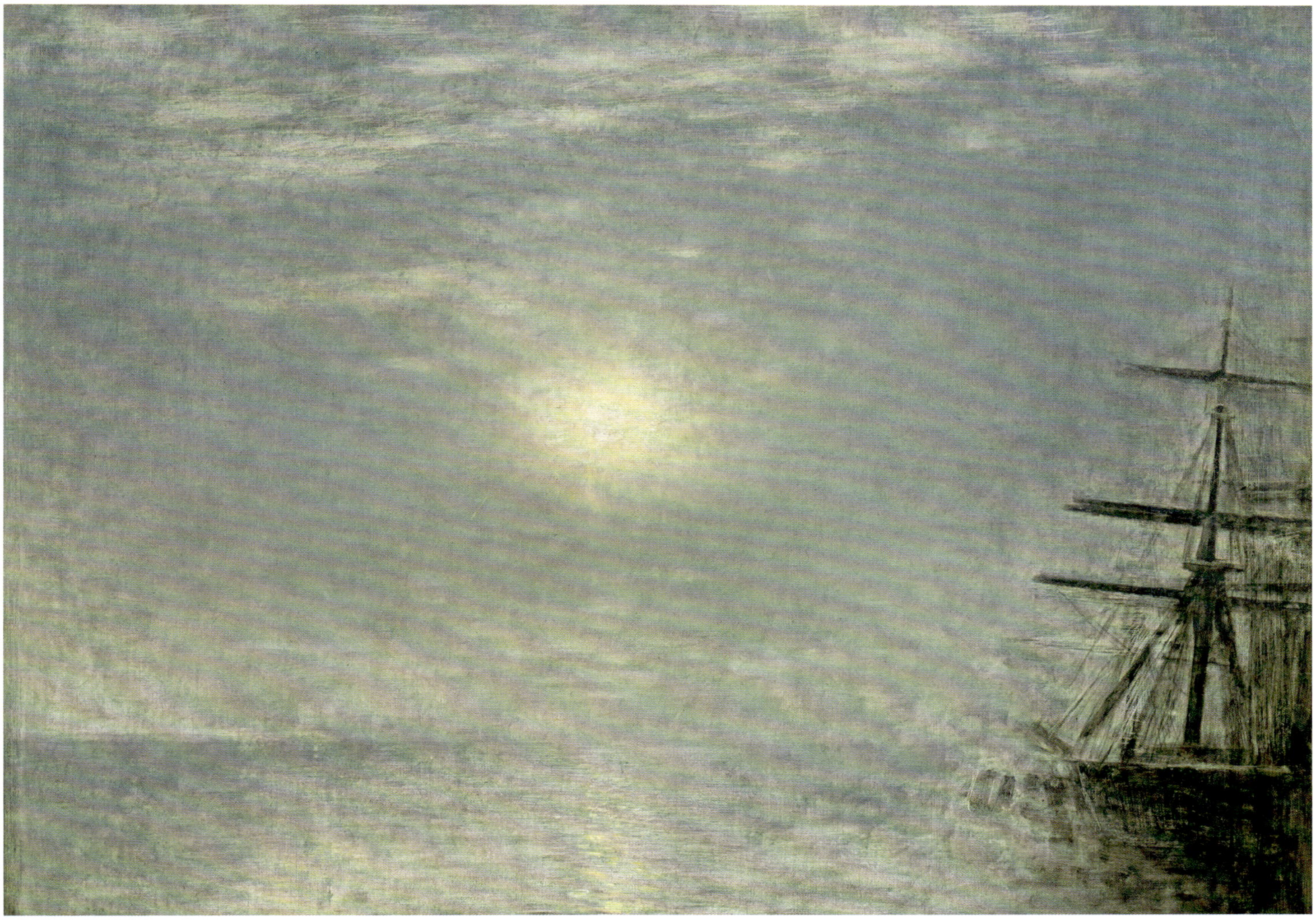

[114]
Valdemar Schønheyder Møller 1864-1905 Danish
Sunset. Fontainebleau 1900
Oil on canvas 116.2 x 88.3 cm
Statens Museum for Kunst

[115]
Vilhelm Hammershøi 1864-1916 Danish
Sun over the Sea c. 1902?
Oil on canvas 54 x 75 cm
Private collection

EPILOGUE:
BACK IN FRONT OF THE MIRROR

In 1911 Hammershøi and his wife spent the summer at the country house "Spurveskjul" near Frederiksdal north of Copenhagen, and in contrast to other summer stays he painted no landscapes there, only pictures from the interiors of the house. The major work was the large self-portrait in which he is standing at the open balcony door [140, p. 199]. But just as significant to his art at this time is the oval *Double Portrait of the Artist and his Wife, seen through a Mirror. The Cottage Spurveskjul* [116].[153] Standing in front of a mirror, he has painted not only himself (with his palette in his right hand as in the reflection), but also his favourite motif: the solitary woman with her back turned, standing in a room where the delicately graduated light floods in the window and door and defines the space. The door is open, but we are not allowed to see what the woman is looking at outside. We can just make out his easel in the right of the picture, but we do not see the picture he is painting – or rather, that is just what we do see: it is the painting we are looking at right now. Perhaps it is quite telling that he has placed himself in the shadow, while his wife in the balcony door stands in the sunlight. As the modest man he was, he did not try to attract any particular attention to himself. The painting is one of a number of self-portraits he painted at the time and is unlikely to be quite finished. But it still seems serene and stands out from the others, as it sums up his artistic endeavours.

Hammershøi has thoroughly scrutinized his own face, but has possibly observed, more than analysed what he saw. It is a man marked by life that we see in the self-portrait. He looks older than his age – just 47. What he did not know when he painted the picture was that a couple of years later he would become seriously ill with the cancer that cost him his life just under five years later. Perhaps he was already marked by the illness when he painted it. Hammershøi's artistic production began to wane significantly as early as 1912, and the double portrait from Spurveskjul can therefore, more than any other painting, be regarded as his artistic testament.

Kasper Monrad (born 1952), Chief Curator at Statens Museum for Kunst, is a specialist on Danish and European art of the 19th century, particularly the so-called Danish Golden Age (1800-50). He has curated a great number of exhibitions of the art of the period. He has written on Hammershøi's art on several occasions and has contributed articles for the catalogues of the Hammershøi exhibitions in Gothenburg and Stockholm (1999-2000) and Hamburg (2003).

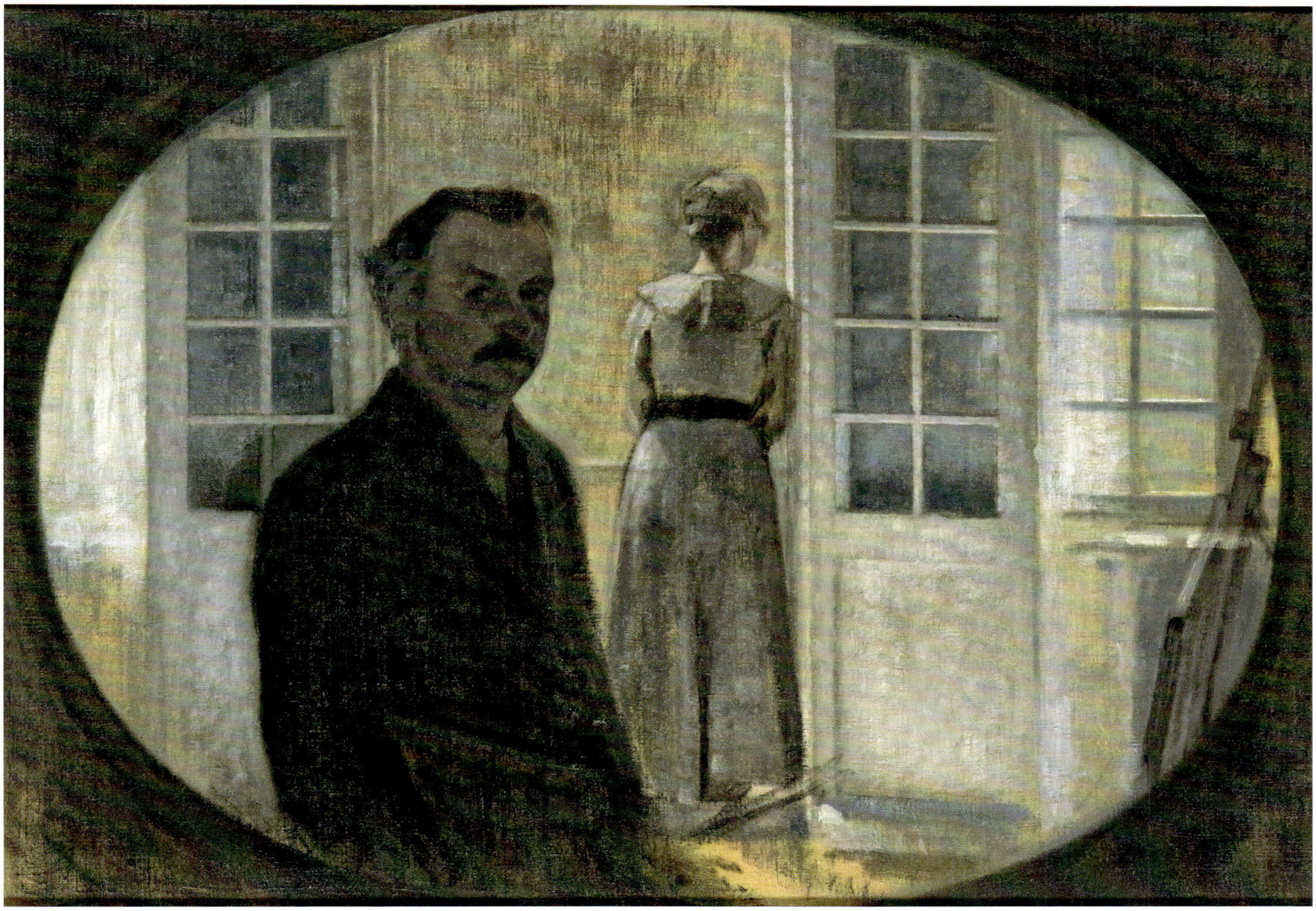

[116]
Vilhelm Hammershøi 1864-1916 Danish
Double Portrait of the Artist and his Wife, seen through a Mirror. The Cottage Spurveskjul 1911
Oil on canvas 55.2 x 76 cm
Private collection, Professor Günther Fielmann – Schierensee Manor

NOTES

1 This section is a reworked version of my article "Stories that are not told," in *Copenhagen, 2000,* pp. 245-257.

2 *Politiken*, 4 June 1886; quoted from *Copenhagen 1983*, p. 13.

3 Hammershøi alternated roughly speaking between two types of interior: on the one hand, pictures where his whole interest was concentrated on the rendering of the light, the atmosphere and the space; on the other, pictures where the interplay between the solitary figure and the room plays the crucial role. But of course the boundaries between the two types are fluid.

4 Cf. Vad, 1988 (1992), pp. 200-203, 204f; Görel Cavalli-Björkman, "Såsom i en spegel. Vilhelm Hammershøi och det holländska interiörmåleriet," in Gothenburg & Stockholm 1999, pp. 20-25; and Anne-Birgitte Fonsmark, "Vilhelm Hammershøi: At the Edge of the Golden Age of Danish Painting," in London 2008, pp. 29-37.

5 Cf. *Dagbladet*, 28 April 1888, quoted from *ibid.*, cat. no. 43.

6 Vad, 1988 (1992), 234, repr. 229.

7 Cf. Vad, 1988 (1992), p. 134.

8 *Politiken*, 4 May 1894; cf. Vad, 1988 (1992), pp. 123f.

9 Mogens Nykjær has discussed the relationship between the figures and has drawn parallels to contemporary Danish Symbolist poetry, although without pointing to direct sources of inspiration; cf. Nykjær, 1991, pp. 147f.

10 It is difficult to tell whether the man's androgynous character is intended by Hammershøi or whether the painter's modesty has prevented him giving the naked man a more decidedly masculine appearance.

11 Cf. Peter Michael Hornung & Kasper Monrad, *C.W. Eckersberg – dansk malerkunsts fader*, Copenhagen 2005, pp. 288-296.

12 One has to be very cautious about drawing parallels between Hammershøi's pictures and his private life. His preserved correspondence with his wife Ida (The Hirschsprung Collection, Copenhagen) is typified by warmth and intimacy.

13 Quote from Vad, 1988 (1992), p. 176.

14 Björn Fredlund's discussion of the subject is in Gothenburg & Stockholm 1999, 88 cat. 23.

15 Review in *Adresseavisen*, 26 April 1902, quoted from Bente Scavenius: *Den frie Udstilling i 100 år*, Copenhagen 1991, p. 78.

16 This was first noted by Wilhelm Wanscher; cf. Wanscher 1915, p. 407.

17 At the Universal Exposition in Paris in 1889 Hammershøi exhibited four paintings: *Portrait of Young Woman* [32], *An Old Woman* [2], *Young Girl Sewing* [3] and *A Baker's Shop* (Vejen Kunstmuseum; Vad, 1988 (1992), pp. 57, 63).

18 Rohde, 1955, pp. 65f.

19 Cf. Emil Hannover's statements from 1893 and 1903, quoted in Rohde 1955, pp. 9, 38.

20 Cf. de Font-Réaulx & Bolloch, 2006.

21 Cf. Bordeaux, New York & Pittsburgh 2000.

22 A comprehensive collection of these photographs is preserved in the Bibliothèque Nationale, Paris.

23 The preserved photos from Hammershøi's photographic collection are kept at The Hirschsprung Collection, Copenhagen. Cf. Svenningsen, 2011.

24 For the discussion of Hammershøi and photography, cf. Vad, 1988 (1992), pp. 369-372; Gertrud Oelsner in Skagen 2001, pp. 85-89 & Oelsner, 2002.

25 See for example Heilbrun, 2008.

26 Cf. Knapp, 1988, & Faber, 2010.

27 Cf. Paris 1889.

28 The painting belongs to the New Carlsberg Glyptotek, Copenhagen; cf. Hornung, 2002, pp. 221-225.

29 Cf. Claus Olsen, "Anna Ancher in Paris 1889" in Hannover, Copenhagen & Skagen 1994-95, pp. 123-129 & Peter Nørgaard Larsen, "Puvis de Chavannes and the North" in Venice 2002, pp. 253-255.

30 Rohde, 1955, p. 77.

31 Paris, 1889, cat. 558. Cf. Paris & Ottawa, 1976, pp. 102f, cat. 77. Further, Copenhagen, 1888a & 1888b, cat. 230.

32 Cf. Vad, 1988 (1992), p. 102.

33 The painting, which belongs to The Hirschsprung Collection in Copenhagen, is today much darkened and can best be judged from the charcoal drawing that Hammershøi did as a sketch for the painting; cf. Vad, 1988 (1992), pp. 39-44.

34 Cf. Paris & Ottawa, 1976, pp. 151-154, cat. 131.

35 The relationship was first pointed out by Peter Nørgaard Larsen in Copenhagen 2000, pp. 24-27, 282, cat. 5.

36 Belongs to the Musée d'Orsay, Paris; cf. Paris 1889, 49, cat. 337; Paris, Ottawa & San Francisco 1982, pp. 173-180, cat. 57.

37 Copenhagen, 1888a & 1888b, cat. 123 & 124.

38 Cf. Paris, 1889, 6, cat. 266; compare Rapetti, 2008, 91, cat. 152, 153, 285 & 286 (however, none of these paintings seems to be identical to the painting exhibited in 1889).

39 Rapetti, 2008, 119, cat. 259.

40 Paris, 1889, 90, 165 & 166. Cf. Young et al., 1980, I, pp. 30-32 (cat. 56), pp. 134f (cat. 242).

41 Cf. Vad, 1988, 414, note on p. 61 (1992, 414 note 61).

42 Cf. Brussels, Salzburg & Boston 2004, cat. 12.

43 Quoted from Vad, 1988 (1992), p. 105.

44 Cf. Krämer, 1999, 74 & Kasper Monrad, "Vilhelm Hammershøi – ein internationaler Künstler" in Hamburg 2003, p. 93.

45 Cf. Vad, 1988 (1992), pp. 116f.

46 Letter from Ida Hammershøi to Frederikke Hammershøi, Amsterdam 13 September 1891. Hammershøi Archive, The Hirschsprung Collection.

47 Here I am thinking especially of the painting *From Christianshavn's Canal*, 1905; The David Collection, Copenhagen; cf. Vad, 2003, pp. 366, 414 & Hamburg 2003, cat. 38.

48 Cf. Brussels, 2005, pp. 42f. Dominique Marechal has kindly drawn my attention to this painting.

49 Cf. Berlin, 1905, cat. 55 (*Die vier Kupfer*, 1905).

50 Cf. Monrad, 1997.

51 There is no overview of what was on display at the Galleria Nazionale d'Arte Moderna in 1902-03 when Hammershøi was in Rome, nor is there a complete catalogue of the Gallery's collections; cf. Monrad, 1997, p. 99 note 23.

52 Cf. Monrad, 1997, 100 note 26.

53 Cf. Vad, 1988 (1892), pp. 190, 193 (pl. 125). Hammershøi varied the subject a few years later when he added a female figure at an open window; cf. *ibid.*, p. 373 (pl. 237).

54 Cf. Copenhagen, 1888a & 1888b.

55 Cf. Copenhagen, 1984.

56 Cf. London & Washington, D.C., 2010.

57 Cf. Copenhagen, 1897.

58 Cf. Copenhagen, 2000, p. 142 note 8.

59 Cf. Copenhagen, 1897, cat. 63 (*Memories (Jeunes filles jouant au tennis)*).

60 Cf. Copenhagen, 1897, cat. 345.

61 Cf. Scavenius, 1983, pp. 41-44; & Vad, 1988 (1992), pp. 33-39.

62 Paris, Ottawa & San Francisco 1982, cat. 22.

63 Rapetti, 2008, p. 112, cat. 227.

64 That Hammershøi may in fact have seen a photo of Carrière's painting is confirmed by a photo taken in 1904 by Heinrich Kühn of his colleague Alfred Stieglitz sitting with a photograph of this very painting; cf. Faber 2010, p. 66, cat. 32.

65 Poul Vad has discussed the possible older models for the painting; cf. Vad, 1988 (1992), pp. 124-131. I myself have earlier pointed to possible sources of inspiration in the French painting of the time, especially Puvis de Chavannes and Gauguin; cf. Gothenburg & Stockholm 1999, pp. 11-15. Peter Nørgaard Larsen has also referred to Puvis de Chavannes; cf. Copenhagen 2000, p. 20.

66 See Copenhagen 1984.

67 Cf. Kasper Monrad in Gothenburg & Stockholm 1999, pp. 11, 13.

68 New York 2002, pp. 175-182, cat. 62.

69 Cf. George Szabo in Copenhagen 1986, cat. 33.

70 Young et al., 1980, cat. 101; London, Paris & Washington 1994, cat. 60; & MacDonald, 2003.

71 Cf. Vad, 1988 (1992), p. 414.

72 Cf. Vad, 1988 (1992), pp. 60-62.

73 Cf. Margaret F. MacDonald & Joy Newton, "The selling of Whistler's Mother," in MacDonald, 2003, p. 65-79.

74 Cf. Vad, 1991.

75 Cf. Kasper Monrad in Gothenburg & Stockholm 1999, pp. 12-14.

76 Cf. Vad 1988 (1992), pp. 142f.

77 Cf. Brussels, Salzburg & Boston 2004, cat. 88.

78 Cf. London 2004, cat. 3.

79 Cf. Peter Nørgaard Larsen in Skagen 2009, p. 25.

80 Cf. Washington, New York & Minneapolis 1982, 211, cat. 78 & Leena Ahtola-Moorhouse in London 1986, cat. 81 & Oslo 1987, cat. 99.

81 Cf. for example London, Boston & New York 2006.
82 Cf. London, Paris & Washington, cat. 65.
83 Cf. Vad, 1988 (1992), pp. 47-54.
84 Cf. Brussels, Salzburg & Boston 2004, cat. 59.
85 Paris, 1889, p. 49. cat. 340. Roger Diederen has kindly drawn my attention to this painting.
86 Vincent Pomarède, "Studies and readings" in Madrid & Lisbon 2009, pp. 238f, cat. 33.
87 Paris, Ottawa & San Francisco 1982, pp. 235-240. Hammershøi is unlikely to have seen the painting in the original, but may have seen a copy or a photograph of it.
88 Rapetti 2008, p. 179, cat. 496.
89 Cf. John Klein, "Portraiture and Assimilation of the 'very singular Vallotton'" in New Haven 1991, p. 110. See also Robert Rosenblum's discussion of Hammershøi's painting in Copenhagen, Paris & New York 1997, pp. 46f.
90 Cf. Rohde, 1955, p. 192.
91 Cf. André Cariou in Vejen, 2010, pp. 20f.
92 Vallotton's tempera painting *Tratsch* (Papotage) from 1902 (private collection) shows three female figures grouped similarly to the three women in Hammershøi's *Three Young Women* from 1895 [39], which suggests that the Swiss artist may really have known the Dane's art; cf. Munich & Essen 1995, cat. 41. Felix Krämer has kindly referred me to this painting.
93 *Politiken*, 4 June 1886; quoted from Copenhagen 1983, p. 13.
94 The painting appears to be unknown today; cf. *Nationaltidende*, 23 December 1886, quoted from Kasper Monrad in Copenhagen 1983, cat. 43; cf. also cat. 77 (Wenzel Tornøe).
95 Cf. Vad, 1988 (1992), pp. 369-371.
96 Cf. Krämer, 2007, pp. 155-157.
97 Cf. Copenhagen, Paris & New York 1997, cat. 67.
98 Cf. Hornung, 1993, pp. 130-132.
99 Cf. Krämer, 2006, pp. 124-152; Zürich & Hamburg 2008, pp. 19-45.
100 Cf. Angelika Wesenberg in London & Washington, D.C. 2001, cat. 62 & Berlin 2002, pp. 122f, cat. 129.
101 Woll. 2008, I, pp. 194f, 284, cat. 192 & 302; Gerd Woll, "Use and Re-use in Munch's Earliest Paintings," in Oslo 2008, pp. 94-97, cat. 107; & Chicago 2009, p. 37, cat. 34.
102 Tøjner, 2000, p. 93; cf. London, 1992, p. 12; Prideaux, 2005, p. 120.
103 Prideaux, 2005, p. 121; Dieter Buchhart in Copenhagen 2009, pp. 13f.
104 Jay A. Clarke in Chicago 2009, pp. 51, 198.
105 The first version of this subject is in a private Swedish collection (cf. Bramsen & Michaëlis, 1918, no. 67; & London, 2008, cat. 9). The version shown here is a copy from the same year (Bramsen & Michaëlis no. 68; cf. Vad 1988 (1992), pp. 62, 73, 401).
106 For Hammershøi's apartment in Strandgade, cf. Vad 1988 (1992), pp. 185-195.
107 In this painting Hammershøi painted a black-clad woman on the left of the table, but the first owner, the painter's close acquaintance Leonard Borwick, was dissatisfied with the figure and folded the painting before 1909 so she could no longer be seen – possibly with Hammershøi's (tacit?) acceptance, since he must have seen the painting at Borwick's home; cf. Vad 1988 (1992), p. 265. The painting now appears closely related to *Study in Sunlight. Strandgade 30* from 1906 (David Collection, Copenhagen; cf. London 2008, cat. 48).
108 Cf. London 2008, cat. 38.
109 Cf. Amsterdam & Brussels 2000, pp. 27-37.
110 Cf. Emily Brown in Washington, New York & Minneapolis 1982, pp. 124, 128 & Kasper Monrad in Hamburg 2003, p. 99, cat. 70.
111 Cf. Vad, 1988 (1992), pp. 318, 388.
112 Cf. Paris 1993, cat. 6 & Copenhagen, Paris & New York 1997, cat. 6.
113 Cf. Vad, 1988 (1992), pp. 241-244.
114 Repr. Vad, 1988 (1992), p. 242.
115 Glasgow & Amsterdam 1990, cat. 55.
116 Copenhagen 1897, cat. 345.
117 Cf. Rohde, 1955, p. 115.
118 Cf. Detroit 1984, cat. 42 & Rennes 2004, cat. 41.
119 Cf. Glasgow & Amsterdam 1990, cat. 105; Reynaerts et al., 2003, pp. 85f.
120 Cf. London, Paris, & Washington 1994, pp. 120-131.
121 *Politiken*, 22 November 1905.
122 David Collection, Copenhagen; cf. Hamburg 3003, cat. 38.
123 Seurat's painting once belonged to the Danish art collector Christian Tetzen-Lund, but he bought it in Paris around New Year 1916-17, i.e. after Hammershøi's death; cf. Lennart Gottlieb, "Tetzen-Lunds samling – om dens historie, indhold og betydning," *Kunst og Museum*, XIX, 1984, p. 42. However, Tetzen-Lund quickly sold the painting again, for as early as 1923 it was acquired by the Národní Galerie in Prague; cf. New York 1991, cat. 170.
124 Musée d'Orsay, Paris; inv. no. PHO 1987 20 149.
125 Cf. London 2008, cat. 71. The painting was formerly called *The Jewish School in Guilford Street, London*, but this title is misleading, and the painting shows *The Jews' College's "Rabbinical Seminary"*, which was in Guilford Street; kindly reported by MaryAnne Stevens.
126 Cf. Glasgow & Amsterdam 1990, cat. 53 & Paris 1993, cat. 7.
127 Copenhagen 1897, cat. 345 (*A Maisonette in Amsterdam*).
128 Cf. Viborg, Hellerup & Næstved 2008, p. 131.
129 This section is indebted to my article "Vilhelm Hammershøis Landschaften" in Cologne 1998, pp. 41-45.
130 Cf. Kasper Monrad, "El ser humano y la naturaleza. El arte nórdico a comienzos de siglo" in Madrid & Barcelona 1995, pp. 23-31 (Eng. transl. "Man and Nature: Scandinavian Art at the Turn of the Century," pp. 286f).
131 Cf. Hamburg 2003, cat. 1 & 2; London 2008, cat. 1 & 3.
132 Brussels, Salzburg & Boston 2004, cat. 152.
133 Cf. Kasper Monrad in *The Golden Age of Danish Painting*. Exhibition catalogue. Los Angeles County Museum of Art & Metropolitan Museum of Art, New York 1993, pp. 17f, 177-190, and in Götz Czymmek (ed.), *Aus Dänemarks goldener Zeit. Landschaftsmalerei des früheren 19. Jahrhunderts aus dem Statens Museum for Kunst, Kopenhagen*. Exhibition catalogue. Wallraf-Richartz-Museum, Cologne 1995, pp. 37-40, 112-125.
134 Cf. Vad, 1988 (1992), pp. 258f, pl. 167; Copenhagen, Paris & New York 1997, cat. 31; London 2008, cat. 36.
135 Cf. Vad, 1988 (1992), pp. 260f, pl. 228; Copenhagen, Paris & New York 1997, cat. 22. For Lundbye's painting from Refsnæs, cf. Stig Miss et al., *Johan Thomas Lundbye 1818-1848. [...] at male det kjære Danmark*. Exhibition catalogue. The Thorvaldsen Museum, Copenhagen 1994, 36, cat. 4 & Lausanne 2005, cat. 62 (the subject is from Zealand, not Jutland).
136 Robert Rosenblum in Copenhagen, Paris & New York 1997, p. 40.
137 Cf. Dabrowski, 1999, p. 17.
138 Cf. Schwartz, 2004, pp. 112-116.
139 London 2004, pp. 24f, cat. 17; Schwartz, 2004, p. 115.
140 Cf. Vad, 1988 (1992), pp. 156-158; & Copenhagen, Paris & New York 1997, cat. 11.
141 Cf. Paris & New York 1991, cat. 79.
142 Cf. Knapp, 1988, pp. 14f, pl. 6.
143 Peter Nørgaard Larsen, in the section "The Tree and the Forest. Allegories of Human Life", in Copenhagen 2000, pp. 85-91, cat. 44.
144 Cf. Viborg, Hellerup & Næstved 2008, p. 127.
145 See especially the chapter "The Evocative Landscape: The 1890s and the Turn of the Century," in Gunnarsson, 1998, pp. 202-269; and Haavard Rostrup in Copenhagen 2002, p. 72.
146 Cf. Detroit 1984, cat. 44.
147 Copenhagen, Paris & New York 1997, cat. 42; & London 2008, cat. 33.
148 Cf. letters from Svend Hammershøi to Anna Hammershøi, undated [summer 1896], quoted in Vad 1988 (1992), pp. 156f.
149 Cf. Oelsner, 2002, p. 36.
150 Cf. resp. Trento 1990, cat. 41; Detroit 1984, cat. 80 & Rennes 2004, cat. 64.
151 The painting is undated, but was probably done in 1902; cf. Vad, 2003, p. 500.
152 Henrik Wivel has tentatively dated the painting as Hammershøi's last, i.e. from 1915, and has interpreted it in the light of his serious illness and imminent death the next year; cf. Wivel, 1996, pp. 60f.
153 Cf. Vad, 1988 (1992), pp. 304-309.

HAMMERSHØI AND ENGLAND[1]

MARYANNE STEVENS

In contrast to other European cities, London was the focus of several extended visits undertaken by Hammershøi. Hitherto, the motivation for these sojourns, and the impact that they may have had on his artistic and personal life have been little explored. By reviewing the existing documentation about his travels and focusing on all the potential contacts he made or may have made during his trips, this article aims to rectify that situation. The result is a far more nuanced and wide-ranging picture of the significance for Hammershøi of his engagement with England.

Hammershøi's visual world was one informed by intensely personal experience: interiors of his apartments, portraits of his family and a small circle of close friends, landscapes and cityscapes derived from familiar locations in close proximity to his places of permanent residence in Copenhagen. Such a repertoire, crafted through a subtly graduated tonal range of greys and imbued with the inner stillness of suspended time, has caused the artist to be perceived as unadventurous, sedentary and averse to travel and unfamiliar or foreign experiences.[2] However, the biographical facts to a certain extent belie this perception. During his life, he journeyed beyond Denmark on twelve occasions, visiting artistic centres in the Netherlands, Germany, Belgium and Italy, and taking up residence for significant periods of time in at least four cities: Paris, Florence, Rome and London. Yet, while he was once resident in Rome (1902-03), and twice in Paris (1889, 1891) and in Florence (1893, 1907), he came to England six times, four of which involved extended sojourns in London. Equally telling is the record of his exposure internationally through group and solo exhibitions. Outside Denmark, his work was included in group exhibitions across Europe and in the United States, from the two Paris International Exhibitions of 1889 and 1900, the Venice Biennale (1903) and the Rome Exposizione Internazionale (1911) to shows in Berlin, Munich, St Petersburg, New York and Chicago, and London (1904, 1907). However, in terms of solo exhibitions outside Denmark during his lifetime, although he had one show organised by Galerie Eduard Schulte which travelled from Berlin to Cologne, Dusseldorf and Hamburg in 1905, it was in London that he not only had a solo show in 1907, but also mounted two private exhibitions for friends and invited guests, in 1912 and 1913.

This apparently disproportionate engagement with England demands closer scrutiny and explanation. To be sure, the author of the major study on Hammershøi, Poul Vad, has touched upon Hammershøi's visits to England,[3] but a perfectly understandable absence of familiarity with the London cultural scene during the period, together with a persistent interpretation of the artist as a shy recluse who seemed to spend his times in London in quasi social and artistic isolation, has led to a misrepresentation of the realities of Hammershøi's English experiences, his level of interest in, and engagement with life in the city, and a somewhat limited understanding of the motives which drove the artist to return with such consistency to this country. Careful study of the archive material pertaining to Alfred Bramsen, Leonard Borwick, and Ida and Vilhlem Hammershøi deposited primarily with The Hirschsprung Collection, consisting of extensive correspondence between the former two and between the Hammershøis and the artist's mother, Frederikke Hammershøi, press cuttings, photographs and postcards cast a somewhat different light on these matters. [4]

Before addressing such issues as Hammershøi's motive, purpose, engagement and ambition in respect of England, it is worth reviewing the facts concerning Hammershøi's six visits to the country.

Hammershøi visited London for the first time, with Ida, his wife, over the winter of 1897-98. Having left Copenhagen on 8 October, and travelling via Amsterdam,[5] Haarlem, The Hague, Scheveningen, Delft and Schiedam to Rotterdam,[6] the Hammershøis arrived in London on 24 October.[7] They stayed initially at Miss Salter's boarding house at 38 Woburn Place, Russell Square, just to the east of the British Museum,[8] and then, from 26 November moved to a two-bedroom apartment nearby at 20 Burton Crescent.[9] After a brief return to Copenhagen for Christmas (from 22 December to early January, 1898), they were back in London probably by 8 January,[10] remaining there until late May 1898;[11] they are recorded to

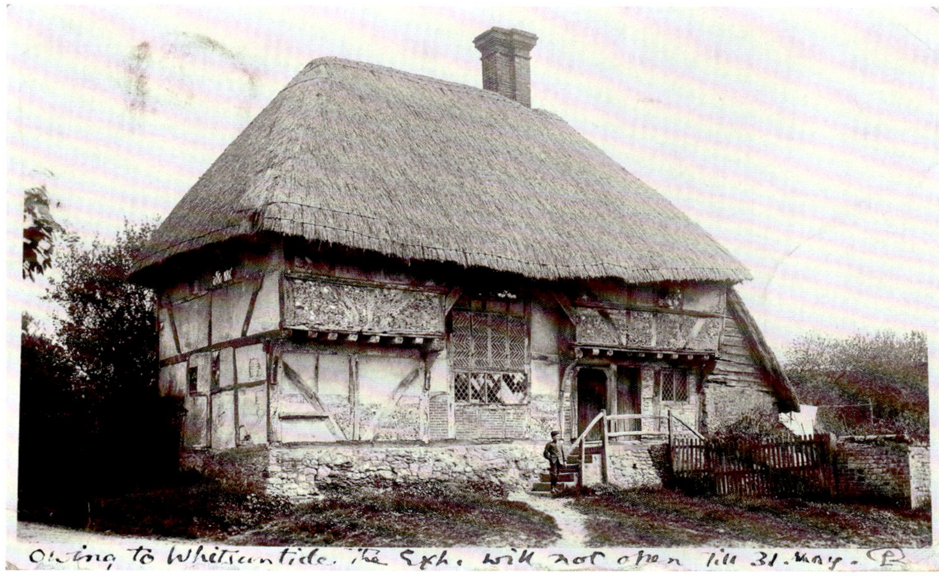

be in Copenhagen on 28 May.[12] Although during the period before Christmas it would appear that the Hammershøis moved almost exclusively in Danish-speaking circles, which included the two children, Henry and Karen, of Alfred Bramsen, Hammershøi's major Danish collector and supporter, who were also boarding with Miss Salter, they started to move in English circles after their return from Copenhagen in early January. This was in part due to a chance meeting on their return trip with the Icelandic scholar and lecturer at King's College London, Dr Jon Stefánsson.[13] This led to introductions to Mrs Ridley, widow of Matthew White Ridley, an erstwhile artist friend of James McNeill Whistler, and to the watercolourist and disciple of John Ruskin, W. G. Collingwood.[14] It was also during this spring that Hammershøi was conducted to the studio of G.F. Watts RA,[15] almost certainly visited the Royal Academy's annual Summer Exhibition[16] and attempted to call in person on Whistler.[17] Hammershøi created five works while he was in London.

Six years were to elapse before the Hammershøis returned to England, orchestrated through the concert pianist and collector, Leonard Borwick (1868-1925), who, one year earlier, had been seduced by the artist's work and had made the acquaintance of Alfred Bramsen in Copenhagen.[18] Through the careful machinations of Bramsen and Borwick,[19] the Hammershøis were invited to spend eight days in mid-September at Borwick's Elizabethan farmhouse at Westburton, Sussex [117],[20] followed by a few additional days in London prior to their return to Copenhagen. During this visit, apart from meeting the English artist, Edward Stott ARA (1839-1918), who lived at Amberley near Westburton, Borwick engineered introductions for Hammershøi to two London art galleries, Obach & Colnaghi, and the Dutch Gallery run by E. J. van Wisselingh.[21]

Exploration of a possible solo exhibition in 1905[22] at one of these two London galleries may have informed Hammershøi's decision to return to the capital later that year. Various letters reveal that the couple arrived from Amsterdam between 9 and 11 November 1905,[23] settling into accommodation at 58 Bloomsbury Street, at the southeast corner of the British

[117]
Unknown photographer
Leonard Borwick's farm house in Sussex 1907
Postcard
The Hirschsprung Collection, Copenhagen

Museum. [24] They remained in London over Christmas, and only returned to Copenhagen in mid February 1906. Christmas itself was celebrated at London's Roman Catholic Cathedral in Westminster and a meal of excellent Danish fare sent by Frederikke, while visits were undertaken to Richmond and Hampton Court.[25] Their social life was guaranteed by the return of Borwick to London after a foreign concert tour, acquaintance with the talented violinist and widow of Sir Charles Hallé, Lady Wilma Neruda Norman Hallé, and attendance at concerts.[26] Artistic activity involved the making of two paintings of the British Museum [87, 121] and further determination to secure a solo exhibition in London the following May.

Logical though it would have been for Hammershøi to visit London during the spring of 1907 in order to enjoy the public exposure of his work in two exhibitions, he chose instead to travel to Florence during the autumn. Indeed, Ida and Vilhelm did not return to the capital until 1912, when the artist records a brief visit to London in June,[27] during which he saw Borwick and had a meeting with the New York dealer, exhibition impresario and critic, Christian Brinton,[28] followed by an extended sojourn lasting from early November to 30 December 1912.[29] Resident at York House, 8 Brunswick Square, Bloomsbury, this visit saw the artist and his wife, once again through an introduction from Leonard Borwick, moving into the circle of Jack and Ada Nettleship (father- and mother-in-law of the artist Augustus John) and their two musician daughters, the singer Ursula and the cellist Ethel,[30] a busy social and concert-going life,[31] and the creation of four important works which were presented in a private exhibition in December.[32] The Hammershøis' final visit to London took place in April 1913.[33] This involved a day trip to Borwick's country house at Westburton,[34] and a private exhibition of the work which Hammershøi had produced in London at the Nettleship's house on Wigmore Street on 10 April.[35]

Having sketched in the frequency and general character of Hammershøi's six visits to England made between 1897 and 1913, it is necessary to address a number of questions. What provoked the initial decision to visit the country? What personal connections did he establish there? What were the implications for his creative practice? What were the artistic opportunities presented to him? What was his critical reception? What was his level of success?

For an artist training in Copenhagen in the 1880s, both at the Danish Royal Academy and with the Paris trained painter P. S. Krøyer, it would have been normal for Hammershøi, who was overtly seeking an artistic language outside that of the academic convention, to have continued his study in Paris like many of his contemporaries. The city was the recognised art capital of the world, providing extensive opportunities for artistic formation within the reformed Ecôle des Beaux-Arts and through a vigorous network of private academies, and for the establishment of a reputation through its state-authorised annual Salons and its burgeoning provision of commercial art galleries. Indeed, Hammershøi would have encountered an extensive international cohort of art students there, including a significant number drawn from Scandinavian countries, including Denmark. Despite a brief visit in 1889 and a sojourn in 1891-2, which included a passing interest in his work from the gallerist and supporter of the Impressionists, Durand-Ruel, Hammershøi chose rather to explore the potential of London as the centre for the establishment of his non-Danish artistic career. But what brought England, and London, to his attention?

Despite no initial mastery of the English language, Hammershøi had developed a taste in his youth for English literature through translation, notably the works of Charles Dickens, for whose *Pickwick Papers* he had provided illustrations.[36] With the establishment of his friendship in 1888 with Alfred Bramsen,[37] Copenhagen dentist, art collector, music enthusiast, and lifelong supporter of, and apologist for Hammershøi, the artist entered a family of anglophiles. Bramsen spoke and wrote English, had English friends such as the concert pianist Leonard Borwick, maintained connections with Danes resident in London, such as W. S. Prior,[38] and evidently encouraged his two musically gifted children, Henry and Karen to further their musical careers not in Germany, as was the norm at the end of the 19th century, but in London: Henry, a cellist,[39] was advised by William Archer, the critic, strong advocate of Scandinavian literature, notably that of Henrik Ibsen, and acquaintance of Georg Brandes, on musical opportunities in London,[40] and Karen, a violinist, studied at the Guildhall School of Music and Drama in the later 1890s.[41] With both children resident at Miss Salter's boarding house in Woburn Place, Russell Square, an establishment which, although evidently providing accommodation for English guests,[42] was run by someone who was possibly Danish,[43] it would have been natural for Hammershøi to have viewed London in a sympathetic light.

Indeed, contrary to Poul Vad's assertion that Hammershøi's "reason for [visiting London] remains unknown",[44] it could be argued that Alfred Bramsen's enthusiasm for London as a proven cultural centre, the presence in the city of a Danish ex-patriot community initially represented by the Bramsen children but swiftly extended to such figures as Oskar Hansen, a journalist,[45] and Dr. Jon Stefánsson, together with the possibility of meeting in person the artist, James McNeill Whistler who was a part-time resident, suggested the city to be a more congenial place for study and the promotion of his career than Paris, whose potential as a capital of the arts he had clearly not appreciated. In addition, he may have understood, again possibly through Bramsen, that, London was potentially as viable an alternative European centre for the visual arts as Paris. The Royal Academy's annual Summer Exhibition provided a platform for the display of over 1200 works, attracted annually an average of 350,000 visitors and provided a conduit for the sale of works and the making of professional reputations. Critically acclaimed alternative exhibiting bodies such as the Grosvenor Gallery (established 1877), the New English Art Club (established 1886), the New Gallery (established 1888) and the International Society of Sculptors, Painters and Gravers (established 1897) provided similar financial and critical opportunities. And the art market was buoyant: it ensured financial success for artists and an ever expanding number of commercial art dealers and galleries, many of whom had international associations with galleries in Paris, Amsterdam and New York. All of these elements provided the structures necessary for the launch of a successful career.

From the beginning of his association with England, Hammershøi appears to have adopted a positive attitude. Writing to his mother from Rotterdam, on 23 October 1897, he records that both Ida and he were much looking forward to living in London.[46] Once he had arrived, despite fears about their inability to speak the language, Ida reports that English did not seem to be so difficult to understand, that she was determined to learn the language and that contrary to the received characterisation of the English as being formal and distant, they were very helpful.[47] This sense of being welcome and at home in England is maintained throughout their six visits: Dr. Stefánsson extended hospitality in 1898 to include the Hammershøis in social events around Mrs. Ridley, invited Vilhelm to lectures and took him to dine at an English Club;[48] Borwick is reported to have been incredibly friendly, kind and hospitable during their September 1904 visit;[49] in 1905 Ida can report that they both "really feel at home",[50] enjoy attending concerts with Borwick and entertaining at a venerable London public house called "Ye Olde Cheshire Cheese";[51] and by 1912, the correspondence reveals a determination by Vilhelm to master English by taking lessons from Ethel Nettleship, as well as a relatively intense social life focused around Borwick, Borwick's recently widowed sister, Mrs. Norman, the Nettleship family, especially Ethel, visits to concerts and the theatre[52] and further entertaining at home and at the "Ye Olde Cheshire Cheese". Set against this level of social integration, it is not surprising, despite Vilhelm's characteristically nervous description, that the two private exhibitions held in December 1912[53] and April 1913,[54] were not only well attended, due to the lists of invitees being drawn up by his well-connected English friends, Borwick and Ada Nettleship, but also, in the case of the latter, could include such distinguished members of the English cultural and critical world as the critics and journalists Clutton Brock and Charles Lewis Hind, collectors, including Frederick Kelly and possibly Robert Witt and society ladies such as the Grimston sisters.[55] Connections with England even extended to Denmark: when selecting work for the exhibition of Danish Art for the Guildhall, the director of the art gallery, Alfred George Temple, through Alfred Bramsen, visited Hammershøi in his Copenhagen studio in 1907, noting that the artist was a "shy man, of rare and sensitive gifts" but whose manipulation of a restricted palette none the less remarkably attained "a sense of occupation and completeness [...] on every canvas".[56]

London also opened up a world of museums, exhibitions, connections with fellow artists, exhibition possibilities, potential collectors and critical acclaim, which responded directly to Hammershøi's interests and could be used to further his own career. From his correspondence, and from his photographic archive and postcard collection, it is evident that Hammershøi was a committed visitor to museums and art galleries whether he was in Amsterdam, The Hague, Munich or Berlin, Italian cities or London.[57] It should be noted, however, that despite the extent and regularity of correspondence generated during his six visits to England, Hammershøi only details such activities during the first visit of 1897-98. By the end of November 1897, for example, the Hammershøis have visited the National Gallery twice, and went daily to the British Museum, where they were especially enthralled by the holdings of Greek (the Parthenon Frieze), Assyrian and Egyptian art, as well as being impressed by "long cases displaying ceramics and glass".[58] Modern and contemporary art was also studied: they probably visited the recently opened Tate Gallery on 25 November,[59] the Royal Academy's Summer Exhibition in May 1898,[60] and, at the invitation of Mrs Matthew White Ridley, another unidentified exhibition with which Vilhelm was decidedly unimpressed.[61] Likewise, the viewing of work by individual contemporary artists was also pursued. Hammershøi's visit to the studio of one of the most celebrated of contemporary artists, G. F. Watts RA, in February 1898 where they "saw a lot of his paintings",[62] took advantage of a facility established by highly successful and sought after artists resident in London such as Frederick Leighton PRA, Luke Fildes RA and J. E. Millais RA, who used part of their architect-designed, purpose-built houses to advertise their art to a discerning public through providing access on specific days in the week to the spaces specifically designed for the display of their own works of art.[63]

Hammershøi did not meet G. F. Watts, nor did he express any interest in the older artist's work. Indeed, although his support of contemporary British art might be assumed through his membership of the committee, together with Alfred Bramsen, that took responsibility for mounting the exhibition of contemporary British art by members of the London based

International Society of Sculptors, Painters and Gravers in Copenhagen in 1909,[64] Hammershøi passed few comments upon his English fellow artists, and those few that he did were not complimentary.[65] Furthermore, he makes no positive reference to the work of the two artists whom we have record that he did meet: W. G. Collingwood (1854-1932) and Edward Stott (1859-1918). Collingwood, a watercolourist, antiquarian, archaeologist and the first "official" biographer of John Ruskin (1893), shared a keen interest in Nordic myth and Norse lore with Dr. Jon Stefánsson. Stefánsson introduced Hammershøi to Collingwood in January 1898[66] at a club (possibly the Scottish Society or the Viking Society) where Collingwood was lecturing about his study visit to Iceland in the summer of 1897, accompanied by a large number of his watercolours, which Hammershøi thought "did not have much to do with art".[67] In the case of Edward Stott RA, whom Hammershøi had met through Borwick in Sussex in 1904, no evaluation of his work is made, although Stott's crepuscular scenes hinting at more abstract ideas, for example the seasons and the passing of time treated in a slightly tachiste technique, such as *Changing Pastures* (1893) [119] and *Starlight: Landscape* (no date) [118], could have resonated with the quiet, distilled subjects and muted palette of the Danish artist.

More perplexing in an account of Hammershøi's relationship to contemporary British art and artists is his failure, on the one hand, to meet Whistler, and on the other, to establish relations with an artist whose work suggests many affinities with his own and which was collected by two of his close friends, Borwick and Bramsen. The history of Hammershøi's failure to meet Whistler when the latter was in London in 1897-98 has been rehearsed by Vad and others.[68] However, Hammershøi's profound admiration for the work of Whistler, substantiated in his work of the mid-1880s, informed his determination both to meet Whistler while in London for the first time and to try to exhibit with the recently established International Society of Sculptors, Painters and Gravers, of which the American artist was the first president. Hammershøi had become familiar with Whistler's work through engravings, the 1889 Paris Universal Exposition and, in London through his acquaintance with Mrs. Ridley, who, apart from having known Whistler through her husband, the artist and fellow student of Whistler's

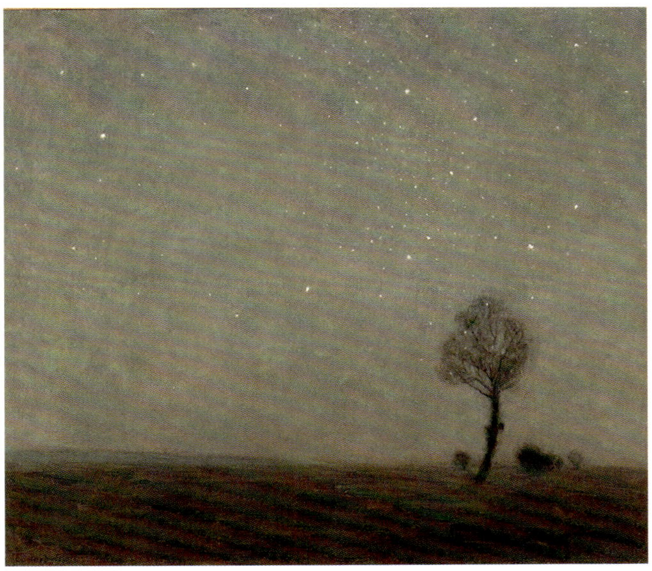

[118]
Edward Stott 1855-1918 British
Starlight: Landscape undated
Oil on canvas 42 x 48 cm
Towner Gallery, Eastbourne
(Presented by Arthur & Helen Grogan through the Art Fund, 2009)

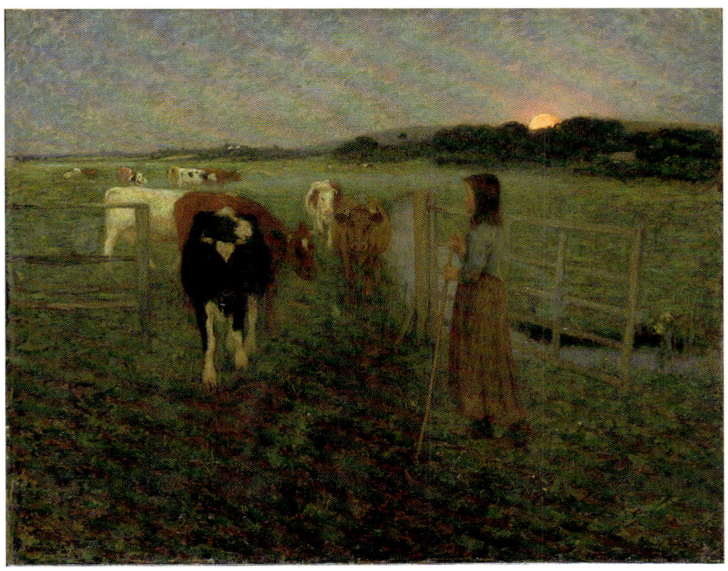

[119]
Edward Stott 1855-1918 British
Changing Pastures 1893
Oil on canvas 70.5 x 87.6 cm
Tate Britain, London

in Paris, Matthew White Ridley, also purportedly owned a painting by the American.[69] Whistler, on the other hand, was introduced to some small, as yet unidentified, works by Hammershøi in the autumn of 1896, delivered on behalf of Alfred Bramsen by his son, Henry, then resident in London, and with which the American artist was clearly impressed: "I trust one of these days I meet the most gifted and sympathetic artist himself."[70] Despite more than one letter and repeated visits to Whistler's studio from late April to 21 May 1898, Hammershøi failed both to meet the artist, who reportedly only returned to London from Paris for a day to attend the opening of the International Society's first annual exhibition on 16 May, and to manage to orchestrate a late inclusion of two of his paintings, *Two Figures. The Artist and his Wife* [14, p. 31], and *Portrait of Karen Bramsen* [120],[71] into the exhibition.

With William Nicholson, it remains surprising that the Danish artist did not seek to establish a relationship with an artist whose subject matter, be it intensely observed still lifes, expressionless single figures in interiors or sparse, simplified landscapes, and subdued tonal range paralleled his own aesthetic. The opportunities were available for a meeting: Borwick owned at least one work by Nicholson made before 1909, and was tempted to purchase a second from the *Exhibition of Paintings by William Nicholson: Rottingdean Landscapes and Other Subjects*, held at the Chenil Galleries, London, June – July 1910.[72] Likewise, Bramsen owned Nicholson's *Behind the Scenes* (1908), acquired another (unidentified) one in 1910,[73] ensured that Nicholson was handsomely represented in the 1909 Copenhagen exhibition of members of the International Society of Sculptors, Painters and Gravers, and published an article on him in the same year.[74] In a letter to Bramsen dated 19 May 1909, Nicholson reports that he has seen works by Hammershøi at Borwick's home: "I paid a visit to Borwick who was most kind and showed me a number of works and reproductions of Hammershøi's. I admired them very much indeed. He has a charm and a dignity."[75] Despite this regard for the Danish artist, there is no evidence that the two artists met during either of the last two visits that Hammershøi made to London in 1912 and 1913.

Hammershøi created a total of eleven paintings (and a map of Scotland)[76] during the course of his six visits to England: five in 1897-98; two during the 1905-06 sojourn, and four during 1912 – early 1913. Apart from a change of geographic subject matter, none reveal any evidence of the artist responding to the new visual and cultural stimuli with which he had evidently engaged. The first sojourn involved the making of two interiors, one commissioned by a Mr. With for 200 DKK and shipped to Copenhagen by 16 April,[77] and another, completed by 9 May.[78] In addition, Hammershøi finished a portrait of Karen Bramsen, violin in hand, at the behest of Alfred Bramsen [120], and the double portrait of himself and Ida: *Two Figures. The Artist and his Wife* [14, p. 31].[79] He discontinued work on the first subject that he tackled after his arrival in London, *Sketch done in a Room of Ancient Greek Art in the British Museum* (1897), giving the work to the Danish journalist, Oscar Hansen, who returned to Copenhagen in December 1897 after 25 years residence in London. [80] In each case, these paintings had precedents in work created previously in Denmark and in Paris. Taking advantage of the classical domestic architecture in proximity to Robert Smirke's great neo-classical British Museum which could be observed from his apartment at 58 Bloomsbury Street, Hammershøi made two views of the British Museum during the sojourn of 1905-06: *From the British Museum. Winter* [121] and *Montague Street in London* [87, p. 112]. The monochromatic palette, the spare geometric architectural forms and the unpopulated urban spaces of these two works directly reflect Hammershøi's earlier treatment of the palaces of

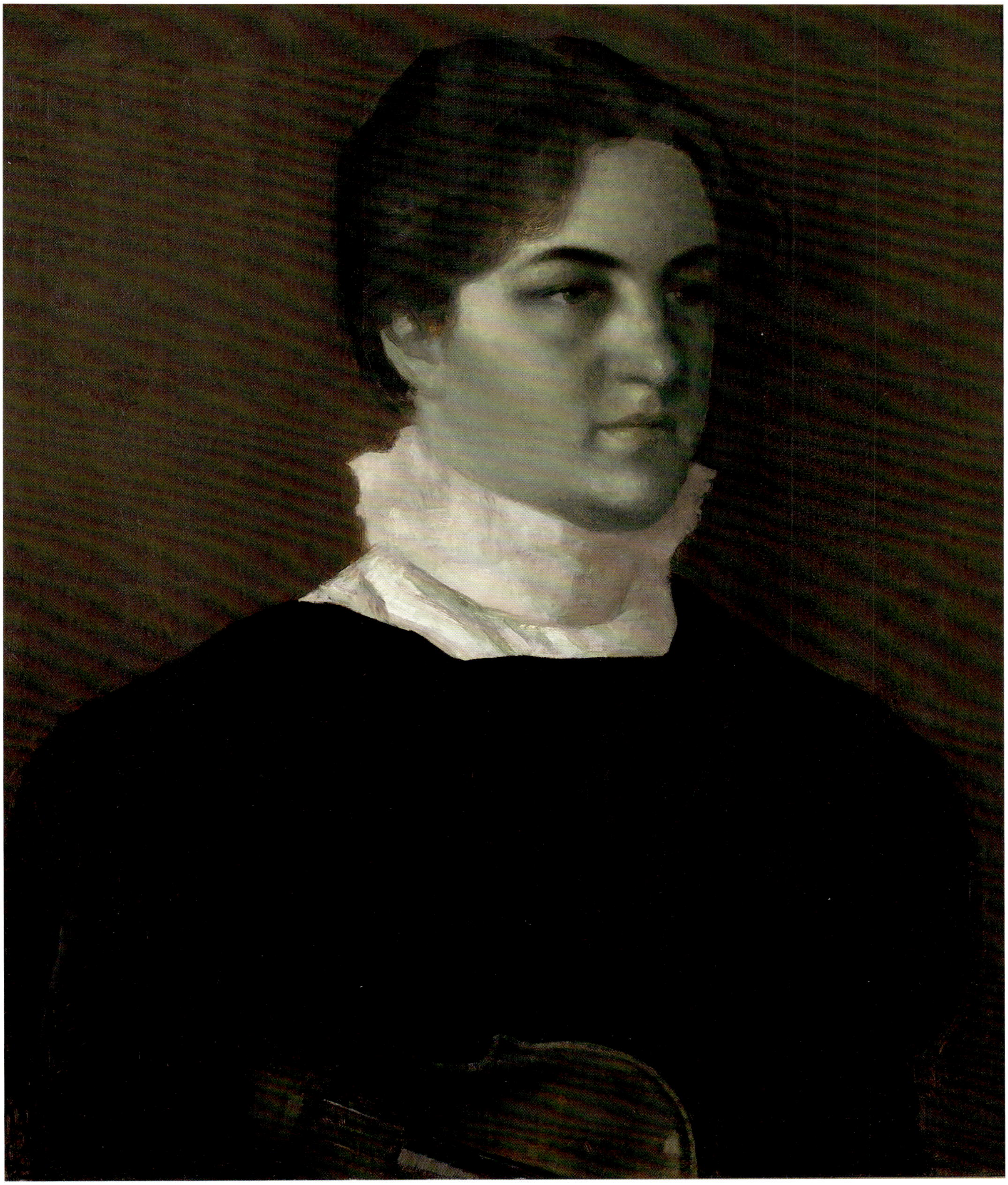

[120]
Vilhelm Hammershøi 1864-1916 Danish
Portrait of Karen Bramsen 1898
Oil on canvas 60 x 50.5 cm
Private collection

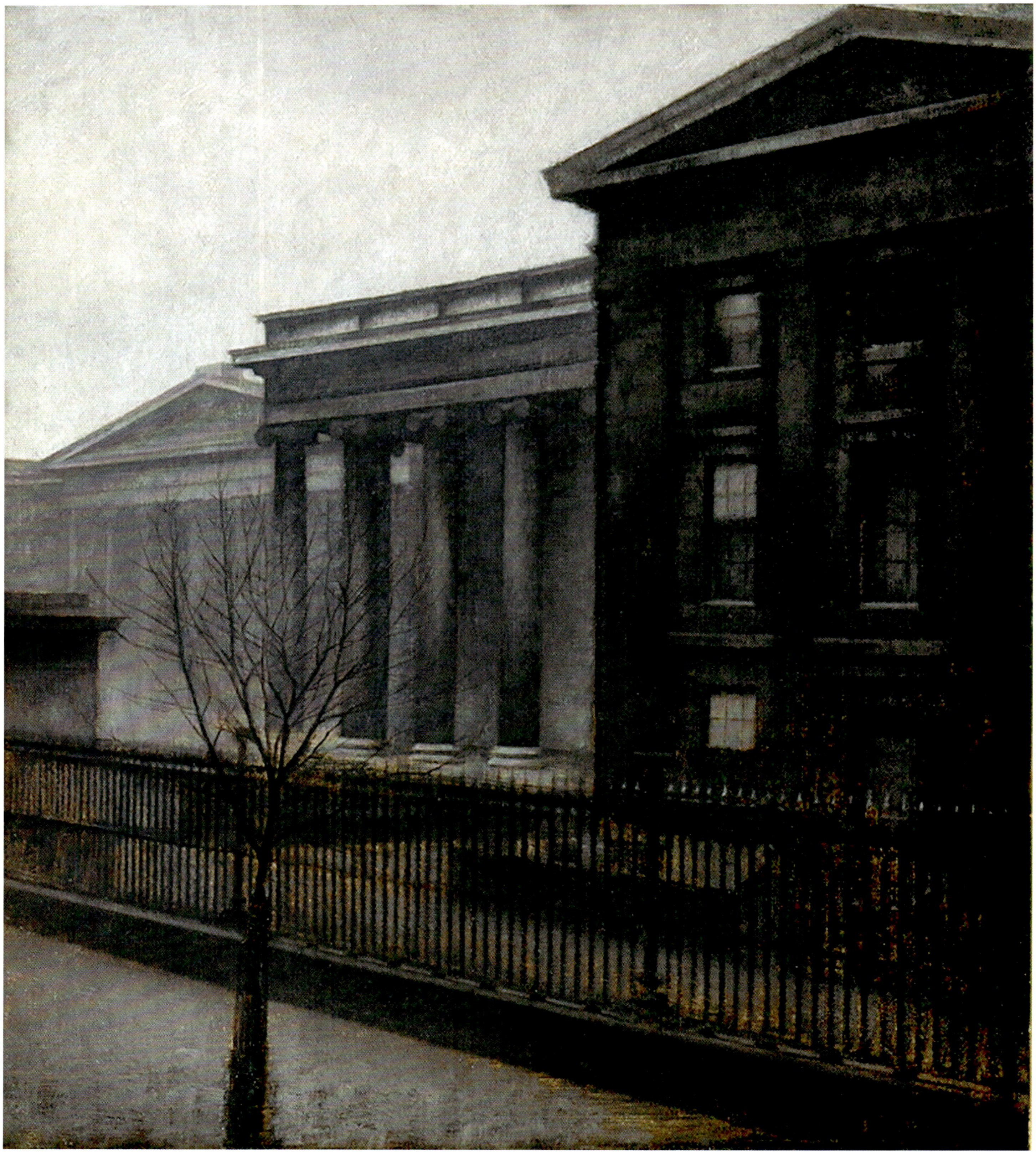

[121]
Vilhelm Hammershøi 1864-1916 Danish
From the British Museum. Winter 1906
Oil on canvas 50.5 x 44.8 cm
Fuglsang Kunstmuseum, Toreby, Lolland

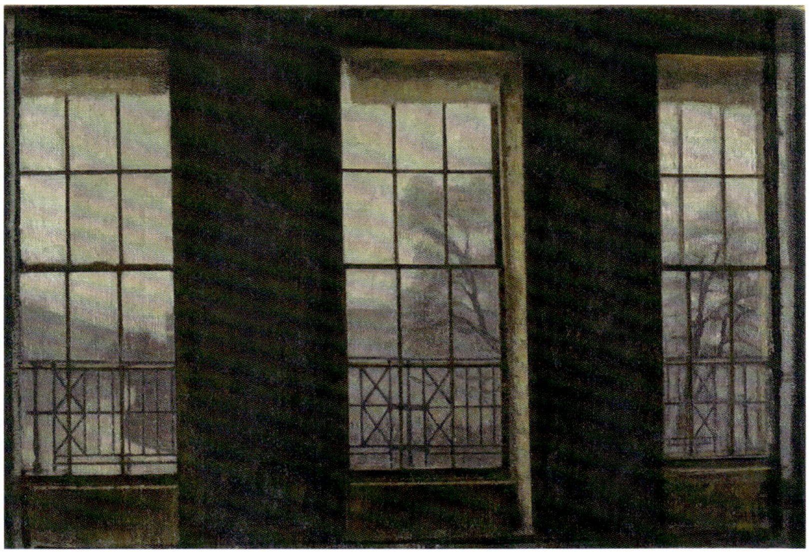

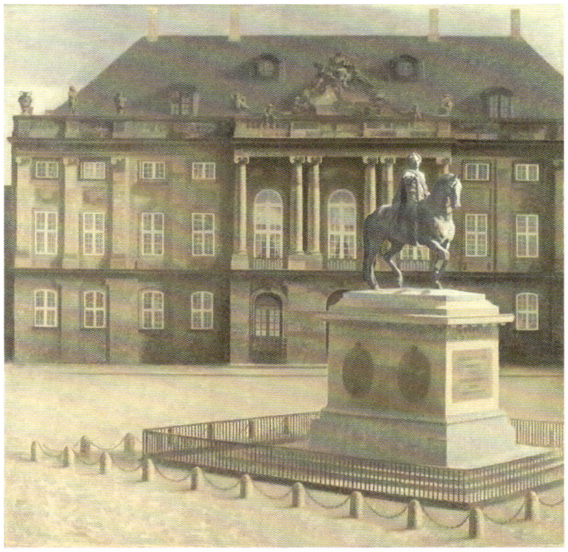

Christiansborg [84, p. 109] and Amalienborg [123] and the façade of the Old Asiatic Company building on Strandgade [86, p. 111]. When Hammershøi returned to the subject of London views during his visit of 1912-13, the continuity of approach to urban scenes found in the 1905-06 paintings persists, as is seen in *Interior in London, Brunswick Square* (1912) [123] and *Jews' College "Rabbinical Seminary" in Guilford Street, London* (1912-13) [94, p. 118].

It could be argued that there was no compulsion for Hammershøi to consider any stylistic shift as a result of his exposure to London or British art, since he enjoyed critical acclaim for exhibitions which showed a representative selection of his work, established a modest but secure market for his paintings, and built up a significant critical following. Although he ultimately failed to have two paintings inserted belatedly into the first exhibition of Whistler's International Society of Sculptors, Painters and Engravers in 1898, the good offices of Leonard Borwick, and indirectly of Alfred Bramsen, secured the inclusion of two works in the International Society's 1904 exhibition: *Interior* owned by Borwick [60, p. 82] (see below) and a small landscape lent by Bramsen.

It appears to have been Borwick, whose friendship with Bramsen was based upon music and a mutual admiration for the artists of the Hague School, Whistler, William Nicholson and Hammershøi, who made an approach to the then secretary of the International Society, George Sauter. He secured the invitation to Hammers-høi to exhibit, arranged the shipping of Bramsen's painting from Copenhagen and ensured that the works were reasonably well hung within the exhibition held at the New Gallery, Regent Street, from January to March.[81] His works were shown within the context of national and international artists of considerable renown, including Guthrie, Lavery, William Nicholson, Jacques Emile Blanche, Monet, Zuloaga, Fritz Thaulow, Charles Cottet, Willem Witsen and Mattjis Maris, and the exhibition itself was dominated by Auguste Rodin's monumental sculpture, *The Thinker.*[82]

In the wake of small but positive critical acclaim, it was Borwick again who busied himself on seeking to arrange a solo exhibition for Hammershøi in London. Correspondence

[122]
Vilhelm Hammershøi 1864-1916 Danish
Interior in London, Brunswick Square 1912
Oil on canvas 53 x 76 cm
Sikorsky Family Collection

[123]
Vilhelm Hammershøi 1864-1916 Danish
Amalienborg Square, Copenhagen 1896
Oil on canvas 136.5 x 136.5 cm
Statens Museum for Kunst

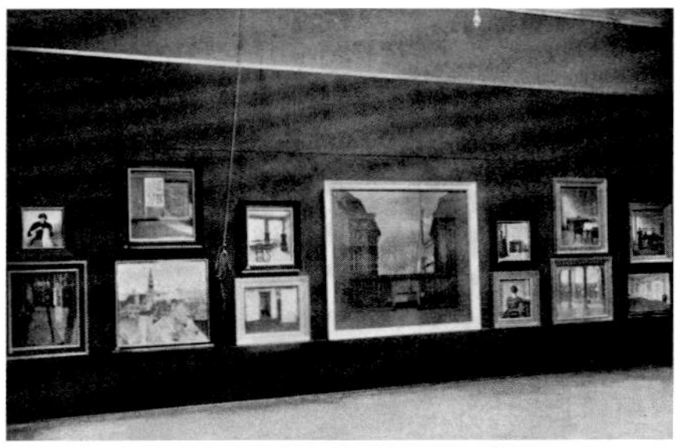

refers to attempts over the period 1904-07, which culminated in a double exposure of the artst's work in the spring of this latter year.[83] Handsomely represented with nineteen works, second in number only to his erstwhile teacher, Krøyer, in Alfred George Temple's exhibition of Danish Art held at the Guildhall Art Gallery, April-May 1907 [124], it was Borwick who was instrumental in determining the selection of the works to be shown.[84] Likewise, it was Borwick who had wisely counselled that the solo exhibition which he had finally managed to arrange at E. J. van Wisselingh's gallery at 14 Grafton Street should be held shortly after the close of the Guildhall Art Gallery exhibition. Opening on 22 May 1907, this latter exhibition presented 13 works, lent primarily by Borwick and Bramsen; its catalogue included an introduction by Borwick.[85] Hammershøi also had two "private" exhibitions in London, one in his apartment at York House, 8 Brunswick Square on 20 December 1912,[86] and the other at Ada Nettleship's house on Wimpole Street on 10 April 1913.[87]

Since Leonard Borwick was central to the propagation of interest in Vilhelm Hammershøi in England, it is important to record the works by the artist which he owned, and the energy which he expended on encouraging fellow collectors to acquire his works. Borwick purchased his first Hammershøi at the Copenhagen gallery of Valdemar Kleis, in March 1903: *Interior with Woman Putting Twigs in a Glass, Strandgade 30* (1900) [125]. He subsequently was given by Hammershøi sometime before the end of January 1906, one of the two works which Hammershøi had created during his London visit of 1905-06: *From the British Museum. Winter* (1905-06) [121],[88] followed by *Interior. Strandgade 30* (1906) [77, p. 100], which he acquired – with a certain degree of reservation about the figure – by 16 November 1905-06.[89] At some point he bought a fourth painting: *Interior* (1899) [60, p. 82]. Borwick also acted as agent and proselytiser of Hammershøi's work in England. In the wake of the critical success of both the Guildhall and van Wisselingh Gallery exhibitions of 1907, Borwick reports in correspondence to Bramsen dated 10 and 23 June 1907, of his abortive attempt to have the National Gallery, London, accept a painting by Hammershøi paid for by public subscription.[90] Borwick however successfully encouraged two of his fellow countrymen to acquire the artist's works: a Scotsman, Mr Adam Black, acquired a work in December 1912,[91] and his close friend, the pianist and composer, Frederick Septimus Kelly, having been invited by Borwick to Hammershøi's private exhibition at the Nettleships' house on 10 April 1013, bought one of the two interior compositions shown there, recording the process in his diary: "went to the Nettleships' house in Wigmore Street [...] to see four of Hammershøi's new pictures. There were two superb interiors, one of Brunswick Square [...] I found the severer of the two interiors just as fine as I did on my first view a week ago and I decided to buy it at £250-0-0."[92] Borwick's correspondence with Bramsen also records an interest expressed in the purchase of Bramsen's small landscape which was exhibited in the 1904 International Society exhibition,[93] as well as Borwick's search for potential purchasers, such as a certain Mr. Spegen who, in September 1906, appears to have been close to the purchase of another scene of an interior.[94]

Hammershøi also realised at least four other British sales. Carl Anton Loevenadler, a Swedish match manufacturer, Honorary Vice-President of the Swedish Chamber of Commerce in London, a member of the Royal Swedish Golfing Club and owner of a substantial property to the southwest of London beyond Hampton Court (to which Ida and Vilhelm were invited to dine), bought an "Interior" from Hammershøi in May 1898 for 450 DKK;[95] John James Cowan, the Edinburgh paper manufacturer and enthusiastic collector of Whistler,

[124]
Unknown photographer
Hammershøi's paintings as installed at the Guildhall Art Gallery exhibition of Works by Danish Painters 1907
Photograph

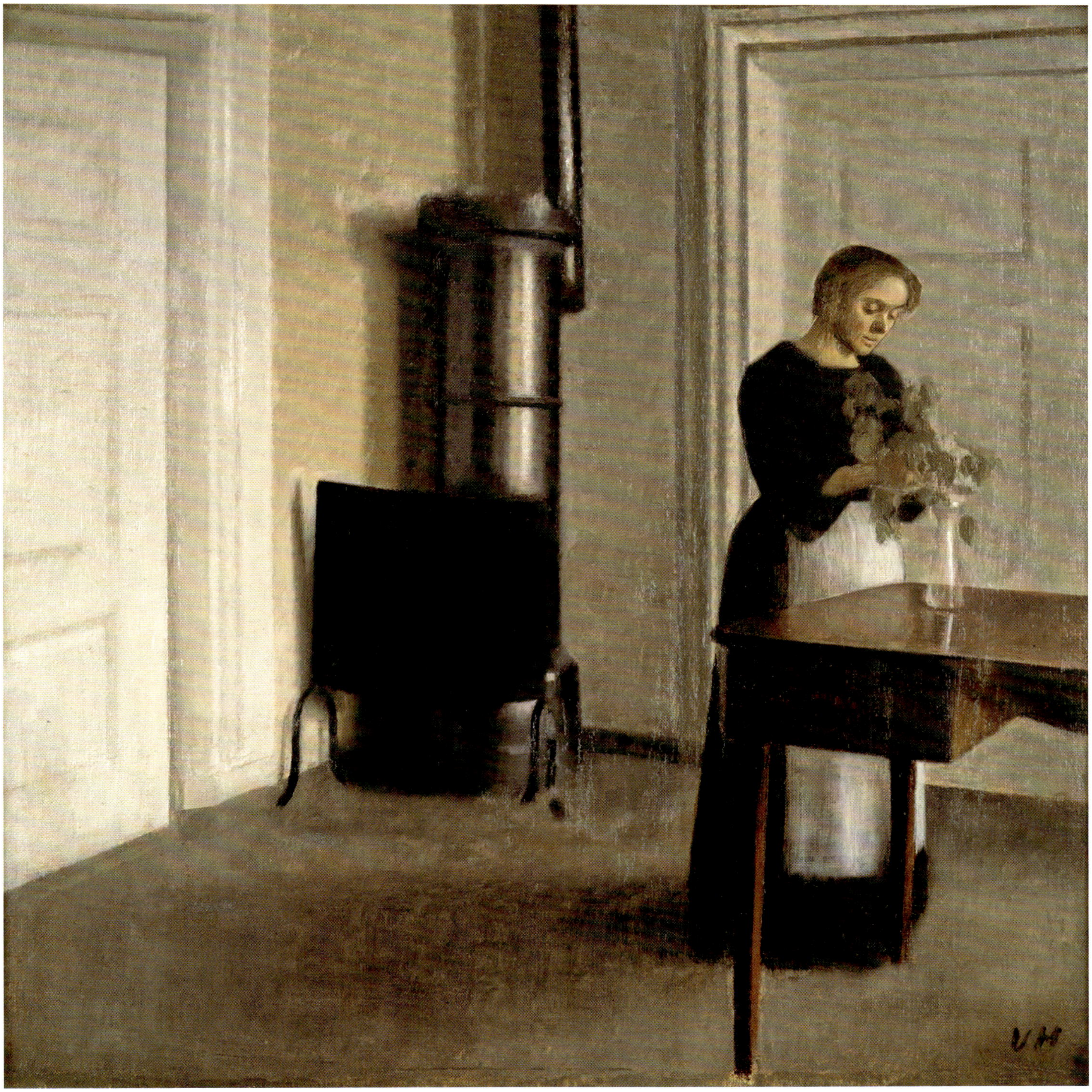

[125]
Vilhelm Hammershøi 1864-1916 Danish
Interior with Woman Putting Twigs in a Glass, Strandgade 30 1900
Oil on canvas 40 x 30 cm
The Ambassador John L. Loeb Jr Danish Art Collection

acquired *The Old Piano, Strandgade 30* (1907) from the van Wisselingh Gallery exhibition in 1907. Two works included in Hammershøi's exhibition held at Galerie Schulte Berlin in 1905 also went to British collectors: Stewart and Company (possibly a London gallery) acquired from Galerie Schulte an unidentified interior in late November or early December 1905,[96] and the British South African gold and diamond magnate, Alfred Beit, purchased *Interior (The Old Cabinet Sofa)* (1905)[25, p. 47], subsequently giving it shortly thereafter to the Nationalgalerie, Berlin in either 1905 or 1906.

The critical acclaim which Hammershøi received in London was generated either directly by the public exhibitions in which his work was presented, or in the wake of such manifestations. Not surprisingly, almost every British critic, untutored in Danish contemporary art, noted a sense of discovery, of revelation of the work of Hammershøi. Some stressed the distinct individuality of his voice, as in *The Times* newspaper's remarks on the 1904 International Society exhibition,[97] or *The Amateur_Photographer*, who in a review of the 1907 van Wisselingh Gallery exhibition, noted that, in comparison to modern British art "represented by such an inferior collection as is gathered year upon year within the walls of the Academy", Hammershøi's works are examples of excellence in their own right.[98] And Clutton Brock, in *The Tribune* opened his review with the words: "This exhibition [...] is truly remarkable because it reveals a new master to us. I, for one, had never heard of Wilhelm [sic] Hammershøi before I saw about twenty of his works at the Guildhall yesterday, but even on so short and imperfect an acquaintance with them he seems to me to be the greatest of living genre painters."[99]

If his uniqueness was noted by some, Hammershøi's distinctly Nordic, or Danish, voice was also certainly identified. *The Pall Mall Gazette* hailed the artist in its review of the Guildhall exhibition of 1907 as "the expression of pure Danish genius",[100] an evaluation repeated in two reviews of his solo exhibition of the same year. Although *The Pall Mall Gazette* had not been overly pleased with the quality of Danish art displayed in the Guildhall exhibition, the reviewer could commend Hammershøi: "Amidst the mediocre artistry of Denmark in painting, as seen at the Guildhall, the works of Hammershøi stood out [...]. The rest we could trace to foreign influence – each lisped with a foreign accent, even the best. But in Hammershøi we beheld a man who had learnt to speak the language of his own people – and it is a golden speech."[101]

What underscored the essence of both Hammershøi's expression of national aesthetic or a unique voice were inevitably his subject matter and his palette. His limited range of subjects – bare spaces, empty rooms, "polished tables and softly gleaming gilt frames and silver bowls and blue china",[102] were consistently commented upon, and well summarised in C. Lewis Hind's evaluation of the artist's distinct modernity. In *The Consolations of a Critic,* the essayist and critic summarised his subject matter thus: "Hammershoy [sic] loves bare spaces where light lingers; grey, empty rooms with severe furniture, in which he delighted to place one figure in perfect harmony with the environment. Hammershoy[sic] is content with things as they are in orderly rooms and byways of his northern capital."[103] Hind's reference to the dominant tonality of Hammershøi's palette reiterates an observation common to all the critics: "Grey and white are his chief colours', wrote Clutton Brock,[104] while *The Sunday Times* referred to the artist's work consisting of "minor melodies of the grey, Northern world".[105] Likewise, the role of light within this world of muted greys is also closely scrutinised and generally admired: "His representation of light is most original, and yet he does not treat objects as if they were merely there for the light to play upon them."[106] It was his treatment of

[126]
Henry Le Sidaner 1862-1939 French
The Table, Gerberoy 1901
Oil on canvas 73 x 70 cm
Musée Petiet, Limoux

the ray of sunlight cast into the room in *Interior. Strandgade 30* [77, p. 101], exhibited in his solo exhibition, which drew the most accolades. *The Pall Mall Gazette* identified it as "a little masterpiece [...] which is so beautiful in treatment [...]; but with what profound insight the sunlight is noted as it gleams through the square panes of the window and flings its reflected light in more restrained and sombre glow upon the walls and door of the shadowed room."[107]

Despite this level of praise, Hammershøi's work also generated concern. His apparently unique voice disturbed some critics, causing them to seek to integrate it within the longer history of art. Of the art of the past, Vermeer and Pieter de Hoogh were most commonly cited.[108] Amongst his contemporaries and near contemporaries, his palette suggested parallels with that of James McNeill Whistler,[109] while his subject matter being concerned with "man's absence rather than his presence" led *The Sunday Times* critic to compare him with his French contemporary Henri Le Sidaner [126].[110] Equally, there were some critics who, while recognising the artist's independent voice, were not unreservedly positive in their reception. For some it was his compositions that appeared wanting. *The Studio* of May 1907 commented upon their monotony and sense of repetition: while recognising that Hammershøi was "a painter of the very highest mark", the reviewer felt that the use of "one figure which he sometimes places in his pictures is unfortunately repeated with monotony, generally with back to the spectator and occupying a space in the picture only as part of the arrangement of the room".[111] Likewise, the subtlety of the grey tonalities of his work could be seen as cold and lifeless: "These sombre, melancholy interiors are [...] cold in the skill of their careful arrangement, and without life, humanity, or inherent beauty of decoration to rouse any real desire for their possession."[112]

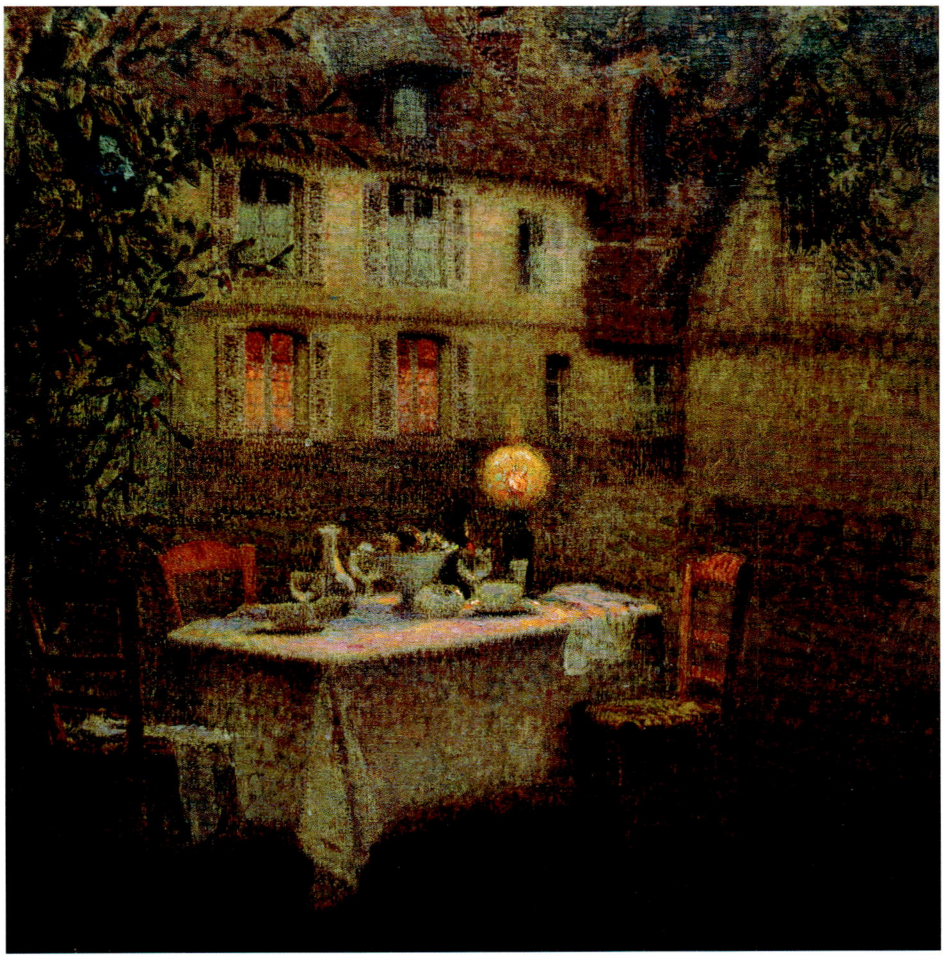

All the criticism generated by the exposure of Hammershøi's work to the British public should, however, be seen within the wider context of the central issue confronting British art during the first decade of the 20th century, namely, what was meant by "modern" art. Contradictory though it may appear, for Lewis Hind, writing one year after Roger Fry's revolutionary exhibition, *Manet and the Post-Impressionists*, the novelty of Hammershøi's quiet, monochromatic vision could be as valid a manifestation of modernity as Matisse's radical, simplified compositions treated in riotous primary colours.[113] It is this awareness of the validity of different modernities which Clutton Brock and the reviewer for *The Pall Mall Gazette* celebrated in their reviews of the Guildhall exhibition, the latter quite comfortably noting that "it is to the modern of the moderns, Wilhelm [sic] Hammershøi, that we must turn ".[114] Equally, it is the identification of the new, the modern, within the context of a new genre of painting, "modern interior painting" which invited T. Martin Wood to consider Hammershøi's work and its place within the specific debate around the meaning of "modern" art. Published in *The Studio* for September 1909,[115] T. Martin Wood uses a new approach to the representation of interior space as a means to define a new, modern aesthetic. No longer an accumulation of realistically defined objects whose presence recounts a story, "modern interior painting" records controlled light falling both specifically upon objects and evenly across the entire space. As such it asserts the intrinsic formal properties of the objects, removes any necessity for finite descriptive accuracy, and suspends all reference to temporality. Identifying the British painter, William Rothenstein as the initiator of this new genre, Wood also acknowledges the contributions of William Orpen, Walter Russel and Jacques Emile Blanche. However, it is Vilhelm Hammershøi, with his quiet interior paintings, whom T. Martin Wood claims to be the true exponent of what is meant by "modern" within the context of a stylistically catholic, contemporary art world. Using *The Old Piano*[116] as his example, Wood declares that the painting "is modern [...]. It is full of a human interest, created by inference alone [...]. And this kind of inference has been made so consciously and successfully only in present times, to a latterly acquired responsiveness in the modern mind."[117] Indeed, Wood provides an eloquent summary of the impact that the exposure of Hammershøi's art in England had made, not least upon a British critic concerned to resolve definitional issues relating to the art of his day:

"In the paintings of Hammershøi, the modern Danish painter, the room that is painted is generally quite empty, but the partly opened door is eloquent of someone who went out. The painter is a poet; we find ourselves wondering what vanished presence is reflected still in the empty room, of the things preferred and arranged there, everything in the room, as in any great interior, bearing witness before all to the life that has been lived in it."[118]

MaryAnne Stevens (born 1947), Director of Academic Affairs, Royal Academy of Arts, London, is a specialist in 18th- and 19th- century British and French art, particularly the history of the Royal Academy and French Impressionism and Post-Impressionism. She has curated major exhibitions in these areas, and has edited and contributed to exhibition catalogues and scholarly journals. She was co-curator of the exhibition, 'Vilhelm Hammershøi: the Poetry of Silence' (Royal Academy of Arts, London and National Museum of Western Art, Tokyo, 2008).

NOTES

1 I wish to acknowledge the invaluable support and assistance of Jan Gorm Madsen, Curator, The Hirschsprung Collection, Copenhagen, who gave unstintingly of his time and skill in locating archival materials and providing and checking translations of text wherever necessary. I would also wish to thank Marianne Saabye, Director, The Hirschsprung Collection, Copenhagen, Dr. Kasper Monrad, Chief Curator, Statens Museum for Kunst, Copenhagen, Dr. Felix Krämer, Curator, Städelinstitut, Frankfurt, and Dr. Naoki Sato, Tokyo University of Fine Arts. Research in Copenhagen was made possible through a grant from the Royal Danish Embassy, London.

2 See Poul Vad, 1988 (1992).

3 See Vad, 1988 (1992), especially pp. 162-177, 263-269.

4 The majority of mss. material quoted in this article resides in the Archive of the Hirschsprung Collection Archive of Artists Letters, Copenhagen (DHS Brevarkiv). It is contained primarily within three specific holdings: the Leonard Borwick Correspondence [Corresp. Borwick]; the Alfred Bramsen Correspondence [Corresp. Bramsen] and the Falck Deposit; and the Ida and Vilhelm Hammershøi Correspondence with Frederikke Hammershøi, deposited by Anna and Svend Hammershøi, 1947, identified by Box and series numbers [e.g Box 83.23]. In addition there is Alfred Bramsen's Scrapbook, and postcards and photographs collected by Vilhelm Hammershøi.

5 Box 83.7, postcard IH, [postmark 8 October 1897].

6 Box 83.9, letter VH, 23 October [1897].

7 Box 83.19, postcard VH, [postmark] 25 October 1897.

8 Ibid.

9 Box 83.13, letter IH, 25 November 1897.

10 Box 83.16, letter IH, 11 January 1898.

11 Box 83.30, letter VH, 21 May 1898.

12 Ibid. in which VH also outlines the schedule for their anticipated date of return to Copenhagen.

13 Box 83.17, letter VH, 19 January 1898. Dr Jón Stefánsson (1862-1952) was Icelandic, received a doctorate from London in English Literature, published with W. G. Collingwood a translation of *The Life and Death of Cormar the Skald*, London, 1901, *Denmark and Sweden with Iceland and Finland*, with a preface by Viscount Bryce OM, London, 1916, and his memoirs in 1949, after his return to Iceland.

14 Ibid.; see also Box 83.20, letter VH, 7 February 1898.

15 Box 83.20, letter VH, 16 February 1898.

16 Box 83.25, letter VH, 2 April 1898.

17 Box 83.27, letter VH, 27 April 1898; 83.28, letter IH, 7 May 1898; 83.29, letter VH, 10 May 1898; 83.30, letter VH, 21 May 1898.

18 Corresp. Borwick to Bramsen, 15 March [1903]: "I have not yet thanked you for the gift of the catalogue and the little account of Hammershøi's work. / The catalogue is a most interesting and valuable possession, and I should like, with your permission, to verify all your pictures with it in hand./ Might I do so on Monday aft.[sic] 23rd or Tuesday 24th? Perhaps you will let me have a line to the Phoenix near the time to let me know if and when it would be convenient to you." Leonard Borwick (1868-1925) was a highly successful concert pianist, acclaimed by Clara Schumann, his teacher, and Johannes Brahms. He had an international career, touring Europe and the United States, introduced Lieder recitals to London in 1893 with the Irish baritone, Henry Plunkett Green (1865-1936), and was closely associated with Joachim and the Joachim Quartet, the celebrated violinist Wilma Neruda Norman, the wife of Sir Charles Hallé, Edward Elgar and the young composer, concert pianist and sculler, Frederick Septimus Kelly (1881-1916).

19 Corresp. Borwick to Bramsen, postcard, 3 August 1904.

20 Corresp. Borwick to Bramsen, postcard, 2 September 1904.

21 Corresp. Borwick to Bramsen, postcard, 19 September 1904: "All went splendidly. They were a great joy to have [....] had Stott to meet him and other neighbours; and have sent them to v. Wisselingh and Obachs in London, and I jope uch for a V.H. exhibition at one or other place next spring.' See also Box 85.19, letter IH, n.d. [September 1904], and 85.20, letter VH, n.d. [September 1904].

22 Corresp. Borwick to Bramsen, postcard, 19 September 1904.

23 Corresp. Bramsen, letter VH to Bramsen, 9 November 1905.

24 Box 85.23, letter IH, 11 November 1905.

25 Box 85.27, letter IV, 29 December 1905.

26 Box 85.20, letter VH, 20 December 1905; 85.27, letter IV, 29 December 1905; 85.28, letter VH, January 1906.

27 Box 85.30, letter VH, 3 June 1912.

28 Ibid. Christian Brinton was resident in New York City with connections with Denmark including acquaintance with Alfred Bramsen. He was central to the organization of the exhibition of Scandinavian Art, in which Hammershøi was represented, which was shown 1912-13 in New York, Toledo (Ohio), Chicago, Boston and Buffalo. He was also a critic. See Corresp. Bramsen, Brinton to Bramsen, letters, 18 October 1912, 20 December 1912, 3 April 1913.

29 Box 85.31, letter IH, 5 December 1912; 85.36, letter IH, 30 December 1912.

30 Box 85.33, letter IH, 30 November 1912.

31 Box 85.34, letter IH, 17 December 1912; 85.35, letter VH, [c. 20] December 1912; 85.36, letter IH, 30 December 1912.

32 Box 85.35, letter VH, [c. 20] December 1912.

33 Box 85. 37, letter IH, April 1913.

34 Ibid.

35 Box 85.38, letter IH, April 1913; 83.39, letter VH, 9 April 1913.

36 Vad op.cit., pp. 13, 162.

37 Bramsen and Hammershøi possibly met at a rowing club in c.1885, but it was in 1888 that Bramsen made his first purchase of a work by Hammershøi, *Young Girl sewing* (1887; Ordrupgaard, Copenhagen); see Bramsen, 2008, pp. 19-20.

38 William S. Prior was a member of one of the most prominent families in Copenhagen; the family owned a shipping company, a bank and electrical cable plant. Prior was resident in London, wrote reviews for Danish newspapers, e.g. *Politiken*, which mentioned, Hammershøi's inclusion in the 1904 International Society of Sculptors, Painters and Gravers London exhibition. He was also to be involved in an abortive attempt to get an article about Hammershøi publiches in *The Studio*, 1909-10.

39 Henry Bramsen (1875-1919) trained in Copenhagen (A Rudinger) and Leipzig (Prof. Julius Klengel), and made his debut as a soloist in 1894. He performed in London, e.g. St James's Hall Concerts, 7 October 1899 (with Dame Clara Butt, and Edward Elgar), and was represented by the leading music agent, Ibbs and Tillett (1914-15). He lived in the United States 1906-10, where he played with the Pittsburgh Orchestra before leading a "players' revolt" in May 1907 and moving to New York to form the New York Trio with Paul Gallico (piano) and Alexander Paslavski (violin). According to his father, he owned a Stradivarius cello (*Varus*, undated published interview with Alfred Bramsen, Bramsen Scrapbook [1900-12], Hirschsprung Archive).

40 Bramsen Corresp. records Bramsen writing to a Mr William Archer in 1885, requesting that he see his son, Henry, to advise him on his career. Presumably this elicited no positive response, since a letter in the Bramsen Archive (Box 112) includes a letter from Georg Brandes to William Archer (1856-1924), dated Copenhagen 2 October 1896, introducing Henry Bramsen, who was already in London, as a talented cellist, and asking Archer to give him advice about his career. William Archer later translated into English Brandes's monumental study of William Shakespeare (Danish edition published 1897-98).

41 Bramsen Scrapbook includes a cutting of an article by Bramsen about his two musical children.

42 Box 83.11, letter IH, 31 October 1897.

43 Box 83.13, letter IH, 25 November 1897.

44 Vad op.cit, p. 27.

45 Box 83.14, letter VH, 7 December 1897.

46 Box 83.9, letter VH, 23 October 1897.

47 Box 83.10, letter IH, 25 October 1897.

48 Box 83.17, letter VH, 19 January 1898; 83.20, letter VH [7 February 1898].

49 Box 83.19, letter IH, [1904].

50 Box 85.23, letter IH, 11 November 1905.

51 Box 85.26, letter VH, 20 December 1905; 85.28, letter VH, January 1906; this venerable London public house (founded after 1666) bears the name of Ye Olde Cheddar Cheese, and is located at 145 Fleet Street in the City of London. It has been the haunt of distinguished men of English letters including Goldsmith, Dickens, GK Chesterton and Conan Doyle.

52 Box 85.32, letter VH, 18 November 1912; 85.33, letter IH, 30 November 1912; 85.34, letter IH, 17

December 1912; 85.36, letter IH, 30 December 1912; 85.36, letter IH, 30 December 1912.

53 Box 85.35, letter VH, [c. 20] December 1912.

54 Box 85.39, letter VH, 9 April 1913.

55 Ibid.

56 A. G. Temple, *Guildhall Memories*, London, 1918, p. 284.

57 Hammershøi's collection of postcards includes two of the British Museum (the Reading Room and the Egyptian Gallery), one of Guildford Place and two of St Bartholomew the Great. His large format black and white photographs mounted on card include images of Tower Bridge, Westminster Abbey, the Houses of Parliament, St Paul's Cathedral and Hampton Court.

58 Box 83.11, letter IH, 31 October 1897.

59 Box 83.13, letter IH, 25 November 1897.

60 Box 83.25, letter VH, 2 April 1898.

61 Box 83.23, letter VH, 21 March 1898.

62 Box 83.20, letter VH, 7 February 1898.

63 See C. Dakers, *The Holland Park Circle: Artists and Victorian Society*, New Haven and London, 1999, and B. Bryant, *G. F. Watts in Kensington: Little Holland House and Gallery*, Studies in the Art of George Frederick Watts 3, Compton, 2009, especially chap. 3.

64 Cf. Copenhagen, 1909.

65 Box 83.23, letter VH, 21 March 1898.

66 Box 83.17, letter VH, 19 January 1898.

67 Corresp. Borwick to Bramsen, postcard, 19 September 1904.

68 See Vad op. cit., pp. 2-163, 168-170, 176.

69 Box 83.20, letter VH, 16 February 1898.

70 The Correspondence of James McNeill Whistler, University of Glasgow, 11089 [September-December 1896?]: JMW to Henry Bramsen, Private Collection, quoted Vad, 1988 (1992), 426 (note 218).

71 Box 83.27, letter VH, 27 April 1898; 83.28, letter IH, 7 May 1989; 83.29, letter VH, 10 May 1898; 83.30, letter VH, 21 May 1989.

72 Corresp. Borwick to Bramsen, letter 24 June 1910.

73 Falck Archive Box 123, William Nicholson to Bramsen, letters 1-3.

74 Cf. Bramsen 1909.

75 Falck Archive Box 123, letter 3.

76 Box 83.21, letter VH, 21 February 1898: a big map made to accompany a lecture delivered by Steffansson given at the Scottish Club.

77 Box 83.26, letter VH, 16 April 1898; "Fortegnelse over Vilhelms Arbejder I 1898 – i London", ms., Bramsen Archive.

78 Box 83.29, letter VH, 10 May 1898; "Fortegnelse over Vilhemls Arbejder I 1898 – i London", ms., Bramsen Archive.

79 Box 83.24, letter IV, 24 March 1898: Ida records that VH had bought her an antique ring for her birthday; the ring figures prominently in the painting.

80 Box 83.14, letter VH 7 December 1897.

81 Corresp. Borwick to Bramsen, letter 7 December 1903; letter 24 January [1904].

82 See Philip Athill, "The International Society of Sculptors, Painters and Gravers", *Burlington Magazine*, vol. 127, January 1985, pp. 21-29, 33.

83 Corresp. Borwick to Bramsen, postcard, 19 September 1904; postcard, 1 February 1906; postcard, 23 September 1906; letter, [c. 29] January 1907; letter, 8 March 1907; postcard, 24 April 1907; see also Box 85.28, letter VH, January 1906.

84 Corresp. Borwick to Bramsen, letter, 19 October 1905; at this stage it would appear that the Guildhall exhibition had initially been planned to be held in 1906.

85 London, 1907b; for further information on E. J. van Wisselingh in London, see J. F. Heijbroek and E. L. Wouthuysen, *Portret vn een kunsthandel: de firma Van Wisselingh en Zijn compagnons, 1838 – heden,* Amsterdam 1999, pp. 59-72.

86 Box 85.39, letter VH [c. 20] December 1912.

87 Box 85.39, letter VH, 9 April 1913.

88 Box 83.28, letter VH, January 1906.

89 Corresp. Borwick to Bramsen, postcard, 16 November 1906; letter 27 November 1906.

90 Corresp. Borwick to Bramsen, postcard, 10 June 1907.

91 Box 85.35, letter VH, [c. 20] December 1912, bought for 450 DKK.

92 *Race against Time: The Diaries of F.S. Kelly*, published by T Radic, Canberra, 2004, p. 293.

93 Corresp. Borwick to Bramsen, letter, 24 January [1904].

94 Corresp. Borwick to Bramsen, postcard, 23 September 1906.

95 Box 83.25, letter VH, 2 April 1898; 83.28, letter IH, 7 May 1898; 83.29, letter VH, 10 May 1898.

96 Bramsen Archive: Corresp. Eduard Schulte to Bramsen, letter 9 December 1905.

97 *The Times*, 1904.

98 "Vilhelm Hammershøi's Pictures at 14 Grafton Street", *The Amateur Photographer*, 11 June 1907, p. 526.

99 Arthur Clutton Brock, "Danish Pictures at the Guildhall – A New Master", *The Tribune*, 9 April 1907, quoted in Vad, 1988 (1992), 407f.

100 "The Danish Painters at the Guildhall", 11 April 1907.

101 *The Pall Mall Gazette*, "Art Notes", 4 April 1907.

102 See note 98.

103 London 1911, 80.

104 See note 98.

105 Reviews of exhibitions in London: "Hammershøi", *The Sunday Times*, 2 June 1907.

106 See note 98.

107 See note 99.

108 See note 99, and Temple op. cit. (note 56), 284 and A.G. Temple, *Introduction to the catalogue of the Guildhall Exhibition*, 1907.

109 See note 101.

110 Ibid.

111 *The Studio*, May 1907.

112 "Danish Art at the Guildhall", *The Queen*, 20 April 1907.

113 Op. cit., 1911, pp. 80-81.

114 See note 99.

115 T. Martin Wood, 1909, 251-256; Borwick and Bramsen had attempted without success to place articles in *The Studio* in 1907 (Corresp. Borwick to Bramsen, postcard 4/5 June 1907), and in 1909-10 (Bramsen Archive: Corresp. W. S. Prior to Bramsen, letter 3 April 1909; leter 15 October 1909; letter 10 September 1910). Two works by Hammershøi were illustrated in this article.

116 Purchased by John Stewart Cowan from van Wisselingh 1907 exhibition.

117 Martin Wood, 1909, 252.

118 Ibid.

THE ESSENCE OF THINGS: HAMMERSHØI AS SEEN THROUGH THE EYES OF RAINER MARIA RILKE

ANNE HEMKENDREIS

The German poet Rilke voiced great admiration for Hammershøi in several letters and was planning to write an article about his art, yet never did so. Based on other writings by Rilke on the subject of art the article discusses what qualities Rilke valued in Hammershøi's works and seeks to find an answer to the question of why he nevertheless refrained from writing about them.

"Hammershøj does not belong among those about whom one may speak rashly. His work is long and slow, and whensoever one studies it, that moment will always be an occasion for speaking about the important and essential in art." [1]

The German poet Rainer Maria Rilke wrote these lines on 10 November 1905 in his final letter to Alfred Bramsen, a patron of Vilhelm Hammershøi. One year previously Rilke had seen the Danish artist's paintings for the first time at the "Internationale Kunstausstellung" (International Art Exhibition) in Düsseldorf.[2] In the years that followed he occupied himself quite intensively with Hammershøi's work, and during his subsequent visit to the south of Sweden he took the opportunity to visit the artist and Bramsen in Copenhagen. His endeavours aimed at preparing an essay on Hammershøi's work, which he himself stated had not ceased to "occupy [him] most earnestly."[3] Even though Rilke was from the very beginning convinced that he perceived "the essence" of Hammershøi's work he would never realise this venture.[4] After his final letter to Bramsen neither Rilke's letters nor his diary entries make references to any further occupation with the art of Hammershøi. What reasons may have lain behind the foundering of Rilke's endeavour?

Writing about the visual arts was not uncharted territory for Rilke around 1904. Having completed his own university studies on art history he had already finished a monograph about the artists' colony in Worpswede in the north of Germany and had been engaged in work on the sculptures and other works by the French sculptor Auguste Rodin (1840-1917). Rilke's work on the visual arts served the purpose of offering a critical way of testing and expanding his own concept of art.[5] His monographs are not so much contributions to art history as they are a transformation of visual art into lyrical language. Rilke's writings on painting evince no objective gaze on art. Rather, he uses them as a medium for communicating his own aesthetic beliefs.

Rilke's work with the art of Hammershøi demonstrates the same endeavour to penetrate and appropriate the artist's paintings. The fact that Rilke's plan founders prompts one to assume that he came across unexpected obstacles in his appropriation process. First of all, Rilke presumably experienced practical problems regarding his access to Hammershøi's paintings.[6] When preparing critical treatises on painting Rilke always took great pains to establish some insight into the personality of the artist in question, believing that it would be reflected in the artist's works.[7] However, during his stay in Copenhagen Rilke only had access to those of Hammershøi's works that were found in Bramsen's private collection. Back in Germany he only had a catalogue of reproductions at hand. These factors undoubtedly hampered the exploration of Hammershøi's works to a considerable extent. What is more, language barriers and Hammershøi's silence impeded the more intimate approach to the artist and his work that Rilke sought.[8]

There is, however, also good reason to presume that Hammershøi's work threw up a semantic obstacle against Rilke's attempts at aesthetic appropriation. Pursuing this thought would mean that Hammershøi's aesthetic did not offer any points of departure for Rilke's neo-Romantic or Symbolist concept of art. Such a contention runs counter to the prevalent belief that Rilke's ongoing work with the Worpswede painters and Rodin quite simply led him to lose interest in Hammershøi.[9] Indeed, Rilke stated in his last letter to Bramsen that the planned essay on Hammershøi remained "a matter close to my heart [...]".[10] The statement only makes it even more surprising that the contrasts in content between Rilke's and Hammershøi's art must have been so compelling that to Rilke they did not allow for an aesthetic approach. Rilke himself describes the problems encountered in his work on Hammershøi's art in indirect terms only. In his last letter to Bramsen he complains that he is not yet "sufficiently thoroughly prepared and initiated" to be able to write about "the essence of this precious master".[11] So even though Rilke initially believed that he had perceived the essential qualities of Hammershøi's work it ultimately evaded his aesthetic yardstick.

According to Rilke, art and poetry performed a mediating function between the subject and the object alienated from the subject – or its surroundings. In this context the work of art becomes a manifestation of the artist's soul. The artist's essence and the object represented by him are reflected in his work.[12] When, during his meeting with Hammershøi, Rilke had difficulty in perceiving his personality, this meant that he also faced insurmountable difficulties as regards his perception of Hammershøi's work. That is why Rilke's last letter to Bramsen sees him stating that he has not yet succeeded in grasping the essence of Hammershøi's paintings.[13]

Quite in line with Rilke, the critics of the time were also in disagreement when assessing the essence and significance of Hammershøi's paintings. For example, a German critic writing in the newspaper *Die Post* described Hammershøi's art as "A vein of painting that offers beauty for the eye, [yet] leaves the soul unsatisfied."[14] However, it is the very emptiness and lack of animation – of soul – in Hammershøi's works that mark out the contrast to Rilke's concept of art.

While Rilke's labours with the art of Hammershøi reached no fruition, his work on the landscapes created by the Worpswede artists resulted in an extensive monograph. The simple fact that Rilke stayed at the artists' colony in Worpswede and entered into a friendship with the individual painters brought about an intensive process of exchange with the artists.[15] One might presume that this helped Rilke to successfully arrive at what he considered the soul or essence of those works of art. A presupposition which in turn leads to the question of how the paintings by the Worpswede artists differ from those of Hammershøi. What special traits in Hammershøi's idioms obstructed Rilke's aesthetic appropriation?

Landscape as the alien: Rilke in Worpswede

Rilke's opinions on the visual arts were initially formed through his contact with the Worpswede artists, a circle that included the sculptor Clara Westhoff, who would later become his wife. Tradition usually counts Fritz Mackensen, Otto Modersohn, Fritz Overbeck, Hans am Ende, Heinrich Vogeler, and Karl Vinnen as the pioneers of the artist's colony. These artists were mainly landscape painters, and at Teufelsmoor northeast of Bremen they found a virtually unspoilt setting that served as subject matter for their art.

Even though the artists worked with a type of landscape similar to the landscapes treated in Hammershøi's art – a flat landscape, rich in water – only the paintings by Overbeck (1869-1909) and am Ende (1864-1918) share a number of traits with Hammershøi in terms of composition and colour. For example, am Ende's portrait-format landscape *Clouds* [127] from 1895, has a monochrome colour scheme similar to that of Hammershøi's *View of Gentofte Lake. Sunshower* from 1903 [100, p. 124]. Overbeck's landscape *On the Moor* (c. 1904) [128] shows a similar interest in cloud patterns, as does Hammershøi's *Landscape, From Lejre* (1905) [17, p. 35]. However, the similarities are too insignificant to lead to any assumption that the Worpswede artists had a direct influence on Hammershøi. This is to say that Rilke is the true link between the Worpswede artists and Hammershøi by virtue of his efforts

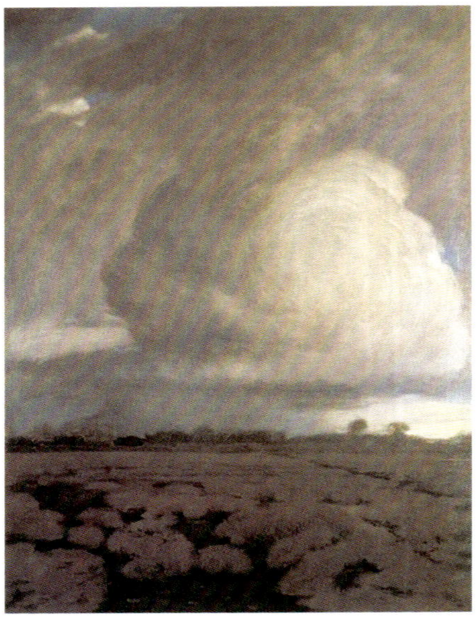

[127]
Hans am Ende 1864-1918 German
Clouds 1895
Oil on canvas
Private collection

to bring the various paintings in line with his theoretical deliberations on the modern subject and its environs.

To begin with, it is striking to note how Rilke describes Overbeck's landscapes – empty of people and filled with a postulated melancholy – as typically Nordic.[16] In so doing he makes an implicit reference to the Danish writer J. P. Jacobsen (1847-85), whose writings served as a role model for his poetry, and whose work he presented to the Worpswede painters.[17] This makes Rilke the only critic of the age to create a link between the Worpswede painters and Danish literature. The absence of people in Hammershøi's paintings also prompt several other contemporaries to be reminded of the writings of Jacobsen, whose novel *Niels Lyhne* (1880) was part of Hammershøi's library.[18]

To Rilke, the evocation of a sense of isolation and of standing apart are the essential properties of the modern perception of landscape. In his monograph about the Worpswede painters, which was first published in 1903, Rilke sees the landscape as something alien, something other.[19] He believes that because of its alien and inapproachable nature, landscape can make the observer aware of how they themselves are distinct and different and, hence, of their own essence. The landscape takes on a constituting significance for the subject. The landscape and the observing subject no longer penetrate each other. Rather, the landscape's lack of engagement allows it to facilitate a sense of isolation for the observer.[20]

According to Rilke, then, landscape painting has a unique ability to create a bridge between the subject and its environs by giving visual form to the essence of nature.[21] Painted images become a medium that mediates between humanity and nature. The gap between the subject and its external world is bridged in art, but it can still be experienced in the interaction with the physical landscape.

Viewed in this light there are essential differences between Hammershøi's landscapes on the one hand and those by Overbeck or am Ende on the other. In the Worpswede paintings Rilke observed a tension between the alien qualities of nature and its appropriation through the artist.[22] By contrast, Hammershøi's landscapes are at first glance characterised by a cool realism, reinforcing the impression of an insurmountable distance between the painting's space and the observer's space. Indeed, the sense of verisimilitude in his landscapes *View of Gentofte Lake. Sunshower* [100, p. 124] and *Landscape, From Lejre* [17, p. 35] seems very clearly accentuated due to the everyday nature of the scenes chosen. The monochrome colour scheme of Hammershøi's landscape *View of Gentofte Lake. Sunshower* represents a clear contrast to Overbeck's intensive palette of vibrant, luminous reds and greens. With his choice of colour Overbeck imbued his landscape with an atmosphere of harmony whereas Hammershøi's landscape evokes a distanced, uninvolved monotony. Here, the grey hue of the lake is reminiscent of a metallic surface, throwing up the flat tongue of land in front of it in sharp relief. The upper and lower halves of the painting are divided by the landscape and no longer appear to have any relationship with each other. Something very different is in play in the landscapes from Worpswede, where the distribution of clouds in the sky determines the lighting conditions on the ground in a natural way.

In Hammershøi's painting the firm materiality of the water stands in opposition to the diffuse structure of the sky arching above the water. This sense of a disconnectedness between the individual levels of the painting becomes even more striking in Hammershøi's *Landscape, From Lejre*, in which the transparent veil of clouds does not cast a single shadow

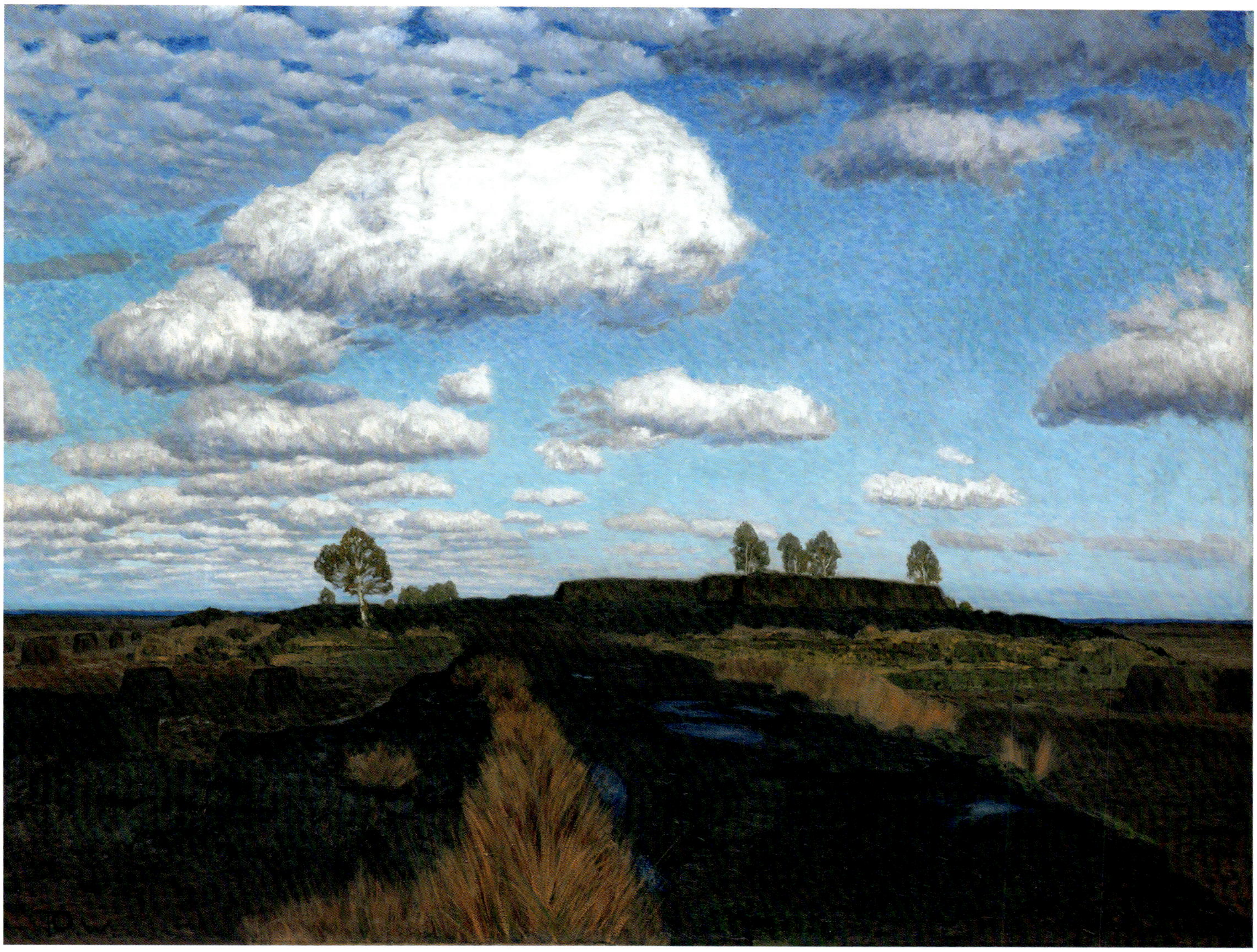

[128]
Fritz Overbeck 1869-1909 German
On the Moor c. 1904
Oil on canvas 156 x 200 cm
Bayerische Staatsgemäldesammlungen,
Neue Pinakothek, München

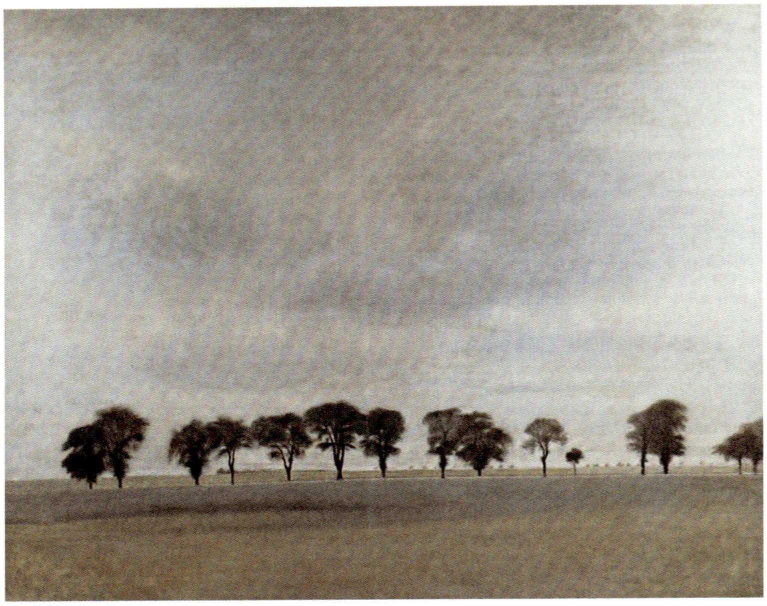

down onto the green hills. In formal terms, the link between heaven and earth is created by means of a uniform rhythm evoked in the softly undulating hills and delicate cloud patterns.[23] Independent of the vagaries of weather, filled with a diffuse light, Hammershøi's paintings cannot be assigned to a particular time of day or a particular season. Rather, and in spite of their everyday-like motifs, they evoke an impression of constancy and timelessness. Their formal, plane-like qualities create a distance to the observer, who notes a break between themselves and the remote landscape.

Unlike the landscapes from Worpswede, Hammershøi's paintings – notwithstanding all their sublime colours and drama – make no appeal to the observer's emotions. By contrast, the art created in Worpswede was regarded as "heartfelt" or "earnest" art and as "atmospheric paintings" even in its own day.[24] Rilke, too, regarded the landscape paintings from Worpswede as having the ability to "reveal [...] and also render immortal that which is true and the essential by means of the matter depicted".[25] Hammershøi's landscapes, which depict typically Danish and rather mundane settings, offer up no references to a hidden truth in their colour scheme or in their everyday-like choice of subject matter. Rather, their distancing and alienating qualities and their accentuation of planes serve to emphasise the gap between man and nature. The alienation between man and nature is suspended in these works of art, but not in the manner favoured by the Worpswede artists and in Rilke's concept of art.

Yet another aspect separates the landscapes by Hammershøi and those of the Worpswede artists. A central issue in Worpswede art concerns its turning to an original, unspoilt nature, which implies a refusal of life as it is led in the age of industrialisation. In their attempt at "maintaining a sense of nature that reality can no longer honour" the artists pursued a Romantic view of art which aimed to re-abolish the distance or alienation between subject and object.[26] Because of this Romantic Utopia they were able to celebrate their greatest success at the well-established, conservative art exhibition at the Münchener Glas-

[129]
Vilhelm Hammershøi 1864-1916 Danish
Landscape (Kongevejen near Gentofte) 1892
Oil on canvas 115 x 147 cm
Private collection

palast.[27] In contrast to such bucolic and largely unspoilt landscapes Hammershøi's paintings show farmed and cultured landscapes near Copenhagen; landscapes which bear clear traces of human activity.[28] For example, the trees shown in the landscape *Landscape (Kongevejen near Gentofte)* (1892) line a street [129]. Despite their sense of loneliness, which gives them a kinship with the Worpswede landscapes, Hammershøi's images show nature as a product of culture. His landscapes lack the Utopian element we see in the Worpswede works, which gives visual form to a subjective sense of nature.

To Rilke, too, the expression of earnest emotion was one of the indispensible functions of landscape painting. Landscape painting was to give visual expression to the common, i.e. the essential, traits of man and nature. By contrast, the distancing and the accentuation of planes inherent in Hammershøi's paintings would seem to exacerbate the gap between the landscape and the subject observing it. The work of art no longer serves to mediate between man and nature. Quite the contrary: The work of art's autonomy is accentuated, pointing to how it is a depiction of nature that is no longer consistent with the nature being depicted. If we follow this logic to its final conclusion, the work of art no longer serves any function for the observer. Rather, it has a heightened degree of autonomy and accentuates its self-sufficient being.

Rilke's contact with Rodin and his artists would serve to further his conviction that there was a break or gap between subject and object, and that this must be mediated in art. Humanity's alienation in the world, an issue that increasingly took centre stage for Rilke, meant that Hammershøi's art was viewed as prefiguring Rilke's late poems, the so-called *Dinggedichte* (1908).[29] As regards Rodin's influence on Rilke, however, there are obvious differences between the poet's views and Hammershøi's aesthetics; the two can only be brought to any degree of mutual harmony at a cursory inspection.

Shimmering surfaces: Rilke and Rodin

As one regards the works of the French sculptor Rodin and the paintings of Hammershøi, the differences between the two media – sculpture and painting – would seem at first glance to preclude any meaningful comparison. Yet when one considers Rilke's monograph and lectures about Rodin from the period 1902 to 1907 one does find relevant points of comparison between the two media.[30]

Rilke's contact to Rodin was mediated through his wife, Clara Rilke-Westhoff, who had worked at Rodin's studio during the early stages of her artistic endeavours.[31] During Rilke's stay in Sweden, over the course of which he also visited Copenhagen, he wrote a letter to Rodin in which Hammershøi does not receive even the most fleeing of mentions.[32] This is to say that Rilke concerned himself with the two artists during the same period of his life, but at first he did so without in any way combining the two.

Rilke's monograph on Rodin and the volume of poems entitled *Neue Gedichte* contain extensive deliberations on the torso figure that can also be applied to Hammershøi's paintings.[33] In 1908, for example, Rilke wrote the poem *Archaischer Torso Apollos*, which is also counted among his *Dinggedichte*. Hammershøi, too, had worked with torsos during an early stage of his artistic career; his body of work includes a drawn study of an antique torso of Aphrodite [131]. In the 19th century, tradition dictated that the education of artists involved the study of the ancients in order to learn and refine their own artistic abilities. Hammershøi's own alma mater, The Royal Danish Academy of Fine Arts in Copenhagen, also put emphasis

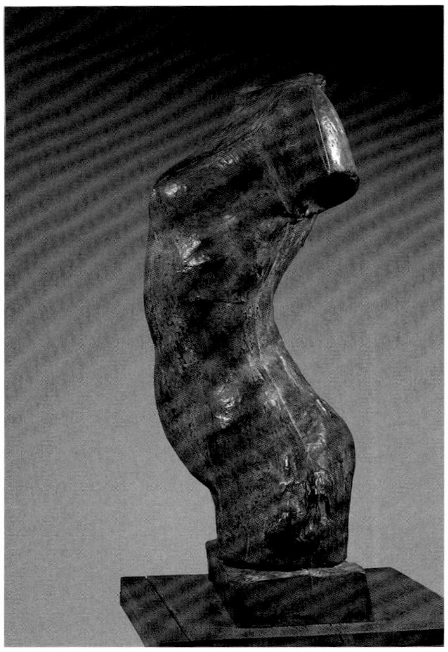

on drawing after Antique art.[34] One distinctive trait of Hammershøi's drawing concerns his undeniably sensual rendition of the motif; this is achieved through the soft lines that imbue the torso with an erotic air. The impression of liveliness and motion is emphasised by the curved lines of the back and the soft accentuation of the ribs. Such re-animation of stiff ancient art objects also reappears in the artist's later works.[35]

In his monograph on Rodin Rilke addressed the treatment of surfaces within the medium of sculpture. To him the special quality of Rodin's works resided in the fact that he transferred the earnestness and sincerity of the works to the surfaces of his sculptures, thereby rendering it visible to observers [130].[36] As Rilke contemplated Rodin's work, focusing especially on the movements of forms, Rilke arrived at a gaze that was oriented towards the material. This change in perception served to enhance the insight stating that the essence of things could no longer be glimpsed or discerned behind the surface; rather, they manifested themselves in their outer, concrete appearance. The sincerity of things could, then, be perceived through the visual observation of their concrete form.[37] It follows that according to Rilke's perspective the artist had an obligation to reproduce reality, i.e. its objective nature, as well as its essence or being.

Surface and sincerity may seem irreconcilable, but the issue is resolved in Rilke's aesthetics regarding the torso. For according to Rilke, it does not follow that a representation of reality must be an exact copy. Rather, the superiority of the artistic form over the real-life body is visualised in the fragmentary nature of the torso.[38] According to Rilke art may well emerge out of the body, but art also expands it because the body fragment attains new life in the recipient's imagination. Within the art of sculpture, then, the torso links nature and art to form a new whole.

In this context Hammershøi's sensuous drawing would seem to correspond to Rilke's concept of art. The blurred surface evokes an impression of life, whereas the break at the sculpture's arm has not been camouflaged. Closer inspection, however, reveals that Hammershøi also depicts the base on which the torso was presented. This renders visible the circumstances under which the torso was observed, which foregrounds the fact that we are observing an object – a work of art – via a painted reproduction. This detail makes it clearly distinct from the work of Rodin, whose sculptures are based on real, living bodies. Hammershøi's drawing, however, points to how it has an object as its motif; an object which is only imbued with life in its drawn representation. The complexity of his multi-media rendition raises the question of what type of earnestness is manifested in Hammershøi's painting. The essence of the original model or the reflection of the sculptor's soul in his sculpture would both be possible contenders. Yet another option might be that Hammershøi inscribes himself in his own work. Hammershøi did not offer any answer to these questions in his drawing; rather, he linked up a realistic rendition of his motif with a technical way of making it come alive.

Such convoluted renditions of art within art did not form part of Rilke's endeavours. Nevertheless his statements offer up certain parallels between the torso and the forest scenes painted by the early Impressionists; parallels that may be expanded to also encompass Hammershøi's landscapes.[39] Rilke defended Rodin's fragmented sculptures, comparing them to the Impressionist landscapes where trees are also not represented in their entirely, but as cropped or fragmented forms. The forest, whose interior cannot be seen in its entirety by the observer, but only as sections, was not randomly chosen by Rilke. Indeed, it

[130]
Auguste Rodin 1840-1917 French
Arched Torso of a Young Woman 1910
Bronze 86 x 48.1 x 32.2 cm
Musée Rodin, Paris

[131]
Vilhelm Hammershøi 1864-1916 Danish
Study drawing of plaster cast of ancient Greek Aphrodite, torso from c. 500 BC c. 1880
Charcoal on paper 75 x 48 cm
The Ambassador John L. Loeb Jr. Danish Art Collection, New York

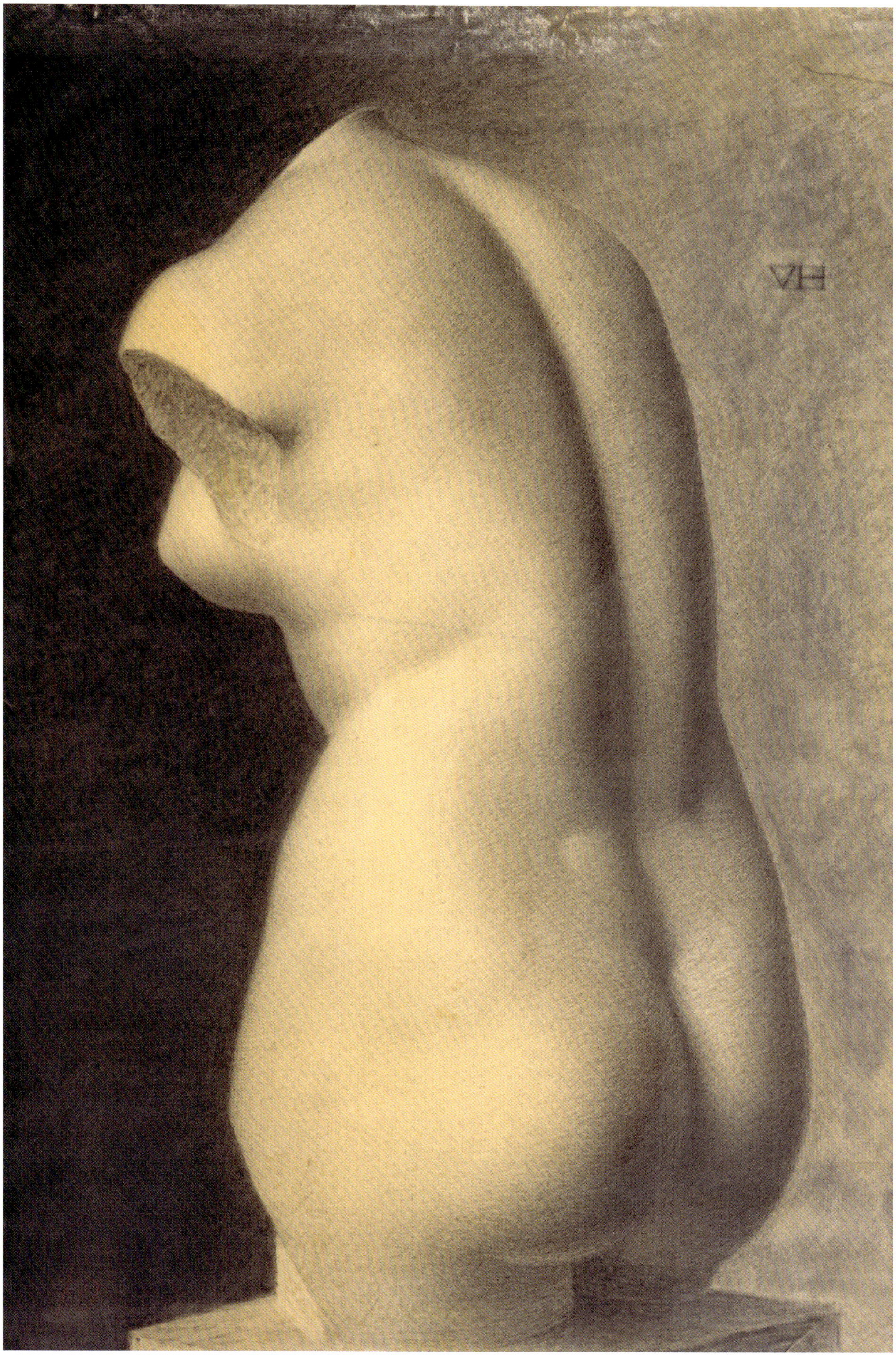
VH

forms a leitmotif running through his lyrical and personal writings, thereby taking on an emotional charge.[40] According to Rilke the towering trunks, the tree crowns evading the observer's gaze, and the observer's position in their midst symbolise the endless creation of nature and, hence, its essence. At the same time the forest interior constitutes a metaphor for the artist's innermost soul. In many of the paintings by late Romantic and Symbolist artists the forest also acts as an idealised sphere for artistic inspiration and earnestness, for example in the works of the Danish artist Valdemar Schønheyder Møller [114, p. 138].[41]

It is striking that to Rilke, the tree trunks are not alone in visualising earnestness; the space between the trunks serves the same purpose. In a letter written to a female friend, Rilke waxed lyrical: "These trees are glorious, but more glorious still is the sublimely elevated space between them; as if it, too, had grown with the trees."[42] The space formed through the interplay of various forms, gradually becoming laden with tension, was something that Rilke also regarded as an essential trait of Rodin's art. According to Rilke the gaze through and between Rodin's sculptures is what leads to a concentration of earnestness and sincerity that reveals the artwork's secret essence to observers in a particularly clear manner.[43] Thus Rilke subjected Rodin's works to a kind of "magical in-between" state which would, in principle, exclude any kind of emptiness. Indeed Rilke made this claim regarding Rodin's art by stating: that "There was no emptiness."[44]

By contrast, emptiness and the lack of a painterly condensation are important properties of Hammershøi's art.[45] This can be demonstrated in Hammershøi's forest paintings, which are in direct opposition to Rilke's theory about the space in-between as well as to the prevalent forest paintings of the time. German art criticism from as far back as 1900 attributed a certain magical quality to Hammershøi's forest scenes, pointing to, for example, a luminous sunset behind the trees.[46] This brought about the erroneous assumption that Hammershøi had indeed tried to depict the essence of things beneath a veil rather than on the surface.[47]

Hammershøi's trees are primarily found in front of an overcast sky unadorned by the warm glow of a rosy evening sun. Only in Hammershøi's landscape *Near Fortunen, Jægersborg Deer Park North of Copenhagen* from 1901 do the trees' soft shadows in the foreground suggest a source of light behind the trunks [113, p. 137]. However, the light is not alluring, but cool and sober. Only the indistinct shadows in the foreground evoke a fleeting sensation of immateriality. In contrast to Rilke's metaphorical treatment of the in-between space, Hammershøi accentuates the linear structure created by the tree trunks and branches. The spaces in between, however, remain lifeless. This is particularly obvious in *Landscape in Snow, Søndermarken* from 1895-96 [108, p. 131]. In this winter scene the foreground and background are both blurred and monochrome, a rendition that further emphasises the almost geometrical shapes of the branches. With this move Hammershøi took a step away from the forest metaphor as a manifestation of the artist's soul. What is more, the geometric qualities of the dark branches do not tally with the aesthetics of the arabesque which had become an expression of earnestness and endlessness in the Romantic era.[48] Rather, his paintings depict a forest as a formally autonomous entity.[49] This is not a forest that has been reproduced to correspond to an actual, specific forest; rather, it is a painted, deliberately stylised forest.

Even though Hammershøi's technique could certainly honour Rilke's insistence that art must make the object depicted come to life, the potential for interpretation represented by Hammershøi's works encompasses obvious examples of the contrary. His landscapes, for example, do not aim for a rendition and evocation of earnestness; rather, they primarily emphasise the formal and technical traits particular to the work as a work of art.

Empty mirror: Reality in and outside of the painting

The self-sufficiency of Hammershøi's pictorial spaces is particularly evident in the empty mirror motif, which is so strongly featured in the painting *Interior* from 1898 [64, p. 87]. Two aspects of the way in which the mirror is depicted are unusual. First of all, the emptiness of the mirror seems grating to us as observers; we would expect the room in front of it to be reflected in the glass, or at least we would expect the mirror to effect a visual expansion of the room.[50] Secondly, the observer's expectations are also stymied in the sense that the empty mirror does not allow for a new perspective on the figure such as the one offered by for example the Danish artist Christoffer Wilhelm Eckersberg (1783-1853) [132].

The mirror metaphor has traditionally held an elevated position within the art of painting because it represents art itself. Within the Symbolist movement it also enters into a very close, even erotic, relationship with the female figure, for example in the pastel *With Grégoire Le Roy. My Heart Weeps for Days of Yore* (1889) by the Belgian artist Fernand Khnopff (1858-1921), whose works may share the greatest affinity with Hammershøi's paintings when viewed in an international context [133].[51] The bridge arches, a frequently used motif in Khnopff's pastels, show how Khnopff used reflections in water to complete geometric figures, thereby creating unified wholes out of for example semi-circular arches. Here, the mirror image fuses with that which it reflects – which in turn is also outside of the image in real life – to form a complete circle. In this manner a new whole is created. This principle of completion can be transferred to the painting and its real-life motif. For example, the merging between subject and object is visualised in Khnopff's pastel by the kiss exchanged between the figure and its mirror image. Even though they are divided by the surface of the mirror it seems as if the figure can experience its other self visually and sensuously. The mirror facilitates a complete experience of the subject and object. The self standing before the mirror recognises its own sensuous nature in its external appearance. Thus, inner and outer life are brought into a state of interplay and harmony through the mirror image.

Rilke also ascribes another function to the art of painting: to mediate between the external, the subject, and inner earnestness. For example, Rilke's *Requiem for a Friend* from 1908, which he dedicated to the late painter Paula Modersohn-Becker, features a similar use of the mirror as an expansion of reality. Rilke writes about the artist from Worpswede and her relationship with painting: "You placed yourself in front of the mirror, immersed yourself in it, except for your gaze, which remained in front of it and did not say 'this is I', no, 'this is'."[52] Here Rilke clearly expresses the view that art should not be regarded as a depiction of reality that completely coincides with that reality. Rather, the subject in front of the mirror recognises the essence of reality without feeling identical to the mirror image. Instead of simply depicting a copy of reality, then, the mirror leads to a recognition of the essence of reality. At the same time it accentuates the separation between reality and its representation in the mirror, or the separation between subject and object. If we transpose this to the realm of painting, Rilke's mirror can be interpreted as a means for accentuating the core of reality through its realistic representation, thereby communicating that core to the observer.

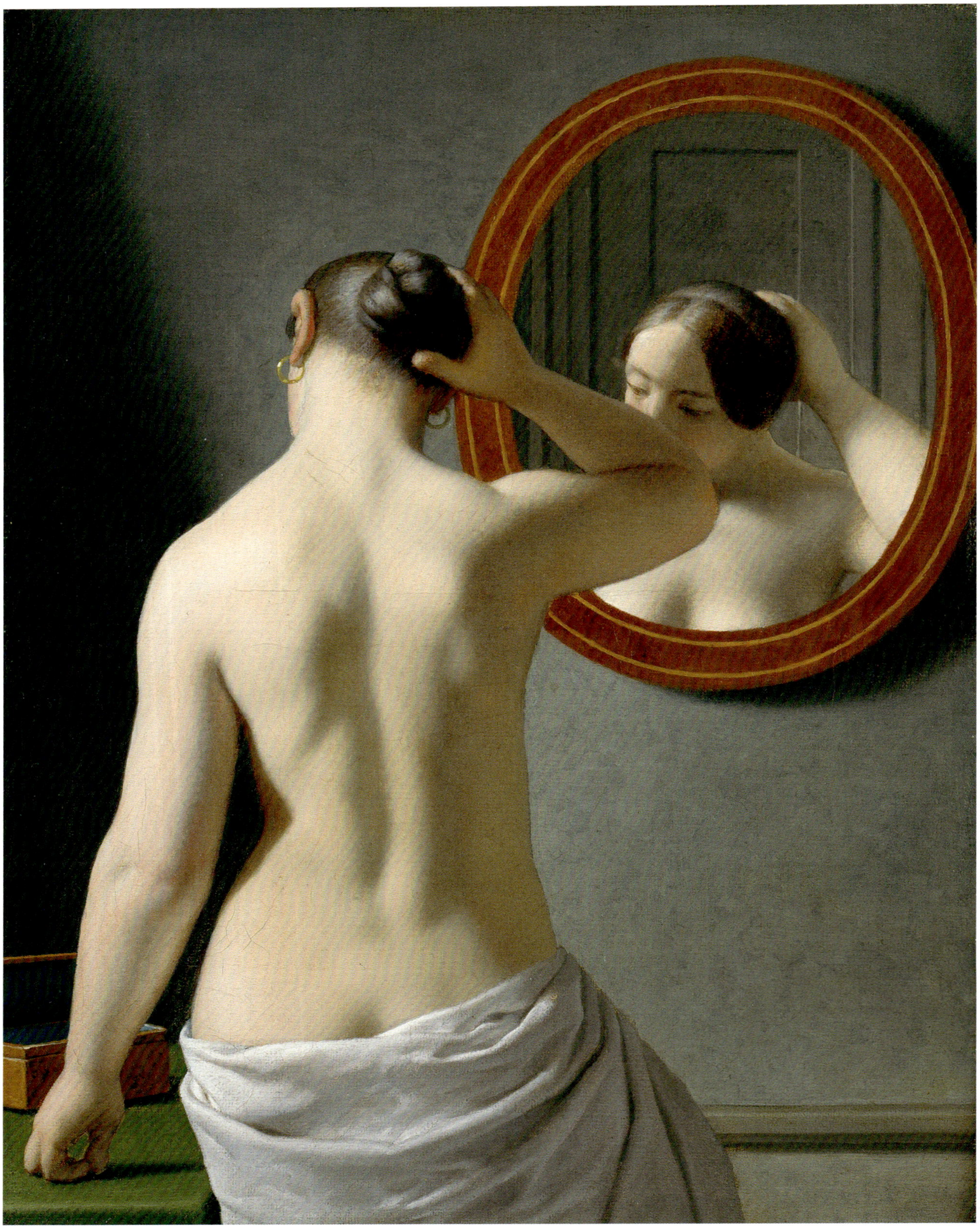

[132]
Christoffer Wilhelm Eckersberg 1783-1853 Danish
A Nude Woman doing her Hair before a Mirror 1841
Oil on canvas 33.5 x 26.0 cm
The Hirschsprung Collection, Copenhagen

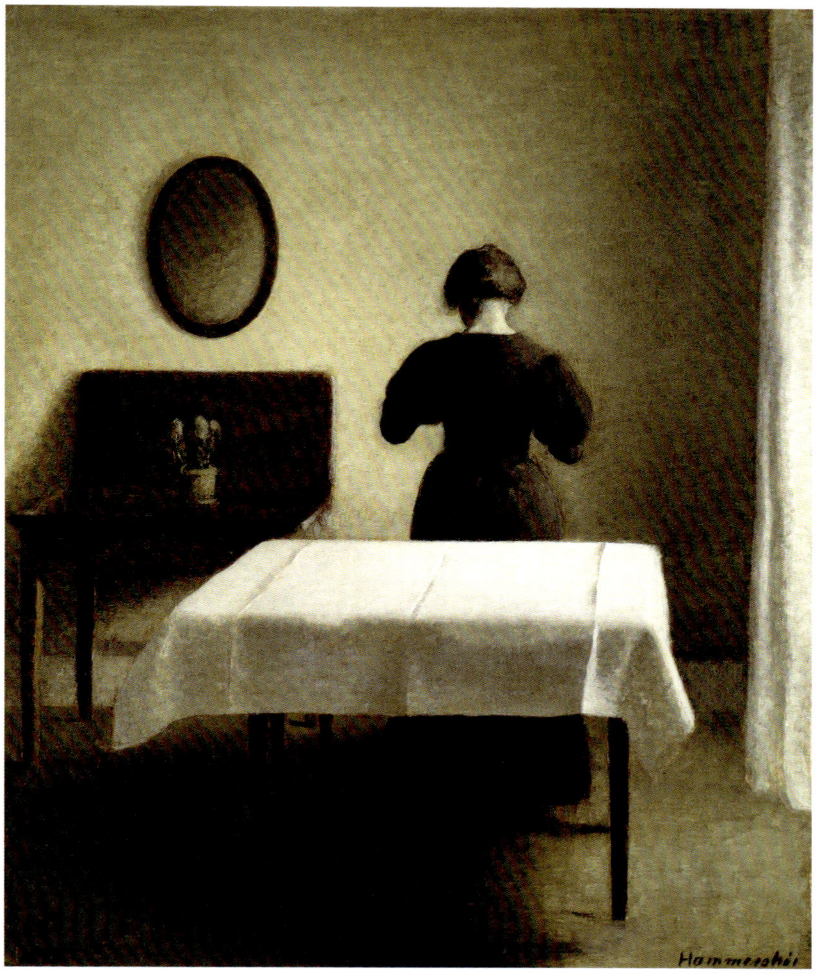

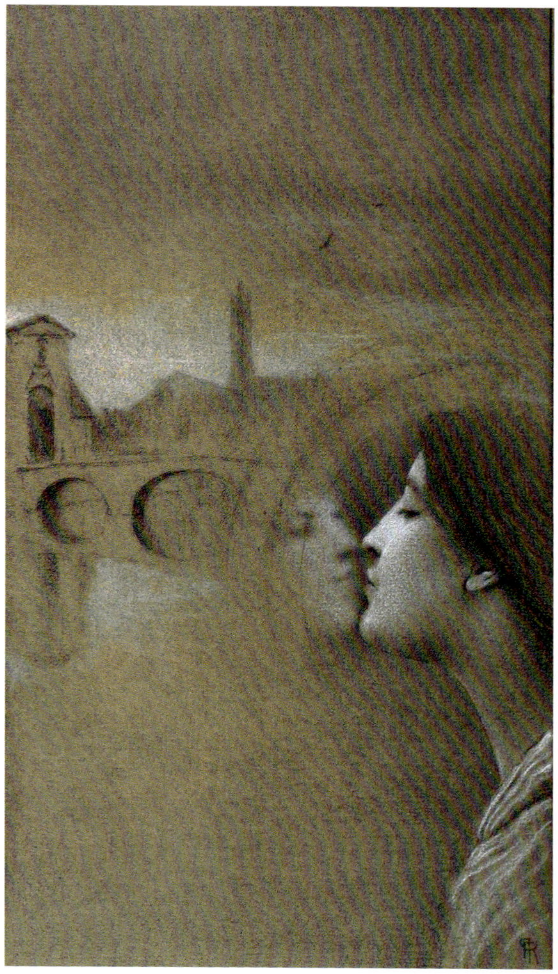

[64]
Vilhelm Hammershøi 1864-1916 Danish
Interior 1898
Oil on canvas 51.5 x 46 cm
Nationalmuseum, Stockholm

[133]
Fernand Khnopff 1858-1921 Belgian
With Grégoire Le Roy. My Heart Weeps for Days of Yore 1889
Black pencil, chalk and coloured pencil on blue-gray paper
23.5 x 14.5 cm
The Hearn Family Trust, New York

The mirror image in Khnopff's pastel is diffusely rendered. According to Rilke, this means that it highlights the difference between subject and object which can only be communicated through art. For the observer, then, the mirror in Khnopff and Rilke always entails an aspect of additional value: As with the landscape, which is experienced as something alien or other, the observer first constitutes himself through the mirror and the ways in which reality differs from the mirror image.

Hammershøi's mirror, however, is empty. As an autonomous form, the surface of the mirror does not enter into any relationship with the figure, the figure's surroundings, or with the observer and the space that surrounds the observer. Thus, the presence of the mirror in the painting entails no added value for the painting and the observer. Rather, the mirror becomes an indifferent sign without reference to reality within and outside of the painting. The introduction of this pictorial element foregrounds Hammershøi's deviation from a realistic as well as a Symbolist concept of art because his mirror neither reflects its surroundings nor links the essential in reality with the essential in art. Here, indifference and emptiness is ascribed value in itself. Even when Rilke later turned to engage with the works of the French artist Paul Cézanne (1839-1906), emptiness without any semantic reference is given no place within his concept of art.[53]

In summary, Hammershøi's work can in many respects be compared with that of other artists of his day as regards motif and technique. In his paintings Hammershøi, too, worked with one of the specific issues of modernity: the subject's alienation from the world around it. In contrast to Rilke, Hammershøi's art ascribes no mediating role to the art of painting.[54] His art gives visual form to "the lack of essence in our present age" and thus to emptiness, its new significant property.[55] As was poignantly stated in one of the newspaper reviews of the time, Hammershøi's pictorial elements are "without essence" or "object-less".[56] Yet the differences between Rilke's and Hammershøi's conception of art are not expressed by Hammershøi's relinquishing of depicting the essence of things. Rather, they reside in the visualisation of emptiness as the modern world's new essence. The divergence between Hammershøi's aesthetics and Rilke's conception of art does not entail an issue of degree; it concerns an essential difference. As Rilke worked intensively with Hammershøi's work he must have realised that it was incompatible with his own convictions, and this may have been the reason why this particular venture into art criticism never reached fruition.

Anne Hemkendreis (born 1984) graduated from the Leuphana University in Lüneburg, Germany, with a thesis on "Vilhelm Hammershøi and the Magic of the Everyday". She teaches at the Leuphana University. In 2010 she completed her master's degree from the Ruhr University in Bochum, Germany, and Trinity College, Dublin, Ireland with distinction. Her research focuses on juxtaposing interior paintings from various periods, with particular emphasis on 19th century painting.

NOTES

1 Rainer Maria Rilke's letter dated 10 November 1905, in Hamburg, 2003, p. 133: "Hammershøj ist nicht von denen, über die man rasch sprechen muss. Sein Werk ist lang und langsam und in welchem Augenblick man es auch erfassen mag, es wird immer voller Anlass sein, vom Wichtigen und Wesentlichen in der Kunst zu sprechen."

2 Felix Krämer, "Dokumentation", in Hamburg, 2003, p. 130.

3 Rainer Maria Rilke's letter dated 22 November 1904, in Vad, 1988 (1992), pp. 404-406 & Hamburg, 2003, pp. 131-132: "innerlich zu beschäftigen".

4 Vad, 1988 (1992), p. 404-406 & Hamburg, 2003, p. 131: "wesentlich zu erfassen".

5 Vad, 1988 (1992), pp. 404-406 & Hamburg, 2003, p. 131.

6 Poul Vad, Vad, 1988 (1992), p. 275.

7 Friederike Felicitas Günther, "Cézanne als dionysischer Künstler: Rilkes Weg von Rodin zu Cézanne", in Hoffmann et al., 2008, p. 125.

8 Hoffmann et al., 2008, p. 275. Even though Rilke mastered written Danish, Poul Vad believes that language barriers may also have been an underlying cause beneath the lack of a connection between poet and painter. Cf. in this context Vad, 1988 (1992), p. 271.

9 Felix Krämer in Hamburg, 2003, p. 131.

10 Rilke, letter dated 10 November 1905, in Vad 1988 (1992), p. 406 & Hamburg, 2003, p. 133: "sehr am Herzen liege".

11 Vad 1988 (1992), p. 405 & Hamburg, 2003, p. 132: "vorbereitet, eingeweiht, durchdrungen genug", "Wesen dieses köstlichen Meisters".

12 Rainer Maria Rilke, "Worpswede", in Bremen, 2003, p. 61.

13 Rilke, letter dated 10 November 1905, in Vad 1988 (1992), p. 406 & Hamburg, 2003, p. 133.

14 "Niederdeutsche Kunst", in Die Post, 10/11, no date, 1900: "[E]ine Malerei, die dem Auge Reize bietet, [aber] die Seele unbefriedigt läßt." From Hammershøi's mother's collection, now housed in the Hirschsprung Collection in Copenhagen.

15 Rainer Stamm, "Paula Modersohn-Becker und Rainer Maria Rilke in Paris", in Bremen, 2007, p. 252. While Rilke lived in Worpswede a special bond existed between Rilke and the artists Clara (Rilke-) Westhoff, Paula (Modersohn-) Becker, and Heinrich Vogeler.

16 Rilke, "Worpswede", in Bremen 2003, p. 87.

17 Weltke-Wortmann, 1979, p. 161 & Ritter, 2009, p. 17.

18 New York & Washington, D.C., 1983, 8. The plans to meet Jacobsen were also the reason underlying Rilke's journey to Scandinavia.

19 Pettit, 1983, p. 130.

20 Rilke, "Worpswede", in Bremen, 2003, p. 60.

21 Sieghild Bogumil-Notz, "Rilke und die Kunst: ein kongeniales Gespräch", in Bremen, 2003, p. 306.

22 Rilke, "Worpswede", in Rilke. Worpswede. Eine Ausstellung als Phantasie über ein Buch, 2003, p. 81.

23 Vad, 1992, p. 260.

24 Schuhmann et al, no year, p. 7: "innerliche Kunst" "Stimmungsbilder".

25 Rilke, 2003, p. 95: "am herangezogenen Stoff das Eigentliche und Wesenhafte frei [zu] legen und [...] auch [zu] verewigen."

26 Boulboullé & Zeiss, 1989, p. 55.

27 Boulboullé & Zeiss, 1989, p. 49. Artists from Worpswede won fame through their exhibition at the Münchener Glaspalast in 1895. According to their own statements, however, they were aware of the discrepancies between the art exhibited at the Glaspalast and Secessionist art.

28 Kasper Monrad, "Stories that are not told – The narrative element in Hammershøi's art.", in Copenhagen, 2000, pp. 253-254.

29 Vad, 1992, p. 277.

30 Günther, in Hoffmann et al., 2008, p. 125.

31 Emde, 1949, p. 90.

32 Rainer Maria Rilke's letter to Rodin dated 11 August 1904, in Luck, 2001, p. 95.

33 Emde, 1949, p. 28.

34 Berman, 2007, pp. 37-38.

35 Felix Krämer in Hamburg, 2003, p. 13. One example would be the three female figures in the painting Greek Relief from 1891, which seem imbued with life because of Hammershøi's rhythmic brushstrokes.

36 Carsten Strathausen, The Look of Things. Poetry and Vision around 1900, London 2003, p. 213.

37 Rainer Maria Rilke, Auguste Rodin. Leipzig 1930, p. 41.

38 Emde, 1949, p. 30-31.

39 Emde, 1949, p. 31.

40 Rainer Maria Rilke, "Verstreute und nachgelassene Gedichte", in Dietrich Bode (ed.): Rainer Maria Rilke: Gedichte, Stuttgart 2009, p. 238.

41 Similar works from the 19th century can be found in the oeuvres of Fernand Khnopff (Belgium), Prince Eugen (Sweden), and Julius Paulsen (Denmark).

42 Rainer Maria Rilke, letter dated 5 August 1919, in Briefe an eine Freundin. 1918-1925, undated, 1944, p. 16: "Diese Bäume sind herrlich, aber herrlicher noch ist der erhabene gesteigerte Raum zwischen ihnen: als hätte mit ihrem Wachstum auch er zugenommen."

43 Rilke, 1930, p. 70.

44 Rilke, 1930, p. 16: "magischem Dazwischen", "Es gab keine Leere."

45 Krämer, 2007, p. 157. Krämer was interested in motivic emptiness. As regards the hollowing out of traditional iconography in Hammershøi's paintings, cf. Monrad, in Copenhagen, 2000, p. 247.

46 E. N. Pascent: "Untitled (Article on Paris exhibition 1900)" in: Kunst für Alle. No. 10, 1900-1901, vol. 16 1901, p. 348.

47 Anonymous, "Kunst und Wissenschaft", in Berliner Lokaler Anzeiger, 29 October 1905. From Hammershøi's mother's collection, now housed at The Hirschsprung Collection in Copenhagen.

48 Werner Busch: Die notwendige Arabeske. Wirklichkeitsaneignung und Stilisierung in der deutschen Kunst des 19. Jahrhunderts, Berlin 1985.

49 Vad, 1992, p. 158.

50 The most famous example would be the Arnolfini portrait from 1434 by the famous Dutch painter Jan van Eyck, now housed at the National Gallery in London.

51 Krämer, 2007, p. 176.

52 Richard W. Pettit, "The poet's eye for the arts: Rilke views visual arts around 1900", in Forster-Hahn, 1996, p. 270.

53 Rilke, 1952, p. 45. Here Cézanne is compared to a dog sitting in front of the mirror, dispassionately regarding its own reflection.

54 Renate Breuninger, Wirklichkeit in der Dichtung Rilkes. Frankfurt am Main, Bern, New York & Paris 1991, p. 104.

55 Ibid., p. 151: "Gestaltlosigkeit der Gegenwart".

56 Emil Heilbut, "Wilhelm Hammershöi. (Ausstellung bei Schulte)", in Der Tag, 7.11.1905, no place named: "wesenslos", "gegenstandslos". From Hammershøi's mother's collection, now housed at The Hirschsprung Collection in Copenhagen.

HAMMERSHØI AND HOMELESSNESS

PETER NØRGAARD LARSEN

A sense of not feeling that you belong, of not being able to find your place in the work permeates Hammershøi's works. In recent years the concept of homelessness has taken on a privileged status. Regardless of whether the issue at hand is migration, gender, homeland, or exile, the analyses all share a focus on notions of cultural identity, of a sense of belonging or a lack thereof. This article is concerned with the notion that homelessness might also be a fruitful concept in the appreciation of Hammershøi's art; perhaps most obviously so in the many interiors which quite literally create a space where modern man can meditate on their own homelessness and difficulties in finding their way home.

Among all of Hammershøi's paintings of architecture *Amalienborg Square, Copenhagen* is the most monumental and grand [122, p. 123]. From a position in Christian VIII's mansion, one of the four mansions that make up the present-day Amalienborg Palace, Hammershøi painted the view towards the equestrian statue of Frederik V, created by the French sculptor Saly, and towards the Christian IX mansion, which now serves as the monarch's residence. The striking lighting scheme with the strongly lit base and rider highlights the monument and prevents it from becoming lost against the architecture and its wealth of detail.

As in this work, Hammershøi's paintings of architecture are usually devoid of human presence. This does not preclude the presence of traces of human activity, yet by mustering his exceptional technical and compositional skills Hammershøi achieves a mastery of his motifs so great that he appears to be draining them of life. As observers we get a sense that time is not just passing with tremendous slowness, but that Hammershøi has successfully stopped time altogether. Hammershøi does not paint modern urban life or new buildings. He favours the classical 18th century face of Copenhagen with its monumental mansions.

Even though Hammershøi scholars do not always agree on how his works should be interpreted, there is no disagreement on the point that aside from the distinctive aesthetic and colouristic sensibilities of his motifs, they also contain more than they appear to. The disagreement among scholars concerns the nature of this *more* – whether the depopulated squares and silent rooms carry an emptiness, melancholia, alienation, eeriness, a repression, or something similar in response to the existential challenges arising on the threshold of modern life. With this text I will seek to outline an outlook that inscribes Hammershøi's works in a distinctly Danish and Northern European embodiment of the sublime (the horror-tinged experience of the beauty of nature, particularly in its grandest incarnations).[1] In so doing, I hope to arrive at stating something useful about how Hammershøi's works can be perceived simultaneously as unique, autonomous visual expressions and as utterances tinted by their own epoch, eloquently expressing a sense of homesickness and homelessness, utterances about how the artist strives to find his place in the world through his painting.

The domesticated sublime

In his comprehensive essay *Det pittoreske øje (The Picturesque Eye)* (2011) on the Danish Golden Age of art (a period which roughly corresponds to the first half of the 19th century), literary historian Klaus P. Mortensen sets out to describe how the sublime in Danish literature, thinking, and art undergoes a gradual shift towards the picturesque during the decades around 1800.[2] Apart from a very few exceptions – such as Jens Baggesen's dizzying poetry in *Labyrinthen ("The Labyrinth")* and Jens Juel's Swiss, stormy landscapes – Danish sentiments veered towards a far more sober approach to nature. Juel's dramatic depictions, anchored in European sensibilities, of man's encounter with a threatening, magnificent nature takes on a rather more cultured feel in Christoffer Wilhelm Eckersberg's interpretation, where the encounter involves rather less life-threatening natural settings such as the Cliffs of Møn [135].

The sublime experience of nature provides a subtext for Eckersberg's painting, but things never get truly dangerous. The encounter between cultured nature and "real" nature becomes a controlled, distanced experience where participants stick to the well-trodden pathways and follow the printed guide. A similar controlled experience of nature lay underneath the new design of the Frederiksberg Gardens in Copenhagen created around the same time. Here, a symmetrical garden design in the Baroque style was transformed into a

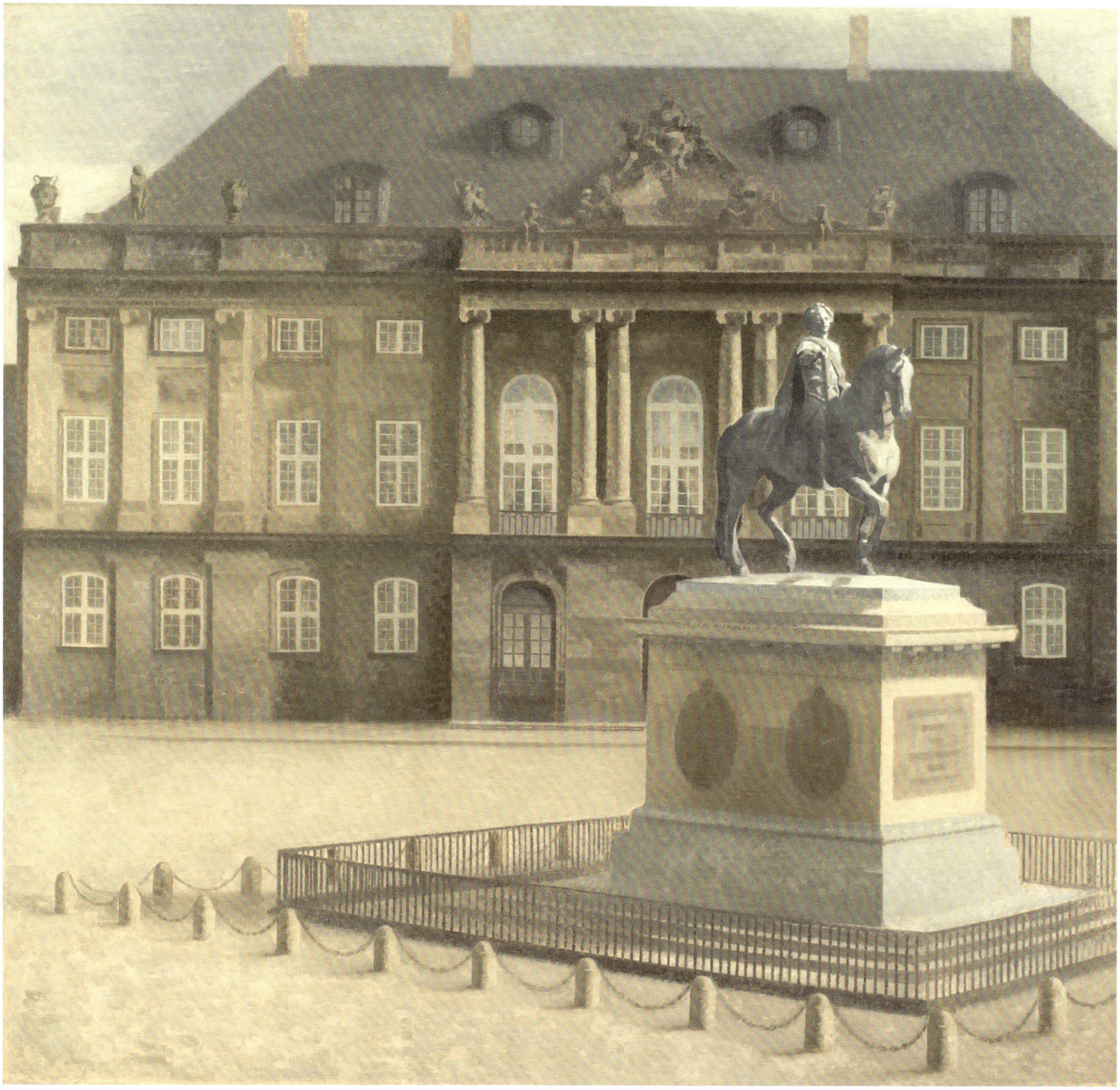

[123]
Vilhelm Hammershøi 1864-1916 Danish
Amalienborg Square, Copenhagen 1896
Oil on canvas 136.5 x 136.5 cm
Statens Museum for Kunst

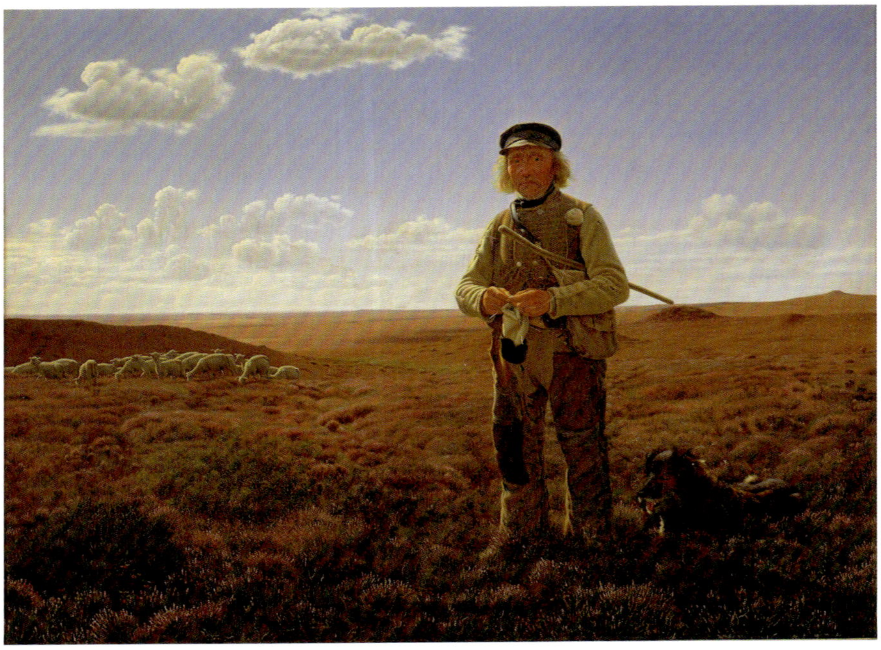

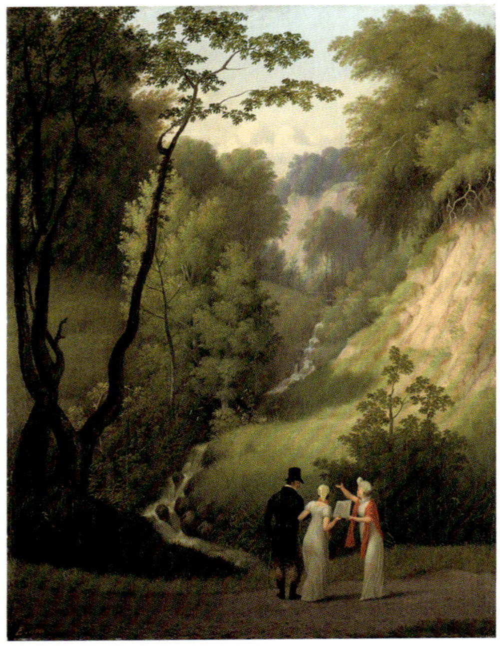

Romantic scene of meandering paths, channels, and picturesque scenes. Everything was carefully designed to provide the perambulating visitors with a walk rich in variety and natural scenery, given additional zest by a sprinkling of architectural elements from the wide world outside of Copenhagen, for example a Chinese gazebo and a Greek temple. This is nature transformed into Legoland, a place where everything has been scaled down and where everything can be taken in and handled in an easily manageable format.

In the decades that followed such carefully orchestrated and controlled experiences of nature became a fundamental precondition for what would subsequently be called The Danish Golden Age. Eckersberg developed his own distinctive theory of perspective as a matrix for the harmonious worldview favoured in the Golden Age. With his systematised depiction of nature and insistence on detailed studies Eckersberg created the foundation of the view of art that greatly infused Danish artists from the Golden Age and through to the advent of Naturalism; a view of art based on verisimilitude in the representation of nature.

An important, yet often overlooked figure from the latter half of the 19th century was the painter Frederik Vermehren. In addition to being one of Eckersberg's students he also carried on the torch as a professor at The Royal Academy of Fine Arts in Copenhagen, where the young Hammershøi was among his students. During his many years as a professor (1873-1901) Vermehren acted as teacher to several generations of artists, and with his resolute insistence on a schematic, realistic idealism that had been passed on to him by Eckersberg he came to appear as something as an anachronism in his latter years – a relic from the old world. Nevertheless, Vermehren was in fact among the very first to recognise Hammershøi's distinctive qualities. Perhaps this was because Vermehren, when regarding Hammershøi's works, once again saw some of the perfectionism and interest in constructive image composition that old Eckersberg introduced to Danish art.[3]

[134]
Frederik Vermehren 1823-1910 Dansk
A Jutland Shepherd on the Moors 1855
Oil on canvas 59.5 x 80 cm
Statens Museum for Kunst

[135]
Christoffer Wilhelm Eckersberg 1783-1853 Danish
View of the Park of Liselund Manor on the Island of Møn 1810
Oil on canvas 54.7 x 41.3 cm
Statens Museum for Kunst

From the 1850s up until his death in 1910 Vermehren endeavoured to reconcile an ever-more insistent reality with an artificial artistic ideality [134]. The conflict was not just artistic in scope; it also concerned existentialist issues and was rooted in its time. By painstakingly accounting for even the smallest details Vermehren tried to create order, to master the conflict between ideal and reality within the manageable format offered by the canvas. As the absolutist worldview began to crack, a sense of division, uncertainty, and abandonment was no longer the exclusive province of the particularly sensitive such as Søren Kierkegaard. From the mid-19th century onwards such sensibilities grew more widespread, eventually becoming a fundamental condition for humanity's view of itself and the world. The works of Vermehren and the late Golden Age of Danish art give visual form to the clash between the old and new worlds and can be perceived as an insistent attempt at maintaining and preserving idealistic contents, transposing them to an increasingly profane concept of art and an increasingly secular world view.

To Hammershøi the situation was different. Science and medicine and the entire positivistic worldview had intervened, blocking the road to the lost Arcadia. The artist was unavoidably affected by modern life and the sense of division that followed in the wake of the old world's breakdown. It is during this period of transit between the 19th and 20th centuries, between tradition and modernity, that Hammershøi paints his works, endeavouring to handle and master the modern world. He did not take the approach favoured by the devoutly Symbolist artists, which would have involved a rejection of the Danish tradition for verisimilitude in favour of Francophile, formalistic experiments and fanciful visions of religious transcendence. Rather, he retained the grid developed by Eckersberg and a matrix that was anchored in reality, effecting a shift by displacing tradition from the familiar and everyday-like towards something else, something more indefinable: the domesticated sublime. From the basis of what is in many ways Hammershøi's artistic and cultural point of departure, his familiar or *heimliche* setting – i.e. the bourgeois interiors and extensive endeavours to create harmony so typical of the Late Golden Age – we see a change and a cleansing in which the homely and familiar shifts towards something *unheimlich*, which is – to varying degrees, depending on the interpretative sensibility – experienced as eerie, uncertain, perhaps even as something that provokes anxiety.

Homelessness

In the Freudian sense of the term, the *Unheimliche* or the uncanny (1919), is associated with a perception of modern life's lack of norms, particularly with modern, godless man's sense that there is no way back to the safe solidity of childhood and the Golden Age.[4] The home as a social womb had been replaced by an awareness of a fundamental loneliness, and in Hammershøi this takes the form of a range of interiors that quite literally allow room for modern man's deliberations on their homelessness and the difficulties involved in finding the way home.

Freud regarded the horrors of World War I as a significant catalyst for the study of *Das Unheimliche*. The homely, safe European civilisation was threatened by a division and destruction which shifted the sense of the uncanny/*Unheimliche* from each individual's own mental maladjustment to a universal socio-cultural state infused with anxiety and a sense of homelessness. A similar diagnosis was made by the German philosopher Martin Heidegger; in 1947, against the backdrop of the Great Depression and World War II, he concluded that "Homelessness is coming to be the destiny of the world!" [5]

In cultural analyses and anthropological studies from the recent decades Heidegger's statement has taken on new relevance, giving the concept of homelessness a privileged status as a key concept. Regardless of whether the issue at hand is migration, gender, homestead, or exile the concept of cultural identity, of a sense of belonging or a lack thereof, is a central feature of the analyses. To me there is no doubt that the concept of homelessness can also be fruitful for the understanding of significant aspects of Hammershøi's art. For example, a sense of not belonging, of not being able to find one's place in the world permeates Hammershøi's works. Perhaps it does so most obviously in the many interiors, but his paintings of architecture can also be regarded from this point of view.

Hammershøi, as we know, did not leave behind any great wealth of biographical material. Quotations are taken from the same few known interviews and letters, and the same fragments and memoirs communicated by contemporary fellow artists are brought into play over and over again. Despite the dearth of material, however, we see a clear outline of a person who, right from his earliest years at the Academy, stood apart by virtue of his art and special talent, but also by virtue of his personality. With his well-bred manners and education Hammershøi seems to have distanced himself from most of his contemporaries at the Academy. He kept himself to himself, maintained a certain reserve and did not say much, neither as a young man nor later in life. This reserved exclusivity, paired with the doubts and insecurities that infused the entire period and its experience of collapse and breakdown, has fuelled a general view of Hammershøi as a gloomy melancholy figure who had difficulties facing the world and shielded himself from it. Undoubtedly this view is to some extent true, but Hammershøi did not in any way isolate himself. He was an active participant on the art scene of his day, he travelled extensively, and most importantly of all he translated his experience of homelessness into art. This is to say that the claim that Hammershøi's works are (also) about homelessness does not suggest that repressed and unconscious issues find expression in his art; quite the contrary: Hammershøi was fully aware of his homelessness, which is exactly why he sought with such insistence to handle it in his paintings.

In recent years the world of contemporary art, particularly the sections engaged with migration-related art, has discussed whether the practice of art can be viewed as an embodiment of the artist's striving to create a special place to where one belongs and in which one feels at home.[6] Often as a response to some kind of maladjustment, a sense of not belonging and a loss of cultural identity. Once again inspiration for this position comes from Heidegger's perception of the concept of *wohnen* (living in the sense of dwelling), which to him involves much more than simply building and living in a home.[7] It also encompasses a sense of being anchored, of being particularly closely connected to something; a place, a region, a city. In English *wohnen* is often translated as *dwelling,* which also suggests a wider sense of belonging. Heidegger developed his concept of *wohnen* to signify that something had been lost within modern society and that this was part of the reason why mankind has become rootless and in need of some guiding principle.

The Interior – the special place

For Hammershøi the art of painting – especially when applied to interiors – became the special place where he could define and create a seemingly well-defined and safe base. The German philosopher Walter Benjamin describes the interior as the private citizen's universe, a framework surrounding a personal self-staging in which you construct and consolidate your

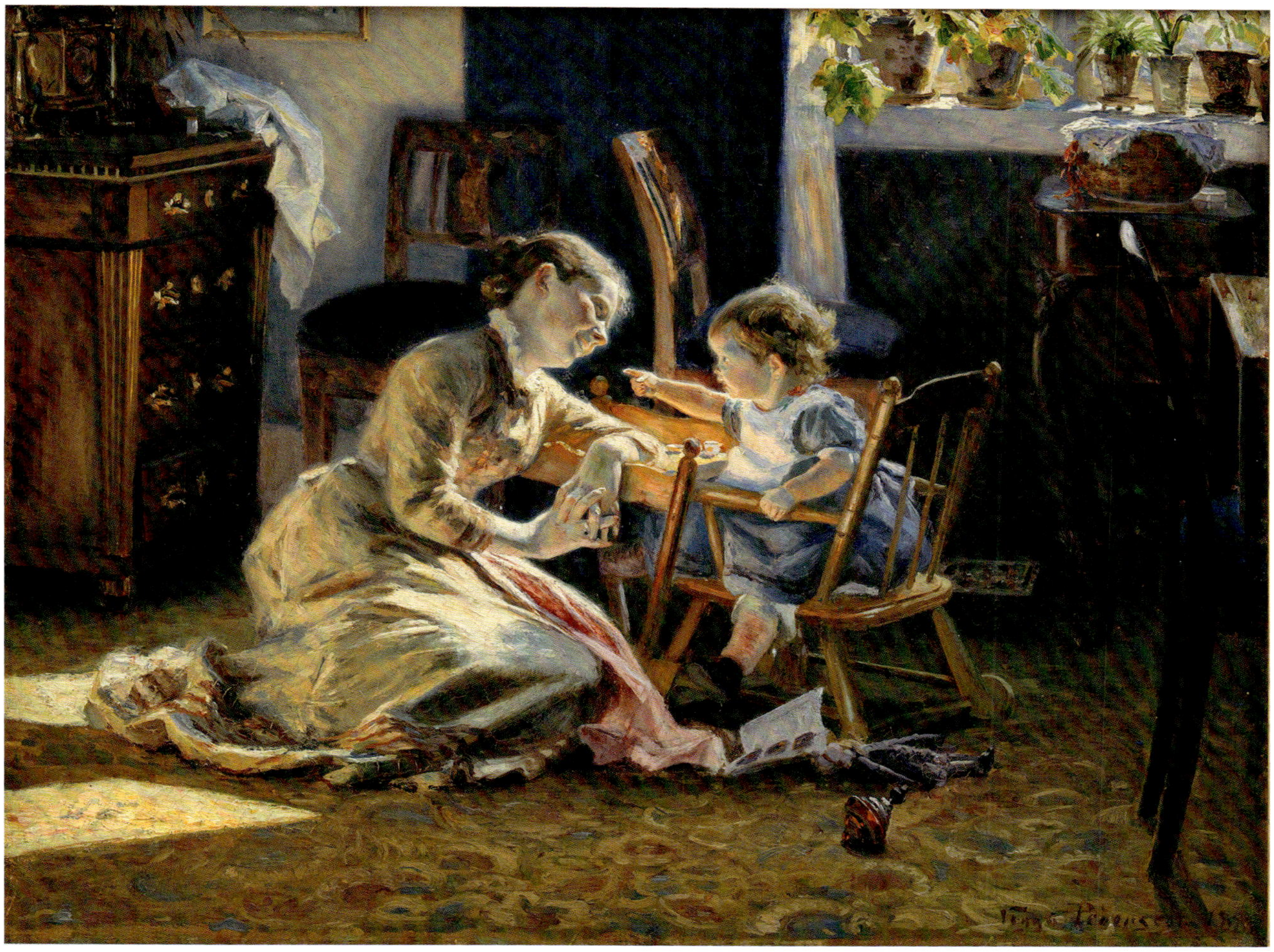

[136]
Viggo Pedersen 1854-1926 Danish
Sunshine in the Living Room. The Artist's Wife and Child 1888
Oil on canvas 35.5 x 45.5 cm
Statens Museum for Kunst

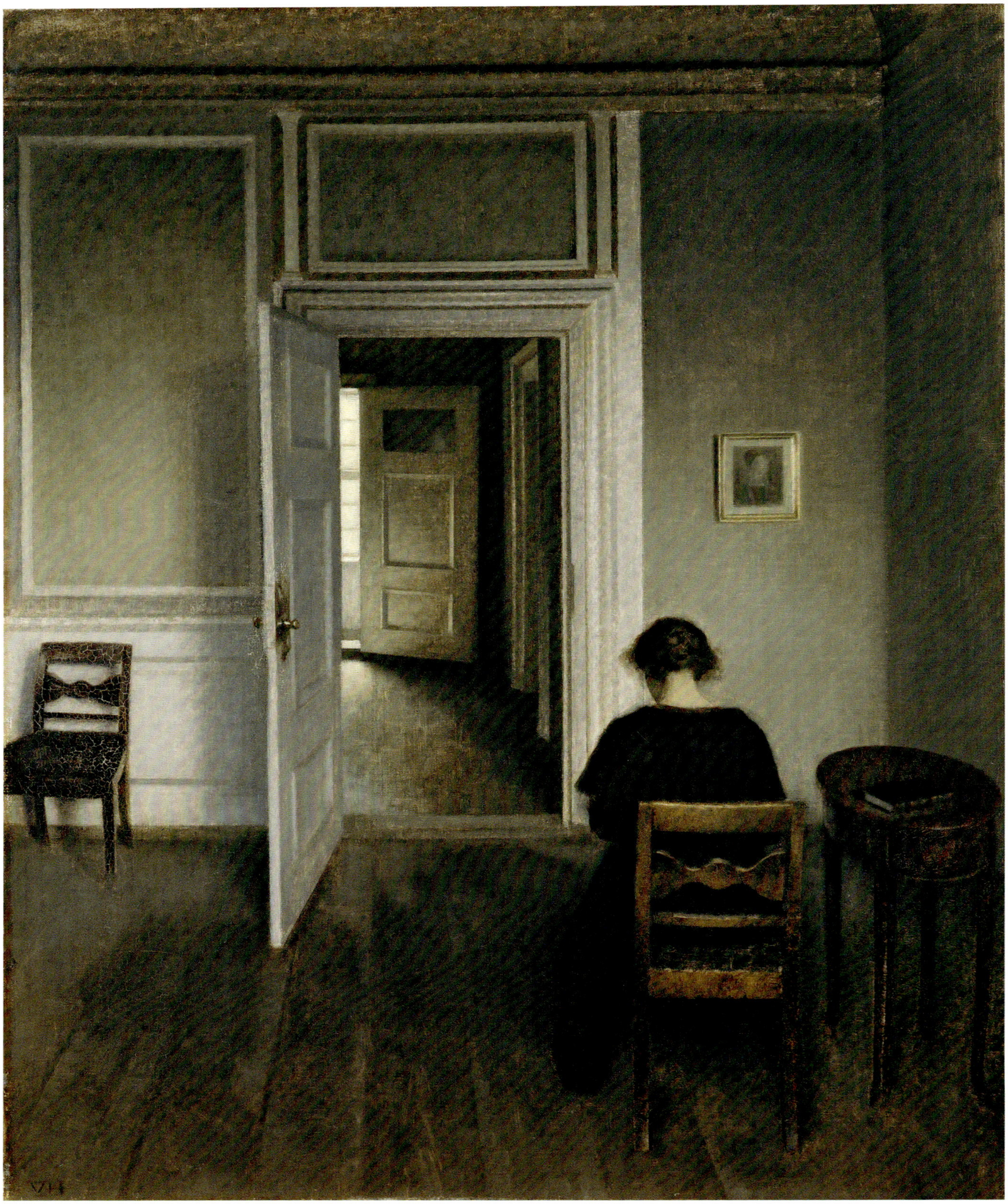

[137]
Vilhelm Hammershøi 1864-1916 Danish
Interior. Strandgade 30 1908
Oil on canvas 71 x 57.5 (79 x 66) cm
ARoS Aarhus Kunstmuseum

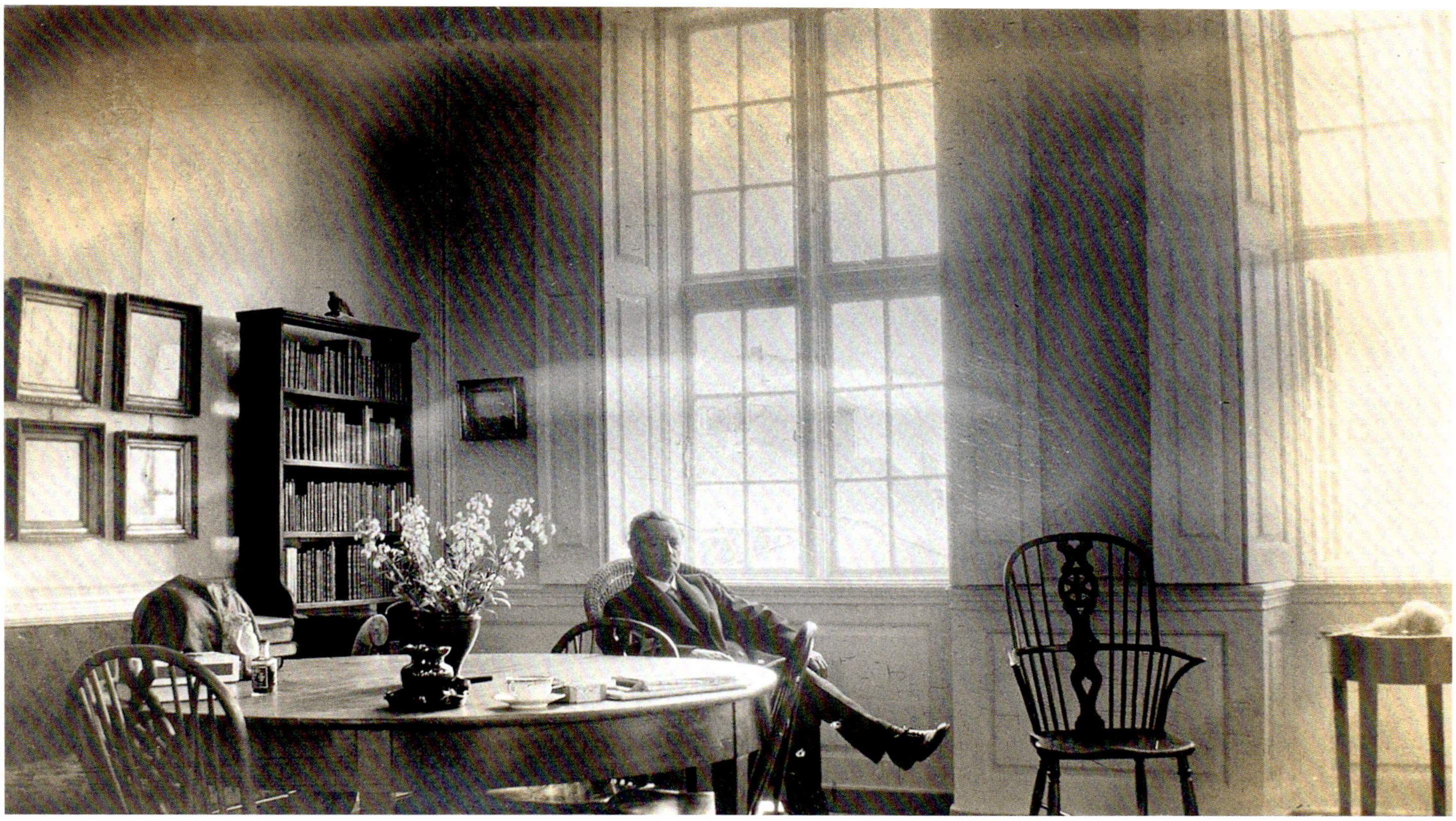

identity and express yourself as a human being.[8] By means of objects and interiors modern man seeks to create a personal space, a place of refuge from the anonymity, rationality, and efficiency that – according to the Swedish ethnologist Orvar Löfgren – infuses public life in the late 19th century.[9] Danish and European art from the time is teeming with interiors, depicting for example social occasions or the artist's own family. Here we see the creation of a seemingly functional and safe setting for modern living within the wider, hectic urban life. Works such as Viggo Pedersen's painting *Sunshine in the Living Room. The Artist's Wife and Child* from 1888 [136] showcase family life, staging it here as a happy tale about the interaction between the artist's wife and their child. The room is messy, toys are strewn on the floor, a piece of linen is falling from the chest of drawers, life is lived and enjoyed in the immediate present. Outside the window the sun is shining, throwing its light not just across the floor, but also upon the mother and child. There is no divide between inside and outside; nature has been invited indoors in the form of the potted plants on the windowsill. Here is no sense of not belonging, quite the contrary: Here is intimacy, a sense of living in the present and of having found one's place in the world.

One could hardly imagine a greater contrast to Hammershøi's interiors featuring his wife Ida [137]. Hammershøi did not have much sympathy for the interior design styles favoured in his day. He had no use for the homely cosiness that many of his fellow artists found expressed in the period's vast accumulations of velvet, ferns and parrots. Hammershøi rejected

[138]
Unknown photographer
Hammershøi's appartment in Strandgade 25 1913
Photograph
The Hirschsprung Collection, Copenhagen

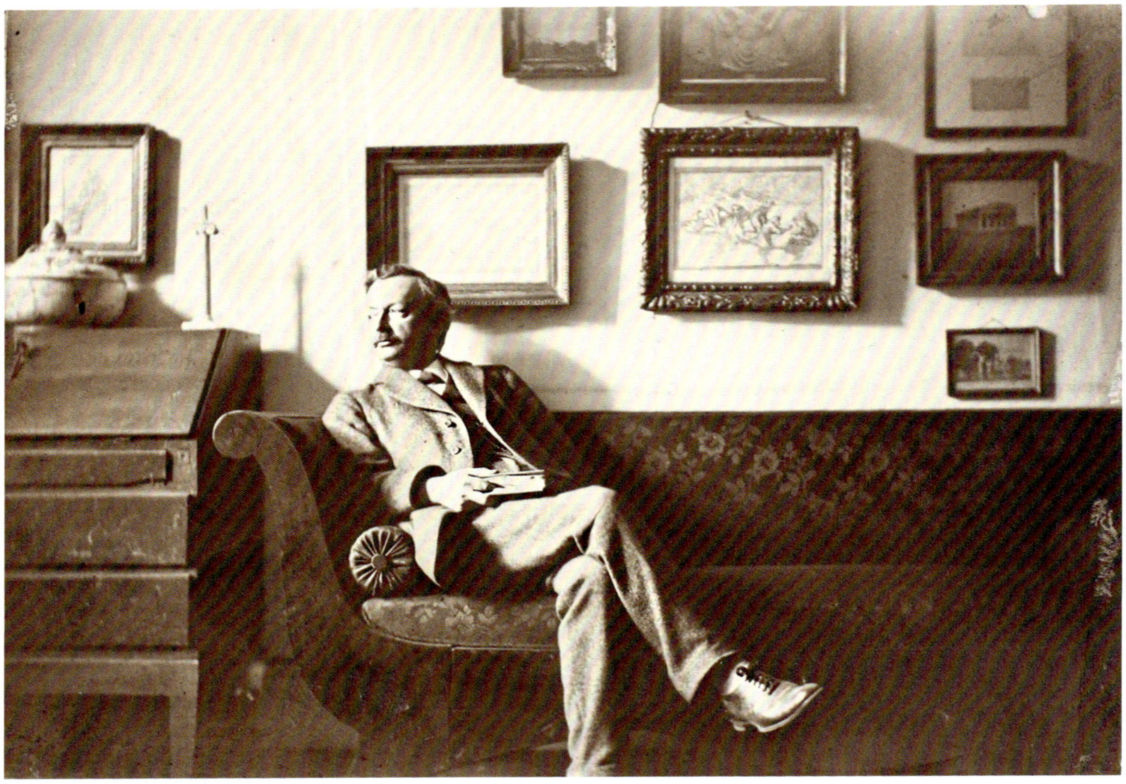

the clutter of upholstered mahogany furniture, heavy draperies and vast flowerpots, preferring instead to decorate his home with very few, distinctive Empire-style pieces and with a general sense of simplicity whose restraint and asceticism mimed the decorating styles of the Danish Golden Age. Hammershøi did not conceal his preferences. In an interview with magazine *Hjemmet* ("The Home") from 1909 with the headline "Vore Hjems Indretning" ("Home Decorating") he is asked his opinion on contemporary decorating styles:

"Well – this question is as interesting as it is difficult to answer [...]. Personally I prefer all things old, old dwellings, old furniture, the quite distinctive atmosphere that resides in such things. At the same time I am not blind to the fact that there is something amiss in favouring the old at the expense of the New – of the *good* aspects of the New, that is. Modern people should live in modern dwellings in keeping with their times. And it is far better to follow modern tastes than to imitate the old."[10]

Photographs from Hammershøi's living rooms show that his paintings almost always show edited versions of reality in which furniture and objects have been moved and rearranged to suit the artist's purpose.[11] And even though he felt only repugnance for ornaments and for what he called "knick-knacks" and "clutter" the photographs show than the Hammershøi home seems to have contained more objects, knick-knacks, and art on the walls that the paintings suggest [138]. The narrative staged by Hammershøi in his interiors is as much about that which *was* as they are about that which *is*. About a modern man who does not feel at home within modern life. About homesickness and a nostalgic yearning for coherence and for

[139]
Unknown photographer
Hammershøi's appartment in Bredgade 25 c. 1911
Photograph
The Hirschsprung Collection, Copenhagen

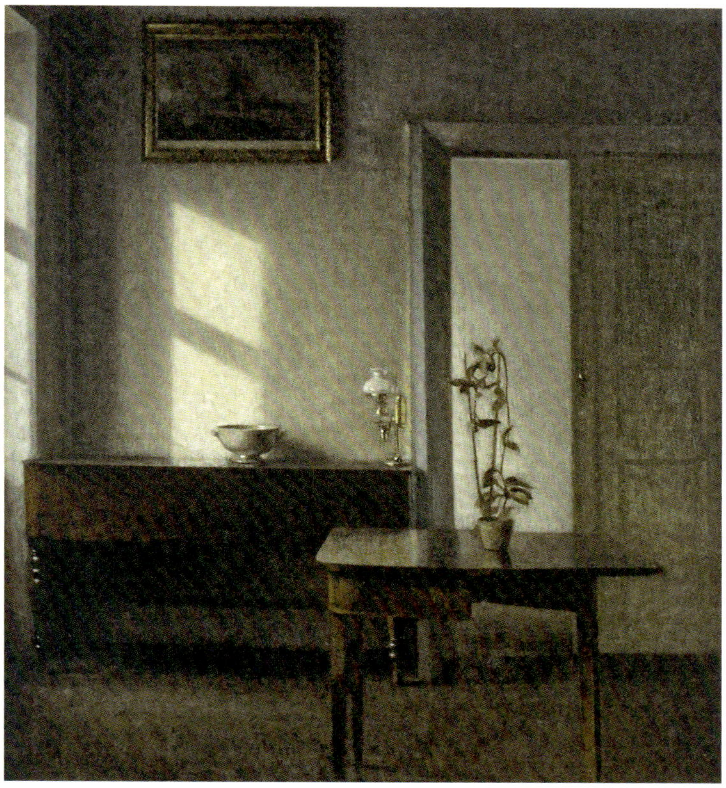

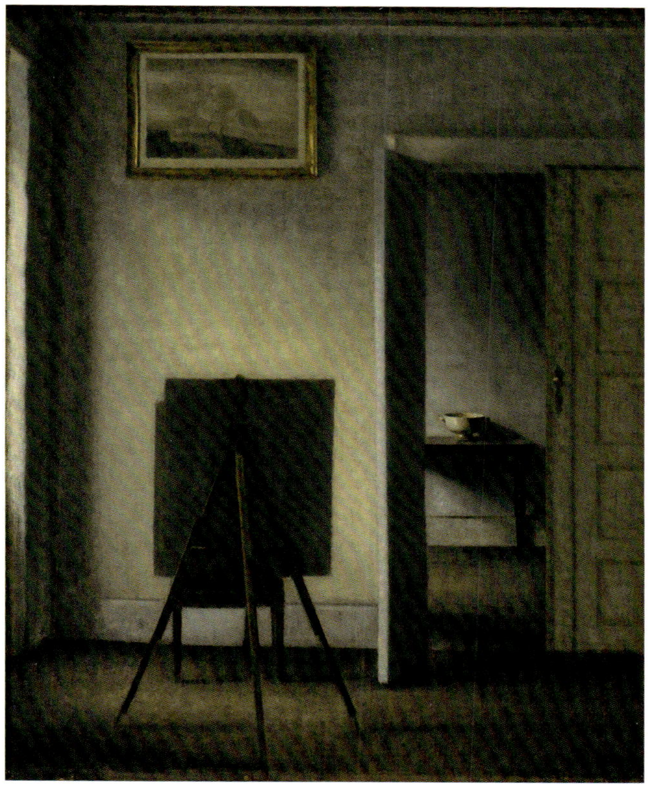

a world that was easy to grasp; such yearnings could not be satisfied in the world outside the painting, but the harmony and coherence it strove for could be composed and staged within the framework of the painting. Hammershøi's response to homelessness was to create a microcosm of repeated compositions infused with an architectural clarity and a firmly controlled balancing of all elements [9, 82]. Horizontal and vertical, doorways and windows, figures and objects, easel and punch bowls; everything is used like set pieces combined to form the most perfect scenes thanks to the supremely gifted touch of the director. In a small text (1969) about Hammershøi's successor Carl Th. Dreyer the French director Francois Truffaut stated that "Each image in *Ordet* possesses a formal perfection that touches the sublime."[12] This is also true of Hammershøi's interiors. Each painting may take its point of departure in this world, but like in an abstract painting by Mondrian they construct a harmony and sense of calm which is not of the world that lay outside of the windows in Strandgade and Bredgade.

Hammershøi's interiors constitute a carefully delimited and controlled domain that he can stage and shape to act as a place of sanctuary and, perhaps, as a kind of fortification capable of holding the outside world at bay. In the paintings his wife Ida and/or his mother are the main figures featured as part of the interior design, but the many known photos of Hammershøi clearly show how he very carefully inserts himself as part of the interior [139]. As in Hans Christian Andersen's fairytale *Everything in Its Place* (1852) Hammershøi, too, found his rightful place in the world: not outside, but inside. As part of the home's ornamenta-

[82]
Vilhelm Hammershøi 1864-1916 Danish
Interior with Potted Plant on Card Table, Bredgade 25 c. 1910-11
Oil on canvas 78.5 x 71 cm
Malmö Museum

[9]
Vilhelm Hammershøi 1864-1916 Danish
Interior with the Artist's Easel 1910
Oil on canvas 84 x 69 cm
Statens Museum for Kunst

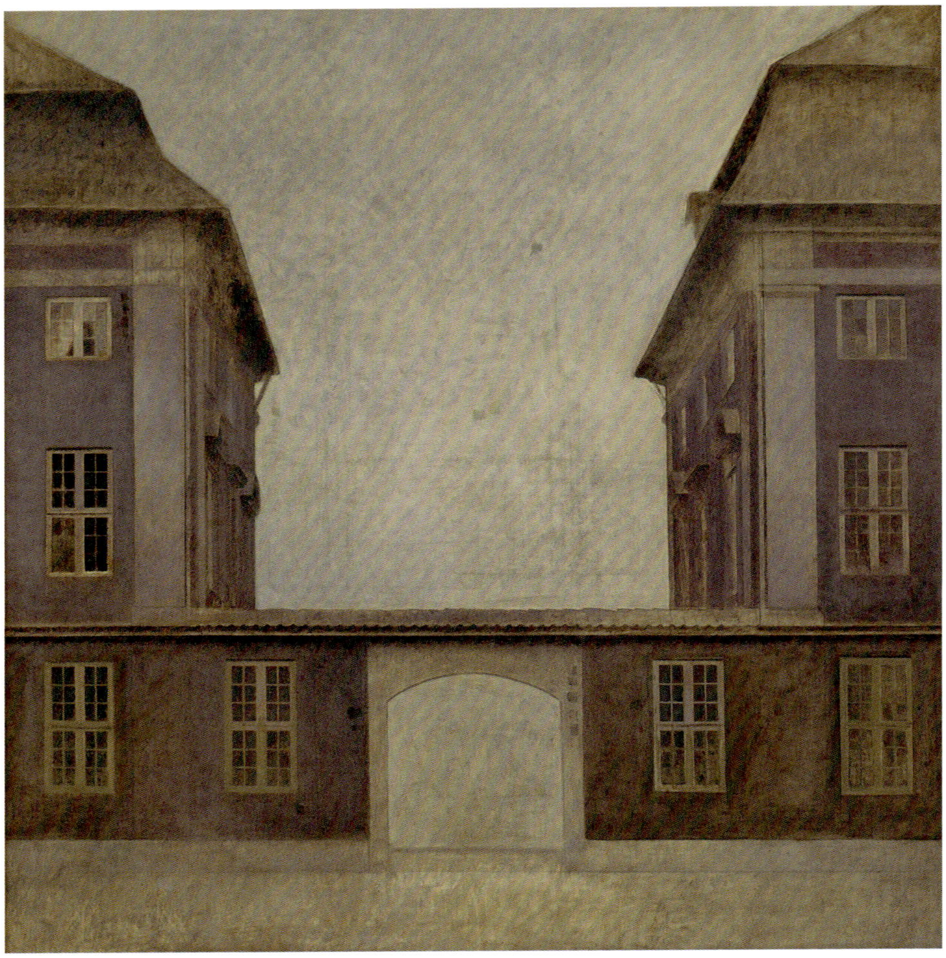

tion and décor Hammershøi falls into place, but he usually stands or sits as something that has been added on, something that latches onto the stability and changelessness of the home. His pose expresses belonging, a sense of being anchored.

The Old World

But this not only holds true for the interiors. Hammerhøi treats landscapes and architecture with the same ambition to master and control things to the point where it reaches an almost sublime perfection. The scene showing the buildings of the Asiatic Company (Asiatisk Kompani) in Copenhagen [86, p. 111] may be the most extreme example. It is reminiscent of Eckerberg's perspective drawings and the architectural scenes of the Golden Age, and it prefigures Mondrian; perhaps the underlying endeavour to translate and capture the external world in a perfect image is a common feature of them all.[13]

As is the case in Hammershøi's other scenes of architecture, this painting sees him painting the face of old Copenhagen in the form of the mansion of the merchant company Asiatic Compagny, a building executed in the late Baroque style and accompanied by a ware-

[86]
Vilhelm Hammershøi 1864-1916 Danish
The Buildings of the Asiatic Company, seen from St. Annæ Street 1902
Oil on canvas 146.5 x 140.5 cm
Statens Museum for Kunst

house that mimics the mansion. Hammershøi inserts 18th century Copenhagen as his frame of reference for urban settings, thereby prefiguring the spate of cultural pessimism that emerged in the interwar years and the yearning back to the sense of community and simplicity offered by village life and one's original homestead. This also applied to his own choice of dwelling. Apart from one year (1897-98) spent at Åboulevarden in a new property designed by the Danish architect Ulrik Plesner, Hammershøi always elected to live in older 18th century houses.[14] The old Christiansborg Palace as it appeared before the fire, its neighbouring church, the Amalienborg mansions, and the Petri Church possessed the simple grandeur and monumental sense of order that obviously had something to offer to those who yearned for the sense of security associated with the old world. At any rate Hammershøi mainly paints monuments – which are effectively memorials – that are drained of life, referring only to the achievements of the past. In most cities a square serves a hub of traffic, a place for gathering. The painting from the Amalienborg square makes no references to the urban space of the era. It is a dead square, referring only to the past and to the dead heroes: the architect Eigtved and the sculptor Saly.

If the interior and the home represents everything that is safe – the stable, the unchanging, that which is *in* in contrast to everything that is unsafe: the *outside*, the city with all its aggression and anonymity – then Hammershøi makes the dangerous "outside" controlled, manageable, domesticated by turning it into a depository of cultural memory, into monuments and memorials.

Governing the world, making it conform to systems, is very much a 19th century preoccupation.[15] In Hammershøi this also seems to influence his gaze on the landscapes he selected as motifs. Several of these – such as the landscapes from Gentofte Lake [100, p. 124] with its straight-edged tree-lined road – repeats the plane-parallel structure that structures the composition of many of the artist's works, whereas others – such as the landscapes from Refsnæs and Lejre [17, p. 35, 102, p. 126] – seem to have been chosen for their monumental simplicity and sweeping lines. Common features include the low horizon, the balancing of sky and earth, and the sense of how the artist's gifted gaze freezes the landscapes, rendering them timeless. Note how the foreshortening of small white summer clouds in *Landscape, From Lejre* forms a well-ordered pattern that helps capture the motif in the same manner as spaces constructed on the basis of a central perspective.

In many ways Hammershøi's air of control and mastery marks a culmination of the domestication of the sublime that was modelled by Thorvaldsen and systematised by Eckersberg in the early 19th century. The generations in between – for example Constantin Hansen and Frederik Vermehren – added more and more narrative and picturesque elements in their endeavours to meet the demands of an audience clamouring for verisimilitude and for edifying and sentimental narratives. Hammershøi cleaned up the anecdotes, reducing the details and "clutter" to a minimum. In so doing he put an effective final flourish on 19th century Danish and Northern European tradition while also opening up portals on a pictorial universe that was purged of ideology and more artistically autonomous.

We continue to be fascinated by Hammershøi's works, probably because we are intrigued by their sublime beauty and order as well as by all the many fissures and cracks that put the sense of doubts and homelessness on display. As Hammershøi says in his interview with *Hjemmet,* he is aware that he is counteracting his own era by preferring the old world, but he does so deliberately and without closing himself up to the present. Nor does he ever close up his paintings, neither in terms of motif nor in his painterly approach, and this is crucial to the sense of perpetual unrest they communicate. Once you have stood really close to a painting by Hammershøi you never forget the distinctive sensuousness that infuses his brushwork. The brushstrokes form dense patterns of multi-hued blobs of colour that echo Seurat's Pointilistic works, creating a sense of pulsating life on the surface and ensuring that the motifs never become overly perfectionist and glossy. The open painterly mode of expression contributes greatly to creating the indefinable shifts in something confidential and private that can no longer be controlled, governed, or harmonised, moving inexorably towards something else, something uncertain that is not yet fully unfolded and categorised; something which exists as a kind of inherent feature of the work, an immanent fundamental atmosphere for the observer to connect with.

Peter Nørgaard Larsen (born 1960), Head of Collections and Research at the National Gallery of Denmark. Has focused on exchanges between Danish and European art in the second half of the 19th century. Has written on and arranged exhibitions of e.g. Impressionist and Post-Impressionist art, Symbolism within European painting, Nordic stemningsmaleri ('mood- painting'), Vitalism, and Puvis de Chavannes' influence on Nordic art.

NOTES

1 In 2001 Aarhus Kunstmuseum showed an exhibition entitled "Intim/sublim" ("Intimate/sublime"). According to the curator, Lennart Gottlieb, this pairing of concepts was intended as a contemporary opposition to the classic dichotomy between the beautiful and the sublime. Most of all because the notion of the beautiful belonged to a different time, while the sublime was very much – perhaps *too* much – a concept that emerged in all manner of contexts. Lennart Gottlieb, "Intim/sublim", in: Aarhus, 2001, 6. The exhibition featured Vilhelm Hammershøi as a key figure juxtaposed with two younger Danish artists: the sculptor Hein Heinsen (born 1935) and the painter Erik August Frandsen (born 1957). The exhibition gave rise to a seminar that featured a range of contributions, each of them addressing the exhibition theme in different ways. The present text is an expanded, and hopefully updated, version of my contribution to the conference.

2 In particular the chapter "Domesticeringen af det sublime" ("Domesticising the Sublime"), in: Klaus P. Mortensen, *Det pittoreske øje (The Picturesque Eye)*. Copenhagen 2011, pp. 55-69.

3 In his memories from the years around 1880 Emil Hannover, who studied at the Art Academy from 1879-83 and would later become director of the Museum of Art and Crafts (now the Danish Museum of Design), describes how Vermehren was one of the first to recognise Hammershøi's distinctive qualities. Cf. Hannover, 1966, pp. 72f.

4 Originally 1919.

5 "Homelessness is coming to be the destiny of the world," Letter of Humanism, Brief über den Humanismus (1947).

6 See for example Lily Markiewicz, "No Place – Like Home", in Sam Durrant & Catherine M. Lord (eds.): *Essays in Migratory Aesthetics: Cultural Practices Between Migration and Art-making*, pp. 37-48, Amsterdam 2007.

7 Martin Heidegger's text about living, "Bauen Wohnen Denken" (1952) can be found in *Vorträge und Aufsätze* from 1954.

8 Benjamin writes about the interior in several contexts, most comprehensively in "Louis-Philippe or the Interior", in *Paris – The Capital of the Nineteenth Century*, originally in German in *Schriften*, Suhrkamp Verlag, 1955, a later English translation is included in *Charles Baudelaire. A Lyric Poet in The Era of High Capitalism*, London 1989 (1973).

9 For example in Orvar Löfgren: "The Sweetness of Home: Class, culture and family life in Sweden", pp. 142-160, in Setha M. Low & Denise Lawrence de Zuñiga (eds.): *The Anthropology of Place and Space – Locating Culture*, Blackwell Readers in Anthropology 4, Oxford 2003.

10 Quoted in Vad, 1988 (1992), p. 402.

11 See especially Vad, 1988 (1992), pp. 185-190.

12 Francois Truffaut: *The Films in my life*, (1975), Da Capo Press edition 1994, pp. 48f. I am indebted to Annette Rosenvold Hvidt for referring me to the quote.

13 In her text "Hammershøis København" Bente Scavenius reproduces a drawing by Eckersberg – an ideal prospect of Charlottenborg – which Hammershøi owned; Scavenius points to the drawing as a possible source of inspiration for the stringent composition for *Asiatic Company*. Scavenius in: Bente Scavenius & Lindhe, 2003, 78. In 1918 the drawing was given to the Royal Collection of Graphic Arts by Ida Hammershøi. As is stated by Poul Vad in his mention of the drawing (Vad 1988 (1992), pp. 242-245), we do not know when Hammershøi acquired it. Indeed, Hammershøi may have acquired the drawing at a later date because it corresponded with his interests, but the first option certainly seems the most likely. The two works were also linked by Erik Fischer in *Tegninger af C.W. Eckersberg*, Kobberstiksamlingen, SMK 1983, cat. 140.

14 Scavenius & Lindhe, 2003, p. 33.

15 As described by for example Michel Foucault and sociologist Norbert Elias, both of whom have linked it to the rise of bourgeois-capitalist society.

LIVING INSIDE THE PAINTING – HAMMERSHØI AND INTIMISM

ANNETTE ROSENVOLD HVIDT

Here, Hammershøi's art is regarded within the context of the Intimism most frequently associated with the art of Bonnard and Vuillard. The article emphasises how Hammershøi works with intimacy and sensory input in his images as a kind of Intimism. The concept of Intimism points to the choice of subject matter as well as to the choice of modes of painting or expression that evoke a sense of closeness and intimacy in the way the paintings appear. Hammershøi applies a photographic gaze directly to his painterly universe, and his particular vein of Intimism is apparent in the care lavished on the appearance of each individual aspect of the painting.

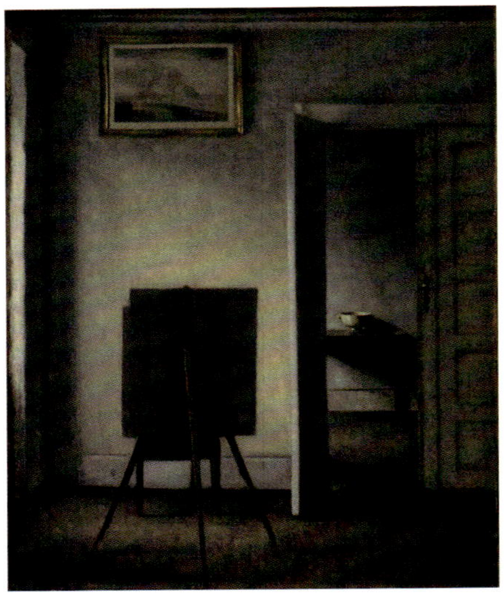

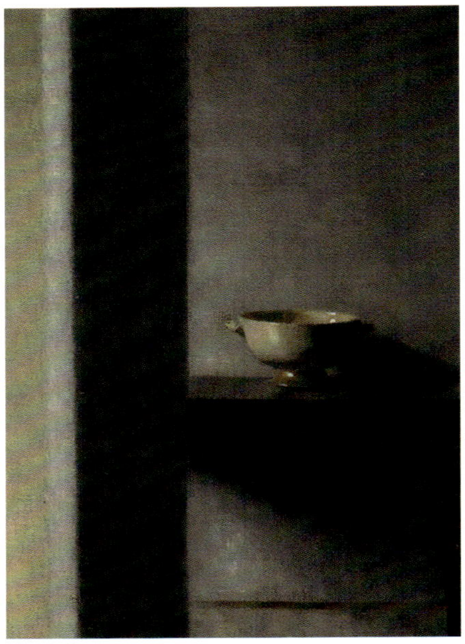

A late self-portrait from 1911 brings us close to the end of Hammershøi's life. The artist looks at us directly while painting, or perhaps while taking a pause from his painting process. He is standing in front of a wall, and on the opposite side of the image we see a door opening up onto a balcony or veranda. Given the fact that the artist is usually not present in his paintings, Hammershøi's presence strikes me at first as somewhat startling, almost inappropriate. He towers in the foreground [140].

The late self-portrait from 1911 was painted at the villa Spurveskjul ("Sparrow's Nest") in Frederiksdal. This was the abode of Hammershøi and his wife Ida in the summer of 1911. The architectural style of the villa, which was originally designed by the artist Nicolai Abildgaard and built in 1805-06, appealed to Hammershøi, who rented the place and used it as a studio for a number of months. The couple entertained thoughts of buying the house, but decided against it as it was too dilapidated.[1] Hammershøi's main motif was rooms, and he would use his homes as studios-cum-subject matter. Together, Vilhelm and Ida sought out older houses whose particular *genii loci* appealed to them. At Spurveskjul Hammershøi worked with variations on open and closed doors and windows and with Ida as a figure; approaches he had often taken before. In *Self-Portrait. The Cottage Spurveskjul*, however, he very obviously painted himself into the room.

The self-portrait from Spurveskjul offers up an interesting relationship between Hammershøi's gaze upon himself and the fact that he looks at the observer at the same time. The observation may be banal in light of the fact that by their very essence self-portraits are founded on this relationship, but nevertheless it can be viewed as a distinctive recurring motif in Hammershøi – accentuated here by the fact that several of his final paintings have a decided focus on a remarkable sense of self-observation and of "being in the painting".

Hammershøi's late works are distinct from the works generally regarded as "classically" Hammershøiesque, i.e. the stylised, aesthetic interiors featuring his wife Ida as a model. It is as if his late works do not quite fit the mould. This may be because Hammershøi works with a greater degree of openness in his late works, and because he himself is more present in the paintings. As in this self-portrait where he stops in the middle of painting, presumably watching himself via a mirror.

And yet he calls attention to his presence throughout his entire body of work. He does so, for example, by having his easel occupy a central position in the painting, and particularly by applying paint in such a careful and obviously structured manner that his imprint, the traces of his presence, becomes very visible in the paintings [9 + detail].

If we look back upon some of Hammershøi's early self-portraits, they also saw him working with ways of representing himself. Yet the distinctive feature of the late self-portraits is the fact that we see him in a larger room and that he is shown with a brush and easel, showing himself engaged in the act of painting [140].

Hammershøi died at the age of 51 in 1916, and we were robbed of the chance to see how his work would have progressed. Was he gradually moving towards evincing a greater degree of sense-recorded existentialism in his paintings? We can but speculate. In this article I offer up a close reading of Hammershøi's way of painting and pursue notions of how he works with traces of life and sensory input in his paintings.

[9]
Vilhelm Hammershøi 1864-1916 Danish
Interior with the Artist's Easel 1910
Oil on canvas 84 x 69 cm
Statens Museum for Kunst

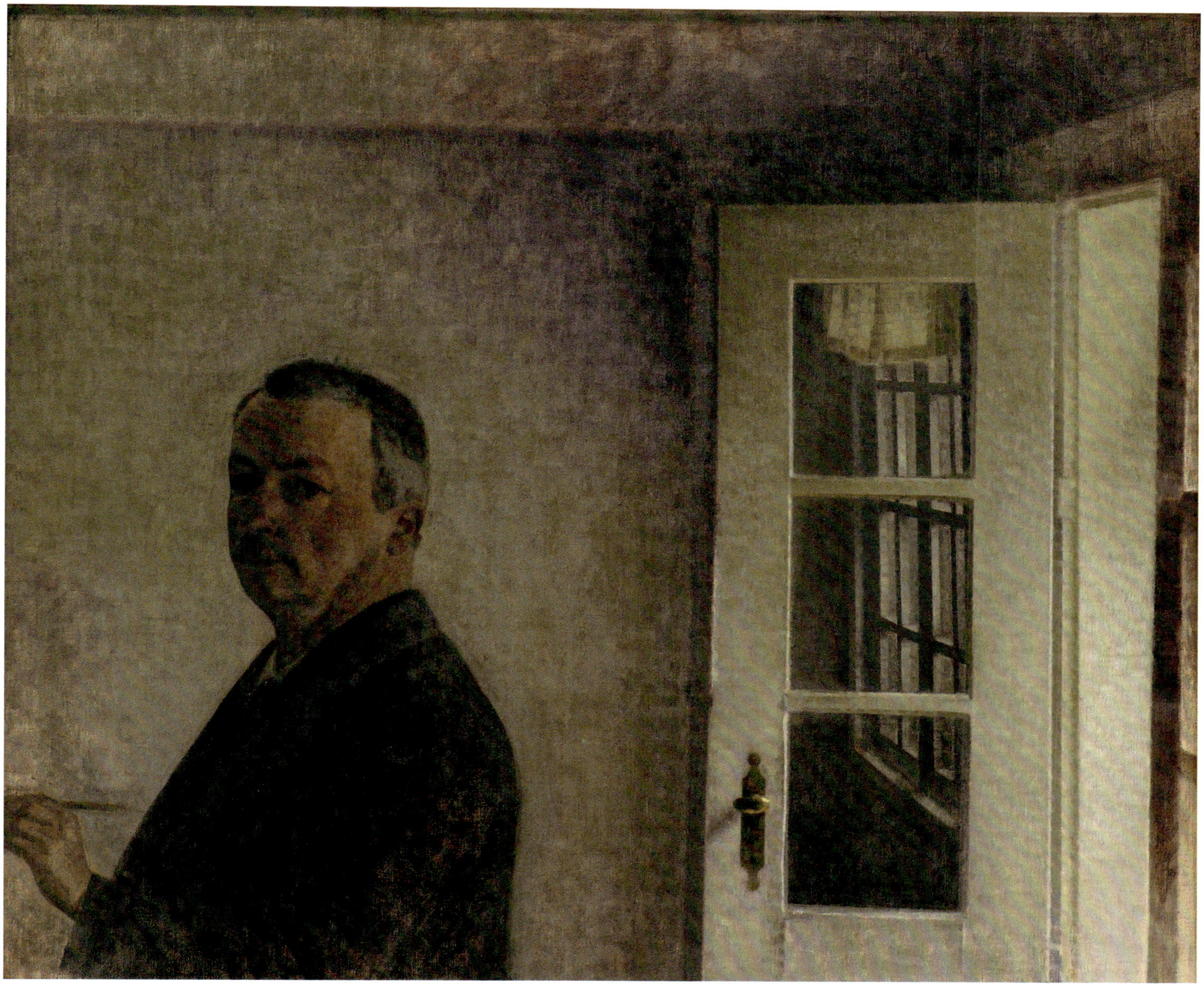

[140]
Vilhelm Hammershøi 1864-1916 Danish
Self-Portrait. The Cottage Spurveskjul 1911
Oil on canvas 126 x 149 cm
Statens Museum for Kunst

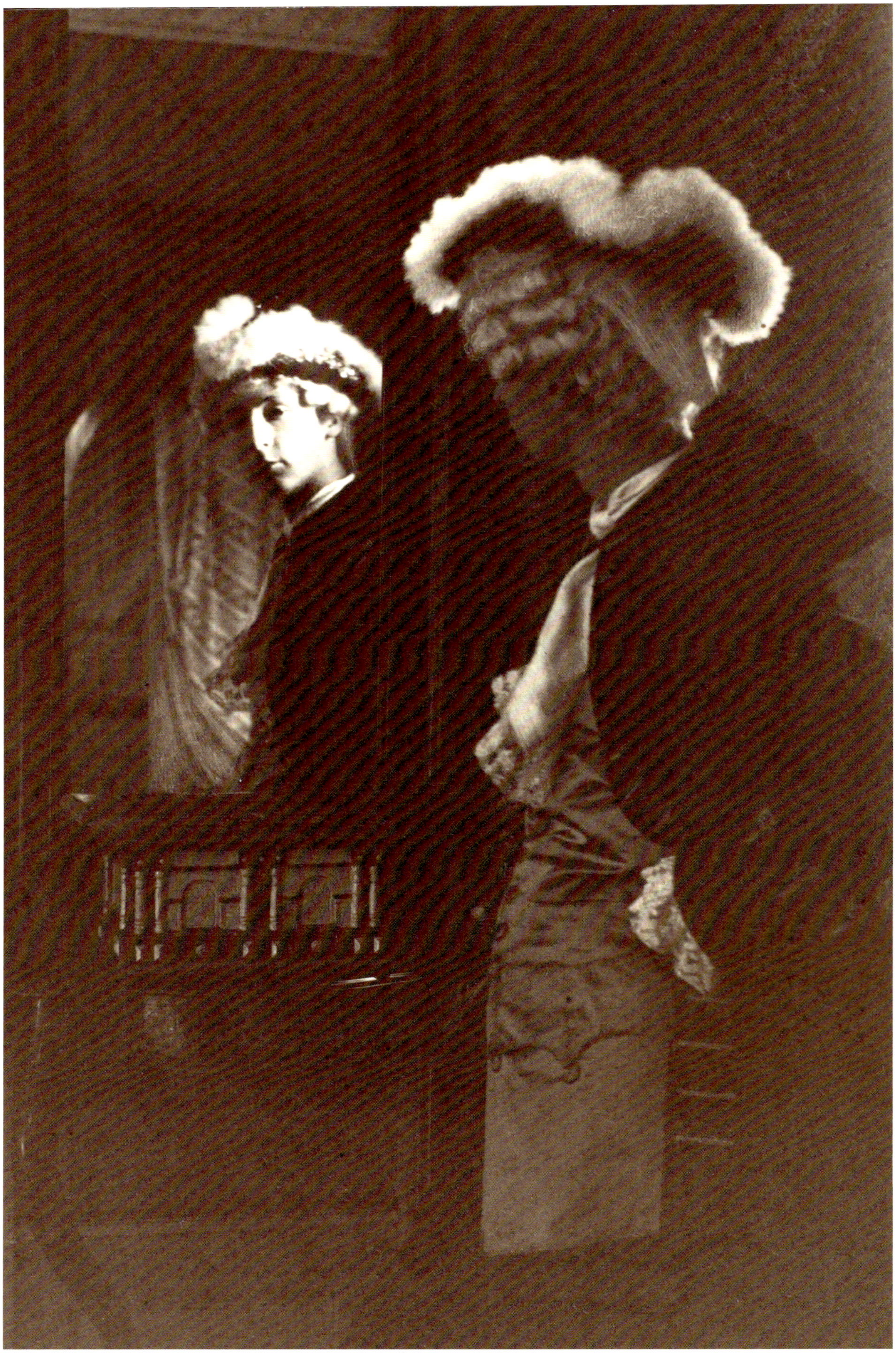

Photographic sensuousness

An early indication of Hammershøi's interest in being present in his paintings can be discerned in the gently sensitive photographic portrait of Hammershøi wearing a wig, an image captured around the time of his debut in 1885.[2] Hammershøi is posing, looking at the photographer in a mirror [141].

This photograph can serve as an entry point for seeing Hammershøi's painting as part of the tendency towards what I term *photographic sensuousness* within the pictorial arts during the period from 1880 to 1920. The artists' use of photography represents more than simply an appendix to their work or mere sketch material – it is an integral part of their work with paintings, and the use of photography can be viewed as an essential clue capable of furthering our understanding of that segment of Modernism of which Hammershøi and several of his European contemporaries are part.

Hammershøi is part of an international modernist movement where domestic scenes such as interiors and figures in rooms become synonymous with investigations into the painterly space. The intimate situation of "painting", i.e. of applying paint to the canvas in order to create specific structures, enters into a symbiosis with the sensuously charged introspection of the motifs themselves. Familiar, recognisable motifs are emptied of narrative contents, giving way to other ways of seeing and approaching things, for example of phenomena such as light, skin, the backs of heads, hands, tree trunks, etc.; phenomena that take on an immense significance in the paintings. The works are gradually moving away from a narrative appeal towards a painterly, sensuous appeal. In the popular parlance, very little happens in the painting, but you feel a great deal when you are in front of them.[3]

The sense of immediacy in the paintings provides a kind of entry point for understanding their *photographic sensuousness.* There is a parallel between the fact that a photograph shows a physical imprint and traces of something pre-existing, and the fact that a painting can make us experience a sense of presence or immediacy by virtue of its manner of painting. By looking at photographs we can get close to something that is or was, and a similar sensation can be evoked in us when standing in front of particular types of painting – in this case many of Hammershøi's paintings.

The writer Poul Vad, who has written extensively about Hammershøi, made the following comment on Hammershøi and photography:

"Photography is one of the phenomena that defines modernity. Undoubtedly the 'photographic' aspect of Hammershøi's paintings holds some of the explanation of why this artist, who was so very bound by tradition, painted paintings that nevertheless belong under the mantle of modernity and still have a modern feel to this day."[4]

Within my optics, the impression of something "modern" described by Vad is closely connected to the sense of immediacy and presence that Hammershøi invests in his manner of painting; as Vad points out, this is directly linked to his photographic gaze upon the work. That is one of the distinctive aspects of Hammershøi's modernity.

In his strokes across the canvas Hammershøi records the effects of light in a photographic manner. For example, one of his best-known works – the canonised *Sunbeams* or *Sunshine. Dust Motes Dancing in the Sunbeams* from 1900 – is awash with light and an all-pervading immediacy and atmosphere where paint mimes and incorporates the effect of light as it may be observed in a photograph [76, p. 100; 142].[5] During this period artists were widely interested in photography's potential as a possible point of entry to painting. The

[141]
Valdemar Schønheyder Møller 1864-1905 Danish
Vilhelm Hammershøi c. 1885
Photograph
The Royal Library, Copenhagen

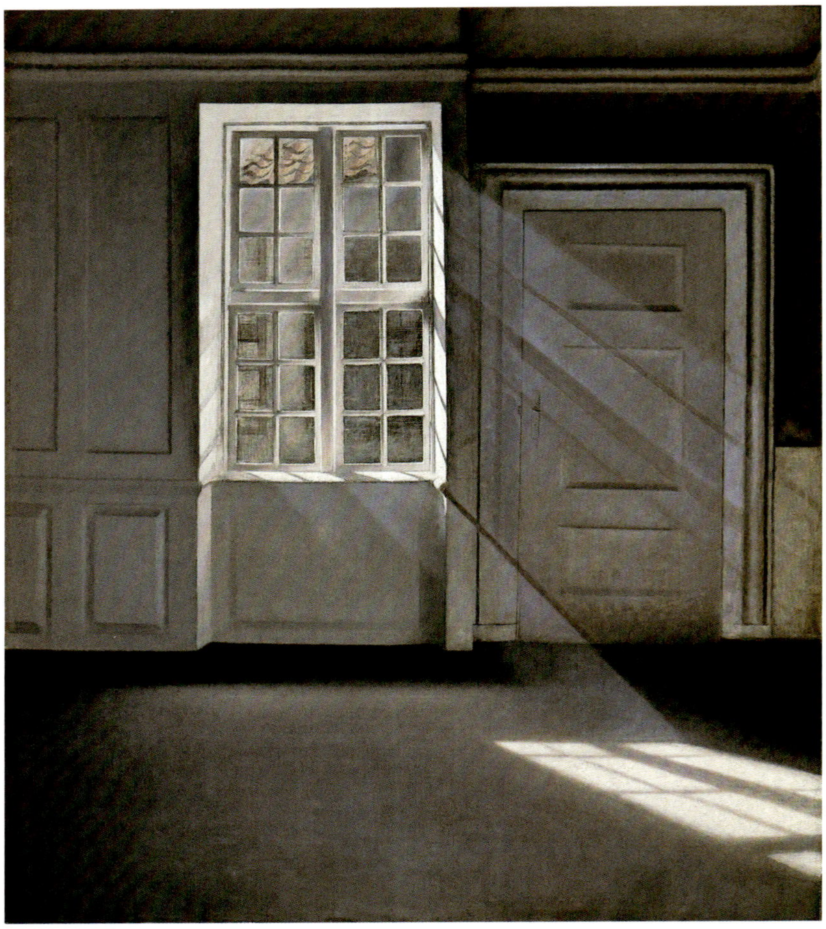

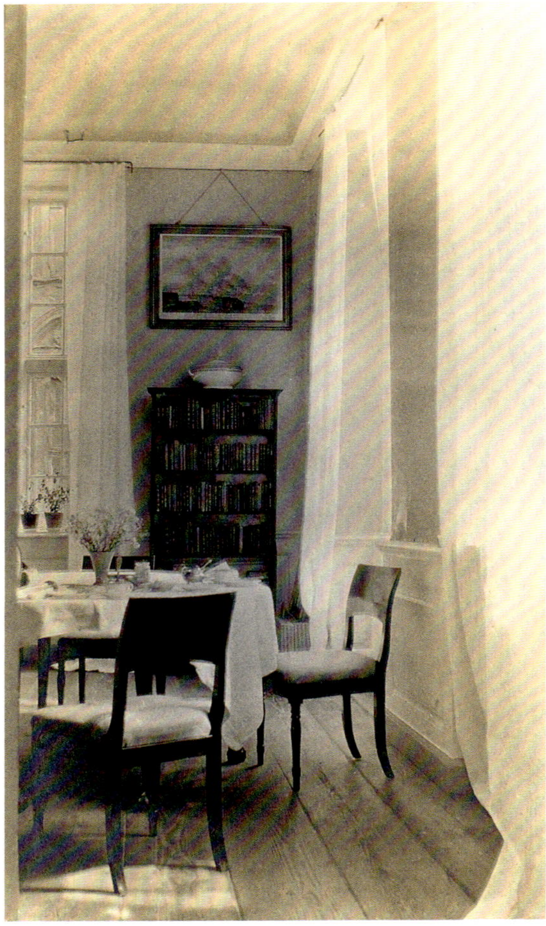

Intimism we see here is not fuelled by random snapshots, but by staged photographs featuring figures positioned in special rooms. The concept of Intimism refers to the intimacy of the subject matter as well as to the modes of painting or expression that evoke a sense of immediacy and intimacy in the paintings. The artists employ a photographic gaze upon their domestic surroundings; a gaze that accentuates phenomena over narrative.

Taking our point of departure in these observations, Hammershøi's paintings can be juxtaposed with those of some of his French contemporaries. Hammershøi never declared himself as a Post-Impressionist, Symbolist or Pointillist. However, he works with a degree of openness, structure, and sensuousness in his approach to painting and motifs that it is interesting to see juxtaposed with paintings and drawings by French artists such as Georges Seurat, Pierre Bonnard, and Édouard Vuillard as well as with works by the Belgian artist Fernand Khnopff. They were all active during the same period as Hammershøi and are described as Intimists, Post-Impressionists, or Symbolists. How might the ways in which these artists treated canvases and paper serve to elucidate Hammershøi's method by means of an ongoing, associative dialogue between the works? That is the subject addressed in the following sections.

[76]
Vilhelm Hammershøi 1864-1916 Danish
Sunbeams or **Sunshine.**
Dust Motes Dancing in the Sunbeams 1900
Oil on canvas 70 x 59 cm
Ordrupgaard, Copenhagen

[142]
Unknown photographer
Hammershøi's appartment in Strandgade 25 1913
Photograph
The Hirschsprung Collection, Copenhagen

The significance of special rooms

Hammershøi had a penchant for painting windows and French doors. The lines of the windows and the graded sequences of light and shadows arising on the window planes are – alongside images of his wife Ida – main motifs in his work. In many instances both are present, Ida and the windows alike.

We might find one parallel to Hammershøi's preoccupation with painting his wife in conjunction with open and shut doors and windows in the works of the French artist Bonnard, specifically his many paintings of interiors of French houses. For example, Bonnard painted interiors from the villa *Le Bosquet* in the South of France and from a house in Vernon. The most striking difference between the two artists concerns the contrast between the vivid colours employed by Bonnard and the subdued colours favoured by Hammershøi. This in spite of the fact that Hammershøi's Spurveskjul paintings belong among his most colourful works; in them a delicate purple and greenish tone emerges within the artist's grey-white-black universe. Compared to his other work, this is positively *wild* [143; 116, p. 141].

To Bonnard the intense colours signify the staggering nature of the intimacy he employs in his painting. As one regards the yellows, purples, reds, blues, and greens they give rise to a sense of allure or repulsion, but whatever the case may be they certainly communicate the sense that Bonnard was present in the rooms he depicts. Partly because of the impact of these colours, these rooms enter into the very bodies of those who view the paintings. This is to a large extent due to the fact that Bonnard applied the paint in a manner which leaves clear brushstrokes and blots in the paintings. Over the course of time these paintings have elicited many responses, negative as well as positive. To Picasso, Bonnard's style and colour scheme expressed a lack of decisiveness. Picasso could not tolerate what I would term the elaborate slowness in Bonnard.[6] Others, such as the art historian John Elderfield, hold the view that Bonnard's paintings embody optic systems that must be seen in specific ways in order to be fully appreciated,[7] whereas art historians such as Mikkel Bogh[8] and most recently Tea Baark Mairey, taking their point of departure in the ideas proposed by the philosopher Michel Serres, believe that the surface of the paintings are what affects the observer's skin and entire body. As Baark Mairey puts it:

"We are invited to use other senses beyond the sense of sight in the perception process. For sight alone does not reach far enough. The painting will not make sense if we try to apply our rational gaze to a representation of a room [...]. We approach the canvas and the planes of the painting in the same manner that we approach the walls, curtains, textiles, and other surfaces in the rooms we ourselves occupy."[9]

Hammershøi and Bonnard both employ interesting ways of letting their figures appear in their interior scenes – in Bonnard's works it often takes quite a while before you actually notice all the figures and see their bodies or faces in the room or how it is all connected. You cannot take in a Bonnard painting all at once – it must be felt and seen repeatedly if you want to grasp all or most of it. Presumably this was one of the reasons behind Picasso's dislike – it cannot be seen as a single whole.

Hammershøi's work is not as organic or malleable as Bonnard's, but the Spurveskjul paintings in particular have an emerging corporeality that becomes insistent and surprising. A case in point would be the self-portrait; as was stated in the above, Hammershøi emerges from the painting's lower edge, holding his brush, painting, and at the same time presumably watching himself in a mirror. His upper body and face form a large, dominant shape within the

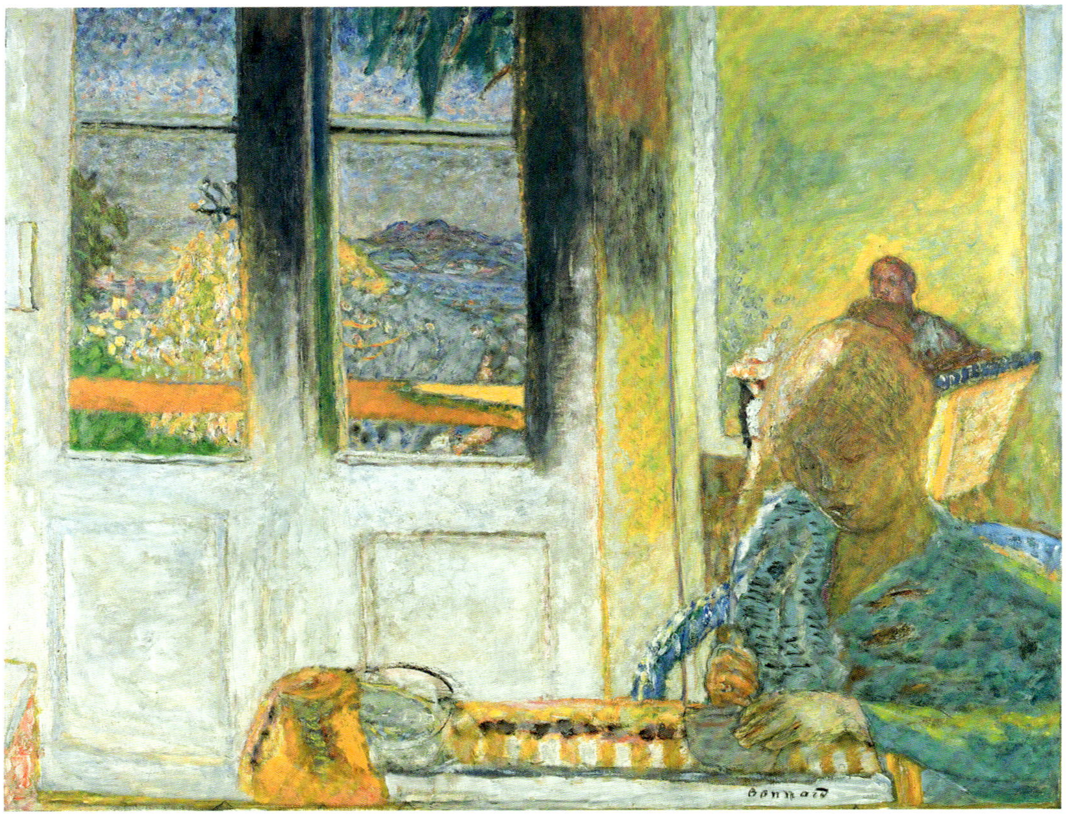

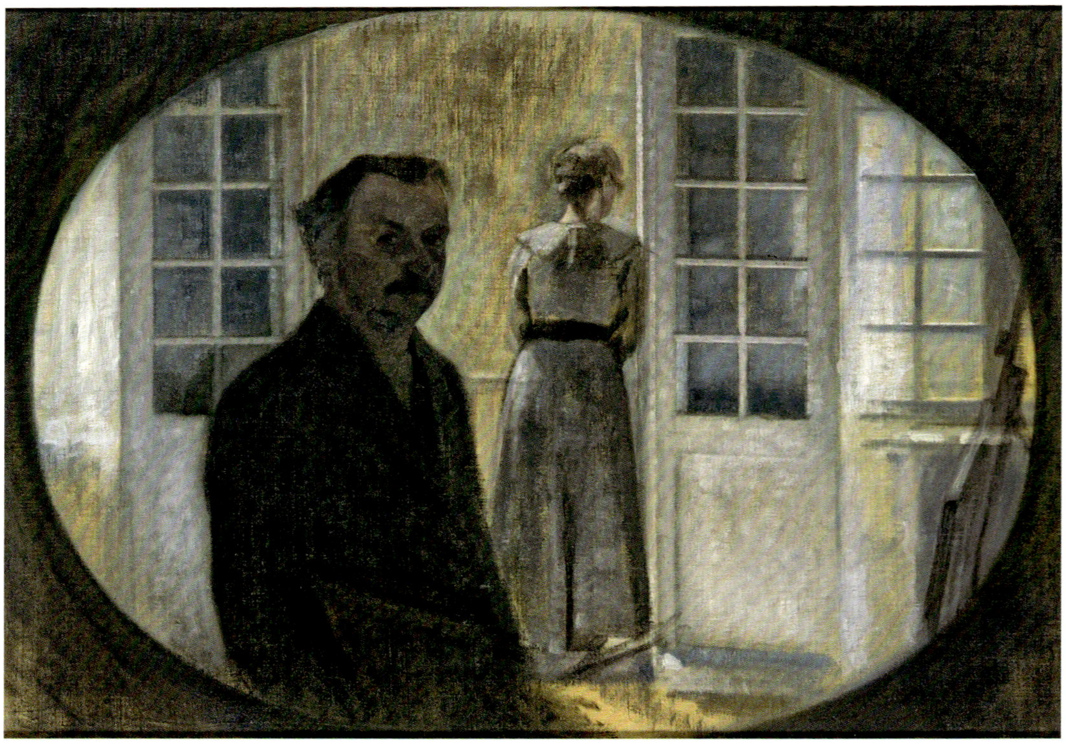

[143]
Pierre Bonnard 1867-1947 French
The French Window
(Morning at Le Cannet) 1932
Oil on canvas 87 x 111 cm
Private collection

[116]
Vilhelm Hammershøi 1864-1916 Danish
Double Portrait of the Artist and his Wife,
seen through a Mirror. The Cottage Spurveskjul 1911
Oil on canvas 55.2 x 76 cm
Private collection, Professor Günther Fielmann – Schierensee Manor

space, whereas the hand holding the brush is remarkably small.[10] The rest of the room is empty, but an open balcony door, through which a window can be glimpsed, demands attention and forms a counterpoint to Hammershøi's own incarnation. Is someone or something behind the door or window? [140]

Perhaps these thoughts arise precisely when one regards Hammershøi's paintings alongside Bonnard's because Bonnard's work hides figures who only appear when you gaze intently upon the canvas for some time – one example would be Bonnard's self-portrait at the back of the painting *The French Window (Morning at Le Cannet)* [143]. An insidious, extreme sensuousness creeps up on you if you devote time to the paintings. The indistinct, sometimes overpainted and blurred areas ultimately attract a great deal of attention, and as observers we may feel as if we ourselves inhabit or become part of the rooms and spaces depicted.

Achieving a corresponding bodily experience is more difficult with Hammershøi's paintings. He employs devices such as oval frames around the motif, making such motifs eminently suitable for a vein of voyeuristic observation where you maintain a certain distance. Some of the Spurveskjul paintings featuring Ida are framed by a dark oval painted onto the canvas. The framing is reminiscent of the ocular perspective of film or of a passe-partout mounting around a photograph in an old album.

By painting himself in the foreground Hammershøi also accentuates the role as observer and voyeur that he himself inhabits as a painter, and Ida, her back turned to us, becomes a pleasant vanishing point in the middle of the painting. If Bonnard paints for our entire body and for our skin, Hammershøi may primarily be painting for our eyes, but he also leaves avenues of approach open for other bodily ways of sensing. Juxtaposing Hammershøi's interiors from Spurveskjul with some of Bonnard's French interiors raises one's awareness of the significance of these special rooms – the rooms have been selected because of their potential for imbuing the paintings with a sensuous air that can also be felt and discerned by the spectator. Instead of being mere backdrops, the rooms take centre stage while the figures subordinate themselves to the room or enter into various correlations with their surroundings. We do not gaze in upon distancing set pieces like those from the world of theatre – rather, we see scenes of an insisting intimacy, always relating immediately to the painting's spatiality and physical aspects. Much attention has been paid to the secondary elements of the rooms, such as the walls, which enables them to engage our gaze and govern our experience in a state of interplay with what would traditionally be the primary elements of such paintings, for example the figures. Reading Hammershøi's paintings in conjunction with those of Bonnard enhances one's sense that the crux of their endeavours resides in their intimate familiarity with what they paint. They paint their home – they live in their paintings.

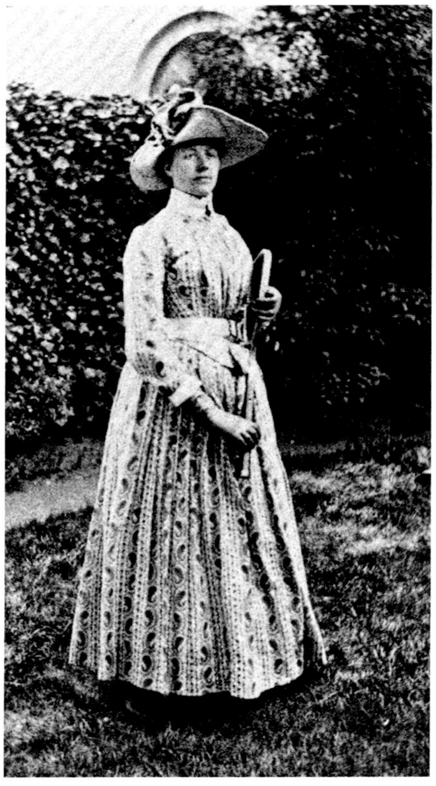

[144]
Fernand Khnopff 1858-1921 Belgian
Marguerite Khnopff c. 1888
Photograph
Musées Royaux des Beaux-Arts de Belgique, Brussels

Floating figures and dream-like moods

The artist Fernand Khnopff is another contemporary of Hammershøi. His monumental pastel *Memories* is based on a series of photographs of his sister Marguerite posing in outdoor settings in a range of outfits, sometimes brandishing a tennis racket [144]. Khnopff painted all these isolated figures into an empty landscape, creating an enigmatic whole. His approach has an affinity with the Hammershøi painting that is often referred to as its creator's only true Symbolist painting: *Artemis* from 1893-94 [145, 10].

Both paintings have an element of artificiality. In the painting *Memories* the artificial qualities concern the figures' position and appearance. They float above the ground in an unreal non-place, looking in all directions without any clear purpose. The fact that the same figure appears repeatedly in different outfits also strikes one as artificial. This is a highly evocative artificiality, and the entire scene has a mysterious and inscrutable air. The title *Memories* plays on this enigmatic atmosphere, and Khnopff uses photography's ability to capture memories as a way of adding a new sense of sensuousness to a Symbolist painting.

In much the same manner that the women's tennis game seems like a handy excuse and as a memory of something feminine and alien in Khnopff, the Artemis myth serves as an excuse or memory in Hammershøi's painting. The reference to mythology resides exclusively in the title and in the crescent moon resting on the head of one of the figures. The figures occupy an empty space. Here, too, we find an evocative, mysterious set-up in which the three elongated, imaginary figures to the left of the painting are almost identical, repetitions of a figure floating in a three-tier movement through the space.[11]

The art historian Emil Hannover appreciated the beauty of the artificial in Hammershøi. In his review of the painting *Artemis* in the Danish newspaper Politiken on 4 May 1894 he accentuated the lines and the dream-like state and spoke of:

"[...] a trembling sensibility for the subtle beauty of each individual line, and it is the presence of this sensibility in even the flawed aspects of the outlines that makes those parts almost as highly priced by the observer as those in which the artist's dreams of beauty have found full realisation on the canvas. It is the sense of this dream that makes the painting arresting."

We do not know whether Hammershøi used photographs during the process of painting *Artemis* the way that Khnopff did for *Memories*; it is more likely that he referred to reproductions of other works of art.[12] Yet when Hammershøi's painting is viewed in conjunction with the photographic eeriness and dreamlike atmosphere that Khnopff introduces in his painting by means of photographs, one sees a similar *memory-laden* photographic atmosphere in Hammershøi's painting. A condensed treatment of the canvas that refers, among other things, to the aura and artificiality that photographs can carry because they are impressions of something real, yet also artificial projections that isolate and capture their subject matter. It is, then, the approach and method of *Artemis* that has a photographic sensuousness. There is not a 1:1, from-study-to-finished-work relationship between a particular photograph and a painting. I believe that this is a sense and a sensibility that cannot and should not be proven rationally. The matter is deliberately diffuse.

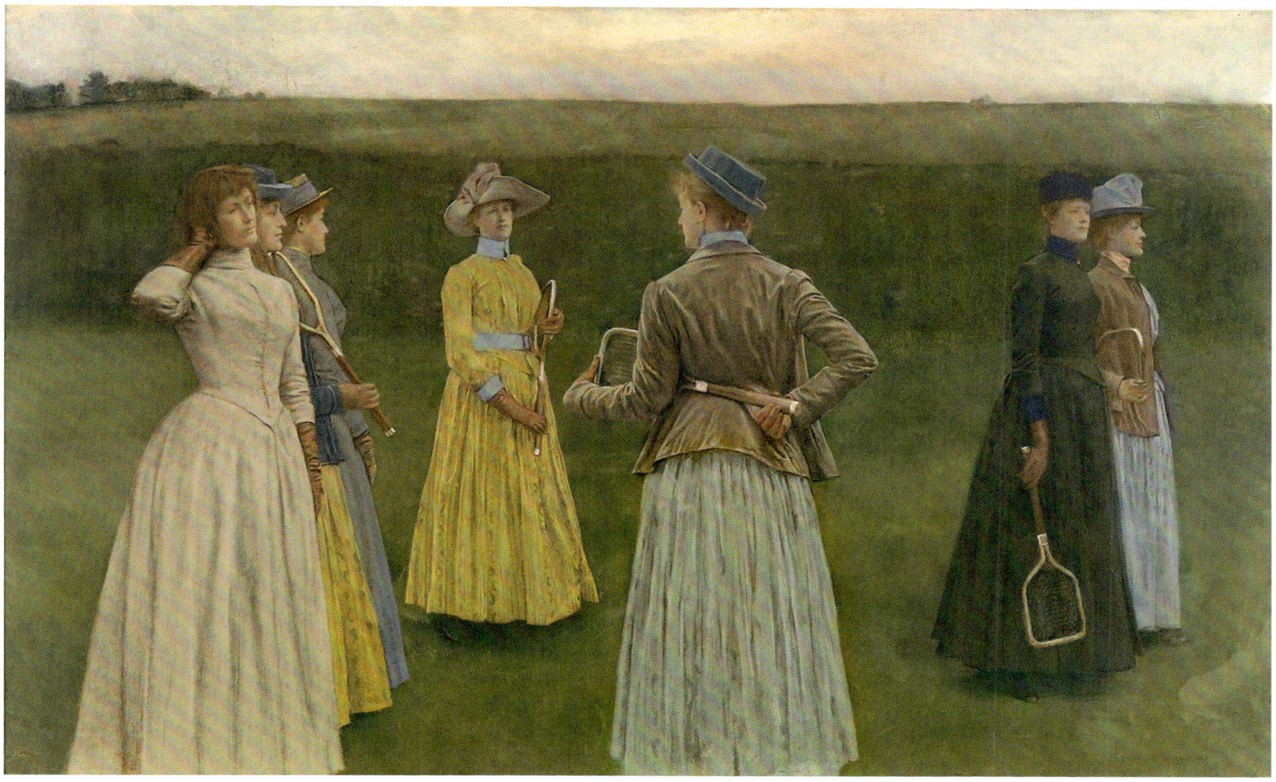

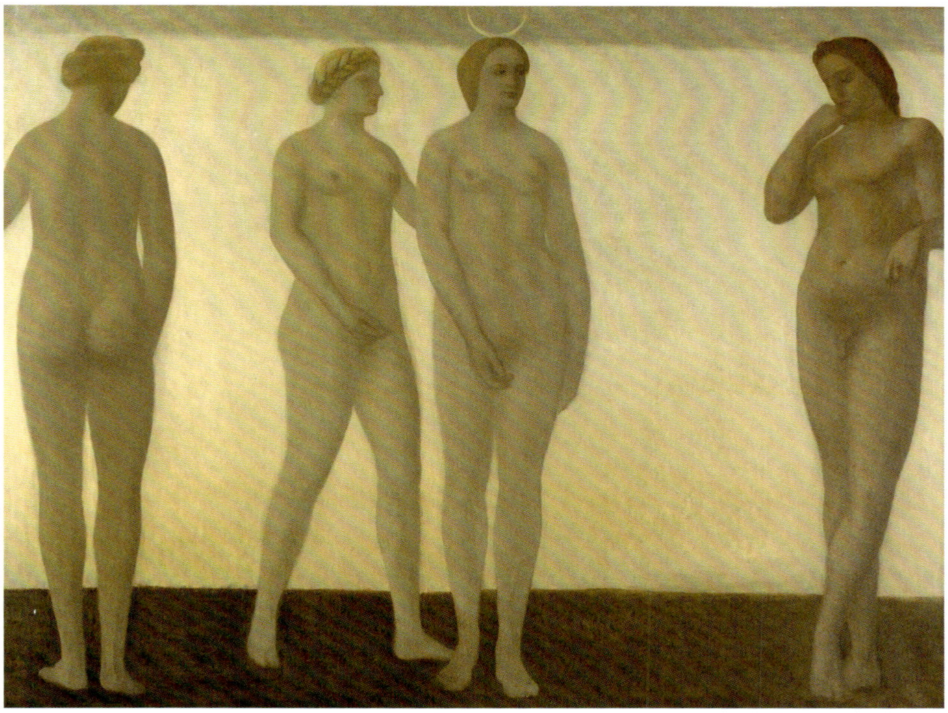

[145]
Fernand Khnopff 1858-1921 Belgian
Memories 1889
Pastel on paper mounted on canvas 127 x 200 cm
Musées Royaux des Beaux-Arts de Belgique, Brussels

[10]
Vilhelm Hammershøi 1864-1916 Danish
Artemis 1893-94
Oil on canvas 193 x 251.5 cm
Statens Museum for Kunst

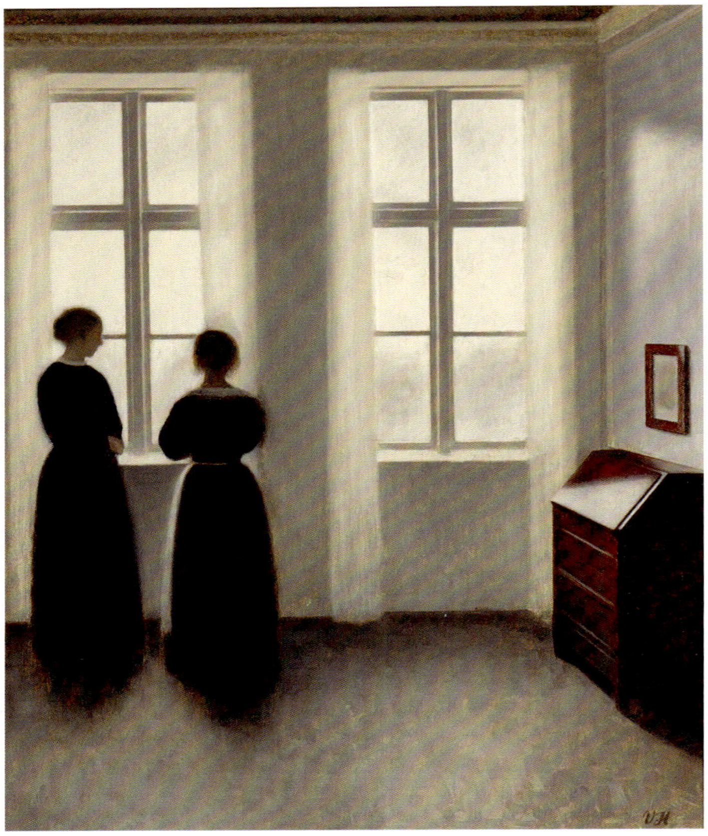

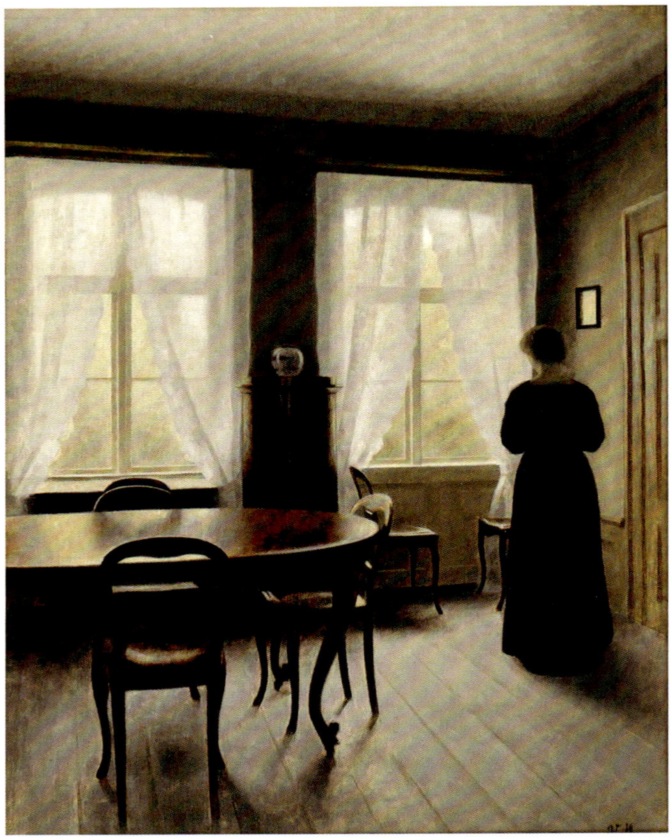

Whiteness

The use of *whiteness* is one of the deliberately diffuse devices within Hammershøi's painting that conjure up a dream-like, film-like atmosphere similar to the moods conveyed by certain type of nostalgic photography heavily laden with sensory input. This is evident in the painting of the two women by a window and in the interior from Hammershøi's family's home in Frederiksberg Allé, where different kinds of whiteness penetrate the rooms and cause everything to float [58, 59].

With their double windows and long white curtains these compositions define the total experience of the spaces shown in the paintings. There is no view; the rooms are dense, concentrated. In the windowpanes Hammershøi reproduces various degrees of saturated whiteness.[13] It might seem as if the windows were more or less covered in paint, and at the same time imbued with associations of clouds, mists, or blurred trees. The whitish layers penetrate the entire painting, spreading out across the furniture and floor. It is as if we are seeing things through a softening whitish lens. The column-like black figures emerge against the white as isolated contrasts, providing clear focal points.

It is hardly surprising that Hammershøi's imagery is often compared to filmic rooms. He is an *auteur*. He has a distinctive style that is entirely his own, and his idiom is always immediately recognisable.[14] The film director Francois Truffaut described the style of fellow director Carl Th. Dreyer as having "a formal perfection that touches upon the sublime."[15] One

[58]
Vilhelm Hammershøi 1864-1916 Danish
Figures by the Window c. 1895
Oil on canvas 55 x 46 cm
Private collection

[59]
Vilhelm Hammershøi 1864-1916 Danish
Interior, Frederiksberg Allé 1900
Oil on canvas 56 x 44.5 cm
Private collection, United Kingdom

might describe Hammershøi in similar terms. The comparison is not entirely arbitrary; Dreyer has been discussed as an important heir to Hammershøi's style on numerous occasions.[16] The remarkable whiteness described in the above and its dominant effect in Hammershøi may be one of the main factors behind Dreyer's interest in Hammershøi's paintings. In his short text about Dreyer, Truffaut points to the fact that he, too, uses whiteness as a powerful marker in films such as *Vampyr*, *Day of Wrath* and *The Word.* Truffaut recalls the whiteness in the various films in a manner suggesting that it is of greater interest to him that the narratives themselves. The controlled whiteness is the main impression left on the retina.

We might venture a comparison between this filmic whiteness and the whiteness in Hammershøi. The whiteness is a dominant feature and is repeated in varying gradations across the canvases. Alongside the impression left by the carefully applied brushstrokes and the graphic palette of blacks, greys, and browns, the whiteness in Hammershøi serves as a foundation for our perception of his paintings as photographically sensuous. The paintings incorporate a photographic impression of space and reality. The marked diffuseness of blurred photographs, the slow observation of the world, the transience, the black-white-brown tinting of the image, and the sensuously seductive qualities of the photographer's gaze are all part of the painterly phenomenon in Hammershøi.

Close-ups

Hammershøi's body of work also encompasses a number of drawings that can stand as works in their own right while also elucidating his method.

During a long sojourn in London in 1897-98 Hammershøi painted a double portrait of himself and his wife Ida [14, p. 3]. During the working process Hammershøi drew a close-up, intimate portrait of Ida [12, p. 30]. Ida's face takes up almost the entire piece of paper – Hammershøi has zoomed in on her in a manner reminiscent of the close-ups of films. In a letter written to his brother Svend in Denmark Hammershøi refers to the painting as "a kind of double portrait of Ida and I", but adds: "that is to say that I myself have my back almost turned; but then these needn't be portraits in the strictest sense of the term."[17]

Between the lines it would appear that Hammershøi was working on an unconventional take on a double portrait. In the drawing of Ida her face emerges gently from the carefully crafted hair and background. Her gaze is turned downwards, and the surface of her face is depicted as a soft shape – a kind of globe – that presents itself for close scrutiny. There is no confrontation here; rather, there is a kind of sympathetic introspection and a certain dreamlike quality. This must be what Hammershøi so discreetly terms "a kind of double portrait", for while his emphasis on the peculiarity of this portrait certainly refers to the way his back is turned, I believe that he is also referring to the accentuated introversion in the image of Ida as one possible take on a new type of portrait; a project that occupies him greatly. Hammershøi's work on portraits featuring introspective people dates all the way back to his early work – one example would be his drawing of his sister Anna from 1886; with its condensed sensibility it heralds what would be a major theme in Hammershøi [146].

A French contemporary of Hammershøi, Georges Seurat, also worked with a "different kind" of portrait in a series of drawings where he focuses on depicting introvert figures. The drawing of the artist's mother, *Mrs. Seurat*, from 1882-83 [147] shows how Seurat employs a distinctive black-and-white close-up technique which sees his mother's face gradually emerging like a luminous presence rising out of the graded black background. Using

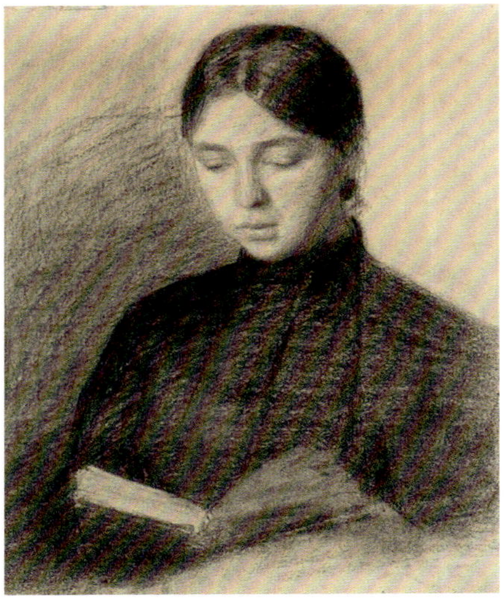

[146]
Vilhelm Hammershøi 1864-1916 Danish
The Artist's Sister Anna, Reading 1886
Drawing, Charcoal 24 x 19.5 cm
Statens Museum for Kunst

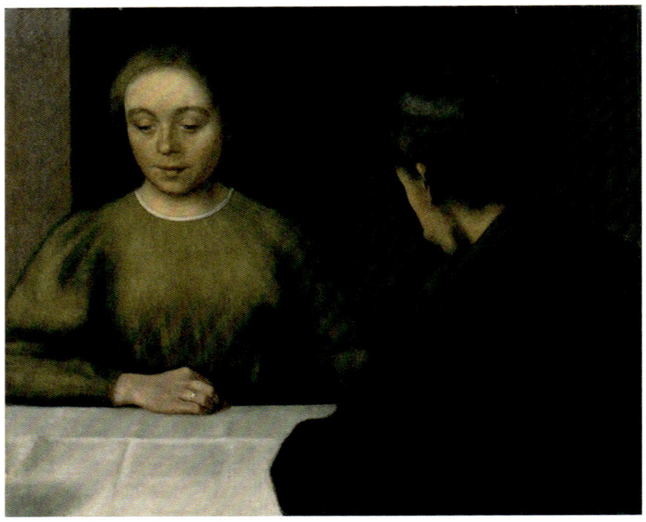

[14]
Vilhelm Hammershøi 1864-1916 Danish
Two Figures. The Artist and His Wife 1898
Oil on canvas 71.5 x 86 cm
ARoS Aarhus Kunstmuseum

simple materials – conté crayon on handmade paper – Seurat conjures up a spectacular emergence of the face. His mother looks down, averting her face and gaze, and the image is suffused with an intimate and intense sense of absorption. The figure may be introvert, but at the same time its aura is very strong, not least because of the tactility of the drawing. The experience of sensing the artist's mother's being and essence may be stronger in this image than if we were regarding a photograph of her, an image where we might be sure that she had posed for the picture in person. The portrait is one example of how a photographic sensibility has been evoked in crayon in a manner which trumps photography's real-life traces of life – its indexicality. The knowledge that the drawing – and, hence, the experience of its aura – is directly linked to the movement of a human hand across paper enhances the sensory impression of an image that is very closely linked to its motif.

The aura effect in Seurat's drawing has a kinship with several of Hammershøi's images of Ida, where Ida's face shines in the darkness and where the frequently monotonous, yet also elaborately rendered backgrounds are reminiscent of the darkness that surrounds the figures in Seurat. In a slightly different kind of drawing by Seurat – his study for the painting *The Models* – his deliberately diffuse drawing technique imbues a nude study with a strangely dreamlike atmosphere. The naked woman is depicted in a staged pose, but at the same time her body enters into a very close relationship with the room. She faces the observer, but her blurred facial features prevent us from meeting her gaze and she remains rooted within the pictorial space [148].

Fernand Khnopff, too, works with close-ups in many of his drawings of women's faces, but in contrast to Hammershøi's work his women direct their gaze directly out of the picture with great intensity. Their gazes seem downright hypnotic, and Khnopff's use of this insisting gaze, a certain diffuseness of drawing, and a slight colouring-in cause these drawings to take on a *made-up* quality that does not appear in Hammershøi and Seurat [149]. According to the art historian Dorothy Kosinski, Khnopff has an overall preoccupation with "seeing" or "not seeing" in his paintings and with the gaze in general. Khnopff shows many

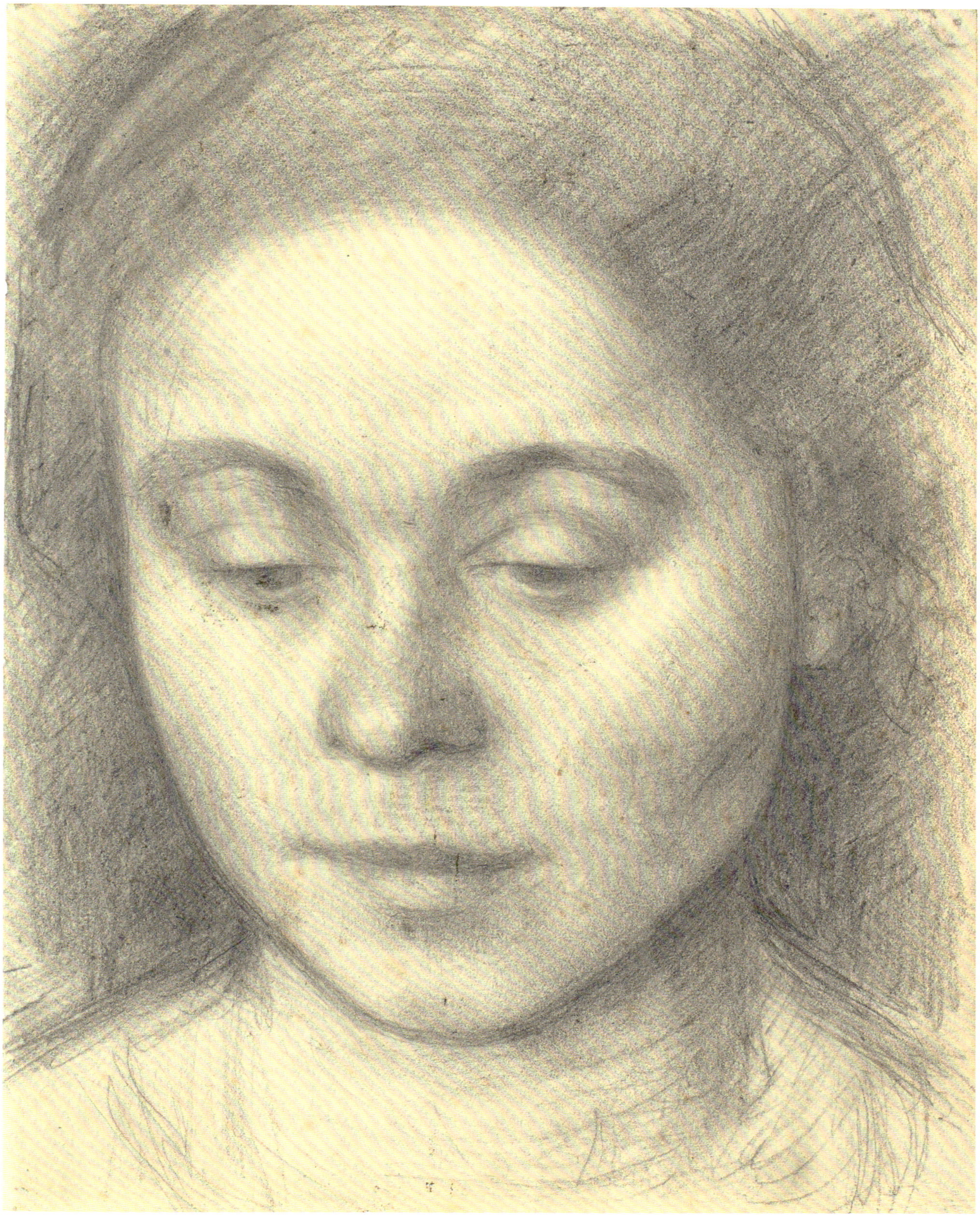

[12]
Vilhelm Hammershøi 1864-1916 Danish
Portrait of Ida, the Artist's Wife 1898
Drawing, pencil 24.2 x 18.8 cm
Statens Museum for Kunst

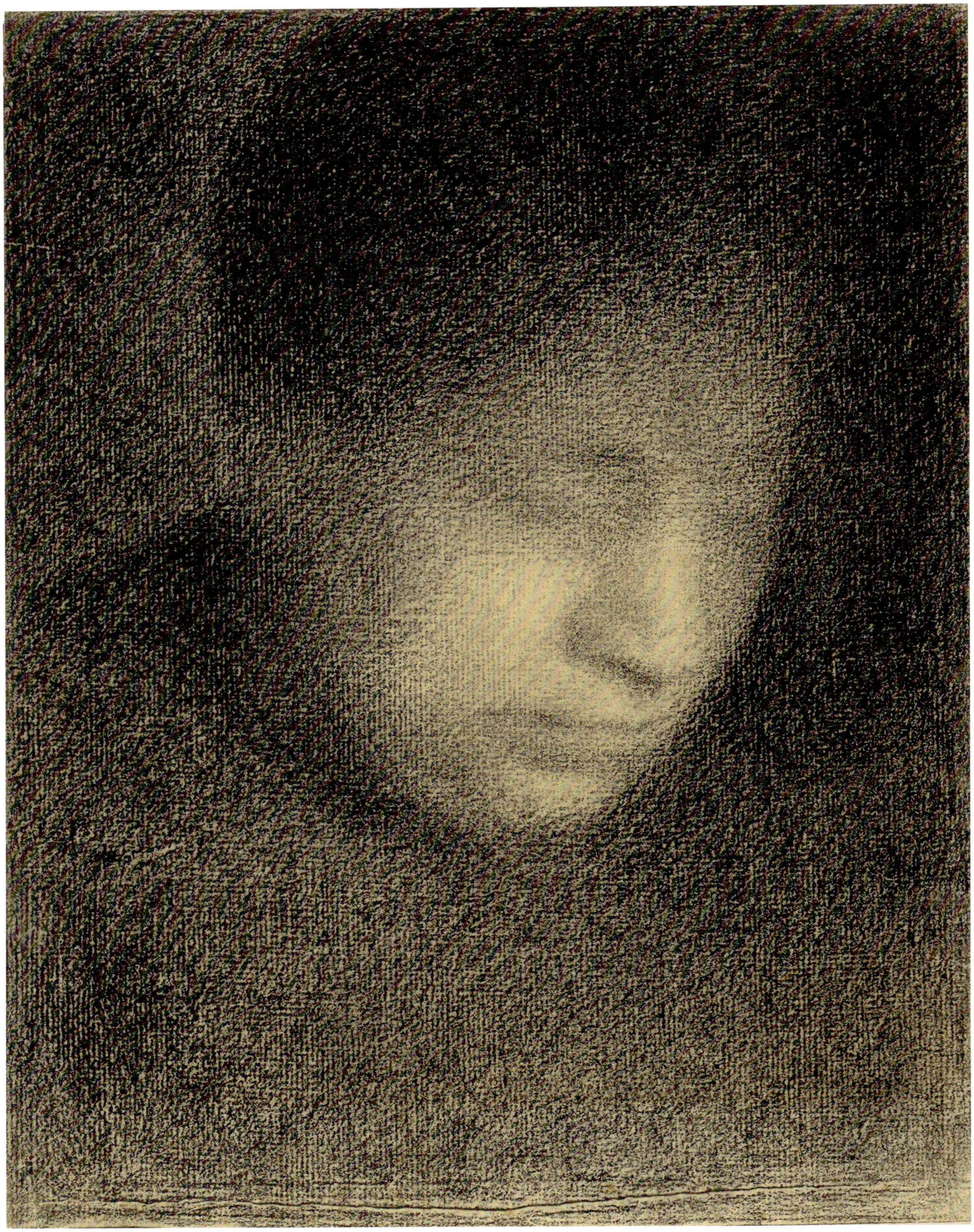

[147]
Georges Seurat 1859-91 French
Mrs. Seurat 1882-83
Conté crayon on Michallet paper 30.5 x 23.3 cm
The J. Paul Getty Museum, Los Angeles

mirrors, windows, eyes, round or eye-shaped forms and reflective bodies of water in his paintings – all elements which somehow refer to the sensing, recording gaze. Kosinski notes that Khnopff does not paint or draw self-portraits in the proper sense of the term; he does not appear as himself in his work, but the staring, idealised, and often androgynous faces may be a kind of alter egos for Khnopff – Kosinski calls them his "avatar-ideals".[18]

As a counterpoint to the hypnotically staring faces Khnopff also works with introspective and mental images – such as in the painting *Memories* [145]. Photographs help Khnopff visualise something mental, something mysterious that he translates into his paintings and drawings. He stages his sister Marguerite in a range of tableaux, and the photographs capture the memories of such scenes while also conveying a sense of something unreal in the midst of all their photographic reality, an effect that Khnopff incorporates into his drawings and paintings. A similarly enigmatic, introspective atmosphere is also an essential part of Hammershøi's art, particularly in those images of Ida and himself that "are not portraits in the strictest sense of the term". Even though photographs may not have formed part of Hammershøi's process, a photographic awareness is embedded in the drawings and paintings; an awareness that the picture has captured more than can be registered at first glance: a mystery, a phenomenon, a memory arising, a play of line and light.

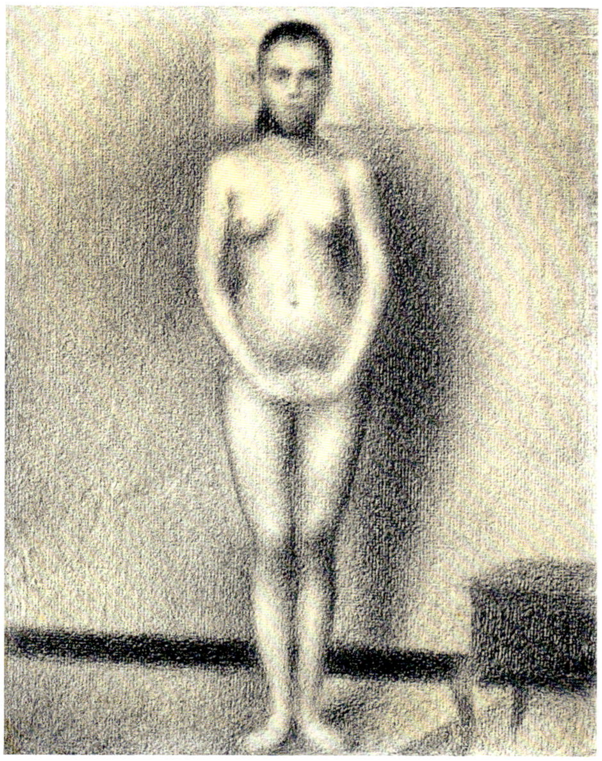

[148]
Georges Seurat 1859-91 French
Study for "The Models" 1886
Drawing, Conté crayon on laid paper 29.7 x 22.5 cm
Metropolitan Museum of Art, New York (Lehman Collection)

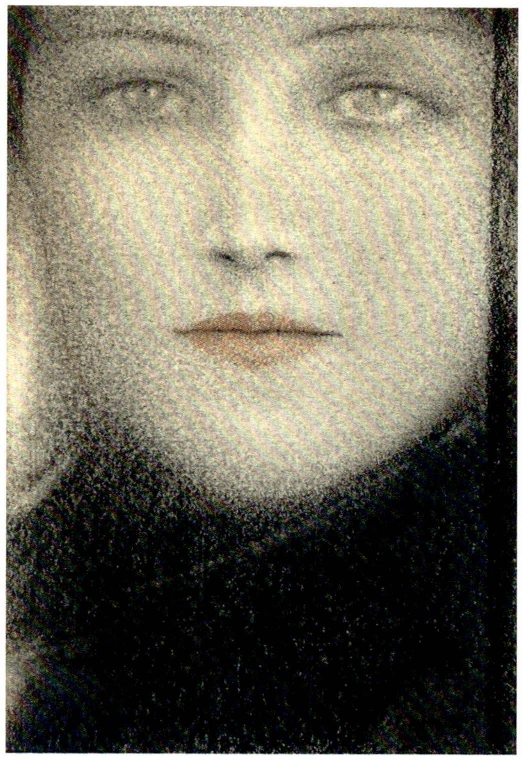

[149]
Fernand Khnopff 1858-1921 Belgian
A Woman's face c. 1892
Pastel, wax crayons and coloured crayons on paper
15 x 10.1 cm
Private collection

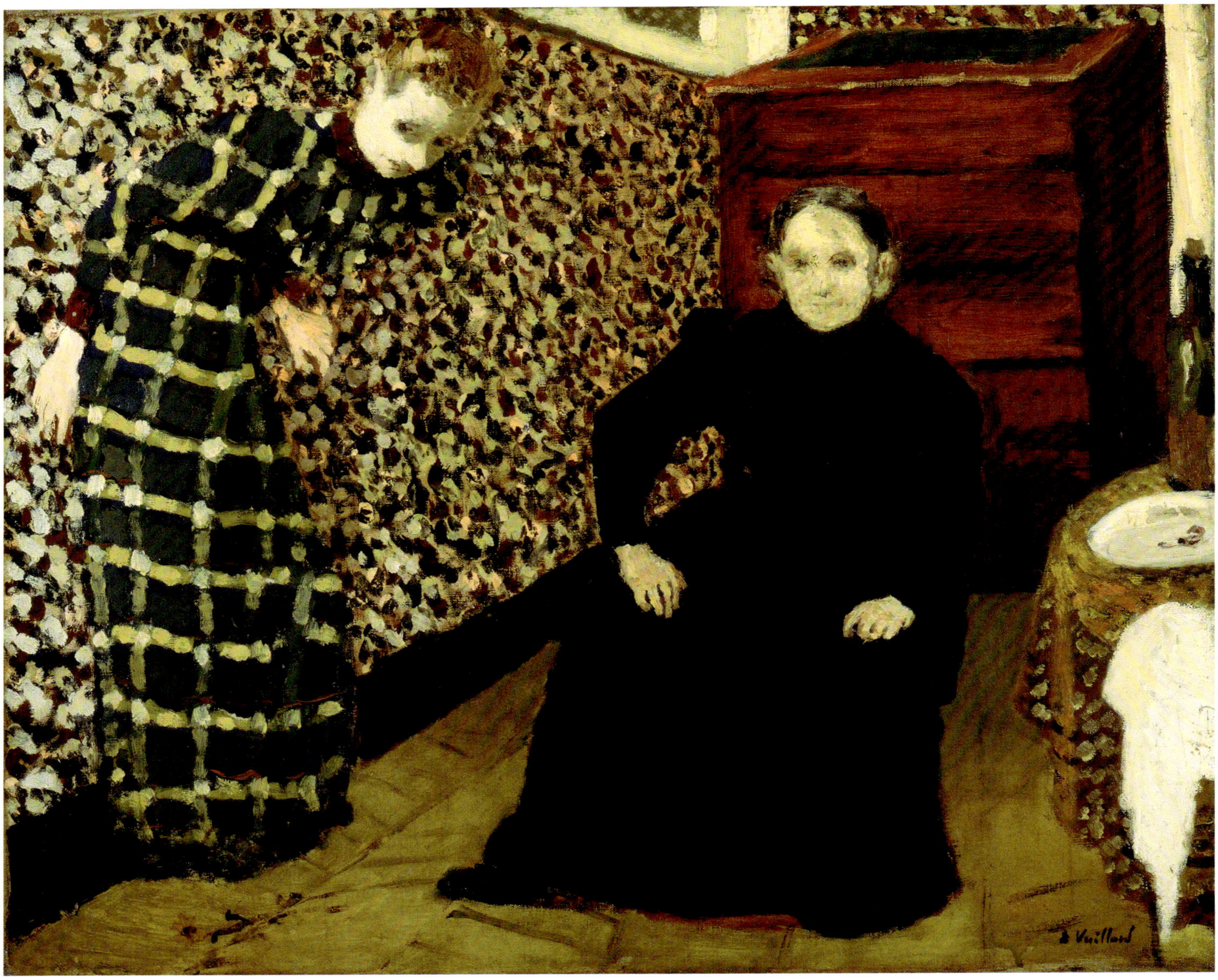

[150]
Édouard Vuillard 1868-1940 French
Interior, Mother and Sister of the Artist 1893
Oil on canvas 46.3 x 56.5 cm
Museum of Modern Art, New York

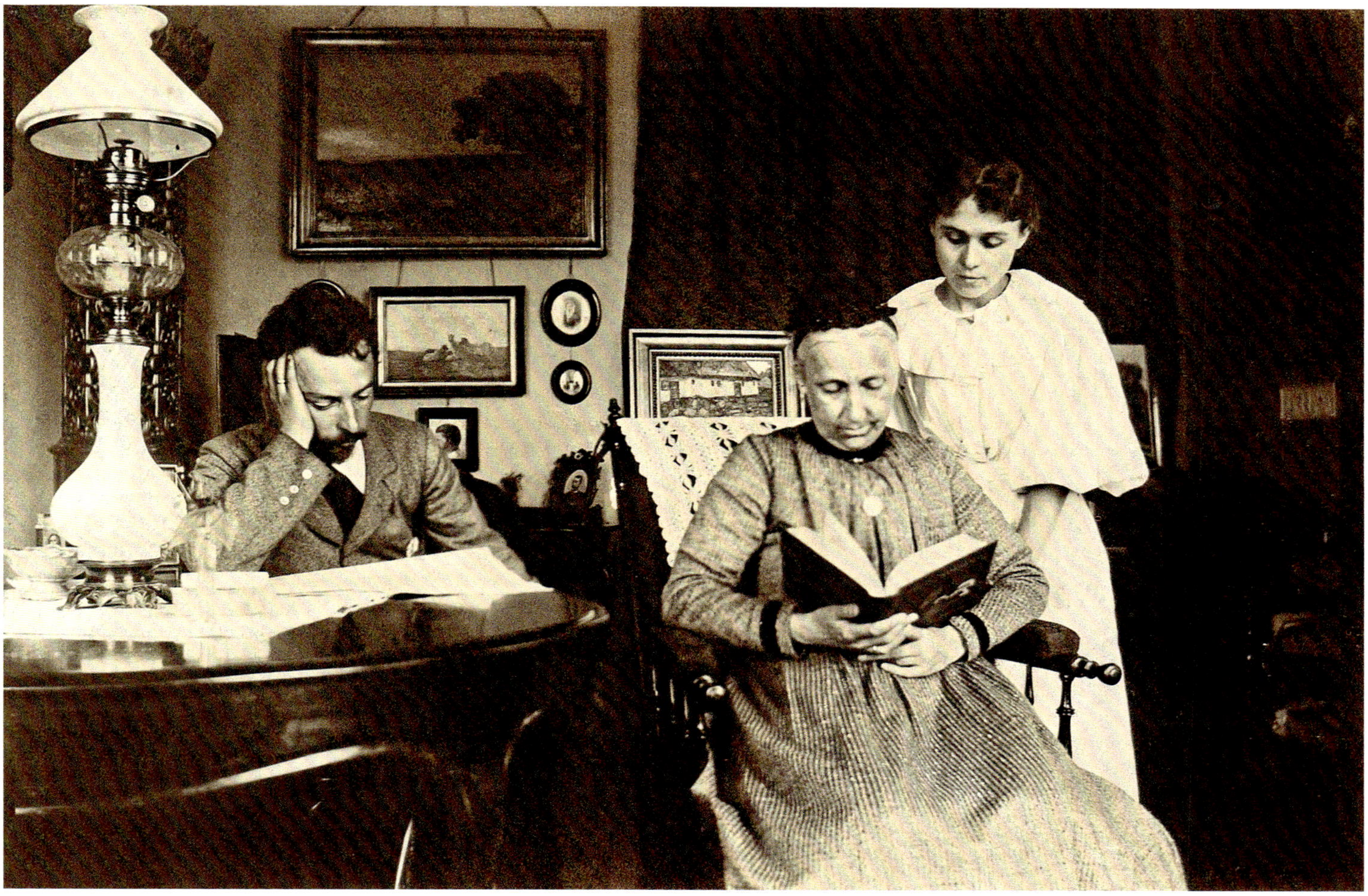

[151]
Unknown photographer
Vilhelm, Frederikke and Ida Hammershøi 1894
Photograph
The Royal Library, Copenhagen

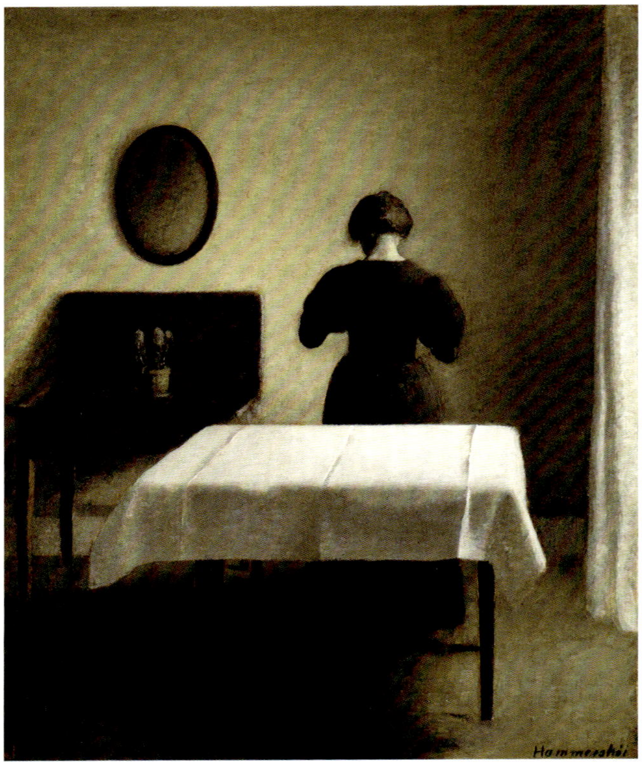

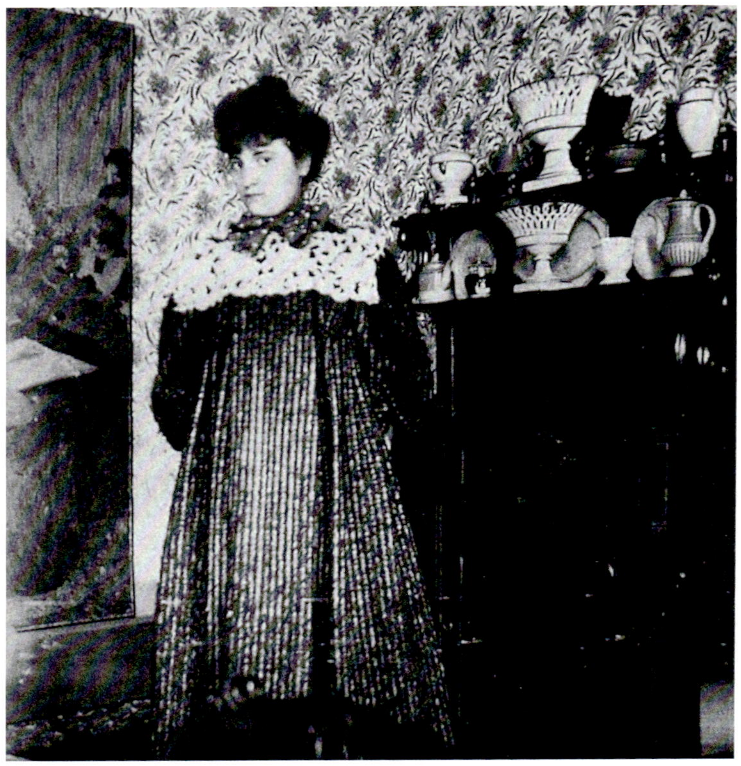

Becoming one with the painting – or being left out

One of the French artists who, like Bonnard, is described as an *Intimist,* is Édouard Vuillard. Intimism is concerned with the artists' choice of everyday scenes in interiors, but also with their interest in new ways of painting that create a density and intimacy in the paintings.

Vuillard's interior with his mother and sister takes the interplay between figures and room to an extreme [150]. The sister is either swallowed by or emerging from the wallpaper while the mother sits heavily and calmly in a chair. The room seems alive; the wallpaper almost appears to grow as you look at it, and the floorboards are undulating up and down. The sense of unease communicated by this painting and its mentally charged energy is also governed by the compressed room that does not really allow enough space for the sister, who bends into the painting while the mother dominates the scene from her firmly rooted, black position.

Hammershøi and Vuillard both collect and stage photographs and use them in their labour to evoke sensuous experiences of rooms in paintings. [152] Vuillard's own body of photographic works is extensive; we know of around a thousand images. The Hammershøi archives, too, are home to a substantial amount of photographs.[19] One example would be a picture showing a scene from the drawing room of the artist's mother, Frederikke Hammershøi; Vilhelm and his mother are engrossed in reading while Ida looks on across Frederikke's shoulder. [151] A seemingly carefully staged private picture in which each person performs the role assigned to them and has been placed in the room in order of significance. But Ida has been positioned awkwardly in this context – somewhat along the lines of Vuillard's sister,

[64]
Vilhelm Hammershøi 1864-1916 Danish
Interior 1898
Oil on canvas 51.5 x 46 cm
Nationalmuseum, Stockholm

[152]
Édouard Vuillard 1868-1940 French
Misia Natanson c. 1897
Photograph
Archives Salomon, Paris, J.M. Routhier

who almost does not fit inside the pictorial space and so, for that very reason, attracts the greatest share of attention. Naturally, the sense of unease and unrest in Vuillard will tint our reading of the Hammershøi family picture when the two are viewed right next to each other. In the photograph Ida does not inhabit the room at the same level as Vilhelm and his mother Frederikke, both of whom are utterly absorbed in their reading. Ida's figure is a surplus presence in the room.

The organic, vibrant, animated qualities of Vuillard's painting is partly a result of his fierce manner of applying paints in large blots and strokes. Hammershøi is less extreme in his method of painting, but he does work with many different variations in his technique – one of which he demonstrates in the interior featuring a woman, her back turned to us, standing behind a table and up against a wall [64].

Each of the small individual areas of paint have been applied in carefully measured doses and have been shaded in by means of greater or smaller quantities of white applied across the plane. One might say that Hammershøi arranges his brushstrokes in the same calculated manner he arranges the furniture and figures in his interiors. This is not to say that such an interior seems lifeless when contrasted with that of Vuillard. Hammershøi's sensuousness and Intimism is evident in the care invested in how each part of the painting appears in the overall image, in the *precision* of the diffuseness and the grading of light and shadow that is so perfectly executed across the canvas. One example would be the white tablecloth, which plays such a tremendous part in the painting. It can be compared to the role played by the wallpaper in Vuillard's interior. A materiality that governs the overall effect of the painting, occupying a position between something real, something seen, something impressionistic *and* an additional effect that highlights the painting as a powerful phenomenon.

Hammershøi does not share Vuillard and Bonnard's dynamic interest in pattern and decoration as visible main elements of paintings. His patterns are subtly integrated in the works, and his figures can be taken out, isolated, from their surroundings. However, the fact that many of his figures have their backs towards us may constitute a different kind of marker for how that figure merges with the interior. By virtue of their position these figures orient themselves inwards in the painting, into and up against the wall that acts as a kind of metaphor for the painting's own canvas surface. They live inside the painting.

Annette Rosenvold Hvidt (born 1963), art historian, art educator at the National Gallery of Denmark. Specialist areas include Danish and French art from 1850-1920; cross-pollination between painting, photography, and film; and digital communication. Has conducted research on Hammershøi's art, e.g. for publications for Ordrupgaard (2005, 2006) and was a curator for the exhibition Hammershøi > Dreyer – Billedmagi, which was presented in Ordrupgaard and in Barcelona (2006-07).

NOTES

1 Bramsen & Michaelis, 1918, p. 70.

2 The picture is part of a series of photographs taken by his friend and colleague Valdemar Schønheyder Møller around the time of Hammershøi's debut in the mid 1880s. Together with Hammershøi's sister Anna they staged and captured a number of different scenes or tableaux whose atmosphere and lighting is reminiscent of his paintings from the same period. I do not believe that the photographs should be regarded as studies for the paintings; rather, they should be considered as works that had a kinship with – and may have provided fuel for – the type of imagery that Hammershøi and Schønheyder Møller worked with at the time. For more on the subject, see Annette Rosenvold Hvidt, "Det ganske mærkelige hos Hammershøi" ("The Strange Thing about Hammershøi"), in Copenhagen, 2006.

3 The art historian Mikkel Bogh offers a phenomenal elucidation in Bogh, 1996.

4 Vad, 1988 (1992), p. 372.

5 In several articles the art historian Gertrud Oelsner has analysed Hammershøi's works in relation to photography as a medium, positing his work within this segment of the art of the period alongside for example P. S. Krøyer and Julius Paulsen. See Gertrud Oelsner, "Øjebliksbilleder" in Skagen, 2001 and "Den hollandske forbindelse", *Passepartout* # 19, 2002, and Oelsner, 2002.

6 Picasso is quoted in Yve-Alain Bois: "Bonnard's 'passivity'", in Paris, 2006, pp. 51-63.

7 John Elderfield, "Seeing Bonnard", in London & New York, 1998, pp. 32-52.

8 See for example Mikkel Bogh: "Interieurer, flader og åbninger – Det intime i maleriet omkring år 1900", working paper for the Department of Literature, University of Copenhagen 1996.

9 Cf. Baark Mairey, 2011, pp. 94f.

10 In his catalogue of Hammershøi's works, Alfred Bramsen, a patron of Hammershøi, also accentuates the differences in scale between the head and hand in the series of self-portraits from Spurveskjul: Bramsen & Michaëlis, 1918, p. 110.

11 Regarding other interpretations of *Artemis* see for example Vad, 1988 (1992), pp. 117-135; Peter Nørgaard Larsen: "Skønheden og døden" ("Beauty and Death"), in Copenhagen, 2000, pp. 17-55 and Holm, 2006, pp. 163-172.

12 For example by Perugino's *Apollo and Marsyas* from 1509 as suggested by Poul Vad, 1988 (1992), p. 128.

13 Cf. Oelsner, 2002.

14 One example of a 21st century interpretation of Hammershøi that focuses on the rooms and figures' particular potential for engaging the imagination would be that of the artists' duo Elmgreen and Dragset. In an interview about their favourite artists presented at the online platform of the Danish National Broadcasting Corporation, dr.dk, they explain their interest in Hammershøi in the following terms: "In the case of Hammershøj his static, empty interiors with their complete lack of action strike us as deeply perverse. His paintings are reminiscent of stage sets for a Bergman film". (Most recently visited in April 2011 at http://www.dr.dk/Nyheder/Kultur/Kunstklub/Kunstnernes_Favoritter/20110321114324_1_1_1_1_1.htm)

15 François Truffaut: "The Whiteness of Carl Th. Dreyer", in *The films in my life*, Da Capo Press edition 1994, pp. 48-49.

16 Poul Vad: "Vilhelm Hammershøi – en introduktion", in Copenhagen, Paris & New York, 1997, p. 9, and Annette Rosenvold Hvidt in Copenhagen 2006.

17 Letter to Svend Hammershøi dated 14 March 1898 – at the Hirschsprung Collection archives.

18 Dorothy Kosinski, "The Gaze of Fernand Khnopff", in San Francisco, Dallas & Bilbao, 1999, pp. 142-155.

19 Photographs from Hammershøi's archives can be found at the Hirschsprung Collection and at the Royal Danish Library.

OVERVIEWS

BIOGRAPHIES
THE EXHIBITIONS
BIBLIOGRAPHY

BIOGRAPHIES

TONE BONNÉN

ANNA ANCHER

Skagen 1859 – Skagen 1935

Born in Skagen into a scene peopled by many of the artists of the day, Anna Brøndum was prompted to develop artistic leanings from her early childhood. From 1875 up until 1879, when she had her debut as a painter at the Charlottenborg Christmas show, she received tuition at the Vilhelm Kyhn Women's School of Painting and Drawing in Copenhagen. Shortly afterwards she gained artistic recognition, and in 1880 her private life also became embroiled with the art scene when she married the artist Michael Ancher, whom she had met in Skagen in the summer of 1877. The couple settled in Skagen, but in the years that followed they would make several prolonged sojourns abroad.

In 1885 they travelled to the Netherlands, Belgium, and Paris, where Anna saw the Salon as well as an exhibition featuring the French Impressionists. In 1888 Anna Ancher received a travel grant that once again brought her and Michael to Paris. They remained here up until the summer of 1889 when she – like Hammershøi – exhibited four works at the Universal Exposition.

During her time in Paris Anna was tutored by the painter Puvis de Chavannes, drawing inspiration from his work on matters such as how to build decorative compositions by means of large areas of uniform colours, but her work also differed from her tutor's; she favoured small-scale formats and realistic subject matter drawn from her domestic surroundings and situations. Anna Ancher was not interested in narratives about the figures in her rooms; she used such traditional motifs to explore the painterly space. She employed other methods to the same end, such as her colour schemes and lighting.

Anna Ancher's focus on light in her painting often prompts critics to describe her as an Impressionist, but in Anna Ancher's art light was primarily a motif, meaning that it was a far more material phenomenon in her works than among the Impressionists [for example 71, p.92]. Anna Ancher painted what she saw and sensed, but she had a controlled gaze that oriented itself towards those colours and motifs that best served her compositions.

Up through the 1890s Anna Ancher received a steady succession of accolades for her work in the form of prestigious medals from the Royal Danish Academy of Fine Arts and invitations to exhibit her work in Denmark and abroad.

Anna Ancher's activity continued to revolve around Skagen the same way that Hammershøi's revolved around Copenhagen. They lived at either end of Denmark and employed very different colour schemes and techniques, but they did share the same choice of motif with their interest in their immediate surroundings, their living rooms and the way light falls through the window, and they also shared an interest in translating what they saw into carefully composed works of art. Anna Ancher died in 1935 and was buried in Skagen next to her husband.

PIERRE BONNARD

Fontenay-aux-Roses,
Paris 1867 – Le Cannet 1947

At the behest of his father Pierre Bonnard began to study law in Paris in 1885. As his own inclinations ran towards a career within the arts rather than the law, however, he also attended courses at the École des Beaux-Arts at the same time. Nevertheless, Bonnard continued his studies at law school when he en-rolled at the Académie Julian in 1887 and at the school of painting at the École des Beaux-Arts later that year. Bonnard was, in fact, in the process of building an artistic career for himself when he graduated from law school in 1888.

At the Académie Julian Bonnard became part of a circle that formed the Nabi group in 1888. The Nabis were directly inspired by Gauguin and by the way in which he used painting as a surface where colours and shapes had a decorative and symbolic function, unfettered by an objective reality. Like Gauguin, the Nabis were interested in delving into something "original" or primordial, and in this regard a crucial event occurred for Bonnard when he visited an exhibition of Japanese art at the École des Beaux-Arts in 1890. The exhibition had a profound impact on him; in fact this impact was such that he was henceforth known as "the Japanese Nabi". Bonnard translated his fascination with the simplified Japanese style into paintings as well as posters, illustrations, textiles, and decorative art. Bonnard had his breakthrough in 1891 at the Salon des Indépendants. Here, he and fellow Nabi Maurice Denis paved the way for the first Nabi group exhibition in Paris later that same year. Bonnard continued to show his work with the Nabis and at the Salons up through the 1890s and well into the first de-cade of the 20th century. In 1892 Hammershøi saw the third Nabi show in Paris, which prompted him to mock their plane-oriented style [p.41]. In his future career as a painter, however, Bonnard gradually abandoned the devices he formerly had in common with the Nabis. Instead, he – like Hammershøi – became engrossed with depicting space and figures within that space while his own homes and his own family served him as particularly favoured motifs.

In 1906 Bonnard had his first major one-man show at the Galerie Bernheim-Jeune in Paris; the exhibition proved to be a success that was repeated during the period 1909-13. Concurrently with these shows he continued to exhibit his works at the Salons, and after 1913 he continued his career by executing a number of major commissions for exhibitions and decorative works. The year 1926 proved a pivotal point for Bonnard's ongoing artistic endeavours; at this point he bought a house on the French Riviera, and this prompted him to explore new motifs. In 1926 Bonnard also went back to staging frequent solo shows at Bernheim-Jeune, a gallery capable of selling Bonnard's works with great ease. And his first solo exhibition in the USA, held at the de Hauke Gallery in New York in 1928, launched Bonnard's international career in earnest.

Bonnard died at the age of 79 in his home in the South of France in 1947. He did not live to see the Museum of Modern Art's major retrospective launched to celebrate his imminent 80th birthday.

EUGÈNE CARRIÈRE
Dournay 1849 – Paris 1906

While Carrière was still a child he and his family moved to Strasbourg where his father made sure that he learned the draughtsmanship necessary to equip him to a career as a lithographer. In 1869, however, Carrière decided to go to Paris to pursue an artistic career. Up until 1877 he studied art at the École des Beaux-Arts under the salon painter Cabanel.

Carrière had his first work accepted at the Salon in 1876 and showed his work there almost every year up until 1884 without generating any great interest. In 1885, however, he achieved his real breakthrough at the Salon with a portrait of his wife and son, *The Sick Child*. Its motif and atmospheric, sentimental qualities were typical of Carrière's approach to painting at the time.

Throughout his entire career as an artist Carrière used his family as subjects and conjured up a distinctive atmosphere in his intimate portraits by restricting his palette to brownish colours and by letting the figures emerge out of a hazy, indefinable background. The dreamlike atmosphere evoked by Carrière gave his paintings a poetic and mystical feel that tied in well with the prevalent symbolism of the time.

Carrière continued to show his works at the Salon each year up through the 1880s, and by the time he was involved in founding the Société Nationale des Beaux-Arts alongside artists such as Puvis de Chavannes and Rodin, who were close friends of his, Carrière was among the most highly regarded and respected artists of his era.

Carrière's restricted palette prompted some of the critics of the time to compare him to Whistler, and in Denmark the Danish art historian Emil Hannover compared Carrière to Hammershøi in 1892. Hammershøi was undoubtedly familiar with Carrière's work. He would have had ample opportunity to see his works at the Salons and at the Universal Exposition in Paris in 1889 and, what is more, Carrière was also well known in Denmark. Mette Gauguin, for example, owned a portrait of Paul Gauguin painted by Carrière, which was not only featured in her collection in her Copenhagen home; it was also exhibited at Den Frie Udstilling (The Independent Exhibition) in 1893.

Up through the 1890s Carrière worked quite extensively with prints. He continued to enjoy great artistic success and exhibited his work regularly up until his death in 1906, which came after he had suffered from throat cancer for years.

HANS AM ENDE
Trier 1864 – Stettin 1918

Hans am Ende was born and grew up in Trier where his father was a priest. In 1872 the family moved to a different part of Germany when his father was appointed to a position in Naumburg. Here am Ende attended school until he was accepted at the Academy of Fine Arts in Munich in 1884. He studied under Wilhelm von Diez and had Fritz Mackensen as one of his fellow students for some time. Mackensen and am Ende became close friends and completed their compulsory military service together after finishing their studies in Munich. After his stint in the military am Ende returned to his studies, this time at the Academy in Karlsruhe.

In 1889 am Ende went to Worpswede near Bremen to live and paint in a state of close communion with nature. He did so in the company of Mackensen, who had regularly spent time in Worpswede since 1884. With the arrival of am Ende and a few other artists in 1889 a true artist's colony took shape.

In 1892-93 am Ende enrolled as a student under the landscape painter Eugen Bracht at the Academy of Fine Arts in Berlin. After his studies, he returned to Worpswede where he got married and acquired a home and studio. Am Ende worked with large formats, capturing the local landscape in paintings and etchings.

In 1895 am Ende exhibited with the Worpswede group at their first group exhibitions at the Münchener Glaspalast and the Kunsthalle Bremen. The exhibitions generated a lot of attention and am Ende was singled out for, among other things, the particularly calm atmosphere of his landscapes. Am Ende worked in a naturalistic vein, but echoed to some degree Hammershøi insofar as he created a simplified mode of expression by means of unadorned, clear compositions.

In 1900 the poet Rainer Maria Rilke visited Worpswede and became keenly interested in the artists and their work, which he subsequently described and gathered in a monograph (1903) about the group. In his essay about am Ende Rilke noted that his paintings contained more than their apparent contents; that they expressed more than they depicted directly. Rilke compared am Ende's paintings with music and stated that they were distinguished by their pauses, by intervals full of reverberations, silence, and uncertainties. This was roughly the same quality – that of slowness – which so attracted Rilke about Hammershøi's works, which he saw for the first time in 1904 at the international exhibition in Düsseldorf.
At the outbreak of World War I in 1914 am Ende volunteered for military service. In 1918 he was injured at the frontline in Belgium and was sent to a military hospital in Stettin, where he died from his injuries. He was buried in Bremen, but in 1945 his tombstone was taken to Worpswede and placed next to his wife's grave.

LOUIS EYSEN
Manchester 1843 – Munich 1899

Eysen was born in Manchester into an affluent German family of merchants. In 1850 his family moved back to Germany, settling in Frankfurt am Main where Eysen began studying art at the Städelschen Kunstinstitut in 1861. Here Eysen would study drawing under Andreas Simons, a professor of architecture. Concurrently with these studies Eysen was privately tutored by Friedrich Karl Hausmann, a painter of historical scenes, and learnt how to create woodcuts from the xylographer Andreas Stix.

Eysen was enrolled at the Städelschen Kunstinstitut up until 1869, after which time he went to Paris. Here Eysen began to paint and was briefly taught by Léon Bonnat. In Paris he became friends with the German painter Wilhelm Leibl, and he met Gustave Courbet, whose realism greatly inspired Eysen. When the Franco-Prussian war grew in intensity in 1870 Eysen returned to Frankfurt. In 1873 he settled in Kronberg, where he painted the local mountains and aimed for objectivity in his depictions. In addition to landscapes Eysen painted a range of portraits of members of his family. The portrait of the artist's mother engaged in domestic chores in an equally domestic interior [72, p.93] was painted shortly before he left the artists' colony in Kronberg in 1878 and moved to Southern Tirol with his mother and sister.

Eysen suffered from poor health and lived apart from the Southern Tirol art scene, continuing to paint landscapes and portraits. His paintings were only shown to the public on few occasions. In 1888 he exhibited at the Ausstellung der Akademie der Kunste in Berlin, and in 1891 he contributed two paintings to the Münchener Jahresausstellung aller Nationen, where Hammershøi also showed a number of paintings. The exhibitions did not lead to any career breakthrough for Eysen, and his health continued to deteriorate. In 1899 he had to commit himself to hospital in Munich for an operation; he died later that year due to post-surgery complications.

The first major presentation of Eysen's work was a memorial show arranged the year after his death; the exhibition was shown in Munich, Frankfurt, Karlsruhe, Berlin, and Meran in Southern Tirol where Eysen lived up until his death.

HENRI FANTIN-LATOUR

Grenoble 1836 – Buré 1904

As a young boy Fantin-Latour moved with his family to Paris. He began his schooling in the art of drawing at the age of 15, and in 1853 he embarked on studies at the École des Beaux-Arts, but quickly abandoned them again. Instead he continued to paint by copying the great masters at the Louvre up through the 1850s. In 1858 Fantin-Latour met James McNeill Whistler at the Louvre. Whistler became a close friend of Fantin-Latour and came to have a strong influence on his subsequent career. Both artists had their works rejected for the 1859 Salon, and Whistler suggested that Fantin-Latour should go to London, which Whistler believed offered better prospects for a career within the arts. In the years that followed Fantin-Latour made several visits to London, where he established good connections and worked with several British artists, particularly within the graphic arts.

Back in Paris in 1861 Fantin-Latour studied under Gustave Courbet. Fantin-Latour absorbed much from Courbet's realism and would subsequently emerge as a painter of realistic motifs himself; flower arrangements and portraits were particularly frequent subjects for him. Fantin-Latour was also associated with several of the rather more innovative Parisian artists of the 1860s and 1870s. He was, for example, part of the graphic arts association Société des Aquafortistes, which was founded in Paris in 1862 and also numbered Whistler among its members. Together with Whistler Fantin-Latour was himself included in the group of important artists that Fantin-Latour depicted in his large-scale group portrait *Hommage à Delacroix* from 1864, which was exhibited at the Universal Exposition in Paris in 1889 – presumably here seen by Hammershøi.

Fantin-Latour was more than just acquainted with the artistic avant-garde. He himself was also an avant-garde figure in his own time, pointing beyond the realms of the realist when he let a focus on overall atmosphere rather than on an accurate likeness govern his portraits. In his many figure compositions from the beginning – and especially from the end – of his career he did not so much evoke realism as something unreal and powerfully atmospheric that would subsequently be viewed as a precursor of Symbolist painting.

Fantin-Latour had his debut as an artist t the Royal Academy in London in 1862. Over the course of the next four decades he regularly contributed works to exhibitions in London and at the Paris Salons. Fantin-Latour's final exhibition took place in London in 1900. He died in 1904 at his and his wife's country residence in Normandy and was buried in Paris in the Montparnasse graveyard.

PAUL GAUGUIN

Paris 1848 – Atuona, French Polynesia 1903

Having finished school the 17-year old Gauguin set out to sea with the French navy. When he returned to Paris in 1871 he became a stockbroker. Gauguin's immediate circle of friends and acquaintances were art collectors, and Gauguin himself became interested in art and built his own collection by purchasing works by contemporary artists. Concurrently with his work as a stockbroker he began to paint floral arrangements and landscapes on an amateur basis. One of Gauguin's landscapes was accepted for the 1876 Salon, and in 1879 the Impressionistic painter Pissarro invited him to take part in the Impressionists' fourth group exhibition in Paris. From this point on Gauguin became an integrated part of the circle and took part in the four subsequent Impressionistic group exhibitions.

In 1883 Gauguin gave up his job to devote himself entirely to his artistic work. In 1873 Gauguin had met and married Danish-born Mette Gad in Paris. In 1884 he moved to Denmark with his wife and the couple's five children. In 1885 Gauguin arranged an exhibition of Impressionist painting at the Kunstforeningen (the Fine Arts Society) in Copenhagen. The exhibition closed down after a brief run, and as Gauguin did not feel that the Danish art scene was open to his artistic insights he went back to Paris that same year. Mette Gauguin, however, stayed behind in Copenhagen, as did large portions of Paul Gauguin's art collection, which Mette gladly showed to people from the Danish art scene and to her circle of friends, which also numbered Vilhelm and Ida Hammershøi.

In 1886 Gauguin moved to Brittany, and in the time that followed he made a radical break with Impressionism and adopted an entirely new style in which unmixed colours and highly stylised decorative surfaces hint at symbolic contents, giving the paintings a timeless quality that points back to Puvis de Chavannes as a major role model. In Gauguin's version of Symbolism, however, the paintings can equally well express private experiences as familiar mythologies. Gauguin himself used the term "Synthetism" to describe this translation of emotions and sensory experiences into pictorial form.

Around 1887 Gauguin met van Gogh, whom he subsequently visited in the South of France in 1888. During this stay Gauguin launched a search for something original and primordial that he pursued further by travelling to Tahiti in 1891 in order to find an unspoilt culture whose everyday life and mythologies he might capture symbolically in his painting.

Ill health prompted Gauguin to return to France in 1893, and that same year his works were exhibited alongside those of van Gogh at Den Frie Udstilling (the Independent Exhibition) in Copenhagen. His way of expressing existentialist contents in painting proved a great inspiration for Danish artists with Symbolist leanings. Hammershøi undoubtedly saw Gauguin's paintings at this exhibition, where Hammershøi himself contributed two paintings.

Nevertheless, Gauguin's work did not meet with the acclaim that he would wish, and in 1895 he returned to Tahiti where he continued to paint and find motifs. In 1901 he went on to the Marquesas islands, where he died in 1903.

SVEND HAMMERSHØI

Frederiksberg 1873 – Frederiksberg 1948

Svend Hammershøi grew up as the youngest of four siblings in the family's home in Frederiksberg Allé. Like his brother Vilhelm, who was nine years his senior, Svend was closely attached to his mother as well as to his siblings. Svend and his sister Anna lived with their parents when their father died in 1893, and both lived with their mother until her death in 1914. After this Svend and Anna, who both remained unmarried for their entire lives, found a new home together in Ludvigsminde in Allégade, Frederiksberg.

Like Vilhelm, Svend had a keen interest in drawing and painting, but Svend's interests also ran towards the applied arts, towards crafts. As a boy Svend considered a career as a carver, and when he saw an exhibition of artist's ceramics in 1888 at The Nordic Exhibition of Industry, Agriculture, and Art in Copenhagen he also became interested in ceramics. Nevertheless Svend commenced on a classic painter's education when he was accepted at the Royal Danish Academy of Fine Arts in Copenhagen in 1890. He studied here for two years until enrolling at Kunstnernes Frie Studieskoler under Kristian Zahrtmann, where he studied until 1897.

Concurrently with his art studies Svend Hammershøi worked with ceramics. He was employed as a so-called "signature-making underglaze artist" at Den Kongelige Porcelænsfabrik (Royal Copenhagen) during the period 1891-94, and he acted as assistant to Thorvald Bindesbøll, who was a close friend of Vilhelm and who would later pose for Vilhelm's *Five Portraits* together with Svend [15, p.32].

While still a student Svend initiated his contact with the Kähler ceramic workshops; after his student days he entered into close and long-term co-operation with Kähler.

Even though Svend continued to work with ceramics after graduating he regarded himself as primarily a painter. In his paintings he was particularly interested in depicting trees and older buildings of cultural and historical significance. Like Vilhelm, he worked with a very restricted palette. Shades of green, brown, and yellow dominate his outdoor scenes, which are devoid of human presences, and this palette is used regardless of whether the subject is landscapes or churches, the latter of which became something of a speciality for him and prompted him to travel to Britain on several occasions.

In terms of exhibitions Svend Hammershøi had his breakthrough at Kleis' Kunsthandel in Copenhagen while he was still a student, in 1892. The following year one of his drawings was reproduced as an illustration in the Symbolist journal *Taarnet*, and he exhibited at Den Frie Udstilling (the Independent Exhibition alongside several artists from that circle in 1895 and on several subsequent occasions up until 1909. Svend entered into a true artist's association when he joined the artists' colony Hellenerne (The Hellenes) on Refsnæs from 1895 up until 1903. He did not, however, celebrate Greek ideals to any great extent; rather, he painted atmospheric landscapes with references to ancient Norse history.

In 1909 Svend Hammershøi had his first solo exhibition at Kunstforeningen (the Fine Arts Society) in Copenhagen. He would later exhibit paintings and ceramic works on an ongoing basis, and he won accolades and awards for his efforts within both areas.

VILHELM HAMMERSHØI

Copenhagen 1864 – Copenhagen 1916

Vilhelm Hammershøi grew up as the second eldest of four siblings in an affluent Copenhagen family which comprised his younger siblings Anna and Svend, Vilhelm himself, his older brother Otto, his father Christian, and at the heart of the family his mother Frederikke, with whom Vilhelm had strong and close bonds up until her death in 1914. Frederikke saw to it that Vilhelm received drawing classes from the age of eight and loyally supported him in his development and career as an artist.

Hammershøi was enrolled at the Royal Danish Academy of Fine Arts in Copenhagen in 1879 and was a student there until 1884, studying under teachers such as Frederik Vermehren. From 1883 onwards he supplemented his studies at the Academy by also enrolling at the newly founded Kunstnernes Studieskoler under P. S. Krøyer. Here Hammershøi developed his distinctive style which was markedly different from the traditional, naturalistic depiction of reality taught at the Academy, but also from the rather more modern, European naturalism favoured by P. S. Krøyer.

As is true of many other artists of the day, Hammershøi's circle of motifs took its point of departure in his immediate surroundings. He would mainly paint his homes and his circle, but to Hammershøi the painterly and compositional properties of these motifs were the main points of interest, not their narrative contents.

In contrast to the painterly traditions prevalent at the time Hammershøi's paintings were purged of narratives and details, and with his subdued grey-white-black palette Hammershøi created an enigmatic and introspective atmosphere that made his style of painting quite unique.

In 1885 Hammershøi had his debut: At Charlottenborg he showed *Portrait of Young Woman. The Artist's Sister, Anna Hammershøi* [32, p.55]. 1885 was also the year that saw Hammershøi's first venture into travelling abroad, and his first journey went to Germany. He would later return often to Germany as he passed through on his journeys to the Netherlands, Belgium, France, Italy, and England. When travelling abroad Hammershøi looked for inspiration for his painterly activities; also he gradually built up substantial exhibition activities abroad.

In 1889 Hammershøi visited Paris in connection with the Universal Exposition and was awarded a bronze medal for what was his first presentation abroad. The four paintings he contributed to the Danish section of the exhibition included *Young Girl Sewing. Anna Hammershøi, the Artist's Sister* [3, p.16], which had been rejected at the Charlottenborg exhibition the previous year; indeed Charlottenborg rejected another Hammershøi painting again in 1890. This prompted Hammershøi to join a group of fellow artists in 1891 to found Den Frie Udstilling (the Independent Exhibition), which remained a significant Danish exhibition platform for Hammershøi throughout his artistic career.

In 1891 Hammershøi married Ida Ilsted (1869-1949), the sister of fellow artist Peter Ilsted. The couple had become engaged the previous year, and in addition to being a supporting spouse Ida also became an important model and travel companion for Hammershøi. Vilhelm and Ida travelled extensively but retained their ties to Copenhagen, where they had their home at varying addresses throughout their marriage. Just after their wedding the couple went to Paris, and upon their return to Copenhagen in 1892 they found their first home together in Rahbeks Allé in Frederiksberg. Here Hammershøi embarked on painting interiors and would often also paint scenes from the nearby Søndermarken park [108, p.131]. Vilhelm and Ida would often spend their summers outside of the city, and while summering in the country Hammershøi would repeatedly paint the landscapes surrounding them [102, p.26].

In 1897 Vilhelm and Ida lived briefly on Åboulevarden before leaving Copenhagen for a prolonged stay in London. Upon their return in 1898 they settled in Strandgade 30. Over the next decade Hammershøi used this flat as the setting for a large number of stringently composed interiors [8, 61, 65, p.23, 83, 88]. Up through the 1890s Hammershøi took part in a number of exhibitions abroad. In 1900 he once again contributed several works to the Universal Exposition in Paris, and this time he was awarded a silver medal. That same year he had his first major solo show at the Kunstforeningen (the Fine Arts Society) in Copenhagen, for which Hammershøi's most important Danish admirer and patron, Alfred Bramsen, prepared a complete inventory of his works. Hammershøi continued to garner the greatest positive acclaim abroad, and he continued to exhibit outside of Denmark during the first decade of the 20th century, for example at the international exhibitions at the Glaspalast in Munich and at several major solo exhibitions in Germany and Great Britain.

Hammershøi enjoyed Britain, and in the winter of 1905-06 he and Ida took yet another prolonged stay in London where he painted a number of scenes depicting the city's streets and buildings [87, 121, p.112, 154] just as he also used the buildings of Copenhagen as the subjects of his paintings [84, 123, p.109, 155]. In 1909 the couple had to move out of Strandgade. They briefly lived at Kvæsthusgade 6 before getting a flat at Bredgade 25 in 1910. Hammershøi also painted several interiors from this home [82, p.106].

In 1910 Hammershøi was appointed a seat on the Academy Council, and in 1911 he was awarded First Prize at the international exhibition in Rome. The following year he received a prestigious commission from the Uffizi in Florence, asking him to create a self-portrait for the museum's collection of self-portraits by famous artists.

Vilhelm and Ida also spent the winter of 1912-13 in London, and upon their return they moved into a flat in the building of the merchant company Asiatisk Kompagni (Asiatic Company) in Strandgade 25 – a building that Hammershøi admired and had painted back in 1902 [86, p.111]. Here, Hammershøi painted his last interiors [83, p.107] and a few other paintings.

Hammershøi was taken seriously ill in 1914, suffering from throat cancer. His illness weakened him greatly up until his death in 1916.

CARL HOLSØE

Aarhus 1863 – Asserbo 1935

The son of an architect, Carl Holsøe attended technical collage in preparation for enrolling at the Royal Academy of Fine Arts in Copenhagen, where he was accepted in 1882. He remained enrolled until 1884, at which point he opted for the Kunstnernes Studieskoler under P. S. Krøyer instead. At both institutions Holsøe was a fellow student of Vilhelm Hammershøi, who also became a close personal friend.

Holsøe and Hammershøi exerted a mutual influence on each other. Holsøe preceded Hammershøi as far as depictions of interiors are concerned: already in 1886 Holsøe attracted attention with a painted interior scene presented at his debut at the Charlottenborg December exhibition. Drawing inspiration from Dutch 17th century masters, Holsøe continued to paint and exhibit unsentimentally depicted interiors of elegant rooms, occasionally incorporating solitary half-turned figures while also employing more colours and more painterly detail than Vilhelm Hammershøi. For example, Holsøe exhibited two interior paintings at the Universal Exposition in Paris in 1889, which garnered a "Mention Honorable", and at the international art exhibition in Munich in 1891 Holsøe, like Hammershøi, was awarded a prize for one of his interior scenes.

Up through the 1890s Holsøe received numerous Academy scholarships and grants, and in the 1900s he exhibited his works at several international exhibitions alongside Hammershøi. In 1901 Hammershøi included Holsøe as one of the figures portrayed in his monumental painting *Five Portraits* [15, p.32]. In terms of his artistic career Holsøe eventually came to stand in Hammershøi's shadow. After 1900 Holsøe's art did not yield any particular innovations, and despite his continued activity he never achieved any great fame. During the last years of his life Holsøe lived a quiet life in Asserbo, where he died in 1935.

PETER ILSTED

Sakskøbing 1861 – Copenhagen 1933

The merchant's son Peter Ilsted was born on the island of Falster, but grew up on the island of Lolland where he attended the private school in Stubbekøbing. He was later apprenticed as a housepainter. In 1878 he was accepted at the Royal Danish Academy of Fine Arts in Copenhagen, graduating in 1883. He had his debut at the Kunstforeningen (the Fine Arts Society) in Copenhagen in 1882 and was a steady contributor to the Charlottenborg Spring Exhbition from 1883 onwards.

Ilsted worked with painting and etchings, and his circle of motifs included landscapes, scenes from everyday life, and portraits. In 1889 Ilsted showed his work abroad for the first time at the Universal Exposition in Paris, where he – like Carl Holsøe, his former fellow students from the Royal Danish Academy of Fine Arts – received a "Mention Honorable" for two interior scenes.

Ilsted and Holsøe both belonged to the circle around Vilhelm Hammershøi; in 1891 Hammershøi married Ilsted's sister Ida, whom he used as a model in many of his paintings. Ilsted himself married the following year, and from that point on he, too, employed his own wife as a model for his realistic depictions of domestic chores conducted in a bourgeois interior.

In 1893 Ilsted took part in the Universal Exposition in Chicago, and from that year onwards until 1905 he acted as an assistant at the Royal Danish Academy of Fine Arts' life school. In 1899 he received the Eckersberg medal, and in 1900 he received a bronze medal at the Universal Exposition in Paris. In 1909 he received a medal at the X. Internationalen Kunstausstellung in Munich, an exhibition that also featured works by Holsøe and Hammershøi, with whom he continued to have a motivic kinship.

Like Holsøe, Ilsted incorporated greater detail in his interior scenes than Hammershøi, but when he began to focus on the mezzotint technique from 1909 onwards he acquired his own distinctive mode of expression, using harmoniously toned colours in his graphic sheets, all while his motifs also took on a greater kinship with Hammershøi.

Ilsted never won the same level of fame and recognition that Hammershøi enjoyed, but throughout his life he continued to exhibit his work in Denmark and abroad. In 1933, the year of his death, he was celebrated with a retrospective held in his hometown of Copenhagen, where he died after a long-lasting illness.

JOHANN EDUARD KARSEN
Amsterdam 1860 – Amsterdam 1941

Eduard Karsen was born into a religious, poor family. His father, Kasper Karsen, was a painter and earned a living by offering drawing classes. From the age of 14 Johann Eduard, too, studied drawing and painting under his father, and four years later he was accepted at the Academy of Fine Arts in his hometown of Amsterdam, where he studied until 1885. During his Academy years he became acquainted with Willem Arnold Witsen, a contemporary of his, and in 1885 Karsen became a member of Witsen's newly founded society for etching, Nederlandsche Etsclub. Witsen was also a co-founder of the journal *De Nieuwe Gids* in 1885, to which Karsen contributed articles for a number of years. During that time Karsen also wrote for the journal *De Amsterdammer,* but he never became an integrated part of the literary scene.

In 1887 Karsen became a member of the artists' association Arti et Amicitiae, thereby winning access to exhibiting his works. In his artistic practice Karsen focused particularly on motifs from Amsterdam and its environs, depicting them in small-scale formats imbued with a densely atmospheric, melancholic air. In Karsen's depictions of farms, gardens, seascapes, and citiscapes he downplays the presence of human beings. Overall his paintings have been purged of all dynamic qualities. This, combined with their blurred contours and subdued colour schemes, means that Karsen's paintings present a subjective view of the world that shares many traits with what we see in Hammershøi.

Hammershøi may have seen Karsen's work during one of his trips to The Netherlands, and when he went to Italy in 1893 he may also have had the opportunity to see the exhibition *Münchener Jahresausstellung von Kunstwerken aller Nationen* in Munich, where Karsen exhibited two works. In 1892 a friend and colleague of Hammershøi, Johan Rohde, saw Karsen's works at an exhibition in Hoorn and described the artist in his travelogues, which means that we can be sure that Hammershøi certainly knew of Karsen's existence. In addition to this Hammershøi himself had yet another chance to see a work by Karsen in 1897 when Karsen contributed to the International Exhibition at the Glyptotek in Copenhagen.

Karsen is a relatively obscure figure within art history. It is believed that he painted around 100 paintings over the course of his career, and most of these are dated prior to 1900, when Karsen moved in with his mother after his father died in 1896. Karsen lived a quiet, isolated life up until his death in 1941.

FERNAND KHNOPFF
Grembergen-Lez-Termonde
1858 – Brussels 1921

As a child Khnopff lived in Brugge, but in 1864 the family moved to Brussels where his father worked within the legal profession, ultimately becoming a judge. In 1875 Khnopff also began studying law, but his true interests ran towards art and literature, so he studied painting under Xavier Mellery too. The next year Khnopff abandoned law altogether in favour of studies at L'Académie des Beaux-Arts de Bruxelles, where he studied drawing and painting up until 1879. At that point he elected to go to Paris to take courses on painting conducted by Jules Lefèbre at L'Académie Julian.

Back in Brussels Khnopff had his debut in 1881 at the Salon de l'Essor, an alternative to the official Belgian Salon. Khnopff exhibited at the L'Essor again in 1882 and 1883, but later that year he was one of the co-founders of Les XX, which offered a new and more open alternative for the experimental art of the day. Khnopff exhibited with Les XX every year up until the group was disbanded in 1893, after which point the group was followed by a new circle with a similar objective, La Libre Esthetique. Khnopff continued to exhibit with the new group.

Via these exhibitions the Belgian Symbolist Emile Verhaeren became interested in Khnopff's paintings, and in 1886 he wrote about Khnopff as a Symbolist in the journal *L'Art Moderne.* Verhaeren was particularly enamoured with how Khnopff introduced literature, psychology, and dreams into his painting and by his focus on inner emotions and moods rather than on a tangible reality. In 1887 the articles were gathered in a volume about Khnopff published by the publisher Monnom, who also asked Khnopff to paint a portrait of his daughter, Marie, that same year [44, p.66].

During the period leading up to 1890 Khnopff painted a number of commissioned portraits in which an external likeness was interwoven with a depiction of the sitter's inner life. Khnopff's other subjects of choice focused mainly on desolate landscape, city scenes devoid of human life, and allegories, all of which he depicted in a range of media.

Hammershøi undoubtedly came across Khnopff in 1889 in connection with the Universal Exposition in Paris, where Khnopff exhibited five works. Khnopff's international exhibition activities continued with a solo show in London in 1890 and with contributions to a wide range of group exhibitions around Europe up through the 1890s. These included The International Art Exhibition at the Glyptotek in Copenhagen in 1897, where Hammershøi certainly saw his work.

In 1898 Khnopff's works met with enthusiastic response from the general public and from the young artists at the first Wiener Secession, and from this point on it was not long before he won official recognition in the form of a major commission for the Belgian city hall in Sint-Gillis. Khnopff kept painting and exhibiting and continued to enjoy successes, but he also entered into a long-term commitment to design costumes and sets for the Belgian Théâtre Royal de la Monnaie. In 1921 Fernand Khnopff died, having achieved a place among the important figures of Belgian Symbolism.

XAVIER MELLERY

Brussels 1845 – Brussels 1921

Xavier Mellery was apprenticed as a house painter before enrolling at the Academy of Fine Arts in his hometown of Brussels at the age of 15. He studied here until 1867, receiving tuition in a range of subjects within the applied arts, sculpture, and painting.

In 1870 he was awarded a grant, "Le Prix de Rome", which allowed him to take a Grand Tour of Italy in 1871 to study the masters of the Italian Renaissance. Mellery returned to Brussels in 1874 and rented a studio, from where he taught a student body that included Fernand Khnopff for a while. In addition to painting, Mellery also worked with drawing and graphic arts. In 1878 he was commissioned to provide illustrations for an article about The Netherlands. This prompted him to visit the small Dutch island of Marken, where he stayed until 1879, creating a range of realistic and detailed depictions of the small fishing community.

In 1881 Mellery was accepted as a member of the Société Royale Belge des Aquarellistes, and from this point on he took part in the group's annual exhibitions. In 1882 he was commissioned to create sculptures for the Le Petit Sablon park in Brussels, and a few years later he created art for the façade of what was then the Palais de Beaux-Arts in Brussels. Throughout the rest of his career Mellery sought to secure more commissions of this kind, but no more projects of this type were realised.

Mellery is regarded as one of Belgium's early Symbolists: From the mid-1880s he pointed to a reality behind the immediate surface; something which is equally evident in gloomy drawings of everyday-like rooms infused with a mysterious calm as well as in bright, allegorical scenes peopled by classically rendered figures against uniformly coloured backgrounds.

On several occasions from 1885 onwards Mellery exhibited his work together with the progressive group Les XX, co-founded by his former student Fernand Khnopff, and Mellery continued to exhibit his allegorical figure images and his renditions of empty, yet soulful spaces with the group when it continued under the name La Libre Esthétique in the early 1890s.

Between 1891 and 1898 Mellery became a member of several important committees, but also upheld his activities outside such official circles.

We do not know for certain whether Hammershøi and Mellery were acquainted with each other's works, but they have certainly to some extent shared the same influences, and Mellery's undated work *The Doors* [80, p.104] clearly shows a kinship between the two artists as regards subject matter, mood, and colour schemes. Mellery remained active and continued to exhibit his work up until his death in 1921, and in 1937 a solo exhibition in his honour was staged at the Palais des Beaux-Arts in his native Brussels.

EDVARD MUNCH

Løten 1863 – Oslo 1944

Edvard Munch grew up in Kristiania (Oslo) and enrolled at The Royal School of Drawing in Kristiania in 1880. However, he soon abandoned his studies in favour of tuition under the realist painter Christian Krohg.

Munch began by painting naturalistic works depicting his family and immediate surroundings and had his debut at the Industri- og Kunstuttstillingen in Kristiania in 1883. That same year he had a work accepted for the annual Høstuttstillingen (Autumn Exhibition) and he continued to exhibit his work here for a number of years. In 1884 Munch was awarded a major grant and the following year he showed his work outside of Norway for the first time, specifically in Antwerp, where a portrait of his sister Inger was featured at the Universal Exposition. That same year he also visited Paris where he found new sources of inspiration.

From 1885 onwards Munch's naturalism gradually took on an increasingly subjective and expressive feel, and in 1886 he caused a scandal at the Høstuttstillingen in Kristiania by showing his semi-Impressionistic painting *The Sick Child*, which was chastised for being too sketch-like.

Munch continued to exhibit in Norway and abroad. In 1888 Munch contributed three paintings to The Nordic Exhibition of Industry, Agriculture, and Art in Copenhagen. On that occasion he met the Danish artist Johan Rohde, and the two men stayed in touch. In 1893 Rohde arranged an exhibition of Munch's works, which had by this point become highly expressive and atmospheric. The exhibition was staged at Kleis in Copenhagen and included the first version of *Night in St Cloud* from 1890, a painting that had also been shown at Høstuttstillingen in Kristiania where it had prompted the critic Andreas Aubert to compare Munch to Whistler, Puvis de Chavannes, and Hammershøi. Being a close friend of Johan Rohde it is likely that Vilhelm Hammershøi saw and was familiar with Munch's works, and he also had the opportunity to see one of Munch's works at the Universal Exposition in Paris in 1889, where both artists presented their work.

After his first solo show in Kristiania in 1889 Munch went to Paris, studying for a while under Léon Bonnat. He spent much of his time in Paris up until 1892. While in Paris he developed the expressive and symbolic idiom for which he is best known today, but which caused a scandal when he first showed works of this type in Berlin in 1892.

Munch lived in Germany from 1892 to 1908, although his stay was interrupted by travels, visits to his native Norway, and a long stay in Paris from 1896-97. In Germany he was part of an art scene that was keenly interested in the modern human condition and the mental life of modern man. Humanity's inner life remained a focus area for Munch, who had gradually become an established artist and was once again represented at an exhibition in Copenhagen in 1906. Munch suffered from erratic mental and physical health, and in 1908 a nervous breakdown prompted him to be admitted to a psychiatric clinic in Frederiksberg. While there he continued to paint and create graphic works, and later that year these works were exhibited at Kunstforeningen (the Fine Arts Society) in Copenhagen.

In 1909 he discharged himself from hospital and went back to settle in Norway, where he finally achieved success with an exhibition held that same year.

Munch had won widespread acclaim and exhibited extensively abroad when he bought the farm Ekely outside of Kristiania in 1916. Here he lived a quiet, yet artistically active life up until his death in 1944 (aged 81).

WILLIAM NICHOLSON

Newark-on-Trent, Nottinghamshire 1872 – Blewbury, Berkshire 1949

At the age of 12 Nicholson began to attend drawing classes. His teacher, William Cubley, encouraged him to pursue a career within the arts.

In 1888 he was accepted at the Herkomer's Art School north of London, where he studied until 1891, at which point he went to Paris to study at the Académie Julian. In Paris Nicholson became greatly interested in Manet and in copying Velázquez at the Louvre. Upon his return to Britain in 1892 Nicholson continued to paint, and in 1893 he married the artist Mabel Pryde, whom he had known since his student days.

Nicholson enjoyed a close relationship with his brother-in-law James Pryde, and in 1894 the two men began to create posters together. The posters had a strong graphic impact with their clear lines and large planes. They were exhibited at the International Poster Exhibition at the Westminster Aquarium in 1894 and 1896, but Nicholson never won any commercial success with his poster production.

In 1896 Nicholson moved to London with his family and also began to work with woodcuts. The first of these, *Persimmon*, was reproduced in the *Magazine of Art* in 1896 and exhibited at the Fine Arts Society where Whistler grew so enthusiastic about it that he urged the publisher Heinemann to embark on producing graphic works with Nicholson. In the years that followed Nicholson enjoyed great success with his woodcuts, which included a series of portraits that was shown at the Universal Exposition in Paris in 1900, where it was awarded a gold medal.

In 1898 Nicholson was invited to exhibit with the International Society of Sculptors, Painters and Engravers, where Whistler was president. Here he exhibited a painting for the first time, and Nicholson continued to contribute paintings to the International Society's subsequent exhibitions in 1899 and 1901. Following this he returned to painting in earnest, and in 1903 Nicholson held his first solo exhibition of paintings at the Stafford Gallery in London. At this point he mainly painted family and friends, but from 1906 onwards – the year of his second major exhibition of paintings in London – he received a number of commissions for portraits, and from 1909 onwards Nicholson would also paint landscapes from the area around his summer residence in Sussex.

In 1909 Nicholson exhibited the painting *Behind the Scenes* at a presentation of English art at the Kunstforeningen in Copenhagen, where it was promptly bought by Hammershøi's patron Bramsen. Thus, Hammershøi certainly knew Nicholson's work and presumably also met him in person and saw his work at exhibitions in London, where Nicholson staged solo exhibitions in 1910 and 1911.

Nicholson was a well-established artist when he lost his wife and second-eldest son in 1918, but when he remarried the next year he no longer depended on portrait commissions to make a living. In the years that followed, Nicholson painted many still lifes and continued to paint landscapes and portraits, albeit using a lighter, more colourful palette. Nicholson was knighted in 1936, and in 1942 the National Gallery in London held a comprehensive retrospective of his works to mark the occasion of his 70th birthday. Nicholson died of old age in 1949 in his home in Berkshire Downs.

JÓZEF PANKIEWICZ

Lublin 1866 – Marseille 1940

Pankiewicz grew up in Warsaw, but moved to St. Petersburg in 1885 to study at the Academy. Dissatisfied, he soon left the Academy and went back to Warsaw where he had his debut at the official salon, in 1887. At this point Pankiewicz painted scenes from everyday life in a realistic style and was awarded a silver medal for such a work at the Universal Exposition in Paris in 1889, which marked the first time that he exhibited his work outside his native Poland.

Like Hammershøi, Pankiewicz lived in Paris in 1889. Here he became acquainted with the French Impressionists and was inspired by their style and techniques in his own works, which were met with severe criticism when he exhibited them in Warsaw in the years that followed. After 1892 Pankiewicz turned to Symbolism for inspiration instead; in terms of subject matter he returned to his point of departure, using his hometown of Warsaw as the mist-shrouded setting for a range of mysterious, atmospheric nocturnes executed in muted colours [89, p.113]. Pankiewicz also painted portraits during the 1890s, and in 1900 he won a silver medal for a portrait shown at the Universal Exposition in Paris.

In 1897 Pankiewicz became a member of the newly founded artists' association Sztuka and exhibited his works with them in Poland and other European countries. These exhibitions prompted Pankiewicz to take several sojourns abroad and he became particularly fond of France, returning to that country numerous times – even after he was appointed professor at the Academy of Fine Arts in Krakow.

While in France, Pankiewicz met Pierre Bonnard in 1908; the two artists proceeded to travel and paint together in the south of France. Here Pankiewicz abandoned his Symbolist idiom in favour of painting still lifes, landscapes, and harbour scenes in a colouristic style similar to Bonnard's. Pankiewicz's new interest in colour stayed with him for the rest of his career. The same held true for his close ties to Paris, where he finally settled in 1925 to head a Parisian branch of the Krakow Art Academy. From his base in Paris Pankiewicz continued his extensive exhibition activity up until his death in 1940, including 11 works for the exhibition of Polish Art at Charlottenborg in Copenhagen.

JULIUS PAULSEN

Odense 1860 – Copenhagen 1940

Julius Paulsen grew up in an affluent, art-loving merchant family in Odense. In 1876 he became apprenticed with a housepainter in his hometown and had learnt his trade by 1879. Paulsen also painted in his spare time, and in 1879 he had his first painting accepted for the Charlottenborg Spring Exhibition. Later that year he moved to Copenhagen to begin his studies at The Royal Danish Academy of Fine Arts. However, Paulsen was dissatisfied with the teaching at the Academy and left the school in 1882. He continued to work independently with his painting, creating works in a style that was not so far removed from the prevalent tastes of the time, and he regularly had his works accepted at Charlottenborg. In 1884 he received the Neuhausen Medal for a classical portrait of his father. This is to say that Paulsen was not just accepted on the art scene; he also won great acclaim for his art even when he was still in his youth. As early as 1885 Paulsen exhibited his work abroad for the first time, specifically at the Paris Salon where he presented the prize-winning portrait of his father.

Paulsen was admired for his technical skill, which he brought to bear on several different types of motif. For his next exhibition in Paris – at the Universal Exposition of 1889, where he received a silver medal – his presentation included landscapes, religious motifs, figure paintings, a portrait, and an interior scene. Paulsen continued this versatility throughout his entire career, and his style, too, bore the traits of varying sources of inspiration drawn from the realms of tradition as well as from the latest Impressionist and Symbolist trends.

From the late 1880s onwards Paulsen created a number of densely atmospheric landscapes; twilight scenes reminiscent of Whistler's nocturnes, which Paulsen had presumably seen. These hazy images – depicting memories rather than a direct rendition of nature – established a link between Paulsen and other Danish artists with Symbolist leanings, including Hammershøi, and prompted Paulsen to exhibit his work with this group of artists at Den Frie Udstilling in 1891. After a few years of being a member of Den Frie Udstilling (the Independent Exhibition), however, Paulsen once again returned to exhibiting his work in the official settings offered by Charlottenborg.

Up through the 1890s Paulsen painted a large number of portraits, and when he married Esther Lange in 1900 she frequently sat for his paintings. She would appear as a solitary figure or as part of large-scale group portraits and depictions of scenes from the couple's social life, for example in the painting *Evening Soiree, the Artist's Home* from 1915, which also features Hammershøi.

Paulsen remained a prolific artist and upheld comprehensive exhibition activities throughout his life; he received several grants and awards and was assigned to numerous important posts. He returned to the Royal Danish Academy of Fine Arts when he was appointed professor in 1908 and was head of his own school of painting up until 1920. Paulsen died from a kidney complaint in 1940; eight years later an exhibition in his memory was staged at the Glyptotek.

PIERRE PUVIS DE CHAVANNES

Lyon 1824 – Paris 1898

Pierre Puvis de Chavannes grew up in a middle-class home in Lyon, moving to Paris in 1840 to study engineering. In 1846, however, he abandoned his studies and travelled to Italy. Greatly inspired by Italian Renaissance frescoes he went back to Paris, and in the years that followed he studied the art of painting under Delacroix, Henri Scheffer, Thomas Couture, and Chassériau. The latter in particular had a crucial impact on Puvis de Chavannes' future career due to his murals.

Puvis de Chavannes struggled to achieve his breakthrough. Throughout the 1850s he painted historic and religious dramas in a realistic, yet romanticised style. He had his first work accepted at the Salon in 1850 but did not win any official recognition until the 1860s, when he abandoned narrative and realism in favour of allegorical scenes presented in a highly simplified formal language.

The true breakthrough for Puvis de Chavannes took place in the wake of the 1861 Salon, where he exhibited – and was awarded prizes for – his two monumental decorative paintings *War* and *Peace*. The recognition garnered here paved the way for a wide range of public commissions for decorative works that saw Puvis de Chavannes develop his distinctive combination of classical tradition and modern formal modes of expression to create a personal idiom.

Up through the 1860s and 1870s Puvis de Chavannes developed and perfected a decorative simplicity characterised by subdued, muted, and harmonious colours and by stylised figures that lend a sense of clarity to serene, rhythmic compositions with a timeless feel. The scenes are most frequently set within Arcadian landscapes, but are devoid of any mythological contents, serving mainly as decorative settings for the compositions.

Puvis de Chavannes' style was unique in its own day, and even though some critics chastised him for his unsubtle renditions of figures, which appeared to be frozen in place, the decorative and classical elements in his painting appealed to many and gave him a unique position within the French art scene. From the 1880s onwards Puvis de Chavannes was a famous and acclaimed artist who was happy to transpose the strategies from his vast decorative paintings to less monumental formats that could be exhibited throughout France and abroad.

Hammershøi was familiar with Puvis de Chavannes's work from the Universal Exposition in Paris in 1889, where both artists exhibited their works. Puvis de Chavannes was also among the artists viewed by the Danish artist Johan Rohde on his journey to Paris in 1892; upon his return Rohde described what he had seen to his fellow artists in Denmark. What is more, Puvis de Chavannes was among the artists featured at The International Art Exhibition at the Glyptotek in Copenhagen in 1897. This is to say that Hammershøi had the opportunity to see and be inspired by Puvis de Chavannes' works, and indeed Hammershøi's use of simple compositions and immobile figures evoke a sense of something eerily unreal that is reminiscent of Puvis de Chavannes. This sense of being removed from reality has positioned Puvis de Chavannes as the father figure of Symbolism and as one of the main foreign role models for Danish Symbolism. Puvis de Chavannes was a famous and celebrated artist when he died in 1898, and in 1899 the Salon staged a large retrospective of his works.

HELENE SCHJERFBECK

Helsinki 1862 – Stockholm 1946

Helene Schjerfbeck began to study drawing at the tender age of 11. She was a pupil at the school of drawing run by the Finnish art society in Helsinki up until 1877, at which point she enrolled at Adolf von Becker's private school of painting.

In 1879 Schjerfbeck had her debut at the art society's annual exhibition, contributing five sketches, and the following year she contributed a history painting. In that year she also received a grant from the art society, which was used to conduct further studies in Paris where her tutors included Leon Bonnat. Schjerfbeck thrived in Paris and applied for grants that would allow her to continue her stay abroad. In 1881 yet another grant from the art society took her to Brittany, where she experimented with genre painting. The following year Schjerfbeck returned to Finland only to go back to Paris in 1883, where one of her works was accepted at the Salon. She spent the winter of 1883-84 in Brittany, this time seeking to use a simplified form of the city and landscape as subject of her paintings. In the years that followed, Schjerfbeck returned to Paris on numerous occasions, including in 1884 and 1888, when she had works accepted at the Salon again, and in 1889, when she – like Hammershøi – took part in the Universal Exposition and won a bronze medal.

Schjerfbeck also spent time in St. Ives before settling in Helsinki in 1890, a city where her work was exhibited on a regular basis. In 1892 she began to teach at the art society's school of drawing. However, Schjerfbeck suffered from ill health in the 1890s, partly due to a hip injury sustained in childhood, and when her contract with the drawing school ended in 1899 she did not apply for an extension.

In 1902 Schjerfbeck and her mother settled in Hyvinge north of Helsinki, where they lived together until her mother's death in 1923. Schjerfbeck no longer travelled, but looked to foreign art journals to keep abreast of current trend developments. She began to use her mother and the local populace as models for stylised portrait paintings characterised by large planes of colour.

In 1913 Schjerfbeck was contacted by the art dealer Gösta Stenman, who bought her paintings and was interested in exhibiting her works. The encounter with Stenman proved to be a turning point in Schjerfbeck's career, reviving her exhibition activities. This included contributions to the Baltic Art Exhibition in Malmö in 1914, where Hammershøi was also represented. In 1917 Schjerfbeck enjoyed success with her first solo exhibition in Helsinki, and after this point there were no slumps in her artistic career.

Following her mother's death Schjerfbeck moved to Ekenäs in 1925. Here she began to create a range of new versions of her own earlier paintings as well as many striking self-portraits. In 1944 Schjerfbeck moved again, this time to the Saltsjöbaden in Stockholm, where she died of uterine cancer in 1946 at the age of 83, an active painter to the last.

VALDEMAR SCHØNHEYDER MØLLER

Aarhus 1864 – Aarhus 1905

Valdemar Schønheyder Møller was born in Aarhus and was apprenticed with a xylographer there at the age of 17. Concurrently with his apprenticeship he studied painting under Johannes Boesen and Harald Foss in preparation for studying at the Royal Academy of Fine Arts in Copenhagen, where he was accepted in 1883. However, he left the Academy again the following year in order to study under P. S. Krøyer at the newly founded Kunstnernes Studieskoler. One of his fellow students was Vilhelm Hammershøi, and the two became close friends. Schønheyder Møller was interested in the potential offered by photography and created a series of photographs of Hammershøi's sister Anna around 1885.

Schønheyder Møller painted *en plein air*, especially landscapes, and in 1885 he had his debut at the Charlottenborg Spring Exhibition where he continued to show his work every year until 1892.

In 1891 Schønheyder Møller went to Skagen in the north of Denmark. Here he painted scenes from the beach and became keenly interested in depicting sunlight [103, p.127]. During his time in Skagen he became acquainted with Anna Ancher, who grew interested in his works and also painted his portrait in 1893. In that year Schønheyder Møller held his first solo exhibition at the Kunstforeningen (the Fine Arts Society) in Copenhagen, and the following year he got married in Copen-hagen. The newlyweds soon moved to Paris, where he exhibited his work at the official Salon every year from 1895 to 1903.

In 1896 the couple settled in Fontainebleau where he continued to work on depicting the light of the sun and the afterimages it creates on the retina. Because of his interest in the sun and the sunlight Schønheyder Møller was called "Peintre de soleil". In 1901 he was taken ill to such an extent that he had to cease his artistic activities and admit himself to the Psychiatric Hospital in his home town of Aarhus. He died here in 1905.

GEORGES-PIERRE SEURAT

Paris 1859 – Paris 1891

Georges Pierre Seurat grew up in Paris. From the age of 15 he studied drawing under Justin Lequien at the École Municipale de Sculpture et de Dessin, where he was enrolled until he was accepted at the École des Beaux-Arts in 1878. Here he received classical tuition on the art of drawing from Henri Lehmann, but Seurat also sought out knowledge and inspiration from the realms of modern painting and science.

In 1879 Seurat saw the fourth Impressionist exhibition in Paris. He subsequently ceased his studies at the École des Beaux-Arts to work independently with Impressionism, developing it in accordance with a stringent and systematic set of rules for painting based on scientific theories of colour and perception that attracted his keen personal interest.

Seurat spent the summer of 1881 in Pontaubert together with a friend, Aman-Jean. Here Seurat painted *The Forest at Pontaubert* [107, p.130] , which is an early example of his experiments with building up motifs by means of closely arranged dots of pigments and a stringently composed picture plane; here, the tree trunks are used as part of a schematic structure reminiscent of Hammershøi's *Landscape in Snow, Søndermarken* from 1895-96 [105, p.131].

In 1883 Seurat made his first and only contribution to the official Salon in Paris in the form of a drawn portrait of Aman-Jean. He had his breakthrough the following year when his monumental *Bathers at Asnières* was rejected by the Salon and he moved on to show it at the newly established Salon des Indépendants instead. Here, critics noted a kinship with Puvis de Chavannes due to the large-scale format, the composition, and the stylised figures and also commented on the painting's affinity with Impressionism in terms of the choice of motif and the broken brushstrokes. The main impact on Seurat's career did not, however, stem from critical response to his work, but from the fact that the exhibition prompted Seurat to meet a number of like-minded artists such as Signac, with whom he continued to co-operate, for example on the foundation of La Société des Artistes Indépendants in 1884.

In 1885 Seurat became acquainted with the painter Pissarro. Pissarro became interested in Seurat's continuation of Impressionism and invited him to exhibit his work at the Impressionist's eighth, and final, group exhibition in 1886. Here Seurat showed the work *Sunday Afternoon on the Island of La Grande Jatte*, in which his theories about the optical effect of colour was given concrete form in a consistent application of a Pointilistic technique that proved a major inspiration for his fellow artists and made him a leading figure within the neo-Impressionist movement.

Hammershøi was not among the artists who drew direct inspiration from Seurat's view of colour and painterly technique, but they shared an ideal of creating harmony by means of carefully composed planes and motifs based on captured and frozen moments.

Seurat died suddenly of diphtheria at the age of 31 in his native Paris at a time when his career was showing great progress and promise.

JAMES ABBOTT MCNEILL WHISTLER

Lowell, Massachusetts 1834 – London 1903

Whistler was born in the USA but spent most of his life outside of his native country. Whistler left the USA at the age of nine when he and his family went to St. Petersburg due to his father's work. The family stayed in St. Petersburg until the father's death in 1849, at which point Whistler and his mother had to go back to America. In the meantime Whistler's half-sister had married an Englishman, and in 1855 Whistler used this connection to travel to Europe with the goal of becoming an artist. Soon after his arrival in London he went on to Paris, where he first enrolled at the École Impériale et Speciale de Dessin; the following year, in 1856, he enrolled at Charles Gleyre's school of painting at the École des Beaux-Arts.

During the earliest stage of his career Whistler subscribed to Courbet's vein of Realism, but he soon became more interested in how a painting is painted than in what it depicts. Thus, Whistler let his compositions govern his subject matter, not the other way around. Whistler's interest in composition is obvious in the painting *At the Piano*, which he painted in 1858 and sought to have exhibited at the Paris Salon of 1859, where it was rejected. That same year Whistler decided to move to London and pursue a career in Britain, and he soon won acceptance for his works there; from 1860 to 1865 he exhibited his works at the Royal Academy in London.

In 1863 Whistler also achieved a career breakthrough in Paris: He exhibited the painting *Symphony in White No. 1: The White Girl* at the Salon des Refusées, where it attracted a great deal of attention.

The use of terms from the realms of music – such as symphony, harmony, and arrangement – in the titles of his paintings was a typical feature of Whistler's work, accentuating his emphasis on painting as a composition rather than a representation. In addition to the composition itself Whistler used specific colour schemes and combinations to evoke a particular atmosphere that place his paintings in a realm removed from the realistic universe, thereby prefiguring Symbolism.

From the 1870s onwards Whistler repeatedly used colour harmonies and simple compositions to create evocative depictions of cities; he called these works "nocturnes".

Whistler gradually won ever-greater acclaim in Paris and frequently contributed to the Salons up through the 1880s. In 1883 he was awarded a prize for his *Arrangement in Grey and Black No. 1 Portrait of the Painter's Mother* from 1871 [40, p.62].

Whistler's significance eventually became impossible to ignore. His rejection of literary and narrative meaning, his evocative aesthetics full of subtly graded greys, and the geometric qualities of his picture planes proved a major inspiration for many young artists – not least for Hammershøi, who had seen Whistler's works at exhibitions in Paris and Copenhagen and who sought to make Whistler's acquaintance in London during his stay there in 1897-98; unsuccessfully, as Whistler was away for the duration. Whistler lived in London up until his death in 1903.

WILLEM ARNOLD WITSEN

Amsterdam 1860 – Amsterdam 1923

Witsen was born in the heart of Amsterdam as the youngest of six children in an affluent family. In 1876 Witsen began his studies at the Academy of Fine Arts in Amsterdam. He was enrolled there until 1884, but would from time to time interrupt his studies to spend time outside of Amsterdam. He would often visit the family's country house in Ewijkshoeve, but he also spent a number of months in Antwerp to attend courses at the Antwerp Academy.

Witsen played an active role on the Amsterdam art scene. In 1881 he was one of the co-founders of the artists' association Sint Lucas, and in 1883 he became a member of a recently established literary association, Flanor. Here he and several young writers and poets conceived the concept behind the journal *De Nieuwe Gids*, which was published for the first time in 1885. The journal was an important organ for the dissemination of new, young art, and Witsen contributed art reviews for the journal. Witsen did not restrict himself to just writing and painting; he also experimented with a range of different graphic techniques. He became particularly interested in etching, and in 1885 he co-founded the etching society known as the Nederlandsche Etsclub.

Even while still a student Witsen began to exhibit his works at a variety of group exhibitions. During the early stages of his career he would mainly paint his friends and family, depicting landscapes and everyday scenes showing farmers at work in the fields, but after his student days he became increasingly interested in the city as motif. But Witsen did not seek to capture urban life as such. Rather, he focused on creating a timeless beauty in a sombre, eerie city devoid of human presence, using the city's architecture as the basis for creating a geometrical sense of order in his pictorial compositions.

In 1888 Witsen exhibited his work abroad for the first time, and later that year he went to London where he depicted the empty city while employing a greyish-brown palette. He filled in the picture plane by means of "empty" fields in a manner that points to considerable inspiration from Whistler, much like Hammershøi.

In 1890 and 1891 Witsen exhibited his London scenes in Rotterdam and Amsterdam, which means that Hammershøi may have seen them as he travelled to Paris in September 1891. In 1891 Witsen moved back to Amsterdam, where he had his first solo exhibition four years later. Throughout his career and up until his death in 1923 his exhibition activities remained consistent, particularly in his own hometown and in his native Netherlands, but he also took part in group exhibitions throughout Europe. In 1897, for example, Witsen was featured at The International Exhibition at the Glyptotek in Copenhagen, where Hammershøi presumably saw his work *Forest Interior*.

PHOTOCREDITS

ARoS, photo: Ole Hein Pedersen, page 31, 70, 189, 210; bpk/Nationalgalerie, SMB/Andres Kilger, 47, 93, 128; bpk/Bayerische Staatsgemäldesammlungen/Sybille Forster, 169; The Bridgeman Art Library, 103, 204, 213; © Bruun Rasmussen Kunstauktioner, 153; © Clemens-Sels-Museum Neus, photo: Walter Klein, Düsseldorf, 113; Conservation départementale de Musées de l'Aude/Patrice Cartier, 159; All Rights reserved, 78, 88, 96, 259; The David Collection, photo: Pernille Klemp, 57, 103, 105; Finnish National Gallery/Central Art Archives, 23, 67; © The Frick Collection, 52; Fuglsang Kunstmuseum, photo: Ole Akhøj, 154; From the Danish art Collection of Ambassador John L. Loeb Jr., 157, 173; Göteborg Kunstmuseum, 64, 96; Hamburger Kunsthalle, 261; Hamburger Kunsthalle, photo: Elke Walford, 51, 102; From the collection of The Hearn Family Trust, 104, 121, 175; The J. Paul Getty Museum, Los Angeles, 212; Det Kongelige Bibliotek, Copenhagen, 200, 215; © Landesmuseum Hannover, 83; © Lyon MBA, photo: Alain Basset, 70; Photo: Johanna Rylander/Malmö Kunstmuseum, 106, 191; Modern Art Press, photo: Lance Cooper, 129; Musée Rodin, Paris, photo: Christian Baraja, 172; Museet Michael Anna Anchers Hus, Skagen © Helga Anchers Fond, 67; Ligier Piotr/ Muzeum Narodowe w Warszawie, 134; Museum für Kunst und Gewerbe, Hamburg, 130; Museum Sønderjylland – Kunstmuseum Brundlund Slot, photo: Kurt Lauritsen, 21; Nasjonalmuseet for Kunst, arkitektur og design, Oslo, 22, 71: © National Gallery in Prague 2011, 117; Photo studio of National Museum in Krakow, 113; Nationalmuseum Stockholm, 35, 77, 87, 216; Ny Carlsberg Glyptotek, photo: Ole Haupt, 52, 94, 112, 258; Odense Bys Museer/Fyns Kunstmuseum, Odense, 49; Ordrupgaard, photo: Pernille Klemp, 16, 17, 90, 100, 107, 134, 202; Prudence-Cunning Associates, 66; © Ribe Kunstmuseum, 65; Collection Rijksmuseum, Amsterdam. Gift of M.C., Baroness van Lynden-van Pallandt, 68; © RMN (Musée d'Orsay)/Hervé Lewandowski, 38, 42, 56, 60, 66, 72, 73; © RMN (Musée d'Orsay)/Jean-Gilles Berizzi, 62; © RMN (Musée d'Orsay)/Michéle Bellot, 89; © RMN (Musée d'Orsay)/ Patrice Schmidt, 116; © Royal Academy of Arts, London, 256, 261; © Royal Museums of Fine Arts of Belgium, Brussels, 38, 45, 68, 206, 207; © 2011, Photo SCALA, Florence – courtesy of the Minestero Beni e Att. Culturali, 50; © 2011, Digital Image, The Museum of Modern Art, New York/SCALA, Florence, 214; © 2011, Image copyright The Metropolitan Museum of Art/Art Ressource/SCALA, Florence, 60, 94, 213; Stiftung Schleswig-Holsteinische Landesmuseum Schloss Gottorf, Schleswig, 118, 257; ©Scweizerisches Institut für Kunstwissenschaft, Zürich, 73; Skagens Museum, 127; Skovgaard Museet, Viborg, 135; SMK-foto, photo: Jakob Skou-Hansen & Riccardo Buccarella, 9, 15, 20, 24, 26, 27, 30, 34, 44, 55, 57, 58, 61 69, 74, 84, 85, 91 92, 97, 109, 111, 116, 119, 125, 131, 133, 137, 139, 147, 155, 156, 175, 183, 184, 187, 188, 190, 191, 192, 198, 199, 202, 207, 210, 211; Stiftung Sammlung E.G. Bührle, Zürich, 38; © Stichting Kröller-Müller Museum, 110, 114; © Tate, London 2011, 59, 82, 101, 151; Thielska galleriet, Stockholm, photo: Tord Lund, 32, 72, 126; Toledo Museum of Art, Gift of The Apollo Society, 200.30, 51; Towner contemporary art museum, 151; Viegaarden/photo: Jørgen Bak Rasmussen, 63.

Pierre Bonnard, William Nicholson, Helene Schjerfbeck/billedkunst.dk
Edvard Munch: © Munch Museum/Munch-Ellingsen Group/ billedkunst.dk 2011
William Nicholson: © Desmond Banks
Pablo Picasso: © Succession Picasso/billedkunst.dk 2011

THE EXHIBITIONS

EXHIBITION IN COPENHAGEN

STATENS MUSEUM FOR KUNST

National Gallery of Denmark
4 Februay – 20 May 2012

HAMMERSHØI AND EUROPE IS SUPPORTED BY:

BIKUBENFONDEN
C.L. DAVID FOUNDATION AND COLLECTION
THE GEORGE JORCK & EMMA JORCK FOUNDATION

EXHIBITION

Concept: Kasper Monrad
Curating: Kasper Monrad and Annette Rosenvold Hvidt
Art education: Annette Rosenvold Hvidt
Architect: Mads Kjædegaard
Graphic design: Mette Secher
Assistant: Tone Bonnén
Exhibition producer: Gitte Kikkenberg
Digital productions: Jack Johnsen, Louise Springborg and Martin Køhler Jørgensen
Registrar/transportation: Thor Nørmark-Larsen
Conservation: Pauline Lehmann Banke, Henriette Heyn Olsen and Christian Balleby Jensen
Art handling: Rosa Hall, Erik Kjærby Jensen, Mogens Kristiansen, Morten Sørensen and Jørgen Trolle

THE EXHIBITION IN MUNICH

HAMMERSHØI UND EUROPA
EIN DÄNISCHER KÜNSTLER UM 1900

KUNSTHALLE DER HYPO-KULTURSTIFTUNG

June 15 – September 16, 2012

HYPO-KULTURSTIFTUNG (HYPO-CULTURAL FOUNDATION)
Management Board: Dieter Rampl, Anne Gfrerer, Heinz Laber, Wolfgang Sprißler, Andrea Varese
Managing Director: Oliver Kasparek
Foundation Office: Gabriele Schubert

KUNSTHALLE DER HYPO-KULTURSTIFTUNG
Theatinerstraße 8
80333 Munich
Germany
www.hypo-kunsthalle.de

Director: Christiane Lange
Curator: Roger Diederen
Exhibition's Office: Bettina Ungerecht
Press and Public Relations: Leonie Mellinghoff
Facility Managar: Winfried Heinz

EXHIBITION

Concept: Kasper Monrad
Curator: Roger Diederen
Exhibition and Graphic Design: Matthias Kammermeier
Assistant: Anja Huber
Conservation: Florian Schwemer

HAMMERSHØI UND EUROPA WAS MADE POSSIBLE WITH THE SUPPORT OF:

HypoVereinsbank, Member of the UniCredit Group

LENDERS

Her Royal Highness
Princess Benedikte
of Denmark

AABENRAA
Museum Sønderjylland -
Kunstmuseet Brundlund Slot

AARHUS
ARoS Aarhus Kunstmuseum

AMSTERDAM
Rijksmuseum

BERLIN
Staatliche Museen zu Berlin,
Nationalgalerie

BRUSSELS
Musées Royaux des Beaux-
Arts de Belgique

COPENHAGEN
The David Collection
The Hirschsprung Collection
Ny Carlsberg Glyptotek
Ordrupgaard
Statens Museum for Kunst

EASTBOURNE
Towner Gallery

GOTHEBURG
The Gothenburg
Museum of Art

HAMBURG
Hamburger Kunsthalle

HANNOVER
Niedersächsisches
Landesmuseum

HELSINKI
Ateneum Art Museum,
Finnish National Gallery

KRAKOW
Nationalmuseum

LE CATEAU-CAMBRÉSIS
Musée départemental
Matisse

LONDON
Tate

LYON
Musée des Beaux-Arts

MALMÖ
Malmö Konstmuseum

MÜNCHEN
Bayerische Staats-
gemäldesammlungen,
Neue Pinakothek

NEW YORK
The Hearn Family Trust
Metropolitan Museum of Art
Metropolitan Museum of Art
(Lehman Collection)

ODENSE
Fyns Kunstmuseum, Odense
City Museums

OSLO
The National Museum of Art,
Architecture and Design

OTTERLO
The Kröller-Müller Museum

PARIS
Musée d'Orsay

RIBE
Ribe Art Museum

ROME
Galleria Nazionale d'Arte
Moderna e Contemporanea

SCHIERENSEE
Privatsammlung Professor
Günther Fielmann –
Schierensee Manor

SCHLESWIG
Schleswig-Holsteinisches
Landesmuseum

SKAGEN
The Helga Ancher Founda-
tion, Michael & Anna
Ancher's House
Skagens Museum

STOCKHOLM
Nationalmuseum
The Thielska Gallery

TOLEDO (OHIO)
Toledo Museum of Art

VIBORG
The Skovgaard Museum

WARSCHAU
Nationalmuseum

Sikorsky Family Collection

– and private collectors

ACKNOWLEDGEMENTS

The curators of the exhibition would like to acknowledge the generous assistance of the following during the making of this exhibition and its catalogue:

HRH Princess Benedikte

Naja Marie Aidt
Dita Amory
Thomas Andratschke
Nienke Bakker
Sofie Bastiansen
Stephane Bayard
Markus Bertsch
Etienne Bréton
Julie Brown
Peter Bysted
Thomas P. Campbell
Anne Christiansen
Maria Vittoria Marini Clarelli
Guy Cogeval
Caroline Collier
Patrice Deparpe
Michel Draguet
Lisette Vind Ebbesen
Elisabeth Alsheimer Evenstedt
Elisabeth Fabritius
Günther Fielmann
Jürgen Fitschen
Dorota Folga-Januszewska
Kjeld von Folsach
Anne-Birgitte Fonsmark
Flemming Friborg
Anette Froesch
Hubertus Gaßner
Zofia Gulubiew
Charles Hack
Gertrud Hvidberg Hansen
Charlotte Hauch
Ernst Haverkamp
Angella Hearn
Allis Helleland
Anne Hemkendreis
Audrey d'Hendecourt
Jenns Howoldt
Joachim Kaak
Katrine Kampe
Liz Kreijn
Felix Krämer
Mette Hjørngaard Lauritzen
Dominique Marechal
Caroline Matthieu
Mette Kia Krabbe Meyer
Agnieszka Morawinska
Larry Nichols
Jolanda van Nijen
Isabella Nilsson
Eva Nygårds
Kristine von Oehsen
Nils Ohlsen
Magnus Olausson
Stéphane Paccoud
Alfred Pacquement
Erik Nørager Pedersen
Wim Pijbes
Robbert M. Pronk
Sylvie Ramond
Jørgen Rasmussen
Patricia Reed
Marika Reuterswärd
Sabine Rewald
Chris Riopelle
Isabelle Rossetti
Matthew Rowe
Axel Rüger
Marianne Saabye
Klaus Schrenk
Margret Schütte
Karin Sidén
Nicholas Serota
Nilly Sikorsky
Marie Arleth Skov
Solfrid Söderlind
Jens Erik Sørensen
MaryAnne Stevens
Evert van Straaten
Jesper Svenningsen
Dominique Szymusiak
Maija Tanninen-Mattila
Gary Tinterow
Barbara Tomassi
Anna Schram Vejlby
Per Erik Veng
Anne-Mette Villumsen
Dagmar Warming
Angelika Wesenberg

WORKS IN THE EXHIBITIONS

Statens Museum for Kunst, Copenhagen
Kunsthalle der Hypo-Kulturstiftung, Munich

○ Munich only

● Copenhagen only

[ ] Catalogue

VILHELM HAMMERSHØI
1864-1916 DANISH

Farmhouse 1883
Oil on canvas 34.7 x 36.7 cm
Private collection, Professor Günther Fielmann - Schierensee Manor
○ [98]

Landscape with a Barn 1883
Oil on canvas 34 x 36.5 cm
Private collection, Professor Günther Fielmann - Schierensee Manor
○ [99]

Back View of a Young Girl, Anna Hammershøi 1884
Oil on canvas 48 x 35 cm
Private collection, London
○ [p. 242]

Interior with the Artist's Mother and Sister 1884
Oil on canvas 40 x 34 cm
Private collection (Dep. Ordrupgaard, Copenhagen)
● [4]

Portrait of Young Woman. The Artist's Sister, Anna Hammershøi 1885
Oil on canvas 112.4 x 91.3 cm
The Hirschsprung Collection, Copenhagen
[32]

Old Woman at the Window 1885
Oil on canvas 34 x 32.5 cm
Schleswig-Holsteinisches Landesmuseum, Schleswig
○ [p. 243]

An Old Woman 1886
Oil on canvas 69.7 x 56.7 cm
The Hirschsprung Collection, Copenhagen
[2]

The Artist's Mother, Frederikke Hammershøi 1886
Oil on canvas 34 x 37 cm
Private collection
[41]

The Artist's Sister Anna, Reading 1886
Drawing , Charcoal 24 x 19.5 cm
Statens Museum for Kunst
[146]

Young Girl Sewing. Anna Hammershøi, the Artist's Sister 1887
Oil on canvas 37 x 35 cm
Ordrupgaard, Copenhagen
● [3]

Interior. An Old Stove. Albertines Lyst, Lyngby 1888
Oil on canvas 61 x 51 cm
Statens Museum for Kunst
○ [75]

From a Bakery Shop 1888
Oil on canvas 60 x 73 cm
Schleswig-Holsteinisches Landesmuseum, Schleswig
○ [p. 243]

Woman seen from the Back 1888
Oil on canvas 63.5 x 55.5 cm
Statens Museum for Kunst
○ [-]

Interior with the Artist's Mother 1889
Oil on canvas 55 x 51 cm
Nationalmuseum, Stockholm
[57]

Seated Female Nude 1889
Oil on canvas 126 x 93 cm
Statens Museum for Kunst
○ [-]

Portrait of Ida Ilsted 1890
Oil on canvas 106.5 x 86 cm
Statens Museum for Kunst
[50]

Self-portrait 1890
Oil on canvas 52 x 59.5 cm
Statens Museum for Kunst
○ [-]

View of Christiansborg Castle. Late Autumn 1890-92
Oil on canvas 115.5 x 147.5 cm
Statens Museum for Kunst
[84]

Self-portrait 1891
Oil on canvas 54 x 42 cm
Private collection
[1]

A Greek Relief in the Louvre 1891
Oil on canvas 96 x 95 cm
Ny Carlsberg Glyptotek, Copenhagen
○ [p. 244]

Evening in the Drawing Room. The Artist's Mother and Wife 1891
Oil on canvas 63 x 49.5 cm
Statens Museum for Kunst
[36]

Portrait of Ida Hammershøi with Needlework 1891
Drawing, black chalk 43.4 x 41.3 cm
Statens Museum for Kunst
[34]

Evening in the Drawing-Room 1891
Charcoal and chalk on paper 57.2 x 44.3 cm
The David Collection, Copenhagen
[35]

Landscape. Falster 1891
Oil on canvas 76.5 x 97.5 cm
Private collection
○ [-]

View of Jægersborg Allé, North of Copenhagen 1892
Oil on canvas 35.3 x 41.8 cm
Statens Museum for Kunst
○ [101]

Interior 1893
Oil on canvas 56.5 x 46.5 cm
The Gothenburg Museum of Art
[42]

Artemis 1893-94
Oil on canvas 193 x 251.5 cm
Statens Museum for Kunst
[10]

The Cello Player 1894
Charcoal and pastel on paper 41.5 x 54.2 cm
Private collection
○ [-]

Three Young Women 1895
Oil on canvas 128 x 167 cm
Ribe Art Museum
[43]

Figures by the Window c. 1895
Oil on canvas 55 x 46 cm
Private collection
○ [58]

Landscape in Snow, Søndermarken 1895-96
Oil on canvas 83.2 x 64.8 cm
The Hirschsprung Collection, Copenhagen
[108]

The Artist's Wife at a Sewing Table 1897
Oil on canvas 61 x 54.5 cm
The National Museum of Art, Architecture and Design, Oslo
○ [-]

Portrait of Ida, the Artist's Wife 1898
Drawing, pencil 24.2 x 18.8 cm
Statens Museum for Kunst
[12]

Self-portrait, seen from behind 1898
Drawing, pencil 24.7 x 18.9 cm
Statens Museum for Kunst
[13]

Two Figures. The Artist and His Wife 1898
Oil on canvas 71.5 x 86 cm
ARoS Aarhus Kunstmuseum
[14]

Interior with a Young Man Reading 1898
Oil on canvas 64.4 x 51.8 cm
The Hirschsprung Collection, Copenhagen
[63]

Interior 1898
Oil on canvas 51.5 x 46 cm
Nationalmuseum, Stockholm
[64]

Interior with a Young Woman Sweeping 1899
Oil on canvas 50.2 x 40.3 cm
The Hirschsprung Collection, Copenhagen
[5]

Interior of Courtyard, Strandgade 30 1899
Oil on canvas 65.7 x 47.3 cm
Toledo Museum of Art, Ohio
(Gift of the Apollo Society)
○ [29]

Interior 1899
Oil on canvas 64.5 x 58.1 cm
Tate: Presented in memory of Leonard Borwick by his friends through the Art Fund 1926
[60]

Interior, Frederiksberg Allé 1900
Oil on canvas 56 x 44.5 cm
Private collection, United Kingdom
[59]

View of Refsnæs 1900
Oil on canvas 63 x 78 cm
The Thielska Gallery, Stockholm
[102]

Sunbeams or Sunshine. Dust Motes Dancing in the Sunbeams 1900
Oil on canvas 70 x 59 cm
Ordrupgaard, Copenhagen
● [76]

Interior with Woman reading. Sunlight on the Floor c. 1900
Oil on canvas 46.1 x 51.5 cm
Private collection
○ [p. 245]

Interior, Strandgade 30 1901
Oil on canvas 62.4 x 52.5 cm
Niedersächsisches Landesmuseum, Hannover
[61]

Interior from Strandgade with Sunlight on the Floor 1901
Oil on canvas 46.5 x 52 cm
Statens Museum for Kunst
[62]

Interior with Woman at Piano, Strandgade 30 1901
Oil on canvas 55.9 x 45.1 cm
Private collection
○ [65]

Near Fortunen, Jægersborg Deer Park North of Copenhagen 1901
Oil on canvas 55 x 66.5 cm
Statens Museum for Kunst
[113]

Five Portraits 1901-02
Oil on canvas 190 x 340 cm
The Thielska Gallery, Stockholm
[15]

The Buildings of the Asiatic Company, seen from St. Annæ Street 1902
Oil on canvas 146.5 x 140.5 cm
Statens Museum for Kunst
[86]

Sun over the Sea c. 1902?
Oil on canvas 54 x 75 cm
Private collection
[115]

Interior with a View of an Exterior Gallery 1903
Oil on canvas 72 x 58 cm
The David Collection, Copenhagen
[79]

View of Gentofte Lake. Sunshower 1903
Oil on canvas 83 x 78 cm
Private collection
[100]

Woman Reading 1903
Oil on canvas 55 x 47 cm
Private collection
○ [-]

Evening in the Drawing Room 1904
Oil on canvas 101 x 123.5 cm
Statens Museum for Kunst
[56]

Tree Trunks. Arresødal, Frederiksværk 1904
Oil on canvas 45.5 x 68.5 cm
Statens Museum for Kunst
[109]

Interior with Punchbowl 1904
Oil on canvas 78.5 x 57.5 cm
Her Royal Highness Princess Benedikte of Denmark
○ [p. 246]

Dunkebakke, Frederiksværk 1904
Oil on canvas 55 x 64.5 cm
Private collection
○ [p. 245]

Interior, Strandgade 30 1905
Oil on canvas 46.5 x 38.6 cm
Hamburger Kunsthalle, Hamburg
○ [p. 247]

Landscape, From Lejre 1905
Oil on canvas 41 x 68 cm
Nationalmuseum, Stockholm
[17]

Open Doors 1905
Oil on canvas 52.5 x 60 cm
The David Collection, Copenhagen
[81]

Interior (The Old Cabinet Sofa) 1905
Oil on canvas 49.7 x 40 cm
Staatliche Museen zu Berlin, Nationalgalerie
○ [25]

Young Lady. "Resting" 1905
Oil on canvas 49.5 x 46.5 cm
Musée d'Orsay, Paris
[66]

Drawing Room. The Four Copper Prints 1905
Painting, Oil on canvas 64 x 61 cm
Private collection, Belgium
[78]

From Christianshavn's Canal, Copenhagen 1905
Oil on canvas 33.1 x 40.8 cm
Statens Museum for Kunst
[91]

Interior courtyard c. 1905
Oil on canvas 80 x 60 cm
Private collection
○ [28]

Interior. Strandgade 30 1906
Oil on canvas 51.8 x 44 cm
Tate: Purchased 1930
[77]

Montague Street in London 1906
Oil on canvas 57 x 64 cm
Ny Carlsberg Glyptotek, Copenhagen
● [87]

St. Peter's Church, Copenhagen 1906
Oil on canvas 133 x 118 cm
Statens Museum for Kunst
[16]

Ida Hammershøi, the Artist's Wife with a Teacup 1907
Oil on canvas 91 x 73.5 cm
Statens Museum for Kunst
○ [-]

Interior with a Woman Reading 1908
Oil on canvas 65.5 x 56 cm
Museum Sønderjylland – Kunstmuseet Brundlund Slot, Aabenraa
[6]

Interior of the Great Hall in Lindegaarden 1909
Oil on canvas 77 x 118 cm
Sikorsky Family Collection
○ [p. 249]

Old Warehouse, Christianshavn 1909
Oil on canvas 68.5 x 56 cm
Hamburger Kunsthalle, Hamburg
○ [p. 248]

Standing Female Nude 1909-10
Oil on canvas 205 x 153 cm
Statens Museum for Kunst
[11]

Interior with the Artist's Easel 1910
Oil on canvas 84 x 69 cm
Statens Museum for Kunst
[9]

Interior with Woman Sitting at a Table c. 1910
Oil on canvas 82.5 x 64 cm
Ordrupgaard, Copenhagen
● [67]

Interior with Potted Plant on Card Table, Bredgade 25 c. 1910-11
Oil on canvas 78.5 x 71 cm
Malmö Museum
[82]

Self-Portrait. The Cottage Spurveskjul 1911
Oil on canvas 126 x 149 cm
Statens Museum for Kunst
[140]

Double Portrait of the Artist and his Wife, seen through a Mirror. The Cottage Spurveskjul 1911
Oil on canvas 55.2 x 76 cm
Private collection, Professor Günther Fielmann - Schierensee Manor
[116]

Interior in London, Brunswick Square 1912
Oil on canvas 53 x 76 cm
Private collection
○ [122]

The Jews' College "Rabbinical Seminary" in Guilford Street, London 1912-13
Oil on canvas 51 x 41.5 cm
Schleswig-Holsteinisches Landesmuseum, Schleswig
[94]

The Four Rooms. Interior from the Artist's Home, Strandgade 25 1914
Oil on canvas 85 x 70.5 cm
Ordrupgaard, Copenhagen
● [83]

A Young sick girl undated
Oil on canvas 33.1 x 27 cm
Fyns Kunstmuseum, Odense City Museums
○ [-]

Interior with the Artist's Wife undated
Oil on canvas 74 x 56 cm
The National Museum of Art, Architecture and Design, Oslo
○ [-]

Landscape, early Spring undated
Oil on canvas 35,5 x 58 cm
The National Museum of Art, Architecture and Design, Oslo
○ [-]

ANNA ANCHER
1859-1935 DANISH

Sunshine in the Blind Woman's Room 1885
Oil on canvas 58.5 x 43.3 cm
The Hirschsprung Collection, Copenhagen
[71]

Portrait of the Artist's Mother, Ane Hedvig Brøndum c. 1893
Oil on canvas 67.8 x 59.8 cm
The Helga Ancher Foundation, Michael & Anna Ancher's House, Skagen
[46]

Interior with Red Poppies 1905
Oil on canvas 56.2 x 65 cm
Skagens Museum
[70]

PIERRE BONNARD
1867-1947 FRENCH

Woman in front of a Mirror c. 1905
Oil on canvas 52 x 37.5 cm
Bayerische Staatsgemäldesammlungen, Neue Pinakothek, München
○ [-]

The Milliner 1907
Oil on cardboard 68.5 x 59 cm
Statens Museum for Kunst
(Dep. Ny Carlsberg Glyptotek, Copenhagen)
[74]

EUGÈNE CARRIÈRE
1849-1906 FRENCH

Winding Wool. The Artist's Wife and Daughter 1887
Oil on canvas 60 x 73 cm
Tate: Presented by Mrs R. M. Dunlop 1927
[37]

The Painter's Family 1893
Oil on canvas 125.5 x 221.5 cm
Musée d'Orsay, Paris
[55]

HANS AM ENDE
1864-1918 GERMAN

Weyerberg with Summer Clouds 1899
Oil on canvas 87.5 x 129.5 cm
Staatliche Museen zu Berlin, Nationalgalerie
[104]

LOUIS EYSEN
1843-99 GERMAN

The Artist's Mother ca. 1877
Oil on canvas 54 x 42 cm
Staatliche Museen zu Berlin, Nationalgalerie
[72]

HENRI FANTIN-LATOUR
1836-1904 FRENCH

Reading (Marie Fantin-Latour) 1861
Oil on canvas 100 x 83 cm
Musée d'Orsay, Paris
[33]

A Corner of the Table 1872
Oil on canvas 160 x 225 cm
Musée d'Orsay, Paris
● [53]

The Reading 1877
Oil on canvas 97 x 130 cm
Musées des Beaux-Arts, Lyon
○ [51]

Around the Piano 1885
Oil on canvas 160 x 222 cm
Musée d'Orsay, Paris
○ [-]

PAUL GAUGUIN
1848-1903 FRENCH

Tahitian Women Bathing 1892
Oil on canvas 109.9 x 89.5 cm
Metropolitan Museum of Art, New York
(Lehman Collection)
○ [39]

SVEND HAMMERSHØI
1873-1948 DANISH

Landscape 1901 1901
Oil on canvas 118 x 144 cm
The Skovgaard Museum, Viborg
[112]

The Garden of Prinsens Palæ, Copenhagen c. 1906
Oil on canvas 63 x 65.5 cm
Statens Museum for Kunst
[95]

CARL HOLSØE
1863-1935 DANISH

Interior with a Girl Reading 1903
Oil on canvas 53 x 46 cm
Statens Museum for Kunst
[69]

PETER ILSTED
1861-1933 DANISH

A Young Girl Preparing Chantarelles 1892
Oil on canvas 66 x 51.5 cm
Statens Museum for Kunst
[68]

EDUARD KARSEN
1860-1941 DUTCH

Beguinage in Amsterdam 1893
Oil on canvas 36.5 x 45 cm
The Kröller-Müller Museum, Otterlo
[96]

View of the Port of Amsterdam c. 1895
Oil on canvas 30 x 44 cm
The Kröller-Müller Museum, Otterlo
[85]

FERNAND KHNOPFF
1858-1921 BELGIAN

Portrait of Marie Monnom 1887
Oil on canvas 49.5 x 50 cm
Musée d'Orsay, Paris
[44]

In Fosset, Rain 1890
Oil on panel 19 x 23.5 cm
The Hearn Family Trust, New York
[97]

Posthumous Portrait of Marguerite Landuyt 1896
Oil on canvas 75.2 x 74.5 cm
Musées Royaux des Beaux-Arts, Brussels
[49]

HENRI MATISSE
1869-1954 FRENCH

Woman Reading 1895
Oil on canvas 61.5 x 48 cm
Centre Pompidou, Paris, on loan to the Musée départemental Matisse, Le Cateau-Cambrésis
○ [-]

XAVIER MELLERY
1845-1921 BELGIAN

The Doors undated
Oil on canvas 72.5 x 58 cm
The Hearn Family Trust, New York
[80]

EDVARD MUNCH
1863-1944 NORWEGIAN

Night in Saint Cloud 1893
Oil on canvas 70 x 56.5 cm
Private collection (Dep. Metropolitan Museum of Art, New York)
[73]

WILLIAM NICHOLSON
1872-1949 BRITISH

Lady in Yellow 1893
Oil on canvas 72.4 x 62.3 cm
Private collection, London
[45]

Viola on the Downs 1909
Oil on canvas board 28.5 x 40 cm
Private collection
● [105]

FRITZ OVERBECK
1869-1909 GERMAN

On the Moor c. 1904
Oil on canvas 156 x 200 cm
Bayerische Staatsgemäldesammlungen, Neue Pinakothek, München
○ [128]

JÓSEF PANKIEWICZ
1866-1940 POLISH

Warsaw Cab at Night 1893
Oil on canvas 72 x 70.5 cm
The National Museum, Cracow
[89]

The Park in Dubój 1897
Oil on canvas 96 x 130.5 cm
The National Museum, Warsaw
[111]

JULIUS PAULSEN
1860-1940 DANISH

Summer Landscape at Dusk, Horneby 1894
Oil on canvas 56 x 62 cm
Ordrupgaard, Copenhagen
[110]

PIERRE PUVIS DE CHAVANNES
1824-98 FRENCH

Young Women by the Sea (small version) c. 1879
Oil on canvas 61 x 47 cm
Musée d'Orsay, Paris
● [38]

Woman by the Sea 1882
Oil on canvas 81.8 x 65.5 cm
Bayerische Staatsgemäldesammlungen, Neue Pinakothek, München
○ [-]

HELENE SCHJERFBECK
1862-1946 FINNISH

The Seamstress 1903-05
Oil on canvas 95.5 x 84.5 cm
Ateneum Art Museum, Finnish National Gallery, Helsinki
● [47]

VALDEMAR SCHØNHEYDER MØLLER
1864-1905 DANISH

Two Boats on the Beach. The Sun Glittering over the Sea beg. of the 1890s
Oil on canvas 29 x 46.5 cm
Skagens Museum
[103]

Sunset. Fontainebleau 1900
Oil on canvas 116.2 x 88.3 cm
Statens Museum for Kunst
[114]

LUIGI SELVATICO
1873-1938 ITALIAN

Morning Departure 1899
Oil on canvas 116 x 169 cm
Galleria Nazionale d'Arte Moderna e Contemporanea, Rome
○ [27]

GEORGES SEURAT
1859-91 FRENCH

The Forest at Pontaubert 1881
Oil on canvas 79.1 x 62.5 cm
Metropolitan Museum of Art, New York
[107]

Study for "The Models" 1886
Drawing, conté crayon on laid paper 29.7 x 22.5 cm
Metropolitan Museum of Art, New York (Lehman Collection)
● [148]

EDWARD STOTT
1855-1918 BRITISH

Starlight: Landscape undated
Oil on canvas 42 x 48 cm
Towner Gallery, Eastbourne
(Presented by Arthur og Helen Grogan through the Art Fund, 2009)
○ [118]

JAMES MCNEILL WHISTLER
1834-1903 AMERICAN

Arrangement in Grey and Black No.1. Portrait of the Painter's Mother 1871
Oil on canvas 144.3 x 162.5 cm
Musée d'Orsay, Paris
● [40]

Arrangement in Yellow and Grey: Effie Deans c. 1876-78
Oil on canvas 194 x 93 cm
Rijksmuseum, Amsterdam
(Dep. Van Gogh Museum, Amsterdam)
[48]

WILLEM ARNOLD WITSEN
1860-1923 DUTCH

The Thames in London c. 1895
Oil on canvas 79 x 100 cm
The Kröller-Müller Museum, Otterlo
[90]

SELECTION OF WORKS, ONLY EXHIBITED AT KUNSTHALLE DER HYPO-KULTURSTIFTUNG

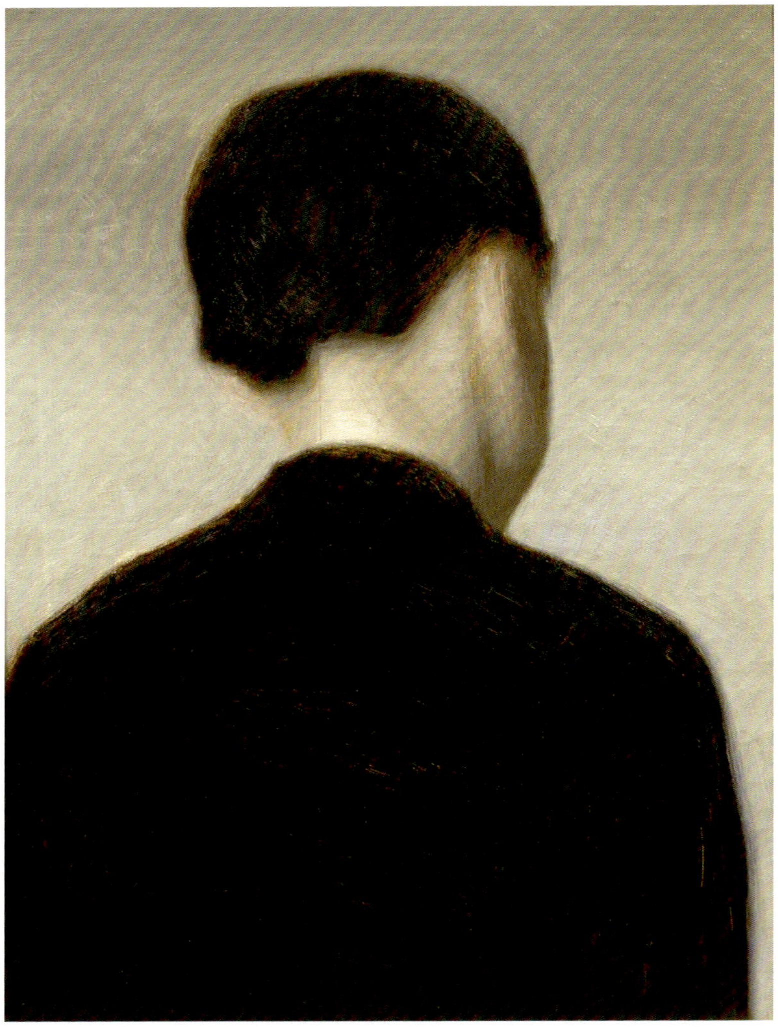

Vilhelm Hammershøi 1864-1916 Danish
Back View of a Young Girl, Anna Hammershøi 1884
Oil on canvas 48 x 35 cm
Private collection, London

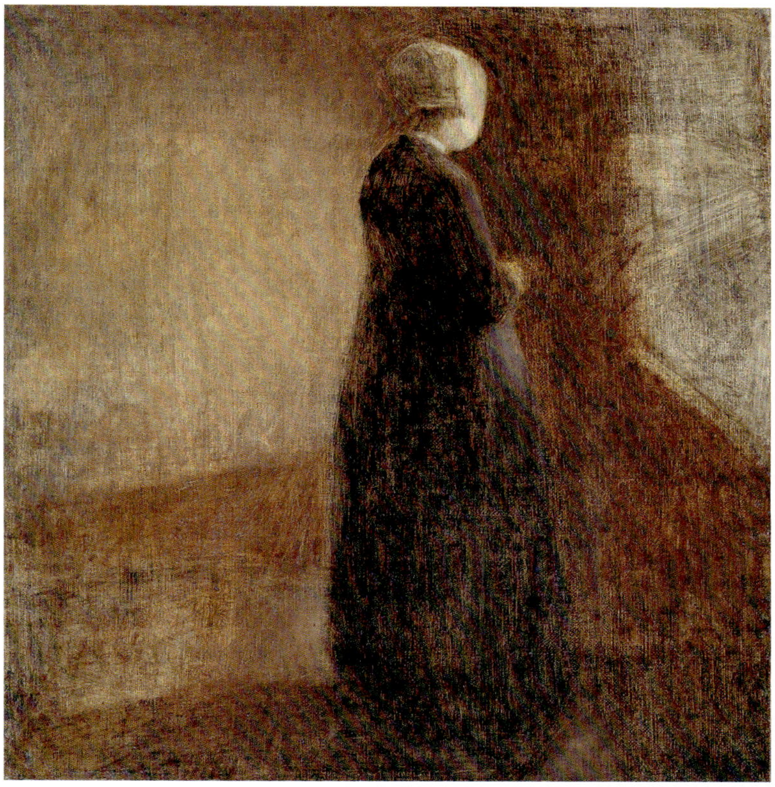

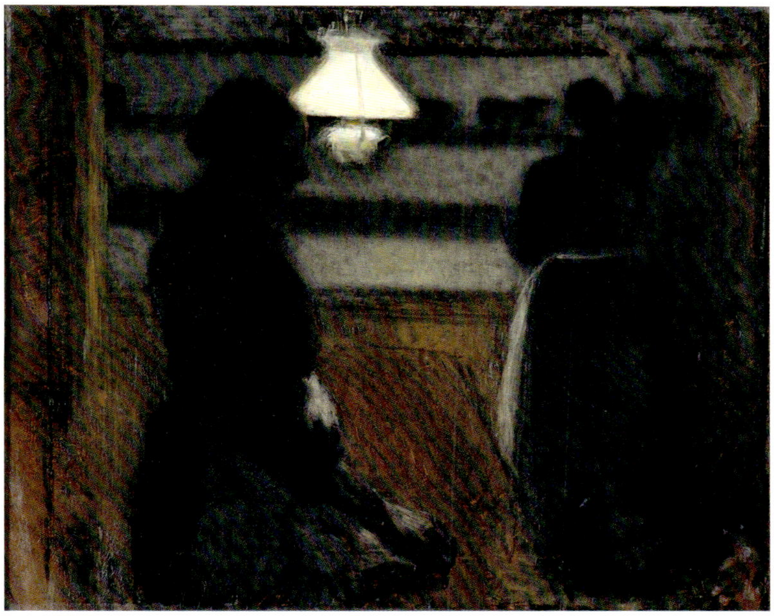

Vilhelm Hammershøi 1864-1916 Danish
Old Woman at the Window 1885
Oil on canvas 34 x 32.5 cm
Schleswig-Holsteinisches
Landesmuseum, Schlesvig

Vilhelm Hammershøi 1864-1916 Danish
From a Bakery Shop 1888
Oil on canvas 60 x 73 cm
Schleswig-Holsteinisches
Landesmuseum, Schlesvig

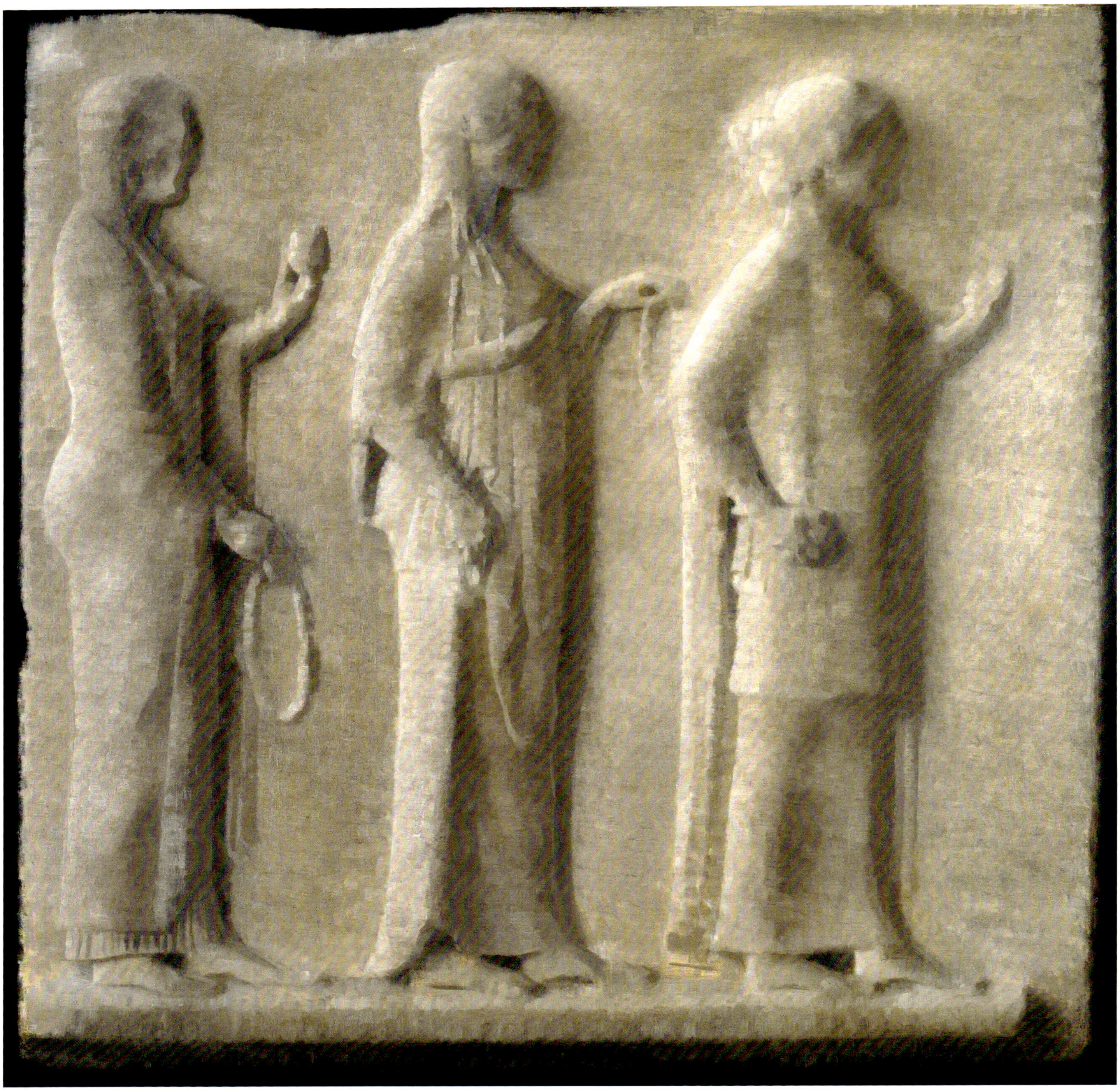

Vilhelm Hammershøi 1864-1916 Danish
A Greek Relief in the Louvre 1891
Oil on canvas 96 x 95 cm
Ny Carlsberg Glyptotek, Copenhagen

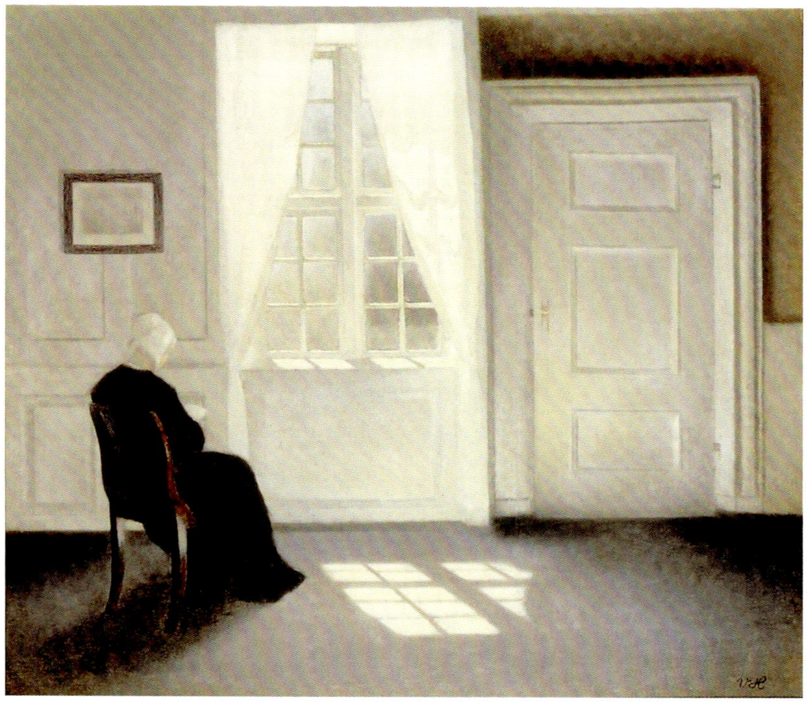

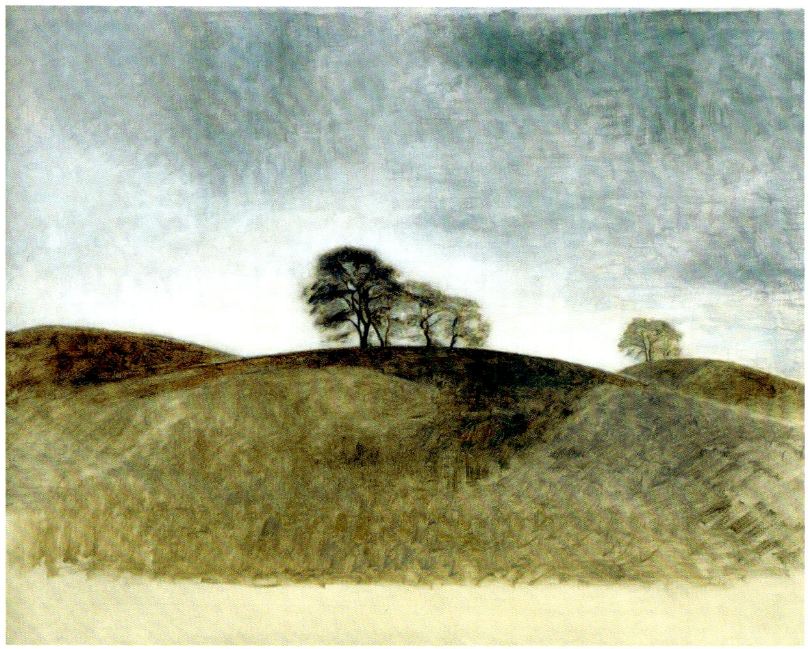

Vilhelm Hammershøi 1864-1916 Danish
Interior with woman Reading. Sunlight on the Floor c. 1900
Oil on canvas 46.1 x 51.5 cm
Private collection

Vilhelm Hammershøi 1864-1916 Danish
Dunkebakke, Frederiksværk 1904
Oil on canvas 55 x 64.5 cm
Private collection

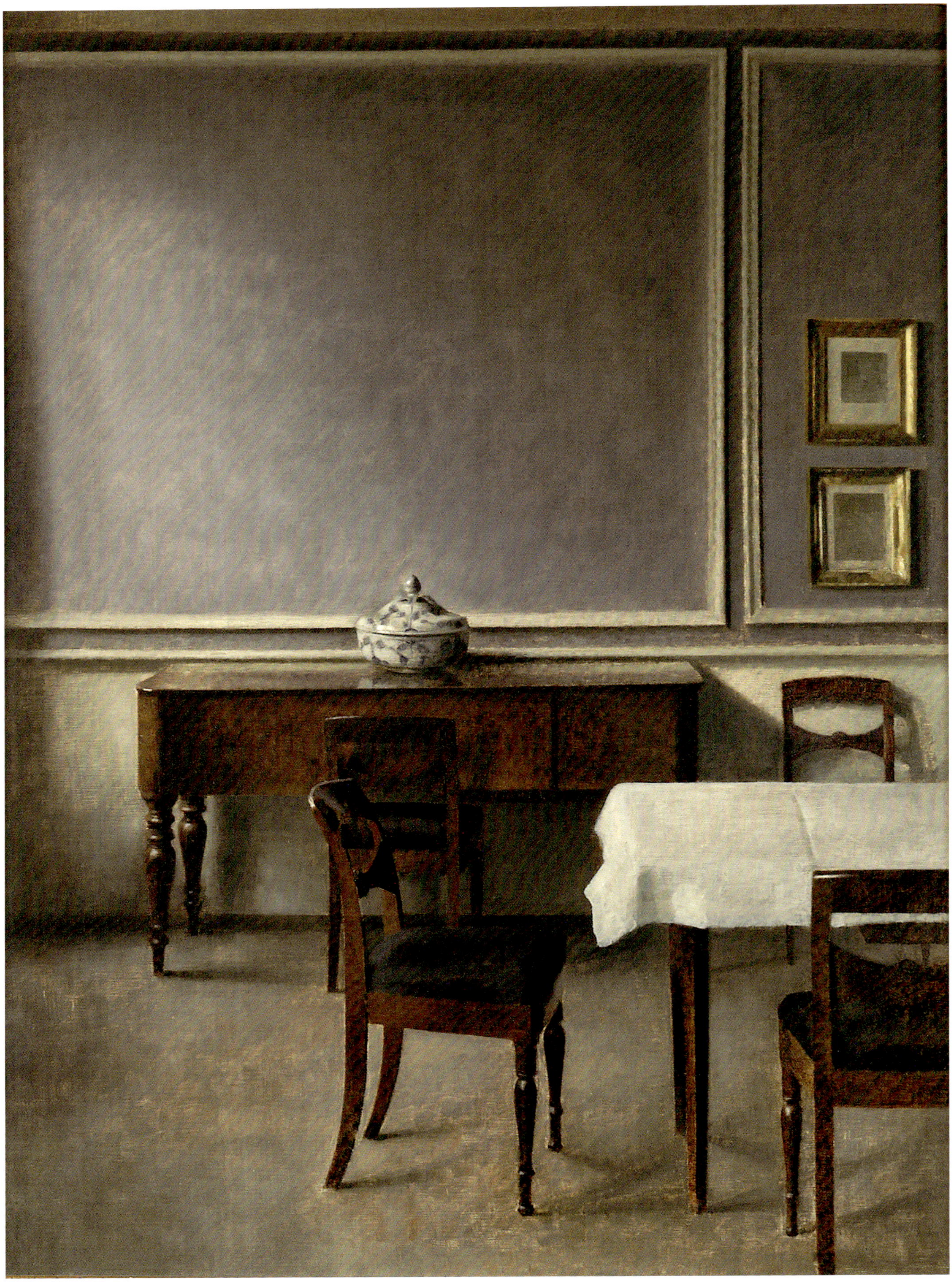

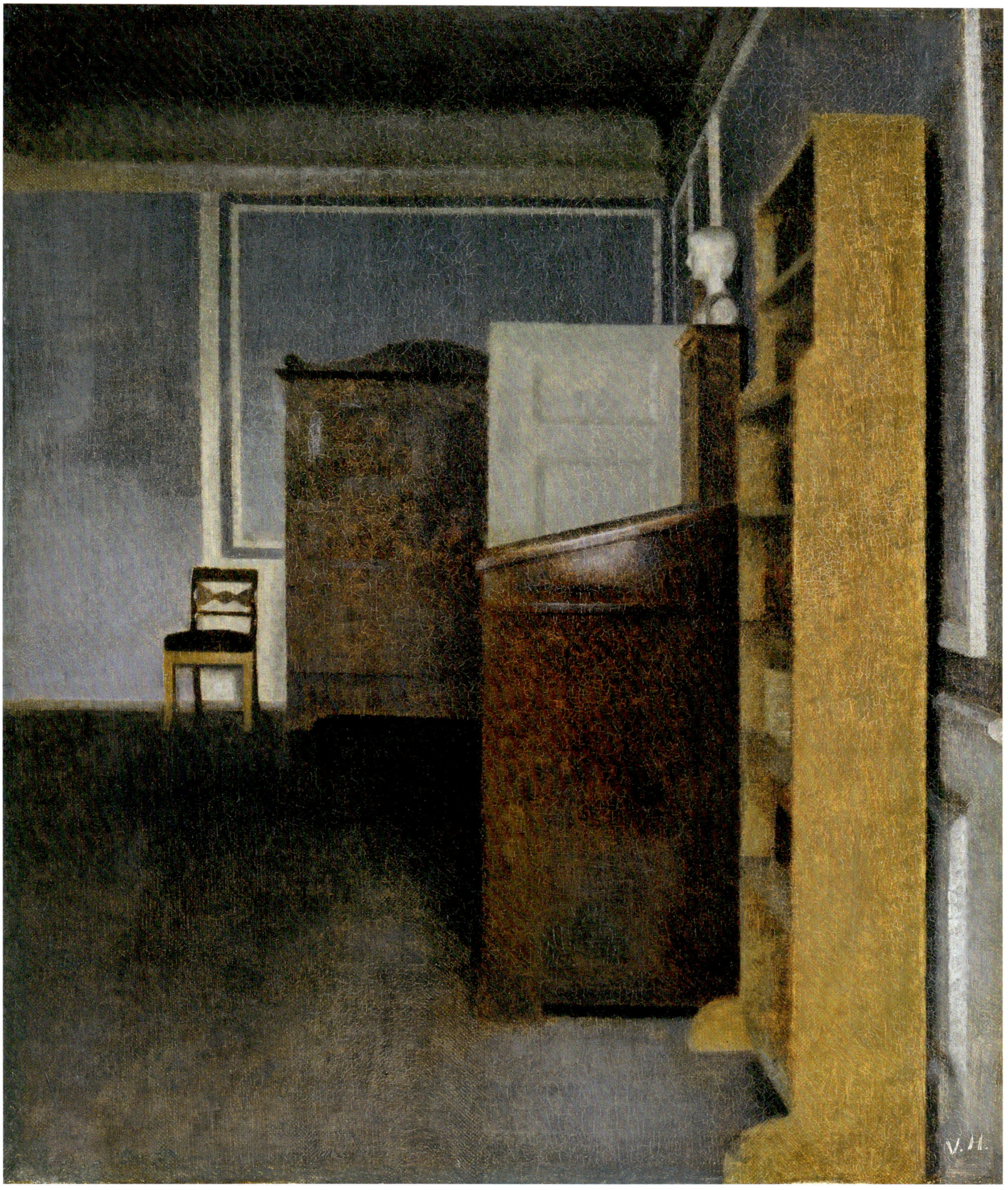

Vilhelm Hammershøi 1864-1916 Danish
Interior with Punchbowl 1904
Oil on canvas 78.5 x 57.5 cm
Her Royal Highness
Princess Benedikte of Denmark

Vilhelm Hammershøi 1864-1916 Danish
Interior, Strandgade 30 1905
Oil on canvas 46.5 x 38.6 cm
Hamburger Kunsthalle, Hamburg

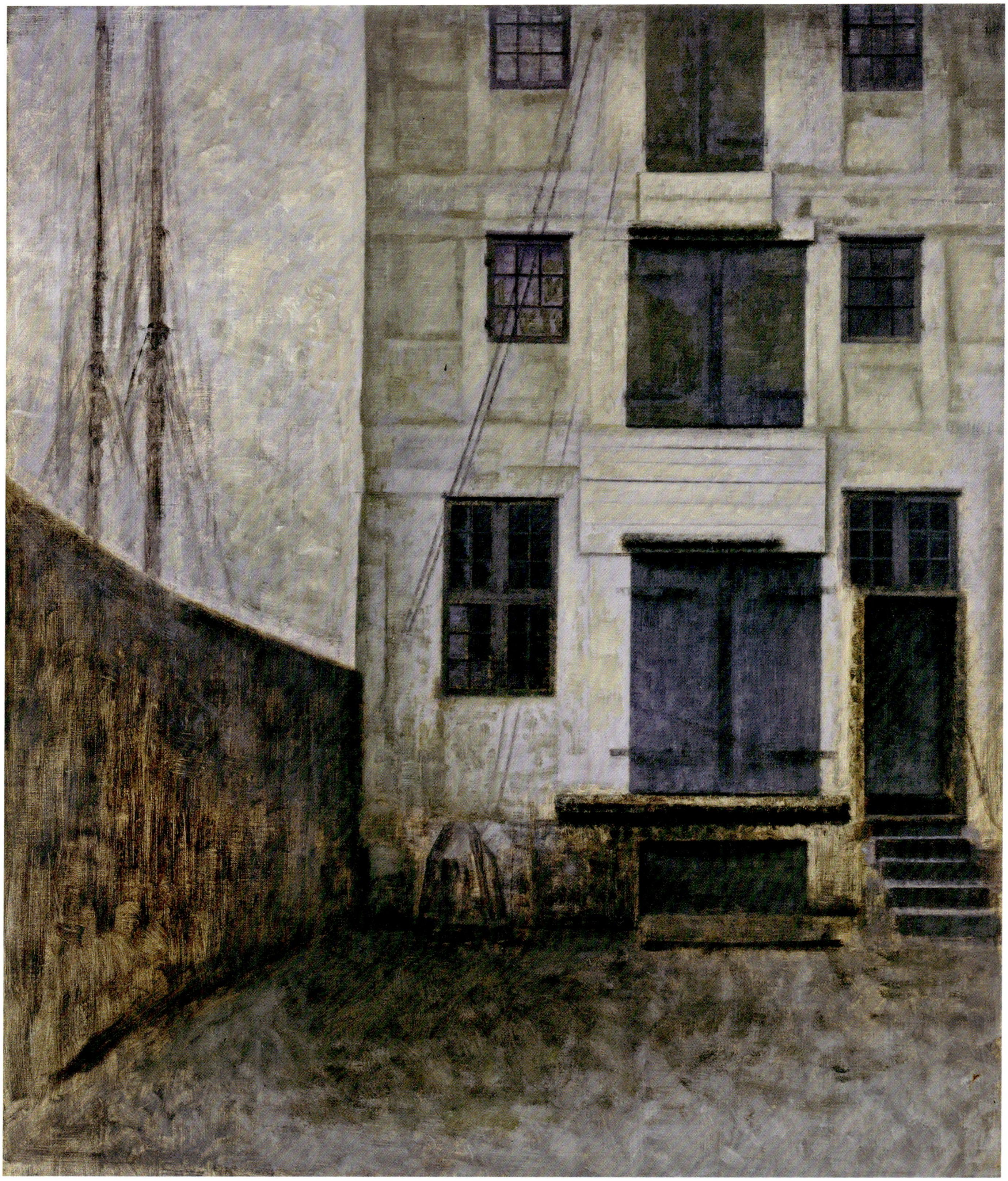

Vilhelm Hammershøi 1864-1916 Danish
Old Warehouse, Christianshavn 1909
Oil on canvas 68.5 x 56 cm
Hamburger Kunsthalle, Hamburg

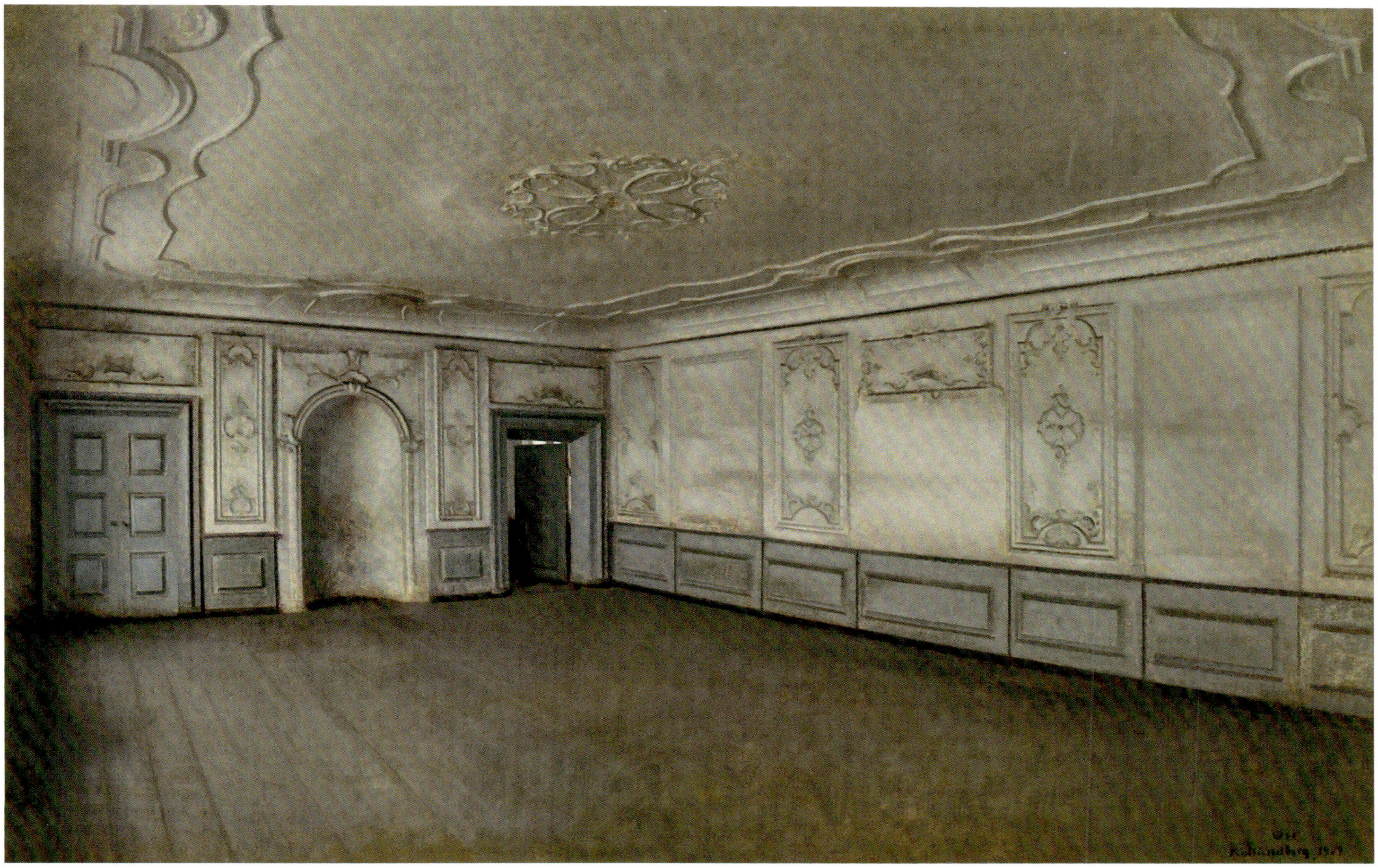

Vilhelm Hammershøi 1864-1916 Danish
Interior of the Great Hall in Lindegaarden 1909
Oil on canvas 77 x 118 cm
Sikorsky Family Collection

BIBLIOGRAPHY

AARHUS 2001
Lennart Gottlieb: "Intim/sublim", in *Intim/sublim. Hammershøi-Heinsen-Frandsen.* Exhibition catalogue, Aarhus Kunstmuseum, Aarhus 2001.

AMSTERDAM 1994
Aimée Brown Price (ed.): *Pierre Puvis de Chavannes.* Exhibition catalogue, Van Gogh Museum, Amsterdam 1994.

AMSTERDAM & BRUSSELS 2000
Vincent Vanhamme: *Xavier Mellery. L'âme des choses.* Exhibition catalogue, Van Gogh Museum, Amsterdam & Musée d'Ixelles, Brussels 2000.

BAARK MAIREY 2011
Tea Baark Mairey: *Hudens æstetik – Intimitet og sanselighed i Pierre Bonnards maleri.* Unpublished advanced master thesis, University of Copenhagen, Copenhagen 2011.

BAJOU 1999
Valérie Bajou: *Eugène Carrière. Intimist Portrait 1849-1906*, Lausanne 1999.

BANTENS 1990
James Bantens: *Eugène Carrière. The Symbol of Creation*, New York 1990.

BERCHTIG 2006
Frauke Berchtig: *Künstlerkolonie Worps-wede*, Munich 2006.

BERLIN 1905
Niederdeutsche Künstler. Hammershöi. Exhibition catalogue, Galerie Eduard Schulte, Berlin 1905.

BERLIN 2002
Peter-Klaus Schuster et al.: *Nationalgalerie Berlin. Das XIX. Jahrhundert. Katalog der ausgestellten Werke*, 2nd edition, Nationalgalerie, Berlin 2002.

BERMAN 2007
Patricia G. Berman: *In another Light. Danish Painting in the Nineteenth Century.* New York 2007 (Danish edition: *Nyt lys over 1800-tallets danske maleri,* Copenhagen 2007).

BOGH 1996
Mikkel Bogh: *Interieurer, flader og åbninger – Det intime i maleriet omkring år 1900.* Paper, Department of Arts and Cultural Studies, University of Copenhagen, Copenhagen 1996.

BORDEAUX, NEW YORK & PITTSBURGH 2000
Hélène Lafont-Coutourier et al. : *Art et Entreprise.* Exhibition catalogue, Musée Goupil, Bordeaux Dahesh Museum of Art, New York & Frick Art & Historical Centre, Pittsburgh 2000.

BOULBOULLÉ & ZEISS 1989
Guido Boulboullé & Michael Zeiss: *Worpswede. Kulturgeschichte eines Künstlerdorfes,* Cologne 1989.

BRAMSEN 1905
Alfred Bramsen: "Weltkunst. Der dänische Maler Vilhelm Hammershøi", in *Zeitschrift für bildende Kunst*, N.F. 16, Leipzig, 1905, pp. 176-189.

BRAMSEN 1909
Alfred Bramsen: "Wm. Nicholson", i *Maaneds-Magasinet*, 1909, pp. 408-413.

BRAMSEN 2008
Christopher Bo Bramsen: "Wilhelm Hammershøi and Alfred Bramsen: the Artist and the Collector", in *FOCUS,* Ordrupgaard, 2008, pp. 18-29.

BRAMSEN & MICHAËLIS 1918
Alfred Bramsen & Sophus Michaëlis; *Vilhelm Hammershøi. Kunstneren og hans Værk*, Copenhagen 1918.

BREMEN 2003
Wulf Herzandenrath & Andreas Kreul von Hauschild (eds.): *Rilke. Worpswede. Eine Ausstellung als Phantasie über ein Buch.* Exhibition catalogue, Kunsthalle Bremen, Bremen 2003.

BREMEN 2007
Anne Buschhoff & Wulf Herzandenrath (eds.): *Paula Modersohn-Becker und die Kunst in Paris um 1900: Von Cézanne bis Picasso.* Exhibition catalogue, Kunsthalle Bremen, Bremen 2007.

BRUSSELS 2005
Eliane de Wilde: *Museum of Modern Art. A Selection of Works*, Musée Royaux des Beaux-Arts de Belgique, Brussels 2005.

BRUSSELS, SALZBURG & BOSTON 2004
Frederik Leen et al.: *Fernand Khnopff.* Exhibition catalogue, Musées Royaux des Beaux Arts de Belgique, Brussels, Museum der Moderne, Salzburg & McMullen Museum of Art, Boston 2004.

CAVANAUGH 2000
Jan Cavanaugh: *Out Looking In. Early Modern Polish Art, 1890-1918,* Berkeley, Los Angeles and London 2000.

CHICAGO 2009
Jay A. Clarke et al.: *Munch becoming Munch. Influence, Anxiety, and Myth.* Exhibition catalogue, Art Institute of Chicago, Chicago 2009.

COLOGNE 1998
Götz Czymmek (ed.): *Landschaft als Kosmos der Seele. Malerei des nordischen Symbolismus bis Munch.* Exhibition catalogue, Walraff-Richartz-Museum, Cologne 1998.

COPENHAGEN 1888A
Katalog over Udstillingen af franske Kunstværker i Kjøbenhavn / Catalogue de l'exposition française des beaux-arts à Copenhague, Copenhagen 1888.

COPENHAGEN 1888B
Illustreret Katalog over den franske Udstilling i Kjøbenhavn, Copenhagen 1888.

COPENHAGEN 1897
Katalog over den internationale Kunstudstilling. Exhibition catalogue, Ny Carlsberg Glyptotek, Copenhagen 1897.

COPENHAGEN 1909
Fortegnelse over Kunstværkerne paa Den Engelske Udstilling. Exhibition catalogue, Kunstforeningen, Copenhagen 1909.

COPENHAGEN 1945
Peter Ilsted, Maleren, Grafikeren. Mennesket (Foreword by Aksel Jørgensen), Copenhagen 1945.

COPENHAGEN 1981
Hanne Finsen et al. (eds.): *Vilhelm Hammershøi. En retrospektiv udstilling.* Exhibition catalogue, Ordrupgaard, Copenhagen 1981.

COPENHAGEN 1983
Peter Michael Hornung & Kasper Monrad: *Dengang i 80'erne. Danske miljøer i malerkunsten 1880-1890.* Exhibition catalogue, Kunstforeningen, Copenhagen 1983.

COPENHAGEN 1984
Merete Bodelsen (ed.): *Gauguin og van Gogh i København i 1893.* Exhibition catalogue, Ordrupgaard, Copenhagen 1984.

COPENHAGEN 1986
George Szabo: *Franske mesterværker. Malerier fra det 19. og 20. århundrede fra Robert Lehman Collection, Metropolitan Museum of Art, New York / French Masterpieces. XIX and XX Century Paintings and Drawings from the Robert Lehman Collection of Metropolitan Museum of Art, New York.* Exhibition catalogue, Ordrupgaard, Copenhagen 1986.

COPENHAGEN 2000
Peter Nørgaard Larsen (ed.): *Sjælebilleder. Symbolismen i dansk og europæisk maleri 1870-1910.* Exhibition catalogue, Statens Museum for Kunst, Copenhagen 2000 (English edition: *Symbolism in Danish and European Painting 1870-1910*).

COPENHAGEN 2002
Anne Cathrine Wolsgaard Iversen et al.: *Julius Paulsen.* Exhibition catalogue, Ordrupgaard, Copenhagen 2002.

COPENHAGEN 2006
Annette Rosenvold Hvidt (ed.): *Hammershøi>Dreyer – Billedmagi.* Exhibition catalogue, Ordrupgaard, Copenhagen 2006.

COPENHAGEN 2009
Dieter Buchhart et al.: *Edvard Munch og Danmark.* Exhibition catalogue, Ordrupgaard, Copenhagen 2009.

COPENHAGEN, PARIS & NEW YORK 1997
Anne-Birgitte Fonsmark (ed.): *Vilhelm Hammershøi.* Exhibition catalogue, Ordrupgaard, Copenhagen, Musée d'Orsay, Paris & Solomon R. Guggenheim Museum of Art, New York 1997.

DABROWSKI 1999
Magdalena Dabrowski: *French Landscape. The Modern Vision 1880-1920*, Museum of Modern Art, New York 1999.

DELEVOY 1987
Robert L. Delevoy: *Fernand Khnopff*, Brussels 1987.

DETROIT 1984
Agnieska Morawinska et al.: *Symbolism in Polish Painting 1890-1914.* Exhibition catalogue, Detroit Institute of Arts, Detroit 1984.

DÜSSELDORF 1986
Leena Ahtola-Moorhouse et al.: *Im Lichte des Nordens. Skandinavische Malerei um die Jahrhundertwende.* Exhibition catalogue, Kunstmuseum Düsseldorf, Düsseldorf 1986.

ELIAS 1915-16
Julius Elias: "Vilhelm Hammershøi", in *Kunst und Künstler*, XIV, 1915-16, 403-08.

EMDE 1949
Ursula Emde: *Rilke und Rodin,* Marbug/Lahn 1949.

DE FONT-RÉAULX & BOLLOCH 2006
Dominique de Font-Réaulx & Joëlle Bolloch: *The Work of Art and Its Reproduction*, Photography at the Musée d'Orsay, Paris 2006.

FABER 2010
Monika Faber: *Heinrich Kühn: Die vollkommene Fotografie*, Ostfildern 2010.

FORSTER-HAHN 1996
Françoise Forster-Hahn (ed.): *Imagining modern German culture 1889-1910*, National Gallery of Art Washington, D. C. 1996.

FRANKFURT & ZURICH 2009
Georges Seurat: Figure in Space. Exhibition catalogue, Schirn Kunsthalle, Frankfurt and Kunsthaus Zürich, Zurich 2009.

GLASGOW & AMSTERDAM 1990
Richard Bionda & Carel Blotkamp (eds.): The *Age of Van Gogh. Dutch Painting 1880-1895.* Exhibition catalogue, The Burrell Collection, Glasgow Museum & Art Galleries, Glasgow & Rijksmuseum Vincent van Gogh, Amsterdam 1990.

GOTHENBURG & STOCKHOLM 1999
Lena Boëthius & Görel Cavalli-Björkman (eds.): *Vilhelm Hammershøi.* Exhibition catalogue, Göteborg Konstmuseum, Gothenburg & Nationalmuseum, Stockholm 1999.

GOTHENBURG 2002
Björn Fredlund (ed.): *Edvard Munch.* Exhibition catalogue, Göteborg Konstmuseum, Gothenburg 2002.

GÖTTE 1996
Gisela Götte (ed.): *Rainer Maria Rilke und die bildende Kunst seiner Zeit*, Munich 1996.

GUNNARSSON 1998
Torsten Gunnarsson: *Nordic Landscape Painting in the Nineteenth Century.* New Haven & London 1998.

HAMBURG 2003
Felix Krämer et al.: *Vilhelm Hammershøi.* Exhibition catalogue, Hamburger Kunsthalle, Hamburg 2003.

HANNOVER 1966
Emil Hannover: *Erindringer fra Barndom og Ungdom* (1914-18). Published by H.P. Rohde, Copenhagen 1966.

HANNOVER, COPENHAGEN & SKAGEN 1994–95
Heide Grape-Albers (ed.): *Anna Ancher 1859-1935.* Exhibition catalogue, Nieder-sächsisches Landesmuseum, Hannover; The Hirschsprung Collection, Copenhagen and Skagens Museum & Michael and Anna Anchers Hus, Skagen 1994-95.

HANNOVER & VIENNA 1986
Worpswede: Eine deutsche Künstlerkolonie um 1900. Exhibition catalogue, Forum des Niedersächsischen Landesmuseums Hannover, Hannover, and Künstlerhaus Wien, Vienna 1986.

HEILBRUN 2008
Françoise Heilbrun (ed.): *La photographie au Musée d'Orsay*, Musée d'Orsay, Paris 2008.

HELLERUP, NÆSTVED AND VIBORG 2008
Iben Overgaard et al. (ed.): *Svend Hammershøi – en kunstner og hans tid.* Exhibition catalogue, Øregaard Museum, Hellerup; Næstved Museum, Næstved, and Skovgaard Museet, Viborg 2008.

HOFFMANN 2008
Torsten Hoffmann et al.: *Lehrer ohne Lehre: Zur Rezeption Paul Cézannes in Künsten, Wissenschaften und Kultur (1906-2006)*, Wissenschaften und Kultur (1906-2006), Freiburg im Breisgau 2008.

HOLM 2006
Henrik Ole Holm: *Analyser af hovedværker i dansk billedkunst fra Nicolai A. Abildgaard til Asger Jorn.* Ph.D. thesis, University of Copenhagen, Copenhagen 2006.

HORNUNG 1993
Peter Michael Hornung: *Realismen,* Ny Dansk Kunsthistorie, vol. 4. Copenhagen 1993.

HORNUNG 2002
Peter Michael Hornung: *Peder Severin Krøyer,* Copenhagen 2002.

KNAPP 1988
Ulrich Knapp: *Heinrich Kühn. Photographien*, Vienna 1988.

KRÄMER 1999
Felix Krämer: *Vilhelm Hammershøi. Strandgade 30, Interieurs.* Advanced master thesis, Hamburg 1999.

KRÄMER 2007
Felix Krämer: *Das unheimliche Heim. Zur Interieurmalerei um 1900,* Cologne, Weimar & Vienna 2007.

LAUSANNE 2005
William Hauptman: *Impressions du Nord. La peinture scandinave 1800-1915.* Exhibition catalogue, Fondation de l'Hermitage, Lausanne 2005.

LAUSANNE 2007
William Hauptman: *La Belgique dévoilée.* Exhibition catalogue, Fondation de l'Hermitage, Lausanne 2007.

LILLE 2008
Annie Scottez-De Wambrechies et al.: *Échappes nordiques. Les maîtres scandinave et finlandais – 1870/1914.* Exhibition catalogue, Palais des Beaux-Arts de Lille, Lille 2008.

LONDON 1907A
Exhibition of a Selection of Works by Danish Painters. Exhibition catalogue, Guildhall Art Gallery, London 1907.

LONDON 1907B
An Exhibition of Oil Paintings by the Danish Artist Vilhelm Hammershøi. Exhibition catalogue, Galerie E. J. van Wisselingh, London 1907.

LONDON 1986
Knut Berg et al.: *Dreams of a Summer Night. Scandinavian Painting at the Turn of the Century.* Exhibition catalogue, Hayward Gallery, London 1986.

LONDON 1992
Mara-Helen Wood (ed.): *Edvard Munch. The Frieze of Life.* Exhibition catalogue, The National Gallery, London 1992.

LONDON 1996
Andrew Nicholson (ed.): *William Nicholson. Painter.* The William Nicholson Trust, London 1996.

LONDON 1997
Andrew Wilton & Robert Upstone (eds.): *The Age of Rossetti, Burne-Jones & Watts. Symbolism in Britain 1860-1910.* Exhibition catalogue, Tate Gallery, London 1997.

LONDON 2004
Sanford Schwartz et al.: *The Art of William Nicholson.* Exhibition catalogue, Royal Academy of Arts, London 2004.

LONDON 2008
Felix Krämer et al.: *Hammershøi.* Exhibition catalogue, Royal Academy of Arts, London 2008.

LONDON, BOSTON & NEW YORK 2006
Kathleen Adler et al.: *Americans in Paris 1860-1900.* Exhibition catalogue, National Gallery, London, Museum of Fine Arts, Boston & Metropolitan Museum of Art, New York 2006.

LONDON & NEW YORK 1998
Sarah Whitfield & John Elderfield (eds.): *Bonnard.* Exhibition catalogue, Tate Gallery, London & Museum of Modern Art, New York 1998.

LONDON, PARIS, & WASHINGTON 1994
Richard Dorment et al.: *James McNeill Whistler.* Exhibition catalogue, Tate Gallery, London, Musée d'Orsay, Paris & National Gallery of Art, Washington 1994.

LONDON & WASHINGTON 2001
Peter-Klaus Schuster et al.: *Spirit of an Age. Nineteenth-Century Paintings from the Nationalgalerie, Berlin.* Exhibition catalogue, National Gallery, London & National Gallery of Art, Washington, D. C. 2001.

LONDON & WASHINGTON 2010
Belinda Thomson (ed.): *Gauguin: Maker of Myth.* Exhibition catalogue, Tate Modern, London & National Gallery of Art, Washington, D. C. 2010.

LUCIE-SMITH 1977
Edward Lucie-Smith: *Fantin-Latour,* Oxford 1977.

LUCK 2001
Rätus Luck: *Der Briefwechsel und andere Dokumente zu Rilkes Begegnung mit Rodin.* Published by Rätus Luck, Frankfurt am Main 2001.

MACDONALD 2003
Margaret F. MacDonald et al.: *Whistler's Mother: An American Icon,* Aldershot & Burlington 2003.

MADRID & BARCELONA 1995
Kasper Monrad et al.: *Luz del Norte/Llum del Nord/The Light of the North.* Exhibition catalogue, Museo Nacional Reina Sofia, Madrid & Museu d'Art Modern del MNAC, Barcelona 1995.

MADRID & LISBON 2009
Vincent Pomarède et al.: *Henri Fantin-Latour (1836-1904).* Exhibition catalogue, Museo Thyssen-Bornemisza, Madrid & Fundaçao Calouste Gulbenkian, Lisbon 2009.

MONRAD 1997
Kasper Monrad: "Vilhelm Hammershøi and the Contemporary Italian Painting", in *The Statens Museum for Kunst Journal,* vol. 1, 1997, pp. 88–100.

MUNICH & ESSEN 1995
Rudolf Koella (ed.): *Félix Vallotton.* Exhibition catalogue, Kunsthalle der Hypo-Kultur-stiftung, Munich & Folkwang Museum, Essen 1995.

NEW HAVEN 1991
Sasha M. Newman et al.: *Félix Vallotton.* Exhibition catalogue, Yale University Art Gallery, New Haven 1991.

NEW YORK 1991
Robert L. Herbert et al.: *Seurat.* Exhibition catalogue, Metropolitan Museum of Art, New York 1991.

NEW YORK 2002
Colta Ives et al.: *The Lure of the Exotic. Gauguin in New York Collections.* Exhibition catalogue, Metropolitan Museum of Art, New York 2002.

NEW YORK 2009
Dita Armory (ed.): *Pierre Bonnard. The Late Still Lifes and Interiors.* Exhibition catalogue, Metropolitan Museum of Art, New York 2009.

NEW YORK & PHILADELPHIA 1971
Allen Stanley (ed.): *From Realism to Symbolism: Whistler and his world.* Exhibition catalogue, Wildenstein, New York and Philadelphia Museum of Art, Philadelphia 1971.

NEW YORK & WASHINGTON 1983
Hanne Finsen (ed.): *Vilhelm Hammershøi. Painter of Stillness and Light,* Wildenstein Gallery, New York & The Phillips Collection, Washington, D.C. 1983.

NYKJÆR 1991
Mogens Nykjær: *Kundskabens billeder. Motiver i dansk kunst fra Eckersberg til Hammershøi,* Århus 1991.

OELSNER 2002
Gertrud Oelsner: "Photographic strategies, perceptual reflections and introvert tendencies in painting around 1900", Statens Museum for Kunst Journal, vol. 6, 2002, pp. 24-43.

OSLO 1987
Knut Berg et al.: *Nordiske stemninger. Nordisk maleri fra århundredskiftet.* Exhibition catalogue, Nasjonalgalleriet, Oslo 1987.

OSLO 2008
Ingeborg Ydstie et al.: *Munch becoming "Munch", Artistic Strategies 1880-1892.* Exhibition catalogue, Munch Museet, Oslo 2008.

PARIS 1889
F.-G. Dumas (ed.): *Exposition Universelle de 1889. Catalogue illustré des beaux-Arts. 1789-1889,* Lille 1889.

PARIS, BRUSSELS AND HAMBURG 1979
Frans Boenders et al. (ed.): *Fernand Khnopff 1858-1921.* Exhibition catalogue, Musée des Arts Décoratifs, Paris; Musées royaux des Beaux-Arts de Belgique, Brussels and Hamburger Kunsthalle, Hamburg 1979-80.

PARIS 1987
Leena Ahtola-Moorhouse et al.: *Lumiers du Nord. La peinture scandinave 1885-1905*. Exhibition catalogue, Musée du Petit Palais, Paris 1987.

PARIS 1993
Françoise Cachin et al.: *1893: l'Europe des peintres*. Exhibition catalogue, Musée d'Orsay, Paris 1993.

PARIS 2006
Suzanne Pagé (ed.): *Bonnard, the work of art, suspending time*. Exhibition catalogue, Musée d'Art Moderne de la Ville de Paris, Paris 2006.

PARIS & NEW YORK 1991
Robert L. Herbert et al.: *Georges Seurat 1859-1891*. Exhibition catalogue, Grand Palais, Paris & Metropolitan Museum of Art, New York 1991.

PARIS & OTTAWA 1976
Jacques Foucart et al.: *Puvis de Chavannes*. Exhibition catalogue, Grand Palais, Paris & National Gallery of Canada, Ottawa 1976.

PARIS, OTTAWA & SAN FRANCISCO 1982
Douglas Druick & Michel Hoog: *Fantin-Latour*. Exhibition catalogue, Grand Palais, Paris, National Gallery of Canada, Ottawa & California Palace of the Legion of Honor, San Francisco 1982.

PETTIT 1983
Richard Pettit: *Rainer Maria Rilke in und nach Worpswede*, Worpswede 1983.

PRIDEAUX 2005
Sue Prideaux: *Edvard Munch: Behind the Scream*, New Haven & London 2005.

RAPETTI 2008
Rodolphe Rapetti: *Eugène Carrière 1849-1906. Catalogue Raisonné de l'oeuvre peint*, Paris 2008.

RENNES 2004
Wojciech Suchocki: *Le Symbolisme polonais*. Exhibition catalogue, Musée des Beaux-Arts de Rennes, Rennes 2004.

REWALD 1990
John Rewald: *Seurat. A Biography*, London 1990.

REYNAERTS ET AL. 2003
Jenny Reynaerts et al.: *Willem Witsen 1860-1923. Schilderijen, tekeningen, prenten, foto's*. Exhibition catalogue, Dordrechts Museum, Dordrecht & Gemeentearchief, Amsterdam 2003.

RILKE 1903
Rainer Maria Rilke: *Worpswede. Fritz Mackensen, Otto Modersohn, Fritz Overbeck, Hans am Ende, Heinrich Vandeler*, Bielefeld & Leipzig 1903 (reprint Frankfurt a.M. 1987).

RILKE 1930
Rainer Maria Rilke: *Auguste Rodin*, Leipzig 1930.

RILKE 1952
Rainer Maria Rilke: *Briefe über Cézanne*, Wiesbaden 1952.

RILKE 2003
Rainer Maria Rilke: *Heinrich Vandeler*, postscript by Bernd Stenzig, Bremen 2003.

RITTER 2009
Ina Ritter: *Die Epiphanie des Augenblicks. Wahrnehmung und Projektion bei Rainer Maria Rilke und Jens Peter Jacobsen*, Reihe XVIII, Vergleichende Literaturwissenschaften, vol. 124. Frankfurt a.M. 2009.

RITTER 2009-10
William Ritter: "La peinture du Danemark, Vilhelm Hammershøi," in *L'art et les artistes*, 10, Paris, 1909-10, pp. 264-268.

ROHDE 1955
Johan Rohde: *Journal fra en Rejse i 1892*, published and commented by H. P. Rohde with foreword by Nils Gösta Sandblad, Copenhagen 1955.

SAN FRANCISCO, DALLAS & BILBAO 1999
Dorothy Kosinski: *The Artist and the Camera – Degas to Picasso*. Exhibition catalogue, San Francisco Museum of Modern Art, San Francisco, Dallas Museum of Art, Dallas & Guggenheim Museum, Bilbao 1999.

SCAVENIUS 1983
Bente Scavenius: *Fremsyn-Snæversyn. Dansk dagbladskritik 1880-1901*, Copenhagen 1983.

SCAVENIUS 1991
Bente Scavenius: *Den frie Udstilling i 100 år*, Copenhagen 1991.

SCAVENIUS & LINDHE 2003
Bente Scavenius & Jens Lindhe: *Hammershøis København*, Copenhagen 2003.

SCHUHMANN U. Å.
Paul Schuhmann et al.: *Die Worpsweder Malerradierer im Urtheil der Kunstkritik,*. undated.

SCHWARTZ 2004
Sanford Schwartz: *William Nicholson*, New Haven & London 2004.

SKAGEN 2001
Annette Johansen et al.: *Harmoni i blåt. P.S. Krøyers stemningsmaleri i 1890erne*. Exhibition catalogue, Skagens Museum, Skagen 2001.

SKAGEN 2009
Mette Bøgh Jensen et al.: *Anna (jeg) Anna. En hyldest til Anna Ancher*. Exhibition catalogue, Skagens Museum, Skagen 2009. (English version: *I am Anna. A Homage to Anna Ancher*).

SMITH 2009
Paul Smith (ed.): *Seurat re-viewed*, Pennsylvania 2009.

ST. PETERSBURG AND WORPSWEDE 1992
Klaus v. Düring: *Worpswede Künstlerkolonie Norddeutschlands*. Exhibition catalogue, Bjelosselskij-bjeloserskij-Palais, St. Petersburg; Grosse Kunstschau and Ludwig-Roselius-Museum, Worpswede 1992-93.

STOCKHOLM, GÖTEBORG AND OSLO 1987
Lena Holger: *Helene Schjerfbeck*. Exhibition catalogue, Prins Eugens Waldemarsudde, Stockholm; Göteborgs Konstmuseum, Gothenburg; Kunstnernes Hus, Oslo 1987-88.

SVENNINGSEN 2011
Jesper Svenningsen: *Hammershøiana. Tegninger, fotografier og andre erindringer/ Drawings, photographs and other memories,* The Hirschsprung Collection, Copenhagen 2011.

TORONTO & CINCINNATI 1984
Roald Nasgaard: *The Mystic North. Symbolist Landscape Painting in Northern Europe and North America 1890-1940.* Exhibition catalogue, Art Gallery of Ontario, Toronto & Cincinnati Art Museum, Cincinnati 1984.

TOKYO 2008
Felix Krämer et al.: *Vilhelm Hammershøi: The Poetry of Silence.* Exhibition catalogue, The National Museum of Western Art, Tokyo 2008.

TRENTO 1990
Gabriella Belli et al.: *Divisionismo italiano.* Exhibition catalogue, Palazzo delle Albere, Trento 1990.

TØJNER 2000
Poul Erik Tøjner: *Munch. Med egne ord,* Oslo & Copenhagen 2000.

VAD 1988
Poul Vad: *Hammershøi. Værk og liv,* Copenhagen 1988.

VAD 1991
Poul Vad: "Vilhelm Hammershøi: Tre unge kvinder", in William Gelius (ed.): *Ribe Kunstmuseum 100 år*, Ribe, 1991, pp. 52–55.

VAD 1992
Poul Vad: *Vilhelm Hammershøi and Danish Art at the Turn of the Century,* New Haven & London 1992.

VAD 2003
Poul Vad: *Hammershøi. Værk og liv,* 5th edition, Copenhagen 2003.

VEJEN 2010
Teresa Nielsen (ed.): *Mogens Ballins værksted.* Exhibition catalogue, Vejen Kunstmuseum, Vejen 2010.

VENICE 2002
Serge Lemoine (ed.): *From Puvis de Chavannes to Matisse and Picasso, toward modern art.* Exhibition catalogue, Palazzo Grassi, Venice 2002.

VIBORG, HELLERUP & NÆSTVED 2008
Anne-Mette Villumsen et al.: *Svend Hammershøi – en kunstner og hans tid.* Exhibition catalogue, Skovgaard Museet, Viborg, Øregaard Museum, Hellerup & Næstved Museum, Næstved 2008.

VIENNA 2007
Agnes Husslein-Arco et al.: *Wien-Paris. Van Gogh, Cézanne und Österreichs Moderne 1880-1960,* Österreichische Galerie Belvedere, Wien 2007.

VIENNA 2008
Michel Draguet et al.: *Der Kuss der Sphinx. Symbolismus in Belgien,* BA-CA Kunstforum, Vienna 2008.

WANSCHER 1915
Wilhelm Wanscher: "Vilhelm Hammershøi", in *Ord och Bild*, 1915, pp. 399-411.

WARSZAWA 2006
Elżbieta Charazińska m.fl., *Józef Pankiewicz 1866-1940. Życie i dzieło. Artyście w 140. rocznicę urodzin.* Exhibition catalogue, Muzeum Narodowe w Warszawie, Warszawa 2006.

WASHINGTON & CHICAGO 1988
Françoise Cachin et al.: *The Art of Paul Gauguin.* Exhibition catalogue, National Gallery of Art, Washington & The Art Institute of Chicago, Chicago 1988.

WASHINGTON, NEW YORK & MINNEAPOLIS 1982
Kirk Varnedoe et al.: *Northern Light. Realism and Symbolism in Scandinavian Painting 1880-1910.* Exhibition catalogue, Corcoran Gallery of Art, Washington, D.C., The Brooklyn Museum, New York & The Minneapolis Museum of Art, Minneapolis 1982.

WEIDINGER 2007
Alfred Weidinger: *Gustav Klimt.* Munich, Berlin, London & New York 2007.

WELTKE-WORTMANN 1979
Silke Weltke-Wortmann: *Die ersten Maler in Worpswede,* Worpswede 1979.

WIVEL 1982
Henrik Wivel: "Den realistiske uhygge. Vilh. Hammershøis og L.A. Rings motivverden", in *Kritik*, 59, 1982, pp. 30-52.

WIVEL 1994
Henrik Wivel: *Symbolisme og impressionisme,* Ny Dansk Kunsthistorie, vol. 5., Copenhagen 1994.

WIVEL 1996
Henrik Wivel: *Vilhelm Hammershøi,* Copenhagen 1996.

WOLL 2008
Gerd Woll: *Edward Munch. Samlede malerier,* I-IV. Oslo 2008 (English version: *The Complete Paintings*).

WOOD 1909
T. Martin Wood: "The Problem of Modern Interior Painting", *The Studio*, vol. 47, no. 198, 15 September 1909, pp. 251-256.

YOUNG ET AL. 1980
Andrew McLaren Young et al.: *The Paintings of James McNeill Whistler,* I-II, New Haven & London 1980.

ZURICH & HAMBURG 2008
Linda Schädler et al.: *Félix Vallotton. Idylle am Abgrund.* Exhibition catalogue, Kunsthaus Zürich, Zurich & Hamburger Kunsthalle, Hamburg 2008.

HAMMERSHØI
AND EUROPE

Published by

Statens Museum for Kunst, Copenhagen
Kunsthalle der Hypo-Kulturstiftung, Munich
Prestel Verlag, Munich

Concept: Kasper Monrad

Editor: Sven Bjerkhof
Editorial assistance: Tone Bonnén
Picture editor: Katrine Thygesen and Pernille Feldt
Proofs: Gitte Hou Olsen
Translations: René Lauritsen, except the articles
by Monrad: James Manley
Graphic design: Mette Secher
Photos: Page 233
Reproduction, printing and binding: Narayana Press, Odder
Fonts: Egyptienne (headings) og Akzidenz Grotesk (text)
Paper: LECTA GardaMatt Smooth, 170 g matt white

MIX
Paper from responsible sources
FSC® C010651

Verlagsgruppe Random House FSC® N001967
The FSC®-certified paper GardaMatt Smooth has been supplied by LECTA.

Front page: Detail of Vilhelm Hammershøi:
Interior from Strandgade with Sunlight on the Floor, 1901

Back: Photo: The Royal Library, Copenhagen

Prestel Verlag
A member of Verlagsgruppe Random House GmbH

Prestel Verlag
Neumarkter Strasse 28
81673 Munich
Tel. +49 (0) 89 4136-0
Fax +49 (0) 89 4136-2335

www.prestel.de

Prestel Publishing Ltd.
16-18 Berners Street
London W1T 3LN
Tel. +44 (0)20 7323-5004
Fax +44 (0)20 7323-0271

Prestel Publishing
900 Broadway, Suite 603
New York, NY 10003
Tel. +1 (212) 995-2720
Fax +1 (212) 995-2733

www.prestel.com

Library of Congress Control Number is available; British Library Cataloguing-in-Publication Data: a catalogue record for this book is available from the British Library; Deutsche Nationalbibliothek holds a record of this publication in the Deutsche Nationalbibliografie; detailed bibliographical data can be found under: http://dnb.d-nb.de

Prestel books are available worldwide. Please contact your nearest bookseller or one of the above addresses for information concerning your local distributor.

ISBN 978-3-7913-5360-9 (English trade edition)
ISBN 978-3-7913-5359-3 (German trade edition)